The Ecology of *Finnegans Wake*

The Florida James Joyce Series

University Press of Florida

Florida A&M University, Tallahassee
Florida Atlantic University, Boca Raton
Florida Gulf Coast University, Ft. Myers
Florida International University, Miami
Florida State University, Tallahassee
New College of Florida, Sarasota
University of Central Florida, Orlando
University of Florida, Gainesville
University of North Florida, Jacksonville
University of South Florida, Tampa
University of West Florida, Pensacola

The Ecology of *Finnegans Wake*

Alison Lacivita

Foreword by Sebastian D. G. Knowles

University Press of Florida

Gainesville · Tallahassee · Tampa · Boca Raton
Pensacola · Orlando · Miami · Jacksonville · Ft. Myers · Sarasota

Copyright 2015 by Alison Lacivita
All rights reserved
Published in the United States of America

First cloth printing, 2015
First paperback printing, 2021

26 25 24 23 22 21   6 5 4 3 2 1

Library of Congress Cataloging-in-Publication Data
Lacivita, Alison, author.
The ecology of Finnegans wake / Alison Lacivita ; foreword by Sebastian D. G. Knowles.
pages cm — (The Florida James Joyce series)
Includes bibliographical references and index.
ISBN 978-0-8130-6062-0 (cloth); ISBN 978-0-8130-6856-5 (pbk.)
1. Joyce, James, 1882–1941—Criticism and interpretation. 2. Joyce, James, 1882–1941. Finnegans wake. 3. Ecology in literature. I. Knowles, Sebastian D. G. (Sebastian David Guy), author of introduction, etc. II. Title. III. Series: Florida James Joyce series.
PR6019.O9F593557 2015
823'.912—dc23
2015008370

Every effort has been made to trace copyright holders and to obtain their permission for the use of copyright material. The publisher apologizes for any errors or omissions and would be grateful for notification of any corrections that should be incorporated in future reprints or editions of this book.

The University Press of Florida is the scholarly publishing agency for the State University System of Florida, comprising Florida A&M University, Florida Atlantic University, Florida Gulf Coast University, Florida International University, Florida State University, New College of Florida, University of Central Florida, University of Florida, University of North Florida, University of South Florida, and University of West Florida.

University Press of Florida
2046 NE Waldo Road
Suite 2100
Gainesville, FL 32609
http://upress.ufl.edu

Contents

Foreword vii
Acknowledgments ix
Abbreviations xi
Textual Note xiii
Introduction: An Ecocritical Joyce? 1
1. Reading the Landscape 41
2. City versus Country 84
3. The Politics of Nature 122
4. Religion and Ecology 160
5. Growing Things 200
Conclusion: New Boundaries of Ecocriticism 221
Notes 233
Works Cited 255
Index 283

Foreword

Once in a blue moon a work comes across an editor's desk that promises to shape the work of a generation. Whoever first read *On the Origin of Species* in manuscript must have felt this way, seeing an entire horizon heave into view. Here comes ecocriticism—led by Alison Lacivita. Lacivita has created an exquisite chapel in her study of the *Wake* and the natural world; the intertwining vines of genetic study and ecocritical reading pleach together in an intricately braided text that is a veritable archipelago of new and hidden discoveries. It is as if James Frazer had actually done his homework: this is *The Golden Bough* for the ecocritical age, an inspirational and breathtakingly original reading that is everywhere supported by close critical engagement with the text. This book provides a necessary redress to the legions of critics who require Joyce to be an urban writer in Aesopian dualism against the Irish literary revival, a town mouse against the country mice of Yeats and Synge, out in their pampooties to murder him. Joyce may have played that distinction up in a particolored way ever since his departure from Dublin, but Alison Lacivita isn't fooled, and she returns James Joyce to the green world where he belongs, leading us to fresh woods and pastures new.

In undergraduate exams on *Ulysses*, I have been known to set two simple questions from the "Ithaca" catechism: "Did he fall?" and "Did it flow?" What follows constitutes the single best possible answer to both questions at once. Lacivita is concerned with nothing more nor less than our post-Edenic existence, and the way that we may make our return to Paradise. Did it flow? Yes, it certainly did: the watery sources of all Joyce's work are revealed in all contexts—genetic, cultural, political, physical, literary, geographical. From paleobotany to post-structuralism, from partridges to peat bogs, from polar bears to Poulaphouca, we are given an encyclopedic topology of the legible landscapes of the *Wake*, including a welcome disquisition on the influence of gaslight on paraheliotropic trees. Lacivita does more than shore up the presence of the River Liffey in the *Wake*; her reclamation of an entire subject from the silted waters of the *Wake* makes her at once charitable mason, landscape architect, and hydroengineer.

Genetic criticism and environmental scholarship can be neatly aligned in ways that make *Finnegans Wake* a perfect study for Lacivita's general argument. Over time and through space *Finnegans Wake* developed like nothing else in literature, allowing Lacivita to shuttle effortlessly between the growth of the text and the text's love of growing things. By the end of Lacivita's book, we come to realize that *Finnegans Wake* allows infinite space to explore the nutshell of the natural world. But that does not make Joyce's work unique; *Finnegans Wake* just makes the general ecocritical argument better than any text ever written. This is the unique quality of Lacivita's scholarship: she makes *Finnegans Wake* a representative work rather than a singularity, a great tree of life instead of a radioactive stone only to be approached in a hazmat suit with a Geiger counter. "Allalivial, allalluvial!" (FW 213.32). "Environs" (FW 3.03) has been hiding in plain sight. Lacivita is our Lucretius, and *The Ecology of* Finnegans Wake our *De Rerum Natura*: through her marvelous work, we are drawn closer to the stars.

Sebastian D. G. Knowles
Editor, Florida James Joyce Series

Acknowledgments

Many individuals and institutions supported this book, and I would like to express my gratitude to all who have helped out along the way. I would particularly like to thank Sebastian Knowles for his encouragement; Sam Slote, my fearless adviser; Philip Coleman; the whole English Department at Trinity College Dublin; John Elder; Niamh Dowdall, for her constant support and faith; the James Joyce Centre; Geert Lernout; Fritz Senn and the Zürich James Joyce Foundation for providing me with a fellowship in 2009; everyone at Foster Place—I hope I got the milk enough times; Kate O'Connor and 2 Maple Drive; my wonderful friends who supported me across the Atlantic—Beth, Kelly, Katie H., Kate P., Kathleen, and Martin; Keel Geheber for his patience when repeatedly being asked to read this over half a decade; and my colleagues and students at the University of Southern Mississippi.

I would like to express my gratitude to Dale and Janet Shearer, who kindly helped support this project. I would like to thank the *Joyce Studies Annual* for permission to reprint excerpts from my article "Polar Exploration in *Finnegans Wake*," from *Joyce Studies Annual* (2013). I would also like to thank David Hayman for allowing me to draw on his work, *The First-Draft Version of* Finnegans Wake, extensively, and Catherine de Courcy, for allowing me to publish information from our e-mail correspondence.

I dedicate this book to my parents, Mark and Audrey Lacivita, who supported me for the seven years I was away from the United States and were always only a phone call away.

Abbreviations

1. Editions of Joyce's Works

BL   Joyce, James. *Finnegans Wake*. Drafts, corrected typescript, and proofs, 1923–1939. British Library, London, Archives and Manuscripts Division.
CW   Joyce, James. *Occasional, Critical, and Political Writing*. Ed. Kevin Barry. Oxford: Oxford University Press, 2000. Print.
D   Joyce, James. *Dubliners*. Ed. Robert Scholes and A. Walton Litz. New York: Viking Press, 1969. Print.
FDV Hayman, David, ed. *A First-Draft Version of* Finnegans Wake. Austin: University of Texas Press, 1963. Print.
FW   (plus page and line number) Joyce, James. *Finnegans Wake*. New York: Penguin, 1999. Print.
JJA (plus volume and page number) *The James Joyce Archives*. Ed. Michael Groden et al. 63 vols. New York: Garland Publishing, 1978–1979. Print.
LI   Joyce, James. *Letters of James Joyce: Volume 1*. Ed. Stuart Gilbert. New York: Viking Press, 1957; reissued with corrections, 1966. Print.
LII Joyce, James. *Letters of James Joyce: Volume 2*. Ed. Richard Ellmann. New York: Viking Press, 1966. Print.
LIII Joyce, James. *Letters of James Joyce: Volume 3*. Ed. Richard Ellmann. New York: Viking Press, 1966. Print.
P   Joyce, James. *A Portrait of the Artist as a Young Man*. Ed. Chester G. Anderson. New York: Viking Press, 1968. Print.
PSW Joyce, James. *Poems and Shorter Writings*. Ed. Richard Ellmann, A. Walton Litz, and John Whittier-Ferguson. London: Faber and Faber, 1991. Print.

SH   Joyce, James. *Stephen Hero*. Ed. Theodore Spencer, John J. Slocum, and Herbert Cahoon. New York: New Directions, 1963. Print.
U   (plus episode and line number) Joyce, James. *Ulysses*. Ed. Hans Walter Gabler et al. New York: Garland Publishing, 1984, 1986. Print.

2. Frequently Cited Works of Joyce Criticism

Buffalo VI.B.   (plus notebook number and page) *The* Finnegans Wake *Notebooks at Buffalo*. Ed. Vincent Deane, Daniel Ferrer, and Geert Lernout. Turnhout: Brepols, 2001– . Print.
EFW   Epstein, Edmund. *A Guide through* Finnegans Wake. Gainesville: University Press of Florida, 2009. Print.
Geni   Slote, Sam, and Wim Van Mierlo, eds. *Genitricksling Joyce*. Amsterdam: Rodopi, 1999. Print.
HJW   Crispi, Luca, and Sam Slote, eds. *How Joyce Wrote* Finnegans Wake: *A Chapter-by-Chapter Genetic Guide*. Madison: University of Wisconsin Press, 2007. Print.
JJ   Ellmann, Richard. *James Joyce*. Oxford and New York: Oxford University Press, 1982. Print.
McHugh   McHugh, Roland. *Annotations to* Finnegans Wake. Baltimore: Johns Hopkins University Press, 1991. Print.
Probes   Hayman, David, and Sam Slote, eds. *Probes: Genetic Studies in Joyce*. Amsterdam: Rodopi, 1995. Print.
TDJJ   Rose, Danis. *The Textual Diaries of James Joyce*. Dublin: Lilliput, 1995. Print.
UFW   O'Hanlon, John, and Danis Rose. *Understanding* Finnegans Wake. New York: Garland, 1982. Print.
WiT   Hayman, David. *The* Wake *in Transit*. Ithaca: Cornell University Press, 1990. Print.

3. Joyce Journals, Print and Online

AFWC   *A Finnegans Wake Circular*
AWN   *A Wake Newslitter*
GJS   *Genetic Joyce Studies*
HJS   *Hypermedia Joyce Studies*
JJQ   *James Joyce Quarterly*
JSA   *Joyce Studies Annual*

Textual Note

References in the text and notes to Joyce's manuscript material as "simplified" mean that I have not included all changes made to a passage, only those that are substantial or relevant to the discussion at hand. Carets (^) in transcriptions of manuscript material indicate Joyce's additions to the manuscript.

The British Library (BL) in London is a major repository of Joycean materials, including annotated drafts, typescripts, and proofs of *Finnegans Wake*. All of the BL citations I present in this study come from the 63-volume James Joyce Archive (JJA). In short citations, such as (BL 47482b-62v), manuscript number (47482b) and page or folio number (62v), sometimes indicating recto (r) or verso (v), follow BL. In long citations, such as (BL 47480-267, JJA 55: 446a, FDV 203.29, FW 380.34), the BL locator is succeeded in turn by (1) location in the James Joyce Archive (vol. and page number), (2) location in the *First-Draft Version of* Finnegans Wake (FDV), and (3) location in *Finnegans Wake* (page and line number). Thus, commas in long citations separate the elements of one citation; semicolons separate discrete citations.

Introduction

An Ecocritical Joyce?

"Time and the river and the mountain are the real heroes of my book." Joyce made this assertion to Eugene Jolas while explaining one version of the structure of *Finnegans Wake*; he continued: "Yet the elements are exactly what any novelist might use: man and woman, birth, childhood, night, sleep, marriage, prayer, death" (qtd. in Jolas, "My Friend" 11–12). This study follows Joyce's direction, presenting the argument, through a genetic examination of environmental themes in the text, that "the river and the mountain" are really the heroes of *Finnegans Wake*. I define "environmental themes" broadly, as themes relating to the natural world or the human relationship to the natural world. Such themes are wide-ranging and include topics such as the city, wetlands, geography, imperialism, animals, agriculture, technology, transportation, engineering, religious tradition, mapping, and the sciences, among others. However, to limit the material, this study focuses only on instances where these themes are clearly grounded in the physical environment.

Through the dual lenses of ecocriticism and genetic criticism, *Finnegans Wake* is situated here in a tradition of modernist inquiries into the relationship between culture and nature. If we broadly define literary modernism as a response to modernity, *Finnegans Wake*'s articulation of an urban ecology, of a self-conscious aesthetic appropriation of nature, and use of experimental form to represent nature make it an exemplary text. During the first years of its composition, *Finnegans Wake* was on its way to becoming the first major text of modernist literature to express profound engagement with the environment. Joyce did not necessarily commence the writing of the *Wake* with this idea in mind. However, from an examination of the earliest sketches and notebooks for the *Wake*, it appears that

Joyce was interested enough in the environment, in a capacity seemingly not yet clear even to him, to record dozens of notes from a wide variety of sources and in very different contexts and to incorporate environmental themes into all of the early sketches.

In this introduction, I provide a brief overview of ecocriticism and its relationship to modernist studies, Irish studies, and Joyce studies. Then I discuss my genetic methodology and provide a genetic approach to three sources in one of the *Finnegans Wake* notebooks as an example of its applications in such a study. Finally, I provide a chapter-by-chapter outline of the book.

An Introduction to Ecocriticism

In the introduction to *The Ecocriticism Reader*, Harold Fromm and Cheryll Glotfelty provide the most frequently cited definition of ecocriticism: "Simply put, ecocriticism is the study of the relationship between literature and the physical environment" (xviii). Since the formative essays of the ecocritical canon were published in the 1970s and 1980s, ecocriticism has steadily expanded in scope, and the traditional approach of examining the role of nature in a particular literary text now encompasses an ever-broadening definition of both "literature" and "physical environment." "Physical environment" has come to mean everything from the deepest woods to the busiest urban areas, and "literature" has become almost any type of text.

As ecocriticism becomes more of an accepted theoretical approach in literary study, the subject matter of which ecocriticism is allowed to speak steadily continues to expand. Along with class, race, and gender, place can now be seen as a determining factor in the understanding of literatures and their production. By "place," I (reductively) mean the specificities of the environment (both built and natural), and their exchange with the culture specific to that particular geographical area. This new focus on place has helped result in the merging of ecocriticism with Marxist criticism (ecomarxism), gender studies, queer theory, feminist criticism (ecofeminism), ethnic studies, and postcolonial criticism.

Though there are presently many different ecocriticisms, two roughly unifying goals behind them all are (1) the exposure of the ways in which the language we use to describe and discuss nature affects our perception of that nature, and (2) the acknowledgment of human inseparability from the nonhuman world. Though early ecocriticism often embraced and perpetuated the timeless "nature vs. culture" binary, such a division is usually now seen as an artificial construct (though oddly not with regard to modernist literature). As Karla Armbruster and Kathleen Wallace argue in *Beyond Nature Writing: Expanding the Boundaries of Ecocriticism* (2001), the focus of earlier ecocritics on personal narratives of the American wilderness is guilty of "seriously misrepresenting the significance of multiple natural and built environments to writers with other ethnic, national or racial affiliations" (7). The culture/nature binary is implicated in the endurance of other damaging discursive binaries as well (white/black, man/woman, colonizer/colonized, urban/rural, human/nonhuman, etc.). As Steven Rosendale argues in *The Greening of Literary Scholarship*, an important idea to keep in mind as an ecocritic is the "human component of the human-nature relationship" (xvii). In the twenty-first century, there is no part of the nonhuman environment that is not affected by human life or vice versa. In short, this dynamic means that the culture/nature and urban/rural divide becomes less and less clear and that the ecocritic must examine all types of environments.

Recent years have brought the constructive interaction between ecocriticism and post-structuralism/postmodernism, though the attempt to bridge the gap between these two approaches has frequently been met with harsh criticism. Early ecocriticism (and much ecocriticism still) sets itself as against theory and in favor of a return to the "real" (once primarily through recourse to nonfiction texts and "nature writing"). Critics of the integration of post-structuralism and ecocriticism often represent post-structuralism as a malicious force that treats nature as solely a linguistic construct. Such critics tend to focus on only the most nihilistic interpretations of post-structuralism and postmodernism, overlooking the ability of these approaches to, for example, decenter the human subject and to query systems of thought and uses of language that reinforce narratives harmful to the environment. While such ecocritics' fear is understandable (radical interpretations of Jacques Derrida or Jean Baudrillard certainly can imply that nature exists only linguistically or culturally and that therefore we do not need to worry about our effect upon it), it is also limiting to the development of ecocriticism's theoretical stance and its larger implications.

Laurence Coupe, in *The Green Studies Reader*, argues that "green studies does not challenge the notion that human beings make sense of the world through language, but rather the self-serving inference that nature is nothing more than a linguistic construct" (3). Coupe accepts the role of language in understanding and formulating the world, but profitably separates this from the destructive belief that the world is only a linguistic construct. Allowing post-structuralism to enter the ecocritical debate on the linguistic level allows for an exploration into the root of our current environmental crisis.

A reassertion of nature's materiality may seem contrary to much philosophy associated with Joyce and with *Finnegans Wake*, but several philosophers associated with post-structuralism and postmodernism do in fact "use" nature to support arguments concerning the decentering of the human, of language, and of the metanarrative. In addition to Martin Heidegger's concept of "dwelling" and Derrida's discussions of the "ani/mal" (in *The Animal That Therefore I Am*), Maurice Merleau-Ponty's work has been the most readily adopted by critics working in diverse areas of ecocriticism.[1] The passages in Merleau-Ponty to which ecocriticism gravitates largely concern language, and David Abram goes so far as to conclude an essay on the phenomenologist by asserting that he stands for an "Eco-Logos," and that "[h]is work suggests a rigorous way to approach and to speak of ecological systems without positing our immediate selves outside of those systems" (97). Such a concept is what defines ecocriticism as a critical approach as opposed to simply a discussion of nature in literature; ecocriticism seeks to uncover assumptions, often buried in language, about the construction of "nature" as a category, and to explore the formal innovations for representing this construction.

Merleau-Ponty, in *The Visible and the Invisible*, provides support for the type of work ecocriticism is now doing when he writes that the goal now for philosophy consists "in restoring a power to signify, a birth of meaning, or a wild meaning, an expression of experience by experience, which in particular clarifies the special domain of language. And in a sense, as Valéry said, language is everything, since it is the voice of no one, since it is the very voice of the things, the waves, and the forests" (155). Continuing, Merleau-Ponty argues that "language is born of our carnal participation in a world that already speaks to us at the most immediate level of sensory experience," and thus, "language does not belong to humankind but to the sensible world of which we are but a part" (274). This detachment of language from the human is crucial when considering, for example, the relationship between language and the current environmental crisis; in a Lacanian sense, the system of language is something into which we have been born, and it exists beyond the control of the individual utterer and utterance.

Merleau-Ponty's attitudes are consistent with the way Joyce portrays language in *Finnegans Wake*; the mixing of languages, both synchronically and diachronically, the malleability of words in different contexts, the difficulties in communication, and the misunderstandings suggest that individuals are not in control of their language or its usage. This lack of control is demonstrated through Joyce's decentering of the human subject, so that several times throughout the *Wake*, language's anthropocentrism is queried, and the text explores the possibilities of other forms of communication, be it through the legibility of the physical landscape or the "speech" of the river and the sea.

Louise Westling, author of *The Green Breast of the New World: Landscape, Gender, and American Fiction* (1998), argues elsewhere that a poststructuralist approach to literary texts can be quite useful to ecocritics, as "it helps to define the human place within the ecosystem by interrogating or erasing the boundary that has been assumed to set our species apart from the rest of the living community" ("Literature" 30). Writing of this boundary, environmental historian Donald Worster argues in *The Wealth of Nature* that "it is a completely arbitrary act to put culture and nature into separate categories, requiring rigidly separate methods of analysis. The polar bear has claws and a fur coat to cope with its environment; we humans use our cultures to do the same" (37). In Worster's view, culture is something directly born out of and dependent on nature, and this idea is integral to the exploration of the ecology of *Finnegans Wake*.

Ecocriticism and Modernist Studies

Though the situation is changing every day (as attested to by the publication of studies such as Bonnie Kime Scott's *In the Hollow of the Wave: Virginia Woolf and Modernist Uses of Nature* [June 2012], or the emphasis on nature in modernism at the 2011 Modernist Studies Association conference, etc.), very few ecocritics address modernist writers, and very few modernist critics address the natural environment. It is only slightly reductive to suggest that prior ecocritical focus on the romantics and nature writing, combined with modernist studies' emphasis on the urban, metropolitan aspects of modernism, has led to a significant gap on both sides. Fairly expansive bodies of ecocritical work already exist on the literature of the early modern period, the romantic period, and the years from World War II to the present, but the period from 1900 until 1950 remains largely unexplored ecocritically. Several studies examine the role of science (largely, physics) in works of modernist art and literature, but few focus on other sciences such as ecology, botany, entomology, zoology, or ethology, or on "nature" as a larger category. J. Scott Bryson, in one of the only attempts to bridge this critical gap, an essay titled "Modernism and Ecological Criticism," also notes this dearth and questions why this is:

> An ecocritical methodology has much to offer as an approach to modern literature, not only because modern artists displayed a significant interest in natural elements in their work [. . .] but also because a central question for artists and intellectuals in the early part of the twentieth century became how humans could somehow render their experiences with a more-than-human world. (591)

This negotiation of the human and the nonhuman or "more-than-human" world can be found, to some extent, in all the central works of modernist literature, but more often than not, these negotiations are overlooked for more predictable modernist themes of despair, alienation, or stylistic experimentation. Such themes can be examined from the perspective of the environment as well, and any ecocritical approach to these tropes of modernist studies would produce propitious new readings. Themes of despair and alienation could be viewed as stemming from "a fundamental uncertainty about the relationship between human and non-human nature" (Bryson, "Modernism" 591), and stylistic experimentations could be understood as attempts to adequately represent a natural world that was receding farther and farther from human life, comprehension, and imagination every day.

To introduce my approach to the definition of an ecological modernism, I turn to Lawrence Buell. In his defining work of ecocriticism, *The Environmental Imagination: Thoreau, Nature Writing, and the Formation of American Culture*, he articulates four criteria for determining the "environmental" quality of a text:

1. The nonhuman environment is present not merely as a framing device but as a presence that begins to suggest that human history is implicated in natural history.

2. The human interest is not understood to be the only legitimate interest.
3. Human accountability to the environment is part of the text's ethical orientation.
4. Some sense of the environment as a process rather than as a constant or a given is at least implicit in the text. (7–8)

Though Buell intended these criteria to apply almost exclusively to "nature writing" and to be unmistakably purposeful in such "environmental" texts, his four criteria can be adapted to examine a wide range of other texts not explicitly "environmental." Despite having the opposite intention, Buell's criteria are particularly suited to more experimental texts; traditional character, setting, and narrative may speak of nature and environmental issues, but will they have the same impact as a text like *Finnegans Wake*, wherein one of the protagonists morphs between woman and river? This study explores how *Finnegans Wake* meets all of Buell's criteria and often draws upon them to guide the ecocritical reading.

Irish Literature and Ecocriticism

Strangely (for a country known as the "Emerald Isle"), ecocriticism is only just beginning to attach itself to the study of Irish literature. There are very few works of Irish ecocriticism, and those that do exist operate almost entirely within fairly tired images of idealized nature, usually through recourse to the Christian nature poets. While this approach may be effective for reclaiming the Irish tradition of nature poetry from the Anglo-Irish–dominated literary revival, it also inhibits contemporary Irish writing from bringing the Irish landscape into the twenty-first century. *Finnegans Wake* deals with all kinds of Irish environments, from inner-city slums to the coasts of Cork and the mountains of Kerry, to the suburban village of Chapelizod and the purgatorial identity of the Phoenix Park, Europe's largest urban park. Joyce also refrains from describing any aspect of nature in the modern world as independent from human interests; he writes of the politics of land, the recurrence of famine, the blessings and curses of agriculture. He often focuses on transitional spaces, on the outskirts of cities, on coastlines, on riverbanks and on bogs, and uses them to explore various boundaries constructed by civilization.

The slow introduction of ecocriticism to Ireland and to Irish literature is also indicative of larger issues related to Ireland and the environment. Though Ireland's popular image may be "green," as Mikael Andersen and Duncan Liefferink argue, Ireland is certainly a "latecomer" in terms of European environmental policy (6). It is not just environmental themes in literature that are overlooked by contemporary Irish culture, but larger environmental issues in the country have also been ignored. Michael Viney, a natural history columnist for the *Irish Times*, explains that, in fact, Ireland ranks very low in international conservation league tables, with "only 1 percent of the national territory given the strict protection of national parks and preserves, compared with an average of 12 percent in other developed countries" (*Smithsonian Natural History* 308). Any reasons for this lack of environmental interest are speculative, but there are a few possible explanations. Viney, in the final chapter of *Natural History of Ireland*, explains that today, in Ireland, "nature conservation is still largely identified with an Anglo-Irish culture" (307–8). John Feehan, a lecturer in environmental resource management at University College, Dublin, expresses a similar view in his essay "Threat and Conservation: Attitudes to Nature in Ireland," arguing that the romantic movement did not have a similar impact in Ireland as it did in England, except "within the walls of the demesnes," and that "this identification of an interest and concern for natural and cultural heritage with the leisured class has persisted down to the present" (583). Though this breakdown is fairly reductive, its logic is sound: the Anglo-Irish had the spare time to stroll about their estates, taking an interest in natural history and conservation, while the tenants tried to make their living and keep their families alive on this same land. What was "sublime" for one was Patrick Kavanagh's "stony grey soil" for another. In order for any redefinition of this conception to occur, there must be a focus on the cultural representations of nature and their ideological origins during the period of English authority in Ireland.

With neither romanticism nor the environmental movement catching on in nineteenth-century Ireland as they did in England, the exploitative policies of the newly formed Irish Free State took hold much easier; Viney explains that "in the impoverished early decades of an independent Ireland, the popular view of nature was urgently utilitarian and land-hungry" (*Smithsonian Natural History* 1). Joyce incorporates this "utilitarian and land-hungry" attitude of the Irish Free State into the *Wake*, referencing the planned destruction of the Bird Sanctuary on Dublin's North Bull

Island, the promotion of peat burning as an effort in energy independence, the methodical attempts at Irish afforestation, and the use of territorially charged rhetoric by Sinn Féin.

More recently, the Celtic Tiger brought Ireland into a sudden wave of prosperity. During this period, Ireland, a nation previously perceived to be archaic by many Western nations, witnessed the arrival of international financial organizations, an influx of workers and immigrants from all over the world, and, overall, a significant rise in the standard of living. During this period, the main interests for a large portion of the population were not environmental conservation but electronics, vacation homes, luxury cars, and designer clothing. Neither was the environment a chief concern for the Irish government, as conservation was seen as a hindrance to further development. The way in which the Irish government responded to environmental concerns during the Celtic Tiger was not dissimilar to its environmental record following the birth of the Irish Free State, another period in the country's recent history where it was struggling to define itself against an inglorious past.

In addition to an urban ecological criticism, a possible way of greening both Irish studies and modernist studies is through a "cultural ecological criticism," an ecological criticism that focuses on the interaction between the human and the environment. In their *Atlas of the Irish Rural Landscape*, F.H.A. Aalen, Matthew Stout, and Kevin Whelan begin by explaining:

> In long and closely settled areas such as Ireland, the human impression is so pervasive that it is appropriate to speak of a cultural landscape. Here, the profusion of human features coalesce and form a virtually continuous layer. This cultural landscape is our major and most productive creation; it is both an artefact, based on foundations of geology and climate, and a narrative, layer upon layer of our history and nature's history intertwined. (5)

It is unrealistic and, frankly, unproductive to speak of any space in Ireland (or, really, any space at all) as unaltered by human intervention. Perpetuating divides between urban and rural Ireland, either geographically or culturally, is irresponsible scholarship. Irish ecocriticism may help to bridge this artificial divide between urban and rural life and, consequently, help to increase general environmental awareness in Ireland.

Ecology during Joyce's Lifetime

During the late nineteenth and early twentieth centuries, a profound change in the way humans viewed their place on earth and their relationship to other living creatures occurred. Clarence Glacken, in his key ecocritical text *Traces on the Rhodian Shore*, argues that the mid-nineteenth century signaled the end of the anthropocentric era, of one in which a "utilitarian interpretation of earth and animals persisted" (704–5).

I argue that in the literary tradition, the aesthetic responses to these events and paradigm shifts can be found in the category of modernism. Malcolm Bradbury and James McFarlane identify two distinct accounts of modernism, the first relating to the aesthetics of form and self-consciousness. In the second definition, modernism is "the art consequent on Heisenberg's 'Uncertainty principle,' of the destruction of civilization and reason in the First World War, of the world changed and reinterpreted by Marx, Freud and Darwin, of capitalism and constant industrial acceleration, of existential exposure to meaninglessness or absurdity. It is the literature of technology" (27). In this definition, modernism is a direct product of the scientific, political, and philosophical contexts of the period, and I expand this definition to include the context of the environment.

The paradigm shift that occurred during this period redefined the human relationship to and understanding of the effect upon the natural world. For example, the nineteenth and early twentieth centuries witnessed the first efforts toward our current idea of environmental conservation with the establishment of the Society for the Prevention of Cruelty to Animals (UK) in 1824, the Sea Birds Preservation Act of 1869 (UK), the establishment of Yellowstone National Park in 1872 (USA), the foundation of the Kyrle Society in 1875 (UK), the establishment of the Society for the Protection of Birds Act of 1880 (UK), the foundation of the Sierra Club in 1892 (USA), and the creation of the National Park Service in 1916 (USA).[2] The National Trust (UK) was founded in 1895 by three Victorian philanthropists who, according to the organization's website, were "concerned about the impact of uncontrolled development and industrialization," and "set up the Trust to act as a guardian for the nation in the acquisition and protection of threatened coastline, countryside and buildings."[3] The modern environmental movement grew from these early efforts in conservation, and this sense of conservation as placing the human in the role of guardian or steward is important to the way in which environmentalism and its associated rhetoric have developed throughout the world.

In the late nineteenth century, one figure in particular stands out in the history of environmental conservation: George Perkins Marsh, an American philologist considered by many to be the first environmentalist. His *Man and Nature, Or, Physical Geography as Modified by Human Action* (1864) was the first text to argue that the success of a civilization was dependent upon its environment. Marsh argued that Mediterranean civilizations collapsed because of the way they treated the land; for centuries, especially in the Judeo-Christian tradition, the prevailing belief had largely been that the earth, its creatures, and its resources were there for human benefit.[4] Anna Bramwell's *Ecology in the 20th Century: A History* explains how, during the late nineteenth and early twentieth centuries, belief in the perfection and indestructibility of God's creation was replaced with the idea of "biological holism." This idea held that "man and animals were interdependent in and on a balanced environment," and, in corollary, anthropogenic effects on the land became increasingly recognized, as the view that "the dissipation of energy might endanger man's existence, or even that of the planet itself" became pervasive (15). Modern geographers also altered the way in which land was perceived; they "examined land settlement and use from the aspect of resources," arguing that "no longer was land a finite resource, but it was slowly becoming a *quantifiable* resource, one that was limited and one that should be preserved" (15). This shift in terms of a sense of responsibility to the world was of enormous consequence; the idea that human actions could have an effect on the world discredited many central Christian beliefs as well as beliefs about the idea of "progress."[5]

Christina Alt, in *Virginia Woolf and the Study of Nature*, provides an overview of the development of the modern life sciences, locating the origin of ecology and ethology in the late-nineteenth-century popularity of "evolutionary history and the new biology of the laboratory" (38). According to Alt, "developments in the late nineteenth and early twentieth-century life sciences [. . .] transformed the way that nature was seen and described, shifting attention from external form to internal functioning, and from the dead specimen to the living organism, its behavior, and its interactions with its environment" (39). The expanding fields of ecology and ethology around the turn of the century also contributed to Joyce's use of nature to articulate changing historical philosophies; popular accounts of nature provided new metaphors (mainly through ideas of organicism, community, symbiosis, and feedback cycles) through which to communicate his "universal history."

Alt also provides an account of the celebrity of several individual works in the life sciences during this period. For example, she discusses the entomologist Jean-Henri Fabre, his *Souvenirs entomologiques* (a series of texts on insects, published from 1879 to 1909), and how his work exploded in popularity: "Thirty-three books based on English translations of Fabre's works appeared in the 1910s and another in the 1920s; additionally, between 1912 and 1922 *The English Review* intermittently printed excerpts from *Souvenirs entomologiques* and extracts appeared as well in the *Fortnightly Review* and the *Daily Mail*" (55).[6] The popularity of entomology during the 1920s may explain where Joyce found some of the information used for "The Ondt and the Gracehoper," or at least where he found some of the ideas, as the *Daily Mail* was a source for the first *Finnegans Wake* notebooks (at least in 1922–1924).[7]

In addition to developments in ethology and entomology, this period also witnessed the first incursions into ecology. The term "ecology" was coined in 1866 by the German zoologist Ernst Haeckel in his *Generelle Morphologie der Organismen*, which was written on the heels of Charles Darwin's *On the Origin of Species*: "By ecology we mean the whole science of the relations of the organism to the environment including, in the broad sense, all the 'conditions of existence.' These are partly organic, partly inorganic in nature; both, as we have shown, are of the greatest significance for the form of organisms, for they force them to become adapted" (qtd. in Merchant, *Columbia Guide* 159).[8] Focusing on the etymology of the word from *oikos*, Carolyn Merchant cites Haeckel's two most important ideas as the "idea of nature as household" and the "economy of nature" (160). Extending from Darwin's theories of adaptation, Haeckel's work urged biologists to take into account the impact of environment and habitat on an organism and eventually led to the development of the idea of the "ecosystem" (Merchant, *Columbia Guide* 159–62). In the following century, the term "ecosystem" was adapted to various contexts, with the main focus being the idea that communities and networks are defined by symbiotic relationships.

The metaphorical use of terms like "ecosystem" is questioned in Dana Phillips's *The Truth of Ecology*, wherein Phillips provides a brief overview of the history of ecology in an attempt to navigate the differing interpretations and connotations of this word over the past century. Phillips tries to rein in what he sees as the humanities' overzealous use of scientific discourse by separating the metaphorical implications of certain terms from their more discipline-specific origins. For example, he explains that the term "ecosystem," as we understand it today, did not fully come into use until 1935 (from the British ecologist A. G. Tansley's paper "The Use and Abuse of Vegetational Concepts and Terms" [61]) and firmly grounds the term "ecosystem" in botany. However, Phillips does not acknowledge Tansley's relationship with Freud, which began in the 1920s and greatly impacted the remainder of Tansley's career.[9] Tansley himself promoted the metaphorical connection between psychology and biology, aligning the concept of the mind as a system with the ecosystem, and drew upon such analogies to study vegetative succession (Cameron, "Ecosystems" 55–56).

The term "ecosystem" suggests, clearly, a *system*, a machine-like version of nature that is integrated and self-regulatory. Such ideas occasionally led to regressive beliefs in nature's permanence and immutability, but Tansley's definition actually suggests otherwise: "Many systems (represented by vegetation climaxes) which appear to be stable during the period for which they have been under accurate observation may in reality have been slowly changing all the time, because the changes effected have been too slight to be noted by observers. Many ecologists hold that *all* vegetation is *always* changing" (Tansley 302). If we keep Tansley's relationship with Freud in mind, this definition of the dynamism of the ecosystem and of steady-state equilibrium suggests that both the human mind and the natural world are always changing yet never changing: an ordered disorder.

Haeckel's definition of ecology also influenced the development of environmental determinism during the late nineteenth and early twentieth centuries, merging ecology with geography, anthropology, and history. A strain of cultural geography, environmental determinism "sought to link human social behavior to determinants in the physical environment (most prominently climate)" (Mitchell 17). A geographical complement to social Darwinism, environmental determinism contributed to early-twentieth-century ideas about the link between a culture, a people, a nation, and their environment (encompassing a wide range of features, from climate to soil to geology and hydrology). Following studies like George Perkins Marsh's, which argued for the relationship between the success of a civilization and its environment, the work of Ellen Churchill Semple (*Influences of Geographic Environment: On the Basis of Ratzel's System of Anthropo-Geography* [1911]), Karl Wittfogel (*Oriental Despotism* [1957]), Thomas Griffith Taylor (*Environment, Race, and Migration* [1937]), and Ellsworth Huntington (*Climate and Civilization* [1915]) explored the interdependence between geography, climate (one of both Haeckel's and Tansley's "inorganic" conditions), and history. Wittfogel established a Marxist dialectic in the struggle between a people and their land in his 1929 article "Geopolitics, Geographical Materialism, and Marxism," which is distilled by Donald Worster to the question: "How does a society's interaction with nature lead to its own restructuring, to its evolution from one form to another?" (*Wealth of Nature* 33). Joyce's own interest in environmental determinism is discussed at length throughout the present study and was sparked by Léon Metchnikoff, a geographer whose *La civilisation et les grandes fleuves historiques* (1889) explored the relationship between progress, civilization, and water sources. This question of the relationship between a society and its environment is addressed throughout the entirety of *Finnegans Wake* as Joyce explores how environment impacts the rise and fall of civilizations.

Technology must also be a key player in any discussion of the relationship between culture and nature in literary modernism. Tim Armstrong, for example, cites the "control of nature" as one of the defining aims of technology (158). In the first half of the twentieth century, several studies appeared concerning the cultural impact of technology, seeking to understand the way in which technology alters the understanding of what it means to be human.[10] Throughout the last century, developments in ecology, ethology, anthropology, biology, chemistry, physics, astronomy, robotics, and cybernetics steadily blurred the boundary line between the human and the nonhuman, calling into question some of the most fundamental beliefs held by mankind. Gilles Deleuze and Félix Guattari, in *Anti-Oedipus: Capitalism and Schizophrenia*, present nature as continuous with the "desiring machine" of man, wherein "every 'object' presupposes the continuity of a flow; every flow, the fragmentation of the object" (6). They propose the dissolution of subject and nature: "Man and nature are not like two opposite terms confronting each other—not even in the sense of bipolar opposites within a relationship of causation, ideation, or expression (cause and effect, subject and object, etc.); rather, they are one and the same essential reality, the producer-product" (5). Deleuze and

Guattari see technology as a force uniting the human and the nonhuman through shared subjugation. This shared subjugation is evident throughout *Finnegans Wake* as Joyce unites the female ALP with the river and the male HCE with Dublin city; each becomes both the exploiter and the exploited in a world focused on progress.

The relatively new awareness of the lasting human impact on nature incited fears throughout the late Victorian period. Joyce may have been alert to the subject of famines because of the emergence of widespread fears of disasters such as "erosion and famine" (Bramwell 7) in early-twentieth-century Europe. The cycles of famine in history suggest famines will continually appear, as they are, after all, negative feedback cycles that control populations and regulate resources such as soil, minerals, and water. Though many believe that technology—in the forms of industry, transportation, medicine, genetically modified organisms, and so forth—will be able to alleviate fears of disasters such as famine, the appearance of these fears in the early twentieth century reveals an underlying distrust in technology's effects and efficacy. In an era when military technology redefined the suffering of war, when national boundaries were being constantly redrawn, when balances of power were continually shifting, there was a fear that nature might also somehow react to its own restraint. Furthermore, this fear is indicative of a shift in perceptions of the environment, moving from a belief in nature as objective to that of nature as responsive to human actions in unpredictable ways.

In the late nineteenth and early twentieth centuries, millions of lives were lost around the world as a result of erosion, famine, disease, floods, earthquakes, tornados, hurricanes, and tsunamis, and with new developments in cinema, these natural disasters were often up on the big screen, thousands of miles away, within days of their occurrence.[11] Additionally, the continually increasing speed with which news was able to reach its audience around the world led to heightened paranoia about such natural disasters. Though natural disasters have obviously always occurred, their newfound fame in the media meant that their frequency seemed to be much greater. The fear that grew from this new awareness clashed with residual faith in the human ability to understand and control nature and put into question confidence in the ability of technology to effectively manipulate and harness natural resources.

As a result of this change in the human attitude toward nature, there was, on the one hand, the decoupling of nature from human responsibility, while, on the other, there was an increase in the sense of humanity's responsibility for the environment. This attitude may seem contradictory, as it certainly is, and it is this contradiction that accounts for the disparity even in current debate over environmental issues. Spiritual beliefs in the benevolent (or not so benevolent) treatment of humans by nature were no longer viable for most, and careful preparations, rituals, or ceremonies (perhaps called superstitions at this point), believed to ensure good weather and, subsequently, good harvests, were irrelevant. Nature would do what it was going to do, regardless of human actions and wishes. For some, this inflexibility was because of the "laws" of nature, but for others, these laws of nature were actually proof of God's design.

The decoupling of nature from religion is one of the most important historical shifts in human attitudes toward the environment. For social policy, medicine, science, literature, art, and nearly any endeavor in the modern world, the separation of the environment from divine providential control is an essential assumption. This shift is a major division between romanticism and modernism, for the providentially controlled wind of William Wordsworth's *Prelude* has become the drought and dry lightning of T. S. Eliot's *The Waste Land*. Nature is uncaring, unforgiving, and uncontrollable. However, nature's ability to *respond* (through such events as famine) replaced its divinity with a different agency, and, as Christa Grewe-Volpp argues, such "responses" mean nature becomes, in a way, "an autonomous actor" (78). She continues, arguing that with this understanding, nature "can no longer be depicted as a mere setting, but becomes a protagonist capable of articulation" (78). Grewe-Volpp takes her point partially from Donna Haraway, one of the principal theorists of the posthuman, who maintains that while nature does not have language in the "human sense," it is capable of articulation, of signification.[12] Grewe-Volpp concludes with Haraway:

> The land, for example, or, more generally, a place, subtly or explicitly influences the psyche and the actual behavior of individual protagonists. Climate, wilderness conditions, technologically altered landscapes, topographies and many other environmental elements—never as pristine nature, never as mere text—function as a powerful force that human beings have to—and do—react to. (Haraway qtd. in Grewe-Volpp 78)

In *Finnegans Wake* Joyce represents the ways in which nature possesses its own agency and its own ability to articulate. Though this articulation is obviously radically different from our own, it is undeniable that nature reacts to human behavior in a way that is not aligned with human beliefs and desires (for example, our current global climate crisis). Through issues of public housing, agriculture, disease, engineering, and famine, Joyce explores the way in which the environment reacts to human manipulation, and through the construction of "place," he also explores how these places define the course of human life and identity.

Interest in the environment and in the human relationship with the environment during the late nineteenth and early twentieth centuries developed from a combination of factors that, while mostly not new, all collided during this period in different ways around the world. Industrialization, technology (radio, telephones, phonographs, cinema, television), X-rays, transportation (railroads, automobiles, airplanes), urban sprawl, famine, quantum mechanics, pollution, the Great Depression, disease, World War I—together, these events and trends forced the questioning of the very idea of progress.

One of the most important reasons to look at works of modernist literature like *Finnegans Wake* from an ecocritical perspective is the ability to connect current environmental concerns with their origins in the late nineteenth and early twentieth centuries. The modern environmental movement is usually seen as a post–World War II product, going hand-in-hand with other civil rights issues. While this view may be partially true, recent scholarship is striving to create continuity from the early twentieth century to the present in terms of our anxieties about the environment and its future. For example, a 2011 study by *Atlantic* senior editor Alexis Madrigal, *Powering the Dream: The History and Promise of Green Technology*, demonstrates how the idea of green technology is not new, but actually originated in the late nineteenth century. Madrigal's history of entrepreneurs interested in what we today know as "renewable energy" covers the last century and a half and proves that the "new" ideas of the past twenty years really are in fact not as new as we think.

In the introduction to *The Environment and World History*, Edmund Burke and Kenneth Pomeranz set out to merge the disciplines of environmental history and world history. They argue that such a merger would help in "reframing the relationship between parts and wholes" (xiii), and they aim for "a more global environmental history and a more environmentally conscious world history" (xiii), arguing that such a redefinition of perspectives has a lot to offer in our era of globalization and international environmental crisis. *The Ecology of* Finnegans Wake argues that environmental history is a principal component of the "universal history" Joyce seeks to present in *Finnegans Wake* and that such a reorientation of a major twentieth-century text contributes to a more "environmentally conscious world history."

James Joyce and Ecocriticism

When Joyce was visiting Denmark in 1936, the journalist Ole Vinding asked, "Do you like flowers, Mr Joyce?" to which Joyce replied: "No. I love plants, green growing things, trees and grass. Flowers annoy me" (JJ 694). While it remains unclear why flowers annoyed Joyce, this love for "growing things" can be traced back to one of the most famous quotations of Joyce's early years, in his identification of a mistranslation of one of Aristotle's tenets: "'Art is an imitation of Nature.' Aristotle does not here define art, he says only 'Art imitates nature,' and meant the artistic process is like the natural process" (CW 145). While this phrase was written when Joyce was very young, it is nonetheless a useful starting point for an examination of Joyce's relationship to the natural world. Lawrence Buell's fourth criterion for an environmental text echoes this dictum from the adolescent Joyce: "Some sense of the environment as a process rather than as a constant or a given is at least implicit in the text" (7–8). Throughout all of Joyce's work, this sense of the environment as implicated in human life is in the background; whether it is through the alignment of Stephen's moods and emotions with the weather in *Stephen Hero*, the snow that unifies Ireland in "The Dead," or the "bird-girl" scene of *A Portrait of the Artist as a Young Man*, Joyce connected nature and climate with artistic inspiration and creation throughout his life. In *Ulysses*, nature and climate are intertwined with issues of Irish nationalism and identity, colonialism, technology, suburbanization, gender, questions of what it means to be human, relationships with other nonhuman animals, and entire outlooks on the world. *Ulysses* is without doubt a novel about the *city* of Dublin, but Dublin, like all cities, is a city whose existence is contingent on its physical setting. Joyce displays this fact acutely in *Ulysses* with the inclusion of the geography of Viking and medieval Dublin, as well as with the constant presences of Dublin Bay, Dublin Port, and the River Liffey (all integral components of the 1904 Dublin economy).

Despite these examples, Joyce has been almost unanimously declared an urban writer, a key representative of the modern world and of the ever-increasing dominance of the city in modern life. Joyce critics working in various different contexts, from different decades and from different countries, almost all emphasize the urban quality of his work and generally frown upon any suggestion that Joyce could have been interested in anything relating to nature. Many critics have referred in passing to nature in their arguments, but they either subordinate it to the urban or seem unaware of the fact they have referred to nature at all. A salient example of this mindset is Clive Hart, who wrote an article on the angles of the sun in *Ulysses*, but who also, in his essay on "Wandering Rocks," openly encourages Joyce's readers to ignore anything not explicitly "urban" in his texts: "Joyce was by temperament an urban man. However he might celebrate, in *Finnegans Wake*, the delights of river and mountain, field and flower, these were projections of fantasy, metaphors of the artistic imagination the tenor of which was always life as he knew it in the urban environment" (Hart and Hayman 181). Nature in Joyce is nothing except metaphor for Hart, for whom nature as an actual part of the human experience appears to be completely removed from the urban. The majority of Joyce scholars confine Joyce within the canals of Dublin's city center, but it is perhaps scholars working to (re-)place Joyce into an Irish context that are most emphatic about his urban quality, a trend that is also indicative of the urban-focused trend of Irish studies in recent decades. For example, John Rickard, in "'A Quaking Sod': Hybridity, Identity and Wandering Irishness," from the *European Joyce Studies* collection *James Joyce and the Fabrication of an Irish Identity*, creates an explicit binary between Joyce, the "urban, cosmopolitan writer" (83), and the "rural" concerns of W. B. Yeats and J. M. Synge. Perpetuating such reductive interpretations of both Joyce and the writers involved in the Irish literary revival is counterproductive, especially given the amount of scholarship arguing that these divisions have been largely fabricated by the repetition of, for lack of a better term, sound bites.

Many Joyce critics have not allowed for the interaction of nature and culture in Joyce's work, choosing, instead, to construct a modernist, Joycean city largely independent of external forces. Correspondingly, ecocriticism only recently began to incorporate the urban and built environments into its definitions of environment. Michael Bennett and David W. Teague, in *The Nature of Cities: Ecocriticism and Urban Environments*, note that although ecocriticism is a steadily growing area of cultural criticism, the movement has been "slow to survey the terrain of urban environments," a point they attribute to the general association of ecocritical literary studies with "the body of work devoted to nature writing, American pastoralism, and literary ecology" (1). They identify the parallel tradition of studying "city" literature, pioneered by Blanche Housman Gelfant's *The American City Novel*. I argue that *Finnegans Wake* is an ideal text for introducing urban studies into ecocritical approaches to modernism because of its focus on the environmental contexts of urban life and explorations of the unavoidable intersections between country and city.

Finn Fordham, in *Lots of Fun at Finnegans Wake*, reviews the variety of critical approaches to the *Wake*, ending with a call to action for the intersection of Joyce studies and ecocriticism. He writes that although ecocriticism has not yet attached itself to the *Wake*, such an attachment is certainly possible as, after all, "*Finnegans Wake* tells the story of the planet—of mountains, rivers, the sky, and of the rubbish, the rivers and mountains of it" (20). Fordham, who has experimented with ecocriticism and *Finnegans Wake* himself, is certainly correct about this possibility. The increasing popularity of ecocriticism is slowly but surely being acknowledged by critics working on Joyce. At the 2011 North American James Joyce Conference in California, there were two panels titled "Joyce and Ecocriticism" and another specifically titled "Nature in *Ulysses*." The 2012 James Joyce Symposium in Dublin saw four Joyce and ecocriticism panels, and a handful of papers on Joyce and nature also appeared at 2012's IASIL (International Association for the Study of Irish Literatures) conference in Montreal. This list is certainly not exhaustive, and based on these appearances it is fair to assume that several other conferences around the world have also been seeing work on Joyce and nature.

From the ecocritical side, the situation is largely the same. There are a few isolated references to Joyce within the confines of the ecocritical community, but, as of 2012, ecocriticism has shied away from modernism as much as modernist studies has shied away from ecocriticism. Joyce rarely appears in ecocritical contexts, though Ursula Heise does mention *Finnegans Wake* twice and *Ulysses* once in *Sense of Place and Sense of Planet: The Environmental Imagination of the Global*. Her most notable mention concerns John Cage's use of "hce," and Heise believes that HCE's designation as "here comes everybody" not only "invites a comparison between the artist and the work of art in the early and late twentieth century and their altered position in the media landscape but also evokes a character whose initials make him merge with an inescapable collective," celebrating "the merging of private space with a global landscape" (88).

In *The Face of the Earth: Natural Landscapes, Science, and Culture* (2011), SueEllen Campbell (writing this section jointly with Richard Kerridge, Ellen Wohl, and Tom Lynch) provides perhaps the only significant mention of *Finnegans Wake* in any work of ecocriticism. Campbell also allows modernism, on a larger scale, to engage with ecocriticism. Echoing John Elder's *Imagining the Earth*, Campbell discusses T. S. Eliot's Thames as "a river of time bearing fragments from the cultural past" (141) like "physical debris on the water" (142), and she foregrounds the river in *The Waste Land*, speaking of the poem's ability to delicately combine "sacred and profane, and past and present." "The river," she continues, "with its dissolving and merging action, makes this possible. Its flow is the poem's flow" (142). Campbell then discusses the *Wake*, and since this seems to be, at present, the only significant mention of *Finnegans Wake* in the work of any ecocritic, I quote the passage at length:

> Another famous Modernist work, James Joyce's *Finnegans Wake*, takes this literary imitation of a river's flow and merging even further. In this extraordinary book—written in a style unlike any other, full of puns that make different kinds of language overlap and merge—the river is Dublin's Liffey, which Joyce identifies with a great female principle encompassing lover and mother that he names Anna Livia Plurabelle. Suggesting with its initial lowercase letter that the story, like the water cycle, has no real beginning, the novel opens with "rivverrun, past Eve and Adam's, from swerve of shore to bend of bay, brings us by a commodious vicus of recirculation back to Howth Castle and Environs." Joyce's Liffey merges everything—mythical, personal, intellectual, carnal, learned, colloquial, sacred, and profane—in the constant punning and shifting of his sentences. It is the river of time and the river of language, image of the endlessly changing forms of language and the way words from the past are carried to us and into the future, with tributaries pouring in from all directions.

> The optimism, wit, and humour of the novel come from its joy in the vastness and endlessness of this great flux, and the river is the natural image for the whole process. (142)

Campbell's brief explanation of *Finnegans Wake* from an ecological perspective spotlights the role Joyce's manipulation of language must play for ecocritical readings of the text. Much like Heise's brief mention of the *Wake*, Campbell focuses on the democratic and leveling tendency of the *Wake*, the ability of the *Wake* to dissolve culturally inscribed boundaries and subsume everything into larger "currents."

Other Joyce critics mention environmental themes in passing but largely, like Hart, relegate them to simple metaphors; the idea of language, time, history, and life itself as a river that is flowing is certainly the most common metaphor attached to nature in the *Wake*. For example, arguing against the reading of the *Wake* as a dream, Derek Attridge explains that Joyce "points rather more clearly to the metaphor of the river and to Viconian cyclic history than to the idea of a dream" (144). He directs readers to Ellmann's claim that Joyce told a friend that "he conceived of his book as the dream of old Finn, lying in death beside the river Liffey and watching the history of Ireland and the world—past and future—flow through his mind like flotsam on the river of life" (qtd. in Attridge 144). However, these readings often end up being as pedestrian as Bloom's mock-advertisement in "Lestrygonians": "It's always flowing in a stream, never the same, which in the stream of life we trace. Because life is a stream" (U 8.95). At this point, critics and readers of *Finnegans Wake* have largely accepted this equation between different things that "flow," and so the role of nature in the *Wake* must now be examined more comprehensively. Surely Joyce must have been thinking of something more for the role of the Liffey in the *Wake* than a hollow analogy between water and prose? This study seeks to uncover what exactly Joyce was doing with nature in *Finnegans Wake* and why.

The Ecology of Finnegans Wake's five chapters each address a different aspect of *Finnegans Wake* and ecology, and each individual chapter proceeds, on the whole, chronologically, demonstrating how these themes appeared and how Joyce developed these themes over successive drafts. The short section titled "The Notebooks," starting on page 28 of this introduction, presents a reading of two of the earliest *Finnegans Wake* notebooks in order to demonstrate the benefits of a genetic approach.

The first chapter, "Reading the Landscape," explores early sketches of the *Wake*, teasing out underlying environmental themes and subjects, and then continues with a sustained examination of the relationship between language, narrative, and landscape as it develops throughout the *Wake*'s composition. As Joyce works on the *Wake*, the narrative, the language, and the personae involved in the telling of the story become ever more entangled with nature and the possibilities of its legibility. In addition to examinations of the earliest *Wake* sketches, this chapter discusses III.3 and Yawn's placement in the landscape, the role of Otto Jespersen, the drafting of I.5 and the "letter," the importance of Edward Sullivan's *The Book of Kells* as a source text for the theme of legibility, the intersections of art and nature, the Ogham alphabet, burial and palimpsests, Breton stone monuments, and Giambattista Vico's merging of nature and language.

The second chapter, "City versus Country," asserts the *Wake*'s importance in the development of an urban ecological criticism. In this chapter, transitional spaces such as suburbs, farmland, riverbanks, and parks are assessed in terms of their cultural construction. The "environs" present in the *Wake*'s first sentence take a central role in this chapter, bringing the topographical and geographical setting of Dublin city to the forefront. The River Liffey's physical and cultural relationship to Dublin city is explored in drafts of I.8, and the relationships between Irish cities and their proximity to water in general are explored with drafts of I.6. The original creation of parks as royal or aristocratic hunting grounds articulates the cultural inscription of landscape as well as the always-already present politicization of land. Additionally, the hunt in the *Wake* engages the coexistence of violence and nature. Notebook VI.B.29 crystallizes topics of urban planning, disease, famine, and public housing, and this notebook's role in drafts of the *Wake* is largely to articulate issues of urban ecology. The final section of the second chapter continues to discuss city planning and focuses on the role of the suburb of Chapelizod in the *Wake*, introducing also the subject of engineering and how engineering projects alter the experience of nature.

"The Politics of the Environment," chapter 3, investigates Joyce's presentation of the ways in which nature is co-opted for various political aims. In *Finnegans Wake*, nature is always political. This chapter argues that Joyce's use of weather and climate in the *Wake* is usually associated with issues of imperialism or nationalism. It also expands the role of the Phoenix Park and uses drafts of III.4 to explain the park's conception as palimpsest, especially in terms of its colonial and military history. The Phoenix Park also introduces the role of class in representations of, and relationships to, nature. Another theme introduced in this chapter is that of self-sufficiency in terms of artistic creation (I.7), energy, and goods.

Chapter 3 also argues that Joyce's use of bogs in the *Wake* is closely aligned with the politics of the Irish Free State, an alignment also of particular importance to the sketch "How Buckley Shot the Russian General." The "Buckley" sketch also unites critical interactions between territory, nationalism, war, and landscape that are particularly developed during the final years of the *Wake*'s composition. The "Norwegian Captain" sketch draws on discourses of exploration, particularly polar exploration, to further explore themes of territory, conquest, and progress. The chapter concludes with a discussion of the tensions between development and conservation.

The fourth chapter, "Religion and Ecology," articulates the relationship between nature and spirituality throughout the *Wake*. Influenced significantly by Vico's work, the *Wake* suggests that religion, like language, was developed from the contact between the human and the environment. In this chapter I argue that Joyce casts weather as a twentieth-century update of Viconian providence. This chapter also draws extensively on works of comparative mythology and religion during the late nineteenth and early twentieth centuries, arguing that Joyce uses universalizing myths of agricultural and fertility rites to show the impact of nature upon the development of religions and their associated traditions and festivals. Finally, this chapter argues that science in the *Wake* is, in some respects, little more than a new form of religion.

The final chapter, "Growing Things," takes its cue from Joyce's comment on the mistranslation of Aristotle. This chapter explores the intersections and overlaps between the representations of linguistic growth, cultural growth, individual growth, sexual growth, national growth, textual growth, and botanical growth. Lawrence Buell's criterion that the environmental text must exhibit some sense of the environment as a process is clearly displayed in this chapter.

Finally, the conclusion presents some sections of *Finnegans Wake* that cut across the themes of the five chapters and looks forward to future ecocritical studies of James Joyce's works.

Genetic Criticism

The Ecology of Finnegans Wake merges ecocriticism with genetic criticism, a branch of post-structuralism that, in its most orthodox application, rejects the authority of the published text and focuses on the *avant-texte* (the notebooks, drafts, proofs, revisions, etc.) that contributes to the genesis of the text. However, I employ an applied genetic criticism, meaning that I use the methodology of genetic criticism, but use this methodology in the aims of ultimately illuminating the development of a central theme. This type of genetic approach not only allows for the presentation of a significant amount of primary material but also provides a more nuanced understanding of how Joyce wrote *Finnegans Wake* and incorporated environmental themes in his text. Additionally, a genetic approach, which itself approaches post-structuralism from a material base through its use of archival material and the attention it draws to the writing process, provides an inroad for negotiating the divide that has existed between ecocriticism and post-structuralism.

This genetic study provides material evidence of Joyce's interest in nature during the years he was working on *Finnegans Wake* and allows the central concerns in this ecocritical reading to be framed in more enriching and substantive ways. In addition to the positivist approach of providing concrete proof of environmental themes in *Finnegans Wake*, a genetic approach to a text with a textual history as complex as *Finnegans Wake* opens up a limitless number of possible readings, inevitably making any reading considerably more comprehensive.

Genetic criticism allows for a reading of the composition methods of *Finnegans Wake* and presents the ways in which avant-texte material was acquired from source texts, copied into notebooks, placed into drafts, revised over subsequent drafts, reconceptualized at different points in the composition process, and interpreted in different contexts. Genetic criticism not only shows the presence of environmental subject matter in *Finnegans Wake*; it also shows how these ideas developed and changed over the years. In short, genetic criticism provides textual terrain in which Joyce's processes can be explored.

Dirk Van Hulle argues that "[a]rchives often arrange the manuscripts teleologically according to the final narrative structure. A genetic study, however, may require a chronological (re)arrangement of the manuscripts" (*Textual Awareness* 5). Within this present study's individual chapters the material is presented chronologically, in order to most clearly demonstrate the development of environmental themes in the *Wake*. Beginning with the first notes Joyce recorded for what would become the *Wake* following the publication of *Ulysses*, and then excavating the successive drafts, notebooks, and revisions, we gain a far different perspective of the *Wake*. For instance, examining the development of the text chronologically allows for small notes, additions, or revisions that occur across different chapters to speak to one another, providing an intertextual reading within the avant-texte of the same work.

Van Hulle also explains that the chronological arrangement of the avant-texte "reflect[s] the type of the writing process, ranging from a carefully planned strategy to a gradual expansion of the manuscript without apparent preconception" (5). It is for this reason that I devote a considerable amount of space to the first five years of work on *Finnegans Wake*, for during this period, Joyce had little strategy but allowed his sources, notes, and drafts to, in a sense, do a lot of the writing for him. If one attempts to read a *Finnegans Wake* notebook as a text independent of the published version of *Finnegans Wake*, or even independent of the drafts in which the notes were used, one can find definite narrative structures and intertextual links within the notebooks themselves. Such structures and links were created as much by the juxtaposition of source texts and their corresponding notes as by Joyce's own intentions, and because of this organic development, the first five years are imperative to understanding the way in which the text took shape.

This idea of the text's growth can be traced back to Joyce's correction of the Aristotle line from *Physics* from whence "mimesis" arose, and is, again, closely connected to Buell's criteria. Through the examination of the *Wake*'s avant-texte, there appears a relationship between Joyce's experiences with the *Wake*'s development and the way he believed elements in nature grow and change over time. Though such a correspondence is often problematic, the desire to find overlap between genetic criticism and ecocriticism is easily understood, with metaphors of organicism and growth dominating the discourse. Buell himself supports the comparison between the "artistic" and the "natural" in *The Environmental Imagination*, where he reads Henry David Thoreau's *Walden* genetically: "To read the published text in light of antecedent drafts and journal material is to see Thoreau undergoing a partly planned, partly fortuitous, always somewhat conflicted odyssey of reorientation" (23). Curiously, especially when taking into account that the writer here is Lawrence Buell, he chooses not to draw explicit connections between the subject of *Walden* and Thoreau's composition process. Such an omission would be welcomed by critics of this type of analogy, represented, perhaps, most vehemently by Phillips, who warns that such parallels can be taken too far, using SueEllen Campbell's celebrated essay "The Land and Language of Desire: Where Deep Ecology and Post-Structuralism Meet" as the scapegoat. Phillips diplomatically calls Campbell's attempt "admirable," but highlights her essay in support of his belief that there must be "lines of resistance" for an interdisciplinary enterprise such as ecocriticism to be taken seriously. Phillips rejects the "realist" ecocritics, "who argue that texts are like the world," and, concomitantly, rejects Campbell's argument that "the world is like a text" (36–37). He calls for critics on both ends of the ecocritical spectrum to recognize the material existence of, in Campbell's case, deer, and to recognize the fact that these deer can "say no even to ecology" by failing "to conform to ecological models" (37). He argues for the necessity of splitting "ecology as a 'point of view' and ecology as a science" and rejects "organic metaphors" (44). Phillips disapproves of the general assumptions of "harmony, balance, unity, and economy in the day-to-day functioning of actual natural systems" (46) and argues that these simplistic models of ecology from the early twentieth century are outdated in the actual field of ecology and should not be used today to critique texts.

While Phillips seems almost to reject the ubiquity (not to mention inescapability) of metaphor in thought and communication, he is largely correct in his argument that adhering to outdated models of ecology is irresponsible scholarship as well as harmful to current environmental literacy. However, in the case of works written before recent research in the sciences, it is necessary to consider the state of the sciences and of environmental attitudes during the period in which the text was produced. In the case of *Finnegans Wake*, earlier ideas in the natural and physical sciences must be studied as influencing the text, though current understandings of these fields can be allowed to inform how readings of these texts are used culturally or pedagogically. Though there are many possible refutations of Phillips's argument, it is for these reasons that my merging of genetic criticism and ecocriticism will be hesitant about theoretically aligning the two and will only relate nature to texts in isolated, specific sections of the *Wake* and its composition.

The Notebooks

This section is intended to illustrate, using examples from *Finnegans Wake* notebooks, the processes of genetic criticism and how such an approach supports an ecocritical reading of *Finnegans Wake*. To provide an introduction to how these notebooks will be used, I present here a close analysis of a few sources from two notebooks Joyce used in 1924, early in the composition of the *Wake* and long before any environmental themes had crystallized in the text.

In the beginning of 1924, Joyce began drafting the Shem chapter, I.7, and the Anna Livia Plurabelle chapter, I.8. It is not possible to know for certain whether Joyce intended the environmental themes that appear in these two chapters, but a close look at the interdependence of some of Joyce's sources in one of the notebooks in use during this period, notebook VI.B.1, provides some insight. The relationships between environment, geography, and the production of narratives found in the first drafts of I.7 and I.8 are supported when one looks to Joyce's sources, the notes he recorded from these sources, the contexts from which the notes originated, and the contexts in which they were used in the drafts for *Work in Progress*. Additionally, there were many notes that Joyce did not use in the *Wake*, but looking at the *Finnegans Wake* notebooks as valuable texts in and of themselves demonstrates that a note does not necessarily have to be crossed out (i.e., crossed through by Joyce and inserted into the drafts) for it to be influential to the *Wake*. Van Hulle explains, "Genetic critics focus on the temporal dimension of writing and regard a work of literature as a process rather than a product. The end result remains inextricably bound up with its textual memory, that is, the numerous textual transformations that preceded its publication" (2). This idea of "textual memory" is important to focus on with regard to Joyce's process, as many of the unused notes from the *Finnegans Wake* notebooks do conceptually find their way into the text.

Van Hulle also argues that "the discovery of a source text provides a context that does not only surround the work and delimit its meanings; it also opens it up" (*Textual Awareness* 6). This being said, the focus will now turn toward specific source texts for *Finnegans Wake* with the intention of "opening up" more possible meanings. Starting on page 13 of VI.B.1, Joyce copies a series of notes from J.B.S. Haldane's *Daedalus*. Geert Lernout, in the introduction to the Brepols edition of VI.B.1, explains the nature of

Joyce's note-taking from this book and concludes that "it is not possible to deduce" the reasons for Joyce's interest in this book, but it is certain that the interest went beyond the title, as "scientific developments in all kinds of fields" were of interest to Joyce or "at least seemed to be relevant to his project, just as the link between anthropology and rivers was central to the next book [Léon Metchnikoff's *La civilisation et les grands fleuves historiques*] he began to read and annotate" (VI.B.1 6). Joyce's Haldane notes begin with a section on the changing perception of death in modern culture because of scientific advances ("death has receded," "vaccination" [VI.B.6: 13]), speculations on the future of science and populations ("Q strain of porphyrococcus escapes into sea, jellies atlantic, climate changes / fish food, sea red" [VI.B.6: 14]), reproduction and sexuality ("octogenic," "reproduction separate from sexual love" [VI.B.1: 14]), and ethics ("science magnify injustice till it is intolerable," "ɯ fluid ethics" [VI.B.1: 15]).

Lernout explains that Joyce then returns to page 40 of Haldane's text, to a section on the mythical Daedalus figure in relation to Haldane's view of the contemporary scientist. One note, "fires { wood / peat / coal / boots } water (no)" (VI.B.1: 16), derives from a passage in Haldane defining the relationship of water to the human organism (whereas fires can be created from various fuels, no other chemical substance can substitute for water), and for Joyce, this fact fosters an interest in sociological implications of water. Several subsequent VI.B.1 entries expand upon this topic with an increasingly biological focus, and Joyce takes notes on plant life, the ability of plants to create their own food, and the way animals break down such compounds with enzymes and bacteria. These systems are then translated to the human context in terms of food production, and Haldane explains the eventual downfall of the agricultural laborer ("strong farmer" [VI.B.1: 17]) to make way for the "key industries" (VI.B.1: 17) that will, according to Haldane, "evolve a stable industrial society" (21–22). These people, he continues, will "inherit the earth" (from which Joyce notes "inherit E" [VI.B.1: 17]).

Haldane then begins an analysis of the limitations of energy resources such as coal and oil, providing a brief vision of future alternative energy technology in Britain. He discounts waterpower as a major prospect because of its "small quality, seasonal fluctuation, and sporadic distribution" and argues, "We shall have to tap those intermittent but inexhaustible sources of power, the wind and the sunlight" (23). He projects that in four hundred years, "the country will be covered with rows of metallic windmills working electric motors which in their turn supply current at a very high voltage to great electric mains. At suitable distances, there will be great power stations where during windy weather the surplus power will be used for the electrolytic decomposition of water into oxygen and hydrogen," and he continues with an explanation of the logistics of the necessary storage system. "Among the more obvious advantages," Haldane projects of such a scheme, "will be the fact that energy will be as cheap in one part of the country as another, so that industry will be greatly decentralized; and that no smoke or ash will be produced" (24).

From these passages, Joyce takes down three notes: "tap wind & sunlight," "⊓ smokes?" and "⊓ HcE chemical" (VI.B.1: 17). Wind and sunlight are reliable, infinite resources in Haldane's scheme, capable of sustaining human life and industrialization. This topic would have been of interest to Joyce at this stage of composition, as water had been recently cast as the renewing, maternal, life-giving source of "Δ" in the drafts of the "Anna Livia Plurabelle" chapter. "⊓" is cast as a type of energy, either a fossil fuel ("smokes?") or the water that will be electrolyzed into its component gases (technically, HcE would become Hc and Ec). The surplus of power of ⊓ would be decomposing Δ.

Two final notes from Haldane revisit themes Joyce touched upon briefly in earlier notebooks as well as in his earlier works: "Columbus / Newton / Einstein} Signs in heavens" (VI.B.1: 17) and "night, distance, surdity / checks to human progress" (VI.B.1: 18). The first note relates to the validation of scientific theories via cosmological "evidence," deriving from Haldane's assertion that "A prophet who can give signs in the heavens is always believed. No one ever seriously questioned Newton's theory after the return of Halley's Comet. Einstein has told us that space, time, and matter are shadows of the fifth dimension, and the heavens have declared his glory" (13–14). Phenomena hitherto attributed to divine origins are simultaneously reduced and elevated by science; given a place in the mechanics of the universe, their patterns become explainable, but their origins remain uncertain (and it is fitting that Haldane continues with a reference to Kantian idealism). The last note derives from a passage concerning the use and abuse of "light" and posits that, within fifty years "there will be no more night in our cities." This development is inevitable, Haldane explains, because "the alternation of day and night is a check on the freedom of human activity which must go the way of other spatial and temporal checks" (17–19). Joyce's note lists three such "spatial and temporal checks" to "human progress" with "night," "distance," and "surdity." In an extension of Kant, "night" becomes a human construct, along with space and time ("distance" and "surdity," respectively). The *Daedalus* notes end here, but Haldane's influence extends to the next text, as it was because of Léon Metchnikoff's writings that Haldane was nearly expelled from Eton (VI.B.1 4).

The next text to discuss is a major source for notebook VI.B.1, Léon Metchnikoff's *La civilisation et les grands fleuves historiques*. This text, discovered as a source by Ingeborg Landuyt, is part of the late-nineteenth-century trend in environmental determinism and explores the development of different civilizations from the perspective of their geography and climate. Landuyt and Lernout provide a description of Metchnikoff and of this text, explaining, "This book by Léon Metchnikoff belongs to a genre that was of obvious interest to an author who was in the process of writing a history of the world and who had just completed the first version of the 'ALP'-chapter. Joyce had an interest in historical and anthropological studies that transcended his interest in Irish history and mythology" (JSA 6: 102). Landuyt and Lernout give a detailed outline of Metchnikoff's text, explaining the major role that the environment plays in his theories and his conceptions of human history. However, they ultimately decide that this is a work of "history," "sociology," or "anthropology," and that Metchnikoff is decidedly a "humanist," despite their explanation that this text may have been intended for Metchnikoff's own class on comparative geography. This interpretation of Metchnikoff's text has endured since this article was published in 1995 and perhaps indicates the general bias that kept *Finnegans Wake* firmly directed away from ecocriticism. It is interesting that in the introduction to VI.B.1, published in 2003, Lernout's description is more generous to the ecological aspects of Metchnikoff: "Why Joyce would read this book at this point is not a mystery: the suggestion in the title of a connection between rivers and human culture must have been relevant for the man who had just written the first drafts of I.8 about the opposition between river and city, nature and culture" (7).

Similar to the nonlinear reading of *Daedalus*, Joyce is erratic in his reading of Metchnikoff, suggesting a more directed, research-like quality for his method of using the source. The examination of Metchnikoff's text in conjunction with Haldane's text reveals a thread through VI.B.1 concerning the relationship between geography, science, progress, and human history. Joyce's notes from *La civilisation et les grandes fleuves historiques* begin on VI.B.1: 13 and continue until VI.B.1: 85, with occasional breaks to consult other sources. On the first page, the note "Mare Tenebrarum / Atlantic 1400" (VI.B.1: 13) derives from the following passage:

> Ainsi, pour citer l'exemple capital, l'Océan, qui rapproche maintenant toutes les nations et qui les fait une par le commerce et les idées, fut jadis le domaine de la Terreur, le chaos d'où s'élevaient les esprits méchants; cinq siècles ne se sont pas encore écoulés depuis que l'on donnait au redoubtable Atlantique le nom de «mer des Ténèbres». (xxi)

Metchnikoff explains how different phenomena and elements in nature have been interpreted differently by different people over time, and he cites the fact that the ocean, vehicle for commerce and for the transmission of ideas, was once seen as a vindictive force of evil and chaos. Joyce's note records the name by which the ocean had previously been called, and the approximate date at which this conception of the ocean as a "Sea of Darkness" existed. The context of this note, Joyce's translation of the text into his notebook, and the juxtaposition of this note with other notes in VI.B.1 together contribute to and construct Van Hulle's "textual memory."

The next note from *La civilisation*, "tropical & arctic / rivers / extrastorico" (VI.B.1: 27), provides a summary of the origins of Metchnikoff's theory. He argues that the success of a population is found in its ability to adapt to change and that this adaptability is learned from the observations of their river throughout the year. People in the extreme climates— whether the tropics, sub-Saharan Africa, or Arctic Siberia—experience the same thing throughout the entire year and thus never learned to adapt and subsequently never experienced the same "progress": "les populations ne sont guère élevées au-dessus de l'état de nature." The rivers (and the people) are "en dehors de la zone historique" (xxiii). The next section of the text deals with the cooperation of peoples in riverside civilizations in defending their society against floods by building dikes and canals. Joyce translates their deluge to his own hometown: "Dublin on the Liffey," "dyke," and "canal" (VI.B.1: 28). The merging of historical cycles (or, in Metchnikoff, "spirales," "∧ zigzag v spiral / corsi ricorsi Vico" [VI.B.1: 29]) with the cycle of the flood and the development of civilizations is a welcome synthesis for Joyce in this phase of *Work in Progress*.

Joyce's attention to etymology is woven into the notes from Metchnikoff beginning on VI.B.1: 29, with Joyce seeming interested in instances wherein a paternal role is bestowed upon nature: "Jupiter Fluvius," "Ararat / Solomon's Throne," and "Kohibaba" (VI.B.1: 30). Jupiter, the Roman god associated with thunder and lightning, is also known as Zeus, or Jove; his name derives from the Latin "Jovis pater," or "Father Jove." He is also Jupiter Pluvius, or "giver of rain," as he is referenced in "Eumaeus" (U 16.41). In this VI.B.1 entry, he is a companion to "Δ," a "Father River." "Ararat," the volcanic peak on what is now the border of Turkey and Armenia, is said to be the resting site of Noah's ark after the Flood; it also lends this note a patriarchal role, as does its association with Solomon's throne. The third entry, "Kohibaba," translates literally as "the father of the mountains," according to the editors of VI.B.1 (VI.B.1 56), and refers to the Koh-I-Baba, an extension of the Hindu Kush Mountains. Additionally, according to *Brill's Encyclopedia of Islam*, "[t]he culminating peaks of Koh-I-Baba overlook the sources of the principal rivers of Afghanistan" (1056), strengthening the relationship between patriarchy and geography. Shortly thereafter, Joyce records "Δ Eg." (VI.B.1: 31), cementing the relationship between the naming of the Nile Delta and its resemblance to the Greek letter delta.

Before beginning a series of increasingly anthropological notes, Joyce summarizes what he has garnered from the text thus far with the simple note "river = synthesis" (Metchnikoff's "synthèse géographique"), deriving from the passage in the chapter titled "Territoire des civilisations fluviales": "Le fleuve, dans tous les pays, se présente à nous comme la synthèse vivante de toutes les conditions complexes du climat, du sol, de la configuration du terrain et de la constitution géologique" (185). Joyce notes Metchnikoff's phases of the development of civilization ("1st period fluvial / 2-maritime" [VI.B.1: 31]) and then writes a set of notes with various versions of creations: "primitive / rivers no mouths," "Noah's ark," "Moses cradle," "lakeborn," and "sources of Nile" (VI.B.1: 32). With regard to the context of the "primitive / rivers no mouths" note, Metchnikoff argues that in "primitive" times, "les grand cours d'eau [. . .] n'avaient pas de débouché du tout," which Joyce translates into "mouths" instead of "ends" or "outlets," suggesting that "aux temps primitifs," rivers, like people, were unable to "speak."

Noah and Moses appear consistently in VI.B.1, and their appearance here places the flood in close proximity to the development of speech and writing. Moses, however, has a "cradle," which links him with "lake-born," which subsequently links him with the earlier ⋒ of "⋒ water baby" (VI.B.6: 127), which links everything back to the river as "origin" (or, extending this further, as *logos*). The notes that follow, "sources of Nile / caput Nili," "mouesi / = lune ou / voleur (qui travaille / à l'aide de la lune," and "only the Pharaoh or chief priest knows 'Head of Nile'" (VI.B.1: 32), expand the river and speech relationship ("chief priest"), return to the "Δ" themes (moon, tide, woman), and return to an earlier series of notes from VI.B.11 concerning Salomé and the veil. The belief that only the pharaoh (or "le scribe sacré," "the sacred scribe") knows the location of the Nile's source begins to provide an explanation for the prevalence of tyranny in early river-centered civilizations and the importance of the "chief priest" or "scribe." Additionally, this belief introduces the Wakean premise of the male scriptor unlocking the voice of the female (primarily, though not limited to, the case of Shem, ALP, and the letter).

The next substantial series of entries concerns the way rivers themselves physically develop, beginning with the formation of "embarrasses" (an archaic term for obstacles or hindrances) that become small wooded islands and force the river underground. In the case of the Nile, this evolution resulted in the creation of the Lower Nile and its floods, which resulted in the birth of ancient Egypt; or, as Joyce records it: "Upper Nile made Lower Nile / Lower Nile made history" (VI.B.1: 33). Metchnikoff also explains that the Nile could have diverted and turned toward the Red Sea at Lake Nasser instead of making the long journey toward the Mediterranean Sea, to which Joyce responds, "if Liffey had turned back?" (VI.B.1: 33)—i.e., could the Liffey have been as grand as the Nile, fostering one of the world's greatest civilizations on its banks? Could it have been, as the Nile was under the pharaohs, "Tsaf-en-Ta (Nourrisseur du Monde)" or "Abou-el-Baraka (Père de la Bénédiction)," that is, "Nourisher of world / benefactor" (VI.B.1: 34)? Maybe so, Joyce concludes, with the note "Ingredient of whisky" (VI.B.1: 34), referring to one of the products that make the Liffey its own unique kind of "Nourisher of world."

Joyce takes a break from Metchnikoff for a few pages of VI.B.1, a couple of which explore the application of Metchnikoff's ideas to Ireland with notes such as, "Iverna / Ierna / Erú Earú land / Irlandia / Ireland," "Suir / Nore / & Barrow} sister," "Brendan's sea," "no earthquake," and "thunder 1 a year" (VI.B.1: 38). With the earlier entry, "tropical & arctic / rivers / extrastorico" (VI.B.1: 27), in mind, this sequence, by aligning Ireland's geography and cold climate, does not shed very positive light upon Ireland's place in civilization. The first entry also suggests "Hiver / Iver" with "Iverna," placing Ireland into the category of places where the flow of the river is "complètement interrompu par les glaces de l'hiver" (Metchnikoff xxiii). While this characterization is not true for Ireland, and does not support the argument on its own, the "no earthquake" and "thunder 1 a year" entries (which *are* currently true) add to the categorization of Ireland as a place "extrastorico." The notes cease with this implication that Ireland's climate has little variation, and another direction is taken with this theme (in this case, toward more ancient Irish history and Giraldus Cambrensis's twelfth-century *Topographia Hiberniae* [*Topography of Ireland*]).

These notes then move to Lough Neagh, whose catchment area includes both Northern Ireland and the Republic of Ireland ("stick pole in Neagh" [VI.B.1: 40]), the Liffey ("Avonliffey" [VI.B.1: 40], with *abhan* being the Irish for "river"), and Saint Patrick's Purgatory ("S. Patrick Purg" [VI.B.1: 41]), in addition to Lough Erne ("fishful Erne" [VI.B.1: 40]) and the River Shannon ("shannon / old river" [VI.B.1: 41]). The Shannon, Ireland's longest river, derives its name from the Irish *Sionainn*, meaning "ancient goddess," but is also very close to *sean abhainn*, the Irish for "old river." These five bodies of water and waterways straddle different points on the map of Ireland, with St. Patrick's Purgatory in Donegal's Lough Derg, the Shannon passing through eleven counties from Cavan to Limerick, Lough Erne in Fermanagh, Lough Neagh in five of the six counties of the North, and the Liffey in Wicklow, Kildare, and Dublin. Then, from Cambrensis, Joyce writes "navel" (VI.B.1: 40), derived from the description of a stone in County Meath near the castle of Kyllari that "is called the navel of Ireland, because it stands in the middle of the country" (qtd. in VI.B.1 71). (This reference explains the "cf SD" before "Meath" on the same page, as "navel" is the omphalos, returning us to the opening of *Ulysses* [1.176]). Together, these notes translate an individual body onto the map of Ireland, an image that dominates much of the *Wake* (with bodies transcribed onto either Ireland or Dublin).

VI.B.1's interest in Irish waterways and geography continues and eventually merges with the historical and ecclesiastical notes on VI.B.1: 42–46. One note, "esker (gravelly hillocks) / ridge—Dub—Gal" (VI.B.1: 46), revisits a VI.B.6 note from Stephen Gwynn's *The History of Ireland* (1923)— "Conn C & Mog Nuadat divide I. / by eskers (Dub to Gal)"—and with the reference to the "navel," these notes suggest a reading of the landscape of

Ireland as a body. The passage in Gwynn from which the two notes derive reads: "Conn's great opponent in Ireland was Mogh Nuadat, and tradition relates that after many battles they decided on a division of Ireland, following the Esker Riada or line of gravelly hillocks (still called eskirs) which runs across the central boggy plain from near Dublin to Maaree on the bight of Galway Bay" (12–13). The difference between the two notes suggests that Joyce returned to Gwynn to look specifically for this note on the esker ridge. We can speculate that this interest derived from the note "Ota w of Turgesius / on high altar / Clonmacnois" (VI.B.1: 45), as Clonmacnoise was founded where the major land route through the bogs, along the esker ridge, crossed the Shannon River. Four notes shortly thereafter—"Eblani," "Dinas Devlin / Doolin Dub" (VI.B.1: 46), "Amnis Lifnius" (VI.B.1: 47), and "Liffeyside" (VI.B.1: 48)—continue referring to the relationship between Ireland's development as a civilization, its history, and its waterways, as do the notes from an article on Dublin's water supply in the 25 February 1924 *Freeman's Journal*: "Water Supply / How Dublin and Districts Are Provided For / Visit to Roundwood." In conjunction with the passage in "Ithaca" wherein the water is traced from Roundwood Reservoir to Bloom's tap (U 17: 93–95), the notes "Roundwood" and "Varty—Callary, Rdwood, Ashford, Broad Lough, Sea" (VI.B.1: 48) are given a heightened significance in this context because of their evocation of a catchment area (and later, Joyce notes "catchment /—basin" [VI.B.1: 123]).

Joyce's Metchnikoff notes begin again on VI.B.1: 51 and explore the interrelation between history, religion, and nature. The notes "City founded after flood," "32 counties under 1 umbrella," "milk cows of heaven," "drought famine," "Manmade parts of Brahma," and "destiny cyclon in Panjab = desolated—tiger = crops eaten by rodents" (VI.B.1: 51–52) all fall into this category. Metchnikoff (along with numerous scholars of folklore, comparative religion, and anthropology during the same period) argues that religions were necessitated by the need to revere nature for the success of the harvest: "Roudra, le chef souverain des vents (Marouts), qui à la voix tonnante de l'orage, vont traire les nuées, les 'vaches célestes,' pour arroser les semailles des Aryas" (308–9). This passage also explains the note "stagnant (cow)?" (VI.B.1: 53); clouds are cows that "need to be milked" for rain (which follows with the note "drought famine," for where the weather benefits one society's harvest, it wreaks havoc upon that of another).

Beginning on VI.B.1: 61, Joyce records several notes exploring arboreal themes—"walnut gunstock," "beetle to rive wood," "poplar match," "slenderleaved [willow]" (VI.B.1: 61), "pear brush," "sycamore bread platter," "beechmast saw," "(ash is elm)," "chesterfield elm," "Ph Park," "spindle tree toothpick," and "Czd poplars" (VI.B.1: 62)—until the Metchnikoff notes commence again. The notes in this section are directed toward familial relationships in *La civilisation*, stemming from the argument concerning the necessity for authority (whether tyrannical or religious) from which notes were taken in the previous section. Here there appear the notes "Fils du Ciel," "no surnames," and "dictated by toothless grandfather to girl," juxtaposed with "1) written tongue / 2) spoken" (VI.B.1: 64), aligning the development of speech and writing in ancient cultures with the voice of the heavens. This idea is developed by a phrase in one of Metchnikoff's footnotes, wherein he expands upon the idea that the names of the rivers, "Hawng-Ho" (Blue River) and "Yangtze" (Yellow River), are closely linked with Chinese cosmogony:

> Hoang-ho signifie litéralement «fleuve Jaune», et ce nom s'applique très bien à ses eaux . . . Mais l'épithète de «fleuve Bleu» n'est donnée au Yangste-kiang que par égard à certaines notions fondamentales de la cosmogonie et de la philosophie naturelle des Chinois. Yang, le principe mâle, actif, éthéré, lumineux, est un équivalent ou une attribution du ciel (tian); Yin, le principe femelle, est passif, opaque, et par excellence, terrestre. Le Hoang-ho est le fleuve de la Terre (ti); le Yangtse, la progéniture du principe mâle, est de la nature du ciel. (343–44n1)

Joyce reduces this note to "yellow E / blue H" (VI.B.1: 65), but the note signals a movement toward an association of rivers and language, as the next notes, "skygrey" and "Fleau des Fils de Han" (VI.B.1: 65), derive from a section on Chinese language, and "monosyllable" describes the way in which, descending from the Chinese cosmogony, "le monosyllabisme, en effet, place cette nation absolument à part de toutes les autres nations historiques" (357). The final note in this section, "flowing water = Govt" (VI.B.1: 65), concisely outlines Metchnikoff's thesis: the Chinese are intrinsically linked to their rivers, and "l'Eau qui coule figure le Gouvernment" (357). Social institutions, language, and government are born from and develop in response to the path of the society's rivers ("delta = public ∆" [VI.B.1: 65]).

Next, Joyce copies the famous quotation from Edgar Quinet:

> Aujourd'hui comme au temps de Pline et de Columelle la jacinthe se plait dans les Gaules, la Pervenche en Illyrie, la marguerite sur les ruines de Numance et pendant qu'autour d'elles les villes ont changé de maitres et de noms, que plusieurs sont entrées dans le néant, que les civilizations se sont choquées et brisées, leurs paisibles generations ont traversé les âges et se sont succédé jusqu'à nous, fraiches et riantes comme au jour des batailles. (Qtd. in Metchnikoff 124)

In a letter to Harriet Shaw Weaver, Joyce comments on this passage: "E. Q. says that the wild flowers on the ruins of Carthage, Numancia etc have survived the political rises and falls of Empires. In this case the wild flowers are the lilts of children. Note specially the treatment of the double rainbow in which the iritic colours are first normal and then reversed" (LI 295). Despite its sentimentality, Quinet's proclamation integrates several motifs Joyce had been exploring up to this stage of composition. As a result, following the Quinet quotation and the culmination of notes from Metchnikoff, Joyce records no fewer than seventy-five separate entries expanding themes that intertwine a civilization's history, culture, and environment.

The remainder of VI.B.1 is inundated with water notes, and, to avoid repetition, many entries will be skipped. To conclude this section, I turn to the end of the notebook, VI.B.1: 177, and to a series of notes linking civilizations to their water supplies. "Maya civilization" and "drought" are the final entries on VI.B.1: 177, with "gorgemaking," "R {Soak in soil / seeps in river / springs feed stream / swing R to L," and "Yellow River / China's sorrow" beginning the next page. The rest of VI.B.1: 178 addresses the breaking of enforced boundaries by water: "overflows levees," "lakes equalise flow," "flood de S. Lawrence / impossible," and "drowned river valley." The next two pages, the last in VI.B.1, present notes derived from the *Encyclopaedia Britannica* and are almost all related to water. Joyce appears to have looked up "river" and recorded "River Brethren / Jacob Engle / trine immersion" (VI.B.1: 179) from the first interesting entry he came across (which deals with Christian communities descended from Swiss settlers). From the category "River Engineering," Joyce records "slope," "rainfall," "gentled fall," and "shingle gravel / sand silt." The latter entry originates in the subsection "Transportation of Materials in Rivers," from a description of forceful currents that can "carry down rocks, boulders and large stones, which are by degrees ground by attrition in their onward course into shingle, gravel, sand and silt" (qtd. in VI.B.1 213). This process of siltation leads to thoughts of bogs and their formation—hence, "bog black rock / spring bright streams," which leads Joyce to the encyclopedia's listings on Ireland's physical geography. The next two notes from this listing, "Foyle" and "Bog of Allen," are followed by more general notes from the listing "Geography": "ekumene = habitable O," "rubbish," "rain wash," and the last entry from the encyclopedia, "Talweg / deepest line along valley." The word "rubbish" and the entry just prior, "R on windward face," come from a passage describing the process whereby streams are created. The rainwater, intent on returning to the sea, is "more mobile and more searching than ice or rock rubbish" (qtd. in VI.B.1 214), and the water, guided by the contours of the land, forms lines that eventually converge into a stream that will "carve its channel deeper and entrench itself in permanent occupation" (qtd. in VI.B.1 214).

The notes discussed in this section on VI.B.1 were not all used in *Finnegans Wake* but have been presented as a demonstration of Joyce's interest in the question of nature and its relationship to human civilization. At this stage, it is not important to consider which notes were used and which were not used, but merely to consider Joyce's methods of note-taking and of approaching a topic from a variety of angles. This examination of just a few of the VI.B.1 sources demonstrates how valuable a genetic reading can be for any interpretation of *Finnegans Wake*, not just the current ecological approach. With specific regard to ecocriticism, genetic criticism uncovers emergent environmental themes in this early notebook, revealing preoccupations with engineering, rivers, the impact of geography on history, renewable energy, the dependence of religion on nature, and much more. During Joyce's lifetime, there was a significant shift in the way the relationship between humans and their environment was perceived and discussed, and examining the *Finnegans Wake* notebooks and their source texts reveals Joyce's concerted interest in these shifts.

Finnegans Wake is deeply engaged with the question of the relationship between culture and the environment, and modernist literature as a whole should be reconsidered in terms of its ecological attitudes, politics, and aesthetics. I argue in *The Ecology of* Finnegans Wake for an ecological modernism that focuses largely on urban ecology—one that does not entirely reject the trope of modernism as metropolitan nor wholly embrace the idea of a pastoral modernism, but one that allows for the uncovering of the complex debates over modernity and nature taking place during this period—from the ways in which humanity was understanding the impact of modernization on the land, to the ways in which nature was politicized, to the ways in which agriculture, transportation, leisure, and domestic life were being redefined.

1

Reading the Landscape

Barry Lopez defines two kinds of landscape: an "outer" and an "inner." "The external landscape," he begins, "is the one we see—not only the line and color of the land and its shading at different times of the day, but also its plants and animals in season, its weather, its geology, the record of its climate and evolution." The external landscape is not just the exterior appearance of the terrain, but it is also comprised of the lives lived there, both past and present. The outer landscape tells a certain narrative as well; it silently stores its biography in its soil, flora, fauna, and climate. Complementing this outer landscape is the inner landscape, which Lopez defines as "a kind of projection within a person of a part of the exterior landscape [. . . the inner landscape] responds to the character and subtlety of an exterior landscape; the shape of the individual is affected by land as it is by genes" (64–65). We are all familiar with this idea; the places in which we were born and raised, live and have lived, shape us, form us, and significantly help to determine who we are. In Lopez's formulation, outer landscapes and genetic codes have an equal role in individual evolution; as genes are expressed, so are inscribed elements of the outer landscape.

To extend Lopez's idea, I point to Neil Evernden, who, in "Beyond Ecology: Self, Place, and the Pathetic Fallacy," expresses the relationship between the outer and inner worlds not only of an individual but of the larger networks of which that individual is a part. He argues that story, geography, and self are intrinsically linked, that landscape is not just "a collection of physical forms" but also a retelling of its history, of "the evidence of what has occurred there" (99). It should be stated that the idea of "reading" history through landscape, while appealing, especially in an ecocritical context, is of course not without its troubles and its critics. While some of the criticism is well founded (because of a few clumsy implications of a landscape's authorial agency), the idea that physical land records its own version of history is viable and useful in many ways. With a landscape feature such as a bog—in which (with the right skills and technology, of course) one can learn of the different species that were living on the land, the frequency of fire, the amount of tree cover, the type of domestic tools used, the type of trade engaged in by the region's inhabitants—such a reading of landscape is possible and can be quite beneficial to our understanding of the history of a place. This first chapter traces the development of inner and outer landscapes throughout the composition history of *Finnegans Wake*, focusing on the legibilities of these landscapes. In *Finnegans Wake*, landscapes tell stories; they act as repositories for language, culture, history, and identity, and they also influence the creation of stories. From the earliest sections composed for the *Wake*, particularly with the influence of source texts such as Sir Edward Sullivan's *The Book of Kells*, Joyce explores alternative ways of reading a text, as well as alternative ways of defining "text."

Throughout the *Wake*, landscape is legible, and legibility, on a larger scale, is closely related to the natural world. Landscapes shape the outcome of history, condition the individual, and influence the way in which cultures develop. This interdependence of individual consciousness and landscape provides an image for the way in which Joyce presents human institutions as contingent upon their environmental context. The legibility of the environment in the *Wake* appears through discussions of mythology, language, writing, religion, history, politics, and natural history and is an important element for understanding the role of the ecological in the "universal history" of the *Wake*.

The early sketches of *Finnegans Wake* introduce the relationship between Ireland and its landscape through a reworking and reimagining of Irish mythology. *Ulysses* had already succeeded in providing a "cognitive map" of the city of Dublin, making the city "legible" (according to the vocabulary of Kevin Lynch's *The Image of the City* [3]), and *Finnegans Wake* brings this legibility to the nation on a larger scale. Kent Ryden argues that "literary cartographers" aim to portray both the visible and the "invisible" landscapes, meaning elements of the landscape not visible to the human eye, but which contribute to its cultural signification. Ryden's definition of an "invisible landscape" is particularly effective: "a world of deep and subtle meaning for the people who live there, one that can be mapped only with words. Their writings, their stories, thus echo the purposes and functions of place-based folklore" (52). He expresses the common belief that "stories—and folklore in general—are inextricably linked with landscapes" and are a "central means by which people organize their physical surroundings" (56). Ryden specifies folklore here, and for the *Wake*, both folklore and myth occupy this role. Both myth and folklore are used throughout the *Wake* as some of the earliest forms of narrative and some of the earliest attempts at ordering space and nature through language. As the *Wake* develops, the relationship between the structures of narrative and the physical landscape begins to inform the creation and re-creation of folklore and myth.

Early sketches for *Finnegans Wake* rework elements of Irish mythology for the twentieth century in a way that purposefully differs from the approach of the Irish literary revival. Though reassessing the Irish relationship to nature, particularly in terms of its mythology, may not have been an original intention of Joyce's, the juxtaposition of the settings of Chapelizod and the Phoenix Park with stories from Irish mythology and legends of early Irish Christianity in the first sketches builds a sustained examination of how Irish myth and history relate to the Irish landscape.

The Irish literary revival often focused on the relationship between mythology and landscape to root its revitalization project firmly in a specific place. Aspects of *Finnegans Wake* extend and revise how the landscape is represented in such revival texts, and query assumptions of how people relate to the landscape. While it is true that Joyce often portrayed the Irish revival and its proponents negatively, this fact should not imply in any way that he rejected the revival in its entirety. Because of the association between the Irish revival and Irish myth, Joyce's relationship with Irish myth has often been overlooked. Gregory Castle's *Modernism and the Celtic Revival* has argued, through recourse to anthropological approaches to folklore, that modernism and the Irish revival should not be considered as mutually exclusive as they typically are. The present chapter supports Castle's reading of the continuity between the revival and modernism and reads Joyce's use of myth and landscape in the early sketches of the *Wake* as an extension of the revival's project.

Aspects of the *Wake* are continuous with elements of the revival through the incorporation of land into Irish historical narratives.[1] Largely because of generalizations about W. B. Yeats, Lady Gregory, and J. M. Synge, the Irish revival is habitually characterized as presenting a romanticized, idealized landscape, and from the point of view of the Anglo-Irish. This simplification of the revival's conception of nature, however, has resulted in the undeserved devaluation of several of its writers including, most significantly for this present study, Synge (whom Joyce admired enough that he staged *Riders to the Sea* in Zürich) and George Moore. Synge's *Riders to the Sea* and Moore's *The Untilled Field* present landscapes altered significantly by famine, agriculture, and emigration and landscapes that are deeply intertwined with the lives of their characters. Greg Winston, in "George Moore's Landscapes of Return," focuses on the implications of the title *The Untilled Field* (e.g., if the field is "untilled," why is it untilled?), argues for the necessity of reading agricultural land as a midpoint between the wilderness and the urban, and presents a harsh landscape that is alien to most assumptions about the revival. *The Untilled Field's* very title implies that the land is a central subject of the stories, and each story addresses a different aspect of how individuals and communities depend on and derive their sense of self from the land. Winston's reading of "The Exile" brings Moore's story in line with concurrent environmental concerns, focusing on monocrop agriculture's determining impact on the severity of the Great Famine and presenting the need for sustainable agriculture to prevent such tragedies.

Likewise, Joy Kennedy-O'Neill's essay on Synge in *Out of the Earth* depicts a very different Synge from the one often mocked for his naïveté while staying on the Aran Islands; Synge is presented as a figure highly conscious of the fragility of lives wholly determined by their environment. Instead of presenting the Irish people as somehow mystically communing with their surroundings, Synge and Moore depict characters whose lives are much more subject to the vagaries of nature. Such a relatively "realistic" view of the cruel actualities of living off the land influences a strand of Irish literature that develops throughout the twentieth century, leading into such works as Liam O'Flaherty's "Spring Sowing," Patrick Kavanagh's "The Great Hunger," or even Flann O'Brien's *The Third Policeman* in the following decades. The *Wake's* representations of agriculture, famine, and the politics of land place Joyce's work in this branch of Irish modernism alongside O'Flaherty, Kavanagh, and O'Brien.

In addition to the relationship between landscape and mythology, which will be discussed at length as this study progresses, another key way in which Joyce explores the relationships between both outer/inner and visible/invisible landscapes is through the relationship between language and nature. Einar Haugen's *The Ecology of Language* (1972) led to the development of "ecolinguistics," which Haugen defines as "the study of interactions between any given language and its environment" (57). Parts of *Finnegans Wake* resemble early exercises in ecolinguistics as they often link words and structures of languages to environmental contexts. This similarity does not necessarily imply a logocentrism (or, perhaps, a "topologocentrism") on Joyce's part, as many of the examples of these links found throughout the *Wake* also focus on the way in which the language has changed because of the influence of environmental and geographical factors.

The relationship between language and nature can be traced to the earliest *Finnegans Wake* notebooks, particularly to VI.B.6, wherein Joyce took notes from Otto Jespersen's *Growth and Structure of the English Language* while also taking notes on the geography of Irish mythology from Stephen Gwynn's *The History of Ireland*.[2] From Jespersen, Joyce records several etymological relationships that relate to nature, such as "Thunresday" (VI.B.6: 67), "holm (ocean)" (VI.B.6: 67), "windeye" (VI.B.6: 67), and "sky (cloud)" (VI.B.6: 68). The "Thunresday" combines "thunder" with "Thursday," or "Thor's Day." "Windeye" derives from the following passage: "Window is borrowed from vindauga ('wind-eye') [. . .] Old English had another word for 'window,' which is also based on the eye-shape of the windows in the old woodenhouses: *eag yrel* 'eye-hole' (cf. *nos yrel* nostril)" (Jespersen 73). "Holm" was once the word for "ocean," and Joyce uses this fact in conceiving of the sea as both origin and final resting place (in terms of the water cycle). The latter entry, "sky (cloud)" in its source context, reads: "It is noticeable, too, that the native word *heaven* has been more and more restricted to the figurative and religious acceptation, while the Danish *sky* is used exclusively of the visible firmament; *sky* originally meant cloud" (Jespersen 75). This difference in "sky" and its implications stems from the original connotation of the term, and helps to explain why similar concepts led to the development of different terms in similar languages.

Joyce also transcribes "plough/pleuch (land measure)" (VI.B.6: 76) from a line in Jespersen describing how the term for "plough," either as noun or as verb, derives from an original description of how to measure the land. Joyce also records "haven (garden)," "havet (sea)," and "sloot dry stream" (VI.B.6: 73), with the first two entries originating in a Jespersen passage wherein the English language is depicted as cannibalistic; that is, it is "more inclined" than other tongues "to swallow foreign words raw"

(150), an idea that Joyce later incorporates to merge the history of Irish invasions with Irish geography and language. "Haven" and "havet" are Danish, and the "-n" and the "-t" are suffixes designating gender, making "haven" (garden) a feminine noun, while "havet" (sea) is neuter. The words were chosen because of their meanings of "garden" and "sea," and because the Danish gender rules end up linking these two concepts orthographically.

The third entry, "sloot dry stream," also relates to the connection between language, nature, and history. The note is from a discussion of the Dutch in South Africa, who, "finding there a great many natural objects which were new to them, designated them either by means of existing Dutch words [. . .], or else by coining new words, generally compounds. Thus *sloot* 'ditch' was applied to the peculiar dry rivers of that country" (Jespersen 151). This instance is an example not only of the resourcefulness of the Dutch language but also of the way in which new words arise out of preexisting structures and the way in which specific terms develop in response to specific elements in the natural world.[3] At the bottom of the same VI.B.6 page, notes from *Criterion* evoke mountainous images ("craggy slope") and lead to "Teuton" (VI.B.6: 88), a portmanteau word signaling "Teutonic" as well as "Teton," the American mountain range that takes its name from the French for "breasts."[4] Jespersen also notes the odd pairing of native nouns and foreign adjectives in English, citing "sun" and "solar" as an example, which Joyce records on VI.B.6: 91. Overall, while there appears to be no clear theme directing the copying of these entries from this source text, Joyce records quite a few nature-related examples and terms from Jespersen's study. What is most important to note is that even though the topic of the text has nothing directly to do with nature, many of the examples Joyce chooses to record do.

In 1912 Edward Sapir published an article titled "Language and Environment" in the journal *American Anthropologist*. Considered to be the foundational text of ecolinguistics, his article argues for how a language's vocabulary "clearly reflects the physical and social environment of its speakers" (Fill and Mühlhäusler 14). Much of Joyce's use of Vico's *New Science* and the presence of the "thunderwords" in the *Wake* can be related to ideas present in this early ecolinguistic theory as, according to Vico, the first words were reactions to the natural environment (e.g., to thunder). Eric McLuhan's *The Role of Thunder in* Finnegans Wake, though a peculiar combination of detailed exegesis of the individual thunders in the

Wake and a reading of the Wake as Menippean satire, does delve into this ecolinguistic territory. McLuhan explains that, according to the "Viconian progression from things to written words, the thunders operate both at the level of things (experiences) and at that of words-as-things" (37); that is, they are both the initial gestural reaction to the thunder and the ensuing symbolic connotations of thunder. Overall, Vico's connecting of history, language, environment, and religion is integral to the Wake. Throughout the present chapter and this study as a whole, ecolinguistics will be called upon to explore Joyce's articulation of the relationship between language and ecology and to explore the ability of landscapes to be legible.

The First Sketches and III.3

The first sketches for *Finnegans Wake* demonstrate the themes of the legibility of landscape through ecolinguistics and environmentally determined narratives (mythologies, histories), and do so in an almost exclusively Irish context. The very first sketch drafted, "Roderick O'Conor,"[5] introduces, in the "place-lore" tradition of the *dinnsheanchas*, the pre-Norman relationship with the land, and the "Tristan and Isolde" sketch introduces invaders arriving to Ireland by sea, as well as the Irish pastoral. "Mamalujo" introduces the relationship between Irish history and geography, and "Saint Kevin" introduces the link between Irish Christianity and landscape.

If one were reading the first drafts of these early sketches without recourse to the *Finnegans Wake* notebooks, it would be easy to cast aside the environmental references in these sketches as strictly ornamental. However, if we keep in mind the themes and trends that grew out of the examination of VI.B.1 and VI.B.6 in the introduction when examining these early sketches, the gradual emergence of themes built around nature's legibility becomes more apparent. It is important to look closely at these early sketches, as they not only contain within them the seeds for the way Joyce will engage with nature throughout the Wake, but they also provide valuable insight into how Joyce merges his experience of composition with the material in the text.

The first two sketches, "Roderick O'Conor" (March 1923)[6] and "Tristan and Isolde" (April 1923), translate ancient heroic Irish figures into the contexts of twentieth-century Dublin. From the first notebook used for the Wake, VI.A (or "Scribbledehobble"), Joyce was creating a male protagonist, Pop, who would be closely linked to the environment and to the attempt to control this environment. David Hayman refers to the heading "A Painful Case" in "Scribbledehobble" for an "early" look at the figure of HCE, who was then, he argues, embodied in "Pop" (*Transit* 25). Three notes under this VI.A heading are: "sleeps in park," "publishes description of Is.," and "protected by beechtree umbrella" (VI.A: 121). "[S]leeps in park," in conjunction with the "A Painful Case" heading, locates the developing *Wake* in the Phoenix Park, and "protected by beechtree umbrella" may refer to the tree under which Mr. Duffy pauses in the *Dubliners* story. Joyce may already have had the historical Roderick O'Connor in mind with these VI.A notes, as O'Connor also has associations with the area; just outside the Knockmaroon Gate to Phoenix Park lies a ruined tower on a hill marking King Roderick O'Connor's headquarters in 1171 (Moriarty 12).

The heading of "A Painful Case" and the note concerning "Is.," or Isolde, also suggest Chapelizod. These two notes are important for the *Wake*'s development not only because they identify a particular location, but because that location is outside of urban, city-center Dublin. This shift in focus from Dublin city center to a rural village on its western fringes, in conjunction with the notes concerning Pop, is not insignificant. Having, in effect, conquered Dublin city in *Ulysses*, Joyce, it seems, decided quite early on that the *Wake* would situate itself at a distance from the urban center.

Chapelizod was a place with which Joyce was quite familiar. Barry McGovern explains how "Joyce himself got to know Chapelizod well from early childhood as the family often went for picnics to the Strawberry Beds" (45). As discussed in the introduction, many critics choose to present a Joyce that never strayed beyond the confines of Dublin city center, but several accounts of childhood peregrinations and subsequent letters and memoirs suggest otherwise. In Joyce's mind, Chapelizod was also primarily connected with his father, once a financial partner in the Dublin and Chapelizod Distilling Company (JJ 16), and David Norris notes, "In the company of Joyce senior, the young James visited various places of refreshment around Chapelizod" (44).[7] Prior to *Finnegans Wake*, Chapelizod had its only starring role as Mr. Duffy's "A Painful Case" residence. In the beginning of the story, Joyce writes:

> Mr. James Duffy lived in Chapelizod because he wished to live as far as possible from the city of which he was a citizen and because

he found all the other suburbs of Dublin mean, modern and pretentious. He lived in an old sombre house and from his windows he could look into the disused distillery or upwards along the shallow river on which Dublin is built. (D 82)

Chapelizod was, and is, a suburb of Dublin. It was not urban in Joyce's day, and it is not urban now. Additionally, one can see a connection to *Finnegans Wake* in the final line of this passage, which figures Dublin's economy and its very existence as contingent upon the river. Toward the end of "A Painful Case," Mr. Duffy walks the "lonely road which leads from the Parkgate to Chapelizod" (D 86), a distance of approximately four kilometers. Chapelizod is chosen as Mr. Duffy's residence because of its *distance* from urban life, and the choice of Chapelizod—not Dublin city—as the centering locale for *Finnegans Wake* at this early stage suggests that Joyce, from the very inception of the *Wake*, was going to be working on a much different type of novel than *Ulysses*.

In the first drafts of "Roderick O'Conor," there is an early version of I.5's "midden heap" with the "grand pile" (BL 47480-267, JJA 55: 446a, FW 318.12), which becomes, on the 1923 fair copy, the "grand old historic pile,"[8] composed of the "colonizers" of Ireland that had preceded Roderick O'Connor: "the unimportant Parthalonians with the mouldy Firbolgs and the Tuatha de Danaan googs and all the rest of the notmuchers." (BL 47480-269, JJA 55: 446b, FDV 203.30–31, FW 381.5–8). These mythological races of Ireland are traditionally credited with the establishment of Celtic society. The Parthalonians were responsible for many "firsts"; from the first foundations of the Celtic legal system to the first adultery and even to the first beer, they gave Celtic society many of its defining features. They also laid the foundations of the Celtic relationship with the environment; Marie-Louise Sjoestedt explains that the Parthalonians take their name from their leader, Partholón, thought to be a god of vegetation (4). Partholón, as god of vegetation, was further believed to have introduced agriculture to Ireland, as, for example (according to Sjoestedt's use of the eleventh-century *Lebor Gabála Érenn* [*The Book of the Taking of Ireland*]), "he found no tiller of the soil before him" and "cleared four plains" (4). Because of this association with agriculture, the Parthalonians were also shapers of the landscape: "When Partholón landed in Ireland," Sjoestedt continues, "he found there only three lakes and nine rivers, but seven new lakes were formed in his lifetime" (4). Partholón and his wife, again according to the *Lebor Gabála* Érenn, lived on an island in the River Erne estuary in northwest Ireland (Macalister 4: 138), presenting an early link between Celtic paganism and Irish Christianity. According to the *Lebor Gabála*, the Parthalonians all died of a plague during the first week of May (beginning on 1 May, also the date of the Bealtaine festival) (Monaghan 376), and it is believed that their remains were buried in the Moy Elta plain, said to be near Howth, according to one of Joyce's sources for *Finnegans Wake*, P. W. Joyce's *A Short History of Ireland* (124).

After the Parthalonians came the Nemed, and then the Fir Bolg. Of relevance to the *Wake*, and more specifically to the "Roderick O'Conor" sketch's association with the Chapelizod area, the Fir Bolg were the first people believed to have lived in this Chapelizod area (McAsey 37). This belief is caused by two cromlechs discovered in the area in the nineteenth century: "one on Knockmary Hill, overlooking Chapelizod, and the second in a sandpit near the village" (McAsey 37). The Fir Bolg were not a particularly successful race, but the mixture of possible provenances and varied linguistic influences serves to complicate the lineage of the Celtic tribes (and thus, to be of interest for the *Wake*). Patricia Monaghan explains that the same Celtic tribes who gave their name to Belgium (Builg, or Belgae) may be related to the Fir Bolg. These tribes "may have traced their descent from a hypothesized ancestral divinity named *Bolg* or *Bulg*, possibly the ruler of thunder, thus their name would mean 'sons of the god/dess Bolg,' or 'sons of the ruler of thunder'" (Monaghan 194). Sjoestedt's account of the Fir Bolg supports this idea of the tribe as believing themselves descendants of the thunder god and in control of nature:

> It is said of their king *Eochaid mac Eirc* that "no rain fell during his reign, but only the dew; there was not a year without harvest." For [. . .] "falsehood was banished from Ireland in his time. He was the first to establish there the rule of justice." Thus there appears with the establishment of the first Celtic communities in Ireland the principle of association between the king and the earth—the king's justice being a condition of the fertility of the soil—which is the very formula of the magic of kingship. (7)

A "pasture loving race," as Carmel McAsey calls them (37), the Fir Bolg were not agrarian like the Parthalonians, but did see themselves as in control of nature, a theme that is important throughout the *Wake* (and throughout this study, particularly in chapter 4) because of the relationship between kingship, fertility of the soil, and agricultural productivity.

The "pasture loving" Fir Bolg were driven to "unproductive lands" (McAsey 37) by the next wave of invaders, the Tuatha Dé Danaan. This race, often known as the first sorcerers in Irish history, also were known to have had the ability to summon nature to their aid, so much so that they even arrived in a "dense cloud upon the coast of Ireland" (Squire 79). Paralleling the inventory in the "Roderick O'Conor" sketch, the Tuatha left behind many relics of their fights, such as stone circles, tumuli, and cairns, which are preserved in the "grand old historic pile" of the landscape. In this manner, it is important to note that McAsey designates the Tuatha Dé Danann as the inventors of Ogham writing (37), the ancient Irish alphabet whose individual letters corresponded to names of trees (developed between the fourth and fifth centuries) that Joyce engages with significantly throughout the *Wake*. Last, with regard to these ancient Irish races, Jessie L. Weston's *From Ritual to Romance* expands the context of the Tuatha Dé Danann and aligns them with the story of King Arthur. Weston explains in her famous source for *The Waste Land* that the "treasures of the Tuatha de Danann and the symbols of the Grail castle go back to a common original" (74). (Throughout the *Wake*, HCE is often aligned with Arthur, specifically in terms of fertility, supporting this connection to Weston.) The appearance of the Tuatha Dé Danann in the first sketch of the *Wake* contributes to Joyce's project of extending the implications of the revival and of exploring universal myths and narratives.

With this account of the Parthalonians, Fir Bolg, and Tuatha Dé Danann in mind, we can see that the "Roderick O'Conor" sketch recounts aspects of each of their histories. "King Art MacMurrough Kavanagh" is aligned with the Tuatha through "Arthur," of course, but is also aligned with the Parthalonians, as Joyce adds "weeping eczema" (BL 47480-269, JJA 55: 446b, FDV 203.24, FW 380.25) to make the line: "took to his pallyass with the weeping eczema" (with eczema being a symptom of a plague). The king eventually died "the year the sugar was scarce and himself down to three cows that was meat and drink" (BL 47480-267, JJA 55: 446a, FDV 203.25–26, FW 380.26–28),[9] suggesting the first famine in times of the agrarian Parthalonians, and providing a link with fertility rituals in Weston as well as in James Frazer's *The Golden Bough*. Then, like Eochaid mac Eirc of the Fir Bolg, who always oversaw a productive harvest, there is "Roderick O'Conor Rex, the auspicious waterproof monarch" (BL 47480-267, JJA 55: 446a, FDV 203.29, FW 380.34). Supported by nature, the King Roderick/HCE figure assumes his patriarchal role over his countrymen: presiding over the harvests, preserving history, and providing liquor.[10] The fact that Joyce has all of these historic races subsumed in the "grand historic pile" from 1923 lays the foundation for the "invisible" landscape of the *Wake*, particularly with regard to I.5's letter and to Yawn embedded in the landscape in book III.

Next, "Mamalujo"[11] shifts the focus to the sea and introduces environmentally determined historical narratives. This sketch introduces the four "historians," the "Four Waves of Erin," who introduce a defining role of geography in history. Jed Deppman notes of the early "Mamalujo" drafts that the "aggregate database is dominated by Irish geography, history, and local culture" (HJW 321), which was partly inspired by Joyce's recent reading of travel guides for VI.B.25. The four historians (also the four evangelists and the four Annalists, among other manifestations) are cast as the "four master waves" (BL 47481-2r, JJA 56: 26, FDV 213.2–6, FW 384.6) early in the composition of the *Wake*, foregrounding the relationship between geography and history.

The four waves of Ireland correspond to different geographical locations on the island of Ireland, and the four historians are each aligned with a specific province of Ireland. This designation of the historians as the four waves unites the story told in the Annals, the story told in the Gospels, and the story told by the sea itself. These three voices of history are weighed almost equally, but each tells a story very different in content, structure, medium, and form. The idea of the waves themselves "speaking" is supported as the history that Mamalujo recounts is actually described as water; they are described as listening "with their mouths watering," "listening & watering," and with "all their mouths making water" (BL 47481-2, JJA 56: 27, FDV 213.23–28, FW 385.34–386.11). Moreover, when the four narrate Ireland's history, it is largely dominated by water (the words relating to this topic are in bold):

> And now that reminds me of poor Marcus Lyons and poor Johnny and the four of us and there they were now listening right enough the four **saltwater** widowers and all they could remembore long long ago with Lally when my heart knew no care the **landing of Sir Arthur Casement** in 1132 and the coronation of Brian by his grace bishop J.

P. Bishop senior in his shovel hat and then there was the **drowning of Pharaoh** and they were all **drowned in the sea the red sea** and then poor Martin Cunningham out of the castle when he was **drowned off Dunleary in the red sea** and thank God there are no more of us. Ay, ay. So he was. and then there was the **Flemish Armada all scattered and all drowned off the coast of Cunningham** and St Patrick & St Kevin & Lapoleon **our first marents** and all they remem**bored** and then there was the French **fleet** in 1132 [...].[12]

The actors arrive in a "fleet," some are "drowned," others land on the coast, and others still are shipwrecked off the coast. The widows of the dead seafarers are "saltwater" widows, the "first marents" are the first parents, but are also combined with "mare" (*mer/mere* sea/mother), thus making the sea an origin (as it is, ecologically and evolutionally). Last, a "bore," often known as a tidal bore, is a phenomenon wherein an incoming tide travels against the direction of a river's current, creating a violent clash between the two opposing flows.

The events described here are not accurate, but hidden in this passage there is the story of Sir Roger Casement, an Irish nationalist who tried to arrange a weapons deal with Germany for the Easter Rising, but was caught while landing in County Kerry; the story of Matthew Kane, a government official drowned off Dún Laoghaire, in south county Dublin, in 1904; and a jumbled account of two other events: the scattering of the Spanish Armada by a storm off the west coast of Ireland in 1588 and a Flemish invasion of Ireland, which likely refers to the 1169 Norman invasion that also included Welsh and Flemish forces.

The significance of this passage is not the actors or the events, but the fact that Mamalujo focuses on the recurrent role of the sea in the course of Irish history (and particularly in terms of its independence). This idea surfaces repeatedly throughout the *Wake*. For example, in a later *Wake* notebook, Joyce records "sea vomits floods of foreigners" (VI.B.29: 108) from a passage in D. A. Chart's 1907 *The Story of Dublin*.[13] This sea-determined history echoes ideas in Metchnikoff, but Joyce's reading of Metchnikoff actually succeeds the drafting of "Mamalujo." Thus, this chronological examination of the *Wake*'s composition (beginning here with the 1923 first drafts) shows that the famous themes present in Metchnikoff's text were something Joyce was, in fact, already working with. The idea of an environmentally determined history actually predates Joyce's discovery of

Metchnikoff's text, as demonstrated by this example of Mamalujo and the sea, and displays Joyce's engagement with Ireland's geography from the earliest phases of the *Wake*'s composition.

John Gordon, in Finnegans Wake: *A Plot Summary*, explains that "[t]he sea adventure of Johnny's monologue becomes, in Marcus's section, emblematic of Ireland's history of invasions and the resulting troubles" (216), and in this early draft of "Mamalujo," the sea is the vehicle for significant events of Irish history (and especially its colonial history). Consequently, when "Mamalujo" is placed alongside other early sketches for the *Wake*, such as "Roderick O'Conor," it is clear that Joyce is establishing the importance of Ireland's physical landscape in the course of its history, thus providing the entire nation with an inner landscape determined by its outer one.

One of the notebooks used in these early stages of the *Wake*, VI.B.6 (which contains some of the abovementioned notes from Jespersen), is filled with environmentally themed notes from a range of source texts. Many of these notes find their way into the early drafts of "Mamalujo." Emily Lawless's *The Story of Ireland* is one of these source texts, and when translating the information on Dermot McMurrough's exile into VI.B.6 notes, Joyce records "Mts or clouds" and "spends winter in Ferns" (VI.B.6: 172). (Ferns is a town in Wexford where Dermot McMurrough founded an abbey in the twelfth century.) Ferns, additionally, is the English translation of *Fearna*, meaning "alder trees," and *fearn* is the third letter of the Ogham alphabet. Concerning Strongbow and Waterford, Joyce records "prisoners with limbs / broken cast into sea" (VI.B.6: 174), and on Henry II and the Church of Ireland he records "wind in Irish sea" (VI.B.6: 176), isolating the geography and climate's role in such decisive historical events. The latter note aligns the outcome of Henry II's visit in Ireland with the weather, deriving from the following passage in Lawless: "The weather that winter was so rough that hardly a ship could cross the channel, and Henry in his new kingdom found himself very practically cut off from his old one. About the middle of Lent, the wind veering at last to the east, ships arrived from England and Aquitaine, bearers of very ill news to the king" (202). The weather's impact on Henry II's ability to travel around his empire allowed the inciting of revolt and ultimately led to the collapse of his empire. This impact of the weather on Irish history appears throughout the *Wake* and will appear again in this study in the context of the Phoenix Park in particular. In "Mamalujo," and in the source texts that inform the material used in the early drafts of the sketch, history and geography are clearly interconnected.

The next sketch drafted, "Saint Kevin," is a retelling of the story of the eponymous saint's sixth-century founding of a monastery at Glendalough, County Wicklow. Drafted during the summer of 1923, this sketch continues to introduce the determining role of environment for Ireland's history, and more specifically, for its religious history. Many notes in VI.B.3 find their way into the first draft of this sketch (which itself appears in VI.B.3), but, returning to the notebook methodology from the introduction, there are many other notes not transferred to the drafts that still provide insight regarding "Saint Kevin." These notes include references to Saint Patrick ("Focluth [wood of]" [VI.B.3: 9]), references to trees preserved in bogs ("bog oak" [VI.B.3: 11]), the name of artificial islands built in bodies of water ("lake dwellings / crannogs" [VI.B.3: 25]), a note concerning the idea of Ireland being a new postdiluvian Eden ("Itself (Tara) centre of world—Ararat Noe" [VI.B.3: 27]),[14] a note linking the HCE figure to Saint Kevin ("Earwicker's bath" [VI.B.3: 38]), another note suggesting postdiluvian Eden ("grass grows on the ark" [VI.B.3: 38]), and last, a note describing an early religious structure constructed out of natural materials ("church of hewn oak & reed roof" [VI.B.3: 40]).[15] Most of these notes speak to the relationship between the nature worship of Celtic paganism and the nature-centric rites, legends, and art of early Irish Christianity. Together, these notes demonstrate the way in which religion often grew out of observed patterns or elements in nature, specifically referring to the motif of rebirth and the rite of baptism.

As in "Mamalujo," geography also plays a principal role in "Saint Kevin," but in terms of the development of early Irish Christianity. Joyce simultaneously glorifies the power of water and mocks its romanticization:

> St Kevin born on the Island of Ireland ^in the Irish ocean^ goes to lough Glendalough to live on an Island in the lake and as there is a pond on the island and a little island in the pond he builds / his hut on the islet and then ^most holy K[evin]^ scoops out the floor to a depth of one foot after which ^venerable Kevin^ goes to the bank of the / pond and fills his tub with water which he emptys time after time into a cavity of his hut thereby forming a pool having done which he ^blessed K^ half fills the tub lets it in the / middle of the pool blessed K pulls up his frock and St Kevin seats himself in the

tub and doctor Kevin meditates with burning zeal the sacrament of baptism of regeneration by water.[16]

Saint Kevin founded the monastic site at Glendalough, which literally translates to the "Glen of Two Lakes," because of its isolation. In Joyce's version, Kevin comically ensures this seclusion by encircling himself with water as many times as possible: already on an island, he seeks another island in a lake on that island ad infinitum. When visiting Glendalough, or even upon seeing an image of the site, the viewer can plainly see that the ecclesiastical site is not so dramatically placed; in fact, it is not in the lake at all. Many other saints discussed in one of the source texts for the Saint Kevin sketch, J. M. Flood's *Ireland: Its Saints and Scholars*, established monasteries proximal to lakes, such as Saint Gall, who established a monastery by Lake Constance (Flood 5). In Ireland, such practices were common, and there are also many monastic sites located on islands within bodies of water; for example, Saint Finbar of Cork established a hermitage on an island in the lake of Gougane Barra (Croker 210), and in the sixth century Saint Molaise established a monastery on Devenish Island in Lough Erne (Co. Fermanagh). Regardless of which saints contributed to the composite version of Saint Kevin, Joyce emphasizes the importance of isolated geographical sites in terms of how the specific brand of Irish Christianity developed. The importance of water in "Saint Kevin" also extends to the baptismal wells of Saint Patrick and Saint Kevin, and to the overall role water plays in Irish history. Kevin's continual fabrication of another body of water in which to perform "the sacrament of baptism," his "regeneration by water," comments on the inevitable human imitation of nature in creative acts as well as concretizes the relationship between ancient pagan traditions and Christianity.[17]

This first version of "Saint Kevin" was followed by "a more sophisticated draft,"[18] to which Joyce added "between rivers" and "with 5 watercourses" (BL 47488-24, JJA 63: 38a, FW 605.19) to the first lines of the sketch. The first fair copies (July 1923) develop the juxtaposition of hagiography with landscape, adding "river Slaney and Liffey River" (BL 47488-25, JJA 63: 38c, FW 605.12–13) as well as several lacustrine elements, the locating of Kevin in the "circumfluent[19] watercourse" (BL 47488-25r, JJA 63: 38c, FW 605.19), and an extension of the baptism and regeneration motif by the addition of "recreated" (BL 47488-25r, JJA 63: 38c, FW 605.7) twice, into the final sentence. In the second fair copy (BL 47488-26, JJA 63: 38d),

Kevin becomes "Hydrophilus" (BL 47488-26, JJA 63: 38d, FW 606.5), pointing the reader back to Stephen Dedalus in "Ithaca" (cf. U 17.1990), and Kevin's sacrament becomes "affusion" (BL 47488-26, JJA 63: 38d, FW 606.11) (wherein water is poured on the head during baptism).

The third fair copy (BL 47488-27, JJA 63: 38e) contains additions from VI.B.25, and the sources for this notebook provide further insight into the direction Joyce was hoping to take "Saint Kevin." Notes from *The Ward Lock Guide* (to Bognor), a travel guide, suggest a need for specific terms and details. For VI.B.25 (of which only a small portion remains), the Bognor guide also provides Joyce with information on fishing (suggesting a possible link to an abandoned passage in the second draft of the sketch, wherein Kevin writes "a prize essay on kindness to fishes" [BL 47488-24, JJA 63: 38a]). In conjunction with "Saint Kevin," the "essay on kindness to fishes" also evokes the story of Saint Kevin and the blackbird, placing Kevin in the line of saints famous for their compassion to members of the nonhuman world.[20]

The use of a travel guide as a source text shows a different aspect of Joyce's interest in specificity of place, in addition to the specific topographical details that appear throughout the composition history of the *Wake*. This attention to topographical detail appears clearly in drafts for book III, the composition of which dominates much of the remainder of 1924.[21] The early drafts of III.3 are situated in rural Ireland and open with Yawn embedded in the landscape and more specifically, "on the hillock" (BL 47482b-62, JJA 58: 3, FDV 228.2, FW 474.2). The word "hillock" itself can mean "a little hill," a "small mound or heap of earth, stones, or the like," or "a hump, bump, protuberance or prominence on any surface." In the context of the *Wake*, each of the three definitions is applicable; the first is self-explanatory, the second contributes to the letter's burial in the "mudmound" in I.5 (to be discussed at length later in this study), and the third relates to the superimposition of body upon landscape. The Yawn figure at the opening of III.3 straddles the entire country of Ireland across its mythical and historical boundaries and connects to Mamalujo as embodied in the four waves and the four provinces of Ireland.

Two central geographical features present in III.3 are the Hill of Usnach and the aforementioned Esker Ridge, both of considerable historical significance in Ireland. The Esker Ridge (as described above) is a stretch of gravel hills formed about ten thousand years ago, when an ice-age glacier covering most of Ireland and continental Europe melted. For the ancient

Celts, the Esker Ridge was the primary route to travel east to west, from Dublin to Galway, and was home to Lucan, Celbridge, Clane, and Clonmacnoise (O.J.R. Howarth 21, 154, 204). The note "Usnach Hill / Centre of I—" (VI.B.6: 180),[22] is used to situate Yawn, and on the second draft Joyce qualifies Yawn's location with the additions of "Esker Ridge" and "near Mullingar" (BL 47482b-62v, JJA 58: 4, FW 475.22), establishing Yawn's location as the Hill of Usnach (located approximately ten kilometers from Mullingar). After a battle in AD 123 near Maynooth, the Esker Ridge became a division of ancient Ireland. Geoffrey Keating's 1723 *The General History of Ireland* recounts the two constituent parts being Leath Coinn, Conn's half (and the upper portion of Yawn), and Leath Mogha, Mogha's share (and the lower portion of Yawn) (10).

VI.B.1 also contains several notes concerning Ireland's historical geography. In this context, the note "Ota w of Turgesius / on high altar / Clonmacnois" (VI.B.1: 45), concerning a Viking raid on Clonmacnoise, present just before "isker (gravell hillocks)" (VI.B.1: 46), refers to Clonmacnoise's famous establishment at the place where the Esker Ridge crossed the Shannon River. This reference appears again with "esker (gravelly hillocks) / ridge—Dub—Gal" (VI.B.1: 46) from Gwynn, demonstrating the alignment between the hillock and the esker, and their importance in early spatial organizations of the Irish landscape. The "esker" also appears in another note from Gwynn, in a different notebook: "Conn C & Mog Nuadat divide I. / by eskers (Dub to Gal)" (VI.B.6: 179).[23] Joyce certainly did not want to forget about the Esker Ridge, and it appears again later in VI.B.14 as "Esker Ridge" (VI.B.14: 176), much in the same context as it did in VI.B.1 and VI.B.6. The passage in Gwynn from which the VI.B.6 and VI.B.1 notes derive is as follows: "Conn's great opponent in Ireland was Mogh Nuadat, and tradition relates that after many battles they decided on a division of Ireland, following the Esker Riada or line of gravelly hillocks (still called eskirs) which runs across the central boggy plain from near Dublin to Maaree on the bight of Galway Bay" (12–13). This is a straightforward passage, but what Joyce has taken away from it is the authority of geography in historical divisions of land in Ireland. The difference between the notes from VI.B.6 and VI.B.1 indicates that Joyce returned to Gwynn specifically to look for this information on the Esker Ridge.

I.5: The Letter, Landscape, and Language

To introduce I.5 and the letter, I begin here with a short overview of the preservational abilities of the Irish landscape because of bogs. E. Estyn Evans, in *The Personality of Ireland: Habitat, Heritage, and History*, explains (somewhat offensively) that "[t]he sight and scent of turf are evocative of traditional rural life, and like the peasant mind, the peat bogs hold the past in their depths" (34). "Thanks to their preservative powers," he continues, "they contain a record of vegetational and human history to supplement the meagre written record" (34).

Accordingly, a key "cultural" feature of the peat bog is its preservational capabilities. Many of Ireland's most famous artifacts were found preserved in bogs (for example, the famous "bog bodies," now on display in the National Museum of Ireland). O.J.R. Howarth, back in his 1911 *Geography of Ireland*, cites the many "magnificent gold ornaments of great antiquity, which have been accidentally dug up in various localities," that are on display in the National Museum in Dublin (190). Several important discoveries were made during Joyce's lifetime, as this was a period of extreme interest in archaeological excavations.

In addition to nearly mummifying artifacts ranging from Paleolithic tools to human bodies, the layers of compressed organic matter that create the bog reveal the natural history of an area, including its changes in climate, terrain, inhabitance, flora, and fauna.[24] In addition to the bog bodies, artifacts like the Ardagh Chalice, various ecumenical texts, bog oak, bog butter, and Celtic gold have also been found in the bogs, and recent discoveries in the bogs continue to revise history. In the 1970s, rock formations discovered in the 1930s underneath a bog in north County Mayo were determined to be the remnants of an ancient agricultural site. This site, known as Céide Fields, provides evidence that agriculture and community life existed in that part of Ireland as far back as six thousand years ago. In mid-2012, the oldest confirmed midden in Clare (and perhaps in all of Ireland) was discovered in a bog in County Clare (Hamilton).

Though recent developments in paleobotany and dendrochronology have allowed that which is preserved in bogs to speak even more fully, the idea that bogs preserved history, both natural and human, would have been widely understood in Joyce's lifetime. For example, Howarth, in 1911, presented an Irish landscape that physically bears remnants of the country's historical geography, explaining how bogs reveal an Ireland that transformed from a heavily forested island to one almost completely barren, and how bogs then encroached upon the newly vacant space. "Wherever the stumps of old trees are found buried in the bogs of the present day (as they often are)," he writes, "there, it may be supposed, a forest formerly grew" (*Geography* 143). Additionally, in the early 1900s, scientists discovered that by studying pollen grains in bogs, the changes in plant life for the region could be revealed.

In I.5 the letter, the mysterious document that will supposedly prove HCE's innocence, is the *Wake*'s central example of the type of legibility of nature provided by bog land. The letter is buried in the ground, which is referred to as a "dump," a "midden heap," and a "mudmound," as well as other terms that emphasize the place of origin of the letter. This designation also suggests processes of decomposition and preservation from the very beginning. Like the "grand old historic pile" in "Roderick O'Conor," the earth in which the letter is buried tells as much of a story as the letter itself. This letter, composed by ALP to defend HCE, but actually written down by Shem, was entrusted to Shaun for delivery. However, the letter gets lost along the way and ends up, somehow, buried deep in the earth. For the drafting of this section, Joyce relied on texts describing Ireland's most famous literary work, *The Book of Kells*, as well as studies of Ireland's history, such as Flood's *Ireland: Its Saints and Scholars*, and he drew upon questions of authorship, design, and textual exegesis articulated in these texts. Then, the sketch known as "The Delivery of the Letter," which became the basis for the entirety of book III, developed out of themes from I.5 and the preceding chapter, I.4. In I.4, Joyce introduces the letter. There is the figure of Kate Strong, who "left, as scavengers will, a filth dump near the dogpond in the park on which fossil bootmarks, elbowdints, breechbowls, kneecaves & fingerprints were all successively found of a very involved description" (BL 47471b-17, JJA 46: 5; BL 47471b-24, JJA 46: 15, FDV 75.20–27, FW 80.4–12). This image of the "dump," the all-encompassing repository for the *Wake*, is also significant for understanding the *Wake*'s themes of language and history through landscape. Though there have been earlier intimations of the "dump" (such as the "grand old historic pile" that appears in the first draft of "Roderick O'Conor" [1923]), this is the *Wake*'s first explicit reference to the "dump."

The first draft of I.5§2, in which the first passage presents the unearthing of the letter, begins:

About that hen, first. Midwinter was in the offing when a poorly clad Shiverer, a ^the^ mere ^merest^ bantling, observed a cold fowl behaving strangely on the fatal dump at the spot called the orangery when in the course of its deeper demolition it ^unexpectedly^ threw up certain fragments of orange peel, the remnant of an outdoor meal of some unknown sunseeker *illico* in a mistridden past. What child but little Kevin would ever in such a scene despondful weather ^in the desponful atmosphere of such biting cold^ have found a motive for the future sainthood ^saintity^ by euchring the discovery of the Ardagh chalice by another innocent on the seasands near the scene of the massacre of most of the jacobiters. (BL 47471b-28v and 26v, JJA 46: 235–36, FDV 86, FW 110.22–111.4)[25]

The source for some of this material is Flood's *Ireland: Its Saints and Scholars*, wherein Flood provides an account of the discovery of two of Ireland's most famous artifacts: "A child playing on the sea-shore near Drogheda found the Tara Brooch, and a boy digging potatoes near the old Rath of Ardagh in Limerick found the Ardagh Chalice" (112). The Shem figure is cast as the boy who found the Ardagh Chalice (one of the most prized artifacts in Ireland, now held at the National Museum in Dublin). The Shaun figure, Kevin, is hoping to find another artifact to outdo his brother. The "jacobiters" and the proximity of Drogheda to the Boyne River explain the inclusion of the "orangery" and the "orange peel" (an allusion to William III's victory at the Battle of the Boyne and the victory's subsequent implications for installing Protestant rule in Ireland) and also add another layer of the geographical preservation of the past. During this period of composition, Joyce was also using Edward Sullivan's *The Book of Kells* as a source for VI.B.6, and the note "Stolen 1006 / found in bog—gold cover" (VI.B.6: 56), concerning the finding of the "large gospel of Colm Cille" (Sullivan 4), supports Joyce's placement of the letter in the ground and supports the alignment of the letter with *The Book of Kells* that pervades the *Wake*.[26]

Using the "Proteus" episode of *Ulysses* to inform a discussion of I.5 strengthens the role of geography in the letter's discovery as well as the relationship between nature and language. In "Proteus," Stephen's acceptance of his teeth as "shells" (U 3.495) and his foregrounding of the "seaspawn and seawrack, the nearing tide, that rusty boot," in the "signatures" (U 3.2–3) he is reading provide a correlation to the discovery of the letter buried along the seashore. If we join this fact with the context provided by Flood's book, the greatest artifacts of Irish history are, on the one hand, detritus or garbage (*Mist* also means "trash" in German). On the other hand, however, they are treasures found embedded in the landscape, and the fact that what appears is a "sheet of letterpaper" (BL 47471b-26v, JJA 46: 236, FDV 86, FW 111.9) creates the sense that within the land, quite literally, history lies buried.

In subsequent drafts of the above I.5 passage, the additions of "strandlooper" and "beachwalker," in addition to the already present "seasands," further link this passage to Stephen's reading of history in the sands and to his examination of decaying matter washing ashore. For Stephen, sand is where "tide and wind have silted" (U 3.298) and where flux and memory transform into history. Marian Eide's *Ethical Joyce* discusses how, in Stephen's meditations in "Proteus," he "envisions language as a heavy sediment whose surface is disturbed by the implacable and constantly changing influences of water and wind" (91). Stuart Gilbert also notes this relationship between nature and language in "Proteus," arguing that "language is always in a flux of becoming, ebb or flow," and that "by the study of language we can often diagnose the processes of change operating in the world about us; for the written signs remain" (129). The fact that both the discovery of the letter in the *Wake* and the "Proteus" episode take place on the seashore is also an important feature to note, as the seashore is often presented as a transitional space. Sand becomes a microcosm for history's mutability as Stephen walks along the strand: "the grainy sand [which] had gone from under his feet" (U 3.147). Stephen's reflection "These heavy sands are language tide and wind have silted here" (U 3.288–89) also looks ahead to the representation of linguistic development in the *Wake*. The "seasands" of this passage from I.5 also emphasize this intermediary placement of sand itself, existing both in the sea and along the shore.

With regard to, in Eide's terms, such "sedimentation" of language, the relationship between landscape (and particularly, bogs) and language appears quite early in the composition process of *Finnegans Wake*, as early as 1925 in the first drafts of III.4. Starting with this early example, one can see how Joyce's own attitude and understanding of Irish land changed from the early drafts (1923–1926) to the final drafts (1936–1939). Bogs appear in the first drafts of the second section of III.4 with "watchman Havelook Seequeersense," which refers to a watchman figure (sometimes Sigurdsen), who is cleaning up and collecting detritus strewn about HCE's pub during the night. Joyce writes: "Seequeersense, punkt by his cursebog, went long adream the way seequestering, for love's propertied offices, loafers purges night leavethings, kikkers, brillers, knappers and bands, handshoes and strumpers, sminkysticks and eddiketsflaskers" (BL 47482a-10, JJA 60: 17, FDV 248.23–27, FW 556.23–27). With this line, peat is used both as a model for the development of language and as a comment on the exploitation of peat as a natural resource.

The choice of "seequeersense" implies both a literal sequestration, in terms of carbon storage in peat bogs, and a metaphorical sequestration, in terms of the historical development, or sedimentation, of language. The list of things the Sigurdsen figure, "punkt by his curesbog," collects, or sequesters, is mostly in Danish, as John O'Hanlon and Danis Rose have observed: "kikkert" are binoculars, "briller" are eyeglasses, "knapper" are buttons, "baand" are ribbons, "handsker" are gloves, "stomper" are stockings, "sminke" is lipstick, and "eddiketflasker" are vinegar bottles (267). The watchman is sequestering Danish words, storing them for later incorporation into Hiberno-English, which echoes theories presented to Joyce by Jespersen.

In *Finnegans Wake*, bogs and language often have similar preservational functions and obey similar models of growth. Over millennia, bogs assimilate dead and decaying material, building layer upon layer. In the same manner, languages assimilate the words of ancient races and cultures, and any one sentence in the English language bears the traces of many languages, cultures, and ideas. This idea of language as repository can be seen clearly throughout the *Wake* in relationship to the types of objects preserved in bogs (e.g., bog bodies, bog oak, Celtic gold) and the way in which a language retains the traces of other languages with which it has been in contact. The role of the landscape in preserving Irish history and bearing the scars of Irish battles is closely related to Joyce's presentation of linguistic sedimentation. In the same way that Hiberno-English preserves the history of Ireland's various inhabitants and influences, bogs preserve the history of Ireland's landscape.

In further support of this argument, on the fair copy of II.2§8, "The Triangle" (1926), ALP's ontological role joins with the discovery of the letter, which also bestows upon her a central etymological role. Joyce adds "midden of the streams" before "muddy delta" (BL 47488-11, JJA 53: 42, FW 297.24) at this draft level, reinforcing the relationship between ALP, the hen, the dump, the land, and the letter. A midden is more than just a dump, as it is so often called in *Wake* criticism; it is a term for a pile upon which the elements of day-to-day life—be that human waste, organic matter, mineral deposits, and so forth—accrue. A "midden heap," a term widely used in the archaeological field, quite literally tells a story in and of itself as the layers are revealed. The word is of Scandinavian origin (Joyce noted the Danish "Kjoekkenmoedding" [*sic*] on VI.B.14: 110), passed down through Middle English, containing within itself layers of history (and in several instances, Dublin's history specifically) through language. In *New Science*, Vico writes:

> [T]he etymologies of native words contain the history of the things they signify following a natural order of ideas. (Thus, at first there were forests, then cultivated fields and huts, next small houses and villages, thence cities, and at last academies and philosophers. This is the order of all progress from its first origins.) By contrast, foreign etymologies merely record the history of words borrowed by one language from another. (15)

This idea of etymology recording the history of words and languages pervades II.2§8, but also I.1, drafted concurrently.

The "midden of the streams" addition appeared contemporaneously with drafts of I.1 (1926), which engages considerably with the "littoral zone" of the Liffey that is central to "The Triangle." VI.B.15, used primarily in 1926 for the early drafts of I.1, contains notes for the exposition of Dublin's early history, both social and natural. There are notes on military figures, alphabets, writing, geography, and hagiography subsumed into larger clusters of notes on Howth, Scandinavian culture, and Chapelizod. In the Mutt and Jute section of I.1, many VI.B.15 notes are turned into a narrative of Dublin's founding (cf. "robbulous & rebus" [VI.B.15: 158]), and embedded within is a demonstration of how various wars and invasions contributed to the language spoken in the country. In the first draft, Joyce uses the land to build a rapport between language, history, geography, and nation: "Walk a look roundward you will see how old the plain From Inn the Bygning to Finnisthere. Punct. Thousand & one livestories have netherfallen here. They are tombed to the mound ishges to ishges, erde from erde. This ourth is not but brickdust. He who runes may read it. But speak siftly. Be in your whist. Whyst? 'Tis viceking's soil" (BL 47482a-97v, JJA 44:41, FDV 56.5–11, FW 17.17–18.13). As with the "olfa" and omega of ALP, this passage also encompasses the span of history from the "Bygning," a word of Scandinavian origin (and Danish for "building"), to the "Finnisthere. Punct." The "Bygning" is obviously "beginning," but as "building" it also evokes Vico's hut-house-village-city order and the construction of homes and walls in the establishment of a civilization. In addition to using the Phoenix Park as the scene of the primary "event" in human history, this passage uses the landscape of the Phoenix Park as historical artifact. The "thousand & one livestories" are buried in the park like the humans buried in mounds, such as the Boyne Valley's Newgrange and Knowth, and all eventually return to the earth, "ashes to ashes" and "dust to dust," or to "brickdust," the destruction of the bricks used for the homes and walls. Combined with the designation of earth as "ourth," with "our" implied, in "ourth is not but brickdust," this passage suggests the earth is not "ours." In the same sentiment as the famous Edgar Quinet passage, this passage suggests mankind and all the things mankind has created will also return to dust. History will still be able to be read through the stones and through the soil, but the "runes" written on these stones will be unreadable and indecipherable (as they largely are today).

Throughout the composition of *Finnegans Wake*, Joyce continues to develop this connection between land and language. From the hundreds of instances wherein Joyce's exploration of etymology ties a word to its landscape, to the clearly articulated relationship between land and language as "landgwage" (BL 47480-2, JJA 55: 3, FDV 182.18, FW 338.5–14) (which also incorporates the "wedge" shapes of the ancient Cuneiform language), the *Wake* articulates the dependence of language upon its environment. However, the relationship in *Finnegans Wake* is more complex than a clear correlation between current speech and environment; the language in the *Wake*, though bearing traces of a possible environmentally inspired origin, also suggests how such an original connection gets absorbed quickly and how new connections continue to build upon it.

Returning again to I.5 specifically, Joyce continues the first draft with references to the "heated residence" and to the "orangeflavoured mound" (BL 47471b-25v; JJA 46: 238, FDV 86, FW 111.26–33). This "mound" is a "heated residence" because of the process of decomposition occurring in the midden heap. The mound is "orangeflavoured" because of the Orangemen and specifically because of Sir Robert Peel, nicknamed "Orange Peel" by Daniel O'Connell (D'Alton, "Daniel O'Connell"). Before Irish independence, anti-Unionists would gather in the Phoenix Park and eat oranges to agitate the Unionists, and thus the buried orange peels are another example of history lying beneath the surface. The orange peels would emit heat as they decomposed in the ground, and their association with the letter in this passage suggests that the letter's decomposition (it is written on paper—made from trees—after all) provides the heat of the "heated residence" that is in contrast to the chilly conditions under which the letter was discovered.

Having established the letter's presence, Joyce then drafts "The Delivery of the Letter" (I.5§4, drafted December 1923 to January 1924). This sketch becomes the basis for book III, and the relationships between I.5, I.7, I.8, and book III that develop at this point in the composition are integral to the evolution of the *Wake*'s ecological themes. "The Delivery of the Letter" is primarily concerned with Shaun's attempt to deliver the letter in a snowstorm: "The unerring zeal with which amid a blizzard with low visibility and on everevenground he sorted & secured for immediate home delivery all packages" (BL 47471b-34v, JJA 46: 293, FDV 90.15–18, not in FW). Details of the letter materialize; its lines run from east to west and from north to south; these "ruled lines along which the traced words can run, march, walk, stumble in comparative safety seem to have been first of all drawn in a pretty checker by using lampblack & a blackthorn" (BL 47471b-40v, JJA 46: 299, FDV 87.12, FW 114.10). Found in a compost heap of sorts, the letter is also written with organic matter: lampblack (as also discussed in Sullivan [47]), or soot, as ink, and a blackthorn branch as a writing instrument. Soot also appears with the addition "for which some blame the cudgel and more blame the soot" (BL 47471b-58v, JJA 46: 317, FW 119.33–34), referring to accounts of giants writing with cudgels and soot in Celtic myth.

With these details, Joyce incorporates Sullivan's focus upon the integration of the natural into *The Book of Kells* both materially (in terms of the ink and of the vellum upon which it was written) and ornamentally (with regard to the leaf and animal designs). For example, in his preface to the third edition of *The Book of Kells,* Sullivan discusses how animals are a main feature of early Irish art and how the presence of certain birds and animals helps pinpoint the provenance of certain manuscripts (ix). He also enumerates the "patterns derived from natural forms—foliage, birds, reptiles, fish, quadrupeds, imaginary or monstrous animals, and man" (15) present in *The Book of Kells* (and also connecting to the above discussion with the "Saint Kevin" sketch about the overlap between Celtic paganism and early Irish Christianity). Sullivan also offers an apposite example of the interdependence of nature and writing, describing how the "general scheme in the foliage panels on the crosses is the long established one of the undulating scroll" (x), with direct correspondence between the scroll and the leaves (both of a tree and of material to write upon) which compose it (cf. also "trefoil" [VI.B.6: 62]).

"Such crossing," the draft of I.5§4 then continues, "is antechristian though the explanation may be geographical quite as easily as domestic economic" (BL 47471b-41v, JJA 46: 298, FDV 87.13–14, FW 114.11–12). "Antechristian" could mean either "opposed" to Christianity or "before" Christianity, and both meanings are plausible for this passage.[27] The transmission of the letter, when embodied as the writing of *The Book of Kells*, is partially "antechristian" (in the sense of both "ante-" and "anti-") in that much of the artistic style derives from Celtic pagan influences ("domestic"), but also derives from Celtic interactions with other cultures ("economic"). Together, the domestic and economic combine as *oikos* (the Greek word from which "ecology" derives), which provides the "geographical" explanation and expands the scope of the text to include the larger territory of Ireland. "[G]eographical" is then changed on the drafts to "geodetic" (BL 47471b-41v, JJA 46: 298, FDV 87.13, FW 114.15), meaning that the text can be used for navigational purposes; that is, it becomes a map (perhaps to guide Shaun the Postman during the blizzard). Additionally, in Brehon Law, blackthorn was the tree that "heralds spring and guards autumn" (Hickie 32), thus serving as a guide through winter.

The presence of the blackthorn tree, in addition to its role in Brehon Law, is also part of the aforementioned Ogham alphabet. Trees begin to appear more consistently in the *Wake* from this stage forward. For example, Joyce adds "more often the arbutus fruit flowering of the cainapple" (BL 47473-26, JJA 46: 318, FW 121.10–11) to the fair copy of I.5§4, deriving from the note "arbutus caithne 2 years Cainapple" (VI.B.6: 61). "Cainapple" may seem to be an invention of Joyce's because of the fortuitous mix of biblical referents, but this note originates in a small piece on the arbutus tree titled "By the Way" in the *Freeman's Journal* from 9 January 1924:

> The arbutus tree is now displaying its beauty in its native districts of Cork and Kerry . . . The tree is one of Nature's curiosities, yielding leaf, flower, and fruit at the same time. "Caithne," its Irish name,

suggests two years old, and may have reference to the fact that the fruit takes two years to develop . . . The "Cainapple," as it is termed locally, has not a very palatable taste. (Qtd. in VI.B.6 8)

The tree in question is commonly known as the strawberry tree; its Irish name is *Caithne*, and its Latin name is *Arbutus unedo*. In Brehon Law it was classified as a "shrub" (H. Fitzpatrick, *Trees and the Law* 1) and is native to Ireland (though now it is increasingly rare and found almost solely in County Kerry [Hickie 24, 68, 130]). In this section of the *Wake*, the tree is used to express a length of time (less than two years), and its other purpose here, in the passage aligning the letter with *The Book of Kells*, is because it is a native Irish tree and a letter of the Ogham alphabet. The berries of the strawberry tree (along with the mountain ash and juniper) were used both as ink for *The Book of Kells* and as part of its design. Sullivan provides a catalogue of the inks used to illuminate the manuscript that are predominantly Irish in origin, providing a literal interpretation of self-creation/creation from self, and the combination of the tree as part of the alphabet, the ink, and the writing surface contributes to nature's legibility.[28]

The Ogham alphabet becomes a clearer focus in VI.B.14 (compiled August to November 1924), a notebook largely dominated by the intersections of culture and the natural world, particularly in terms of the ways in which humans leave behind evidence of their existence. VI.B.14 concludes with a list of the trees constituting the Ogham alphabet, in both Irish and English, as well as the equivalent character:

ailm
b beith birch
c coll hazel
d dair oak
e eadhadh aspen
f fearn alder
g gort
h uath whitethorn
i iodha yew
l luish quicken
muin
n nuin ash
o oir broom

p peith dwarf elder
r ruish elder
s suil willow
t teithne furze
u ur heath (VI.B.14: 223–24)

VI.B.4 also contains a second list of the Ogham alphabet that Joyce had already listed in VI.B.14 and also included in the 1925 letter to Weaver discussed below (LI 225–26). The fact that the trees themselves are continually identified in the notes and appear in the drafts suggests that these specifically Irish trees were of considerable importance to Joyce and to his vision for the *Wake* and were not purely ornamentation. Moreover, the existence of an alphabet composed entirely of tree species connects directly to Joyce's conception of the interdependence of culture and nature.

In addition to the Ogham alphabet, VI.B.14 displays several topic clusters and source texts integral to the understanding of landscape's legibility in the *Wake*. VI.B.14 contains notes from varied sources, but almost all of the dominant themes concern the landscape or the relationship between culture and landscape, whether that relationship is evident through language, religion, monuments, literature, politics, or mythology.

In a 27 January 1925 letter to Weaver, Joyce explains that "The Irish alphabet (ailm, beith, coll, dair etc) is all made up of trees" (LI 225–26), signaling that this fact is something Weaver should know for her understanding of what was being written for the *Wake* during this period. Neither the Ogham list nor "runes made of [twigs]" (VI.B.14: 18) were crossed, but across this draft level Joyce incorporates examples of the materiality of early writing in terms of what was written (the Ogham alphabet), what was used to write (berries, flowers, twigs, etc.), and what was written on (stones, trees, caves, etc.).

To the first typescript of III.2, Joyce adds: "I don't want your ugly gobs round the hobs robbing leaves out of my book. Once upon a drunk and a fairly good drunk it was and all the rest of your blatherumskite" (BL 47483-119, JJA 57: 186, FW 453.21) and "memory's while leaves are falling" (BL 47483-121, JJA 57: 188, FW 460.20).[29] These additions relate to "wind turns over pages" (VI.B.14: 18), found on the same page as the "runes" note, as well as continue the theme "winter turned leaves of book of nature" from the first *Wake* notebook (VI.B.10: 47).

In drafts of III.4, also from 1925, trees are abstracted beyond their role in the Ogham alphabet. In these drafts, Joyce describes the "wind then mong them treen" (BL 47482a-16v, JJA 60: 30, FDV 266.34–35, FW 587.2) (the wind among the trees, possibly echoing Yeats's "Down by the Salley Gardens"), one of the first examples of the trees "speaking" through the rustle of their leaves. In the same way that Stephen imagines the "wavespeech" in "Proteus," Joyce in this next passage imagines what I will call "treespeech": "See yews. All see, together. Hers? saw hymn? Him saw. So and so. Hers, cease to cease. Kindly turn the new leaves thinning over, lisperingly. Cease to cease. Rustle off now. Spake the sooth folly volanty to us? Were you there? Where who were?" (BL 47482a-8v, JJA 60: 14, FDV 267.1–6, not in FW). The trees are questioned, but they do not reply; they only make some sounds ("s" and "o" sounds) as the wind passes through them, which are mistaken for English words. The holly and ivy are queried, their "climbing," "creeping," and "clinging" to the wall (the magazine wall, city walls) misinterpreted as commemoration of the human events that have passed there ("then Yule remember me. O") (BL 47482a-8v, JJA 60: 14, FDV 267.9, FW 508.5). The four old men inquire about HCE, whom they translate into foliage through the name "old honeysuckle" (BL 47482a-8v, JJA 60: 14, FDV 267.23, FW 587.19),[30] in an attempt to win over the trees, hoping that they will reveal the answer. "We sort of gathered he was in sugar," they continue, translating HCE's sexual arousal to arboreal terms, referring to the flowing of sap in spring, and further trying to align themselves with the imagined concerns of the trees.

The weather conditions, highlighted in the composition and discovery of the letter, appear again in this section addressing human inquiry into nature. Specifically, it is foggy; the narrators claim, "it was low visibility" (BL 47482a-8v, JJA 60: 14, FDV 267.21, FW 587.28), defending their own lack of knowledge and placing blame on nature for not revealing the answer, for being illegible. "Hollymerry, iveysad, were you there?" they ask again, only to be answered: "Nobody's here to hear, only trees, such as these, such as those waving there, the Barkertree, the O'Brientree, the Rowantree, the O'Corneltree, all the trees of the wood that trembold, humbild, when they heard the stoppress from their Someday's Herold" (BL 47482a-8v, JJA 60: 14, FDV 267.25–29, FW 588.27–34). As nature does not provide the desired answer, it is ignored, demonstrated by the transformation of the trees into new species with human names. However, two of the names, "Barker" and "Rowan," serve to show the preservation of the tree in the surnames.

Two much later additions to drafts of II.1 revisit the Ogham alphabet, its trees a reminder throughout the *Wake* of the enduring role of nature in Irish culture. Joyce inserts two notes from VI.B.29, "bushments" and "underwoods" (VI.B.29: 89), at this draft level (II.1§6 revisions ca. 1931–1932), incorporating them into the addition: "Underwoods spells bushment's business. So if you sprig poplars you're bound to twig this. 'Twas my lord of Glendalough benedixed" (BL 47477-135, JJA 51: 127, FW 248.28–30). This line refers to Saint Kevin again, the "lord of Glendalough." The two VI.B.29 notes, from Samuel A. Fitzpatrick's *Dublin: A Historical and Topographical Account of the City*, refer to Irish rebels hiding in the forests of Wicklow. Both Kevin and the Irish rebels ("woodkerne") are aligned through this ability to "speak tree" (the Ogham alphabet). "Sprig" is *spreche* or *sprichst* (German, "speak"), and "twig" is Hiberno-English for "understanding" or "knowing" (deriving from the Irish *tuigeann* [Dolan 245]). Joyce also adds at this draft level: "that the turtling of London's alderman is ladled out by the earful to the regionals of pigmy land" (BL 47477-129, JJA 51: 130, FW 253.10). Poplar, alder, twig, and sprig work together to assert the place of nature in culture through language and narrative, returning to another orthographical link in the *Wake* between the German words for book (*Buch*), beech (*Buche*), and letter (*Buchstabe*).

Joyce's attention to trees is present throughout the entire composition of the *Wake*, and the final years of its composition witnessed an even more focused interest. Building on the "tree" additions already discussed in this chapter, Joyce also wrote to Weaver in July 1934 about a text by H. M. Fitzpatrick titled "The Trees of Ireland: Native and Introduced": "Léon began to read to me from a scientific publication about Irish trees. The first sentence was to the effect that the oldest tree in the island is the elm tree in the demesne of Howth Castle and Environs" (LIII 308). This note leads to the designation of HCE as "haught crested elmer, in his valle of briers" (FW 73.36–74.2), and the specification of the "demesne" further informs the political role of trees and of HCE as Anglo-Irish landlord on the final drafts and proofs. The subtitle of Fitzpatrick's text, "Native and Introduced," provides concrete material for the *Wake*'s alignment of invasions with invasive species, and also provides specific detail for the botanical levels of "husbandry" concerning ALP, Issy, and the "flower-girls."[31]

On the galleys for II.1 (January 1938), Joyce added: "Tree taken for grafted. Rock rent" (BL 47477-272, JJA 51: 396, FW 221.31–32), referring to the grafting of one plant species onto another. "Rock rent" in this context is "rack rent," alluding to HCE as a landlord, "laird of Lucanhof" (FW 253.32, VI.C.4: 171). This line continues with the addition: "The oakmulberryeke with silktrick twomesh from shop sowry, seedsmanchap. Grabstone [. . .]" (BL 47477-272v, JJA 51: 396, FW 221.33–34), referring to HCE's "sowing" of his seeds. A passage further on in II.1, concerning the ownership of a large estate, has "boskiest of timber trees" (BL 47477-281v, JJA 51: 414, FW 235.15) added to the description of the estate, leading the way for the many trees that Joyce will add here in the long addition composed largely from notes from Fitzpatrick's text. The addition incorporates several types of trees, some native to Ireland and some not, which can all be found on the island: "Oncaill's plot. Luccombe oaks, Turkish hazels, Greek firs, incense palin edcedras. The hypsometers of Mount Anville is held to be dying out of arthataxis but, praise send Larix U'Thule, the wychelm of Manelagh is still flourishing in the open, because its native of our nature and the seeds was sent by fortune" (BL 47477-281v, JJA 51: 414, FW 235.16–21). The specific choices of Ranelagh ("Manelagh") and Dundrum ("Mount Anville") also relate to the colonial heritage of many of Ireland's invasive (introduced) species. The name "Ranelagh" dates "from the establishment of the Ranelagh Gardens towards the close of the 18th century" (W. Joyce 157), and Dundrum, the "rural hamlet" with its "reviving scenery," was also an Anglo-Irish enclave with its Norman castle and accompanying "private grounds [. . .] almost entirely concealed by trees" (W. Joyce 163). While on the one hand, this addition evokes the Anglo-Irish importation of foreign plants to Ireland for their gardens, it also articulates the question of native trees, relating to the discussion of "Cyclops" and Sinn Féin that appear in the third chapter of this study. This insertion merges Irish locations with other world locations through the detailed attention to trees: the presence in Dundrum and Ranelagh of trees from Turkey, Greece, Tasmania, and elsewhere challenges such nationalistic nativism, providing a type of botanical internationalism. Like Quinet's flowers that know no human boundaries, the trees ignore national borders. If the tree can survive in the conditions in which it sets its roots, then the tree is indifferent as to whether it is native or introduced.

The third typescript of II.3§6, from 1938, displays several more tree additions, and as the end of the story of II.3§6 is reached, Joyce adds: "He beached the bark of his tale; and set to husband and vine: and the harpermaster told all the living conservancy how that win a gain was in again"

(BL 47480-246v, JJA 55: 378, FW 358.17–19). The end of the tale is the "bark," the outer layer of the tree, which also, in seafaring language, is "beached"; the tale itself becomes the bark of a decayed tree washed on to the shore.

In *Finnegans Wake*, the environment is legible because of its ability to preserve artifacts and records of both human and natural history, its ability to be recorded in linguistic structures and subsequent changes, its presence as a subject in works of art, and its use as the material with which art and language are created.

Burial and Palimpsests

The decomposition and recomposition of the letter in I.5 mirrors the burial and unearthing of HCE in I.4, and both contribute mutually to themes of resurrection, excavation, and the legibility of landscape. Joseph Campbell and Henry Morton Robinson's *A Skeleton Key to* Finnegans Wake refers to the beginning of I.4 as "the prehistory of HCE" (81). As I.4 develops, this prehistory expands to encompass a kind of prehistory of Ireland, a trend that can be traced to Joyce's early assertion in "Ireland, Island of Saints and Sages" that "Nations have their ego, just like individuals" (CW 154). The first draft of I.4 (November 1923) introduces two new figures, Kate Strong and Festy King (Shaun), as well as the third Viconian institution, the burial of the dead (here, of HCE). The second paragraph of the first draft reads: "The coffin was to come in handy later & in this way. A number of public bodies made him a present of a grave which nobody had been able to dig much less occupy, it being all rock. This he blasted and carefully lined the result with bricks & mortar, encouraging public bodies to present him over & above that with a stone slab" (BL 47471b-8v, JJA 46: 3, FDV 75.6–11, FW 76.11–77.25). HCE peculiarly creates his own grave by blasting through the rock and building a structure in the resulting hole with "bricks & mortar." The designation of "bricks & mortar" also evokes the building of a wall or a house. This reference again casts HCE in his role of the great patriarchal figure, as the construction of a wall is often represented as a first action in the establishment of a civilization and the demarcation of a city's boundaries, and a house is key to establishing the institutions of community and family. The "stone slab," along with "the other spring offensive" (BL 47471b-8, JJA 46: 4, FDV 65.12, FW 78.15), in the next paragraphs, aligns HCE with Christ and prefigures an eventual resurrection,[32] which also, syllogistically, attributes the idea of rebirth to the discovery of the letter.

The Christian imagery of the "spring offensive" continues in I.4§1 as Joyce moves to the Phoenix Park as the location of original sin and to HCE's rise and fall. This section addresses the role of the Phoenix Park as palimpsest. The Phoenix Park was walled in 1663 to protect deer and fowl intended for hunting (Nolan 7), and HCE's grave/wall encloses him in a similar way, also giving power to his accusers and pursuers. The connection between HCE's grave, Christian mythology, and the Phoenix Park becomes clearer as the draft, and the *Wake* on the whole, continues. Joyce specifies that the events in question occur "on that resurfaced spot" (BL 47471b-17, JJA 46: 5, FDV 75.27, FW 81.12–13), the phrasing indicating that the spot itself was buried and has just now "resurfaced," and also implying that the history of what had happened on that particular spot had been buried along with the spot itself. "Resurfaced" also suggests resurrection, but also applies to the above description of Kate Strong, who "left, as scavengers will, a filth dump near the dogpond in the park on which fossil bootmarks, elbowdints, breechbowls, kneecaves & fingerprints were all successively found of a very involved description" (BL 47471b-17, JJA 46: 5; BL 47471b-24, JJA 46: 15, FDV 75.20–27, FW 80.4–12). The physical land in the Phoenix Park has preserved past events and records of earlier people, as all the artifacts discovered in the above passage are unequivocally human. The "dogpond in the park" is the Dog Pond, otherwise known as the Citadel Pond, found alongside the Phoenix Park's Chesterfield Avenue. According to the Office of Public Works Ireland (the body responsible for overseeing the Phoenix Park), this pond is "partly located on the site of the former Star Fort (also referred to as Lord Wharton's fortifications) from the early 18th century" ("The Phoenix Park" 101); thus, the pond presents part of the park's colonial and military history through its presence. The Phoenix Park's landscape is replete with remnants of its past in the *Wake* and becomes a repository of its own historical waste.

In his essay "Large Parks: A Designer's Perspective," landscape architect George Hargreaves argues that parks are palimpsests and that their design should strive to retain their history, both cultural and natural (122). In the first drafts of III.4, the idea of Phoenix Park's possessing its own narrative expands with the passage simultaneously describing HCE's bottom. The park is described by the second narrator, Mark (of Mamalujo):

Is it not that we have here from back, woman permitting, a profusely fine birdseye view from beauhind this park? Finn's park has been much the admiration all of the stranger ones, Greekish & romanos, who arrive to here. The road down the centre (see map) bisexes the park which is said to be the largest of its kind in the world. On the right prominence confronts you the handsome viceregal lodge while, turn we the other supreme piece of cheek, exactly opposite is the equally handsome chief secreatory residence. The black & blue markings indicate the presence of sylvious beltings. Grassrides herearound lend themselves out for rustic cavalries. Any pretty deers are to be caught inside. A dandelion now shows the site when formerly the first murder were wanted to take place. Some hystorical leavesdroppings may also be garnered up with Sir Shemus Swiftpatrick in archfieldchaplain of Saint Lucan's. At the lowest end do not fail to see and to point to yourself a depression, called the Hollow. It is often quite gloamy and gives bad thought to the head but the band of the Metropolitan Policingforcers bassoons into it on windy Woodensdays their wellsounding wolvertones. (BL 47482a-35v, 36v, 37v, JJA 60: 68, 70, 72, FDV 253.33–254.15, FW 564–65)

This description of the Phoenix Park presents the idea of the park as palimpsest in several different ways: the Greek and Roman versions of the pastoral appear with the juxtaposition of "Greekish & Romanos" with the Latinate "sylvious"; the "pretty deers" caught "inside" allude to the establishment of the park as hunting grounds by Lord Ormonde in 1662, including the importation of deer to stock the park and the subsequent construction of the wall; and the word "park" is etymologically linked to the Latin *parricus*, or "fence." The Viceregal Lodge and Secretary's Lodge ("secreatory residence") are further imprints of English rule, and "Swiftpatrick" may allude to Swift's joke about the construction of the Magazine Fort. "Sir Shemus Swiftpatrick" is an amalgamation of Shem, Jonathan Swift, and Saint Patrick. "Wolvertone" contains "Wellington" as well as "Wolfe Tone," referring, of course, to the Wellington Monument in the Phoenix Park and to Wolfe Tone's visits to the park's military barracks. Then, the single dandelion marks the spot where the "first murder" took place (Abel), or, more currently, the 1882 Phoenix Park murders. In the same way that this dandelion's presence contains a story, one may look to other parts of nature, to "leavesdroppings," to unearth the "hystorical."[33] One place to search is the "archfieldchaplain," composed of both "field" and "champlain" (*champs*, French for "field" or "plain").

The road that "bisexes" the park is Chesterfield Avenue. This road, with the Viceregal Lodge on one side and the Chief Secretary's Lodge on the other, is named after the Earl of Chesterfield, who, according to Weston St. John Joyce in *The Neighbourhood of Dublin*, is the name most closely associated with the park.[34] This bisecting road is also the line between the cheeks of HCE's bottom, as the "black & blue markings" are bruises, signs of "sodomy."[35] Thus, the Earl of Chesterfield's imposition of order—both in terms of British political control and in terms of the ordering of the park itself—are acts of violence. However, the "markings" are also "sylvious beltings," or "sylvan belts," groups of trees in the park as well as remnants of past wilderness and images of current suburban development (discussed further in chapter 2 of this study).

"Finn's Park" refers to the giant, Finn, stretched across the landscape, but also to the Anglicized "*Fionn Uisge*," a fact Joyce recorded in two different notebooks during this period as "Phoenix (Fionn Uisge)" (VI.B.6: 81), "ᗰ Mr Phoenix," and "(Fionn Uisge)" (VI.B.1: 34). In a 14 August 1927 letter to Weaver, Joyce discusses this famous mistranslation, explaining: "As to 'Phoenix.' A viceroy who knew no Irish thought this was the word the Dublin people used and put up the mount of a phoenix in the park. The Irish was *fiunishgue* = clear water from a well of bright water there" (LI 258). It may have seemed humorous to Joyce that an English viceroy was responsible for the association of Dublin's major park with images of resurrection and rebirth. Thus, Hargreaves's idea of the park as palimpsest is effective for understanding this passage of the *Wake*; Joyce presents a space where the landscape and even the language bear inscriptions of each previous occupier.

Another theme of the aforementioned VI.B.14 notebook, derived from sources on Breton culture, language, and folklore, continues to engage this idea of the landscape as palimpsest. While Joyce's original interest in these Breton sources may have originated with Saint Patrick's possible Breton heritage, the extensive notes taken from the Breton sources show that Joyce strayed quite far from this topic of inquiry. The notes Joyce chose to record from these sources demonstrate a clear interest in how culture develops both from and alongside its landscape and climate. These VI.B.14 notes were recorded while Joyce was on holiday in Saint-Malo,[36] and the attention to Breton culture also situates Joyce among other modernists who looked to "primitive" cultures, such as that of the Bretons, for, in theory, authenticity and universal truths. In *The Golden Bough* Frazer also attributes to Breton culture (and to French peasant culture in general) the belief in the connections between nature and divinity.[37] Accordingly, if Saint Patrick is still an interest in VI.B.14, the Breton notes also connect to the earlier Irish races of "Roderick O'Conor."

Many of Joyce's Breton sources in VI.B.14 identify affinities between Breton and Irish culture through the continuity of their cultural geography. Deane, Ferrer, and Lernout explain that this note-taking begins with "Les Prairies de Cézembre / par / l'Abbé Mathurin," the title of a small article in *Annales de la Société historique et archéologique de l'arrondissement de Saint-Malo* (1901). They provide the following gloss on the context of this piece and its possible appeal to Joyce:

> Cézembre is an island that Joyce could see from Saint-Malo. In the early Middle Ages, according to Mathurin, Cézembre was still linked to the coast by a plateau ("the meadows of Cézembre") that was progressively obliterated by the sea. The farming leases to these fertile lands remained a subject of litigation long after the actual ground disappeared beneath the waves. This idea of a submerged territory that survived in (legal) fiction may have appealed to Joyce. At any rate, the Brittany that he was interested in had a somewhat similar status: it was a land that had very little to do with current reality, a misty legendary land that no longer existed, and to some extent a land that had never existed outside of tourist guides or the imagination of Celtophiles and Romantics. (VI.B.14 4–5)[38]

Little more than the title of this book was recorded in VI.B.14, but the idea of Cézembre advances ways in which Joyce conceptualizes territory, geography, and Celticism as the *Wake* progresses.

Cézembre is also relevant to developments in the *Wake* concerning land and territory because of its association with Celtic beliefs that the underworld lies beneath the water (Ó hÓgáin 169). The focus on the "shared Celtic culture" is achieved through notes expressing similarities between the Breton and Irish coasts, bridging the spatial divide caused by the rupture and migration of landmasses themselves. Joyce's continued interest in a shared Celtic heritage present in VI.B.14 is also apparent with the use of Abbé Millon's *Les Pierres Bretons et leurs legendes*, a text discussing the preservation of Breton history in formations such as the stones at Carnac and describing the folklore and superstitions surrounding such megalithic monuments (e.g., dolmens, cromlechs, and menhirs).[39] Deane, Ferrer, and Lernout explain that the significance of these sources for Joyce was their explanation of the syncretism of myth and of the attempted answering of enigmas about the pre-Celtic megaliths through folklore; hence, of having "signs of a very remote past interpreted through conceptions belonging to a recent past (folk tales that were still current at the end of the nineteenth-century)" (VI.B.14 5). Joyce takes notes such as "5000 menhirs in B" (VI.B.14: 1), "dolmen & couloir" (VI.B.14: 1), "cromlech 17 in B" (VI.B.14: 4), "circle of menhirs" (VI.B.14: 4), and "Louannec, Dolmen, S Yves' bed" (VI.B.14: 4), as well as records other specific details about Breton stone monuments that can also be applied to Ireland. Appearing amid these Breton notes are also "T & I write names" (VI.B.14: 22) and "write O" (VI.B.14: 29); such megalithic stone monuments were early forms of communication, and the relationship between the megaliths and narrative also relates to lithography (Greek, *lithos*, "stone" and *graphein*, "writing"), one definition of which is "the art of engraving on precious stones."[40]

VI.B.14's notes on communication and commemoration through stone monuments support both the idea of language originating through responses to the physical environment and the idea of language and writing originating from environmental conditions. Following a cluster of notes relating to prehistoric man (e.g., "Man Cro-Magnon," "Ape Chancelade," "idiot Grimaldi" [VI.B.14: 137]), Joyce copies four pages of notes from William James Perry's *The Origin of Magic and Religion*. Perry's introductory notes to his study provide analysis of what he considers as major indicators of culture, with one indicator being whether a group of people "had reasoned about their relations to the outside world" (3) through the creation of ritual, mythology, religion, or art. Perry locates the origins of both toolmaking and artistic expression in hunting and the fear of becoming hunted oneself, a theory related to Joyce's notes "food gathering" (VI.B.14: 138) and "head hunting" (VI.B.14: 140). Referring to early cave art, Perry explains that the majority of images were animals, either "those hunted for food" or "dangerous beasts of prey" (3). "It seems certain," he continues, "that, in both cases, the aim of the paintings was to enable men to gain control over these animals, to cause the animals that were eaten to be captured the more easily, and, in the case of the dangerous beasts, to gain some measure of protection from them" (3). Representing the animals as visual images creates a certain power over the subject through the translation of the live animal into a static image on rock. Additionally, these early paintings provide a record of the most important preoccupations of a particular society. In this case, the arresting of the animal through the image is intended to lead to the capture of the elusive food sources required to sustain life; thus the origin of art and the need to procure food are closely linked. In the images left on the rock, we learn about those who came before us.

Mountainy Mots

The relationship between languages, the legibility of the environment, and historical cycles in *Finnegans Wake* derives partially from Joyce's engagement with Vico in VI.B.12. Andrew Treip provides an instructive look at Joyce's use of Vico (filtered through the translation of Michelet) from 1926 to 1929. In VI.B.12, Joyce records notes pertaining to Vico's tripartite structures, such as "theocratic obscure / heroic fabulous / human historic" (VI.B.12: 13). Subsequent VI.B.12 notes support Treip's assertion that at this stage in the *Wake*, Joyce's interest in Vico had undeniably extended to an interest in his linguistic theories (63). One particularly relevant note is "first words gestures" (VI.B.12: 13), which prefigures the notes Joyce later takes from Marcel Jousse, but in VI.B.12 refers to Vico's theory that "divine" language was comprised solely of gestures.[41] The "heroic" language was one composed of the same objects that were deified:

> Les signes par lesquels les hommes commencèrent à exprimer leurs pensées furent les objets mêmes qu'ils avaient divinisés. Pour dire *la mer*, ils la montraient de la main; plus tard ils dirent *Neptune*. C'est *la langue des dieux* dont parle Homère. Les noms des trente mille dieux latins recueillis par Varron, ceux des Grecs non moins nombreux, formaient le vocabulaire *divin* de ces deux peuples. (Michelet qtd. in Treip 66)

From this passage, Joyce records: "mountainy mots / plain language / littoral sense" (VI.B.12: 13). What Joyce takes away from this passage is that language and religion were first born out of the human response to the external world. The "littoral sense" relates to the "equilittoral" triangle of II.2§8 (further discussed below) as well as to "literal"; the "divine" language of the sea (resulting in "Neptune") is literal (from the origin) as well as "littoral" (*mer/mère*).

The group "mountainy mots / plain language / littoral sense" (VI.B.12: 13) also parallels Vico's three linguistic stages as they appear in the following passage:

> Le premier principle qui doit nous guider dans la recherche des etymologies, c'est que la marche des idées correspond à celle des choses. Or, les degrées de la civilisation peuvent étre ainsi indiqués: *Forêts, cabanes, villages, cités* ou sociétés de citoyens, *académies* ou sociétés de savants; les hommes habitant d'abord les *montagnes*, ensuite les *plaines*, enfin les *rivages*. Les idées et les perfectionnements du langage ont dû suivre cet ordre. (Michelet qtd. in Treip 68)

The "mountainy mots" correspond to the *divine*, the "plain language" to the *heroic*, and the "littoral sense" to the *human*. In a translation of *New Science*, the aforementioned line appears as: "This was the order of human institutions: first the forests, after that the huts, then the villages, next the cities, and finally the academies" (98). This order of human institutions provides another way of understanding the role nature plays in the histories of civilization in the *Wake*. The forests begin as "Edenic" or primeval space, and then they are translated into ordered parks, estates, and hunting grounds and into cultivated land for agriculture and stockbreeding. Then the movement is made to the cities, further separating the human from the natural, and before all becomes overgrown again by forests, the academies develop, to formalize and codify "knowledge."

Ecotaph

Later in the composition process, Joyce turns again to the famous "Upfellbowm" passage of FW 503 (which will be discussed at length later in this study), adding a lengthy piece to the galley proofs for book III. The tree is qualified as "an overlisting ashtree" (BL 47487-68v, JJA 62: 132, FW 503.30), enforcing its connection to the Yggdrasil. There is also the addition to Yawn's answer about the "tree stuck up": "Besides the Annar. At the foot of Slieveamond. Oakley Ashe's elm. With a snoodrift from one beerchen bough. And the grawndest crowndest consecrated maypole in all the reignladen history of Wilds. Browne's *Thesaurus Plantarum* from Nolan's. The Prittlewell Press, has nothing alike it. For we are fed of its forest, clad in its wood, burqued by its bark and our lecture is its leave. The cram, the cram, the king of all crams" (BL 47487-68v, JJA 62: 132, FW 503.30–504.2). The tree was located beside the "Annar," Anna (the Liffey), and at the foot of a mountain, which in Irish is *Slieve*. "Annar," however, is also part of "the three marriages of night" in Scandinavian mythology, where "night first marries Naglfari and then Annar," and Annar is also "Day" (Byock 134). The tree may have been an oak, an ash, an elm, or a birch, but regardless, the tree became a symbol for man and woman (ash and elm, in Scandinavian myth), the symbol of spring's arrival with May Day rituals, and a political pawn ("reignladen history"). "Browne's *Thesaurus Plantarum*" is William James Browne's 1881 introductory textbook, *Botany for Schools and Science Classes*. This book contains chapters on the specific parts of plants (e.g., "The Root," "The Stem," "The Leaf," "The Flower," and "The Fruit and Seed") and presents a diagram of a flowering plant on the fourth page (accompanying the section "General Structure of a Flowering Plant" [5]). Browne's text, or a similar textbook, could likely have provided some of the detail for II.1 and II.2 (see below, chapter 5), and may also contribute to the botanical additions appearing throughout these final drafts.

Last, the "reignladen history of Wilds" is a history of the wilderness and its growth (rain) and its control (reign). Joyce presents this idea succinctly with the final line of the above passage: "For we are fed of its forest, clad in its wood, burqued by its bark and our lecture is its leave." Summoning the Viconian structure again, this line provides an image of the "Wilds" providing not just food and clothing, but also family names ("burque" may be the surname "Burke"[42] and the Germanic *burg*,[43] which also adds shelter to the list of food, clothing, and shelter) and literature. "Our lecture is its leave" brings readers, reading, and texts together with the implication of the French *lecteur/lecture* with the English "lecture." All of these textual processes depend on the tree and its leaves; nature provided the first stories, words, and religions, but also the first paper and ink. It also provides our metaphors for reading (we still "leaf through" a book, and the French word for pages is the same as leaves, *feuilles*) and provides us always with something legible.

To the galleys of book III, Joyce inserts: "Their livetree (may it flourish!) by their ecotaph (let it stayne!) with balsinbal bimbies swarming tiltop" (BL 47487-13, JJA 62: 23, FW 420.11–12). "Ecotaph" implies, of course, both "ecology" and "epitaph." An epitaph is a written inscription upon a tomb,[44] a tomb being, of course, a place of burial, usually within the earth. "Ecology" comes from the Greek *oikos*, meaning "house" or "dwelling," and "ecotaph" (*oikotaphos*) thus becomes a place of burial, a home, a return to the earth. The written aspect of an epitaph also suggests that nature writes upon itself, upon the place of interment.

This relationship is also evident on the galley proofs of book III: as Jaun is preparing to leave, Joyce adds, "Daughters of the heavens, be lucks in turnabouts to the wandering sons of red loam!" (BL 47487-45v, JJA 62: 88, FW 469.3). According to *The Brown-Driver-Briggs Hebrew and English Lexicon*, the word for "red" in Hebrew is "*adom*," which is also linked etymologically to "*adam*" (man) and to "*adamah*," meaning "ground" or "earth" (726). Max Oelschlaeger also discusses this relationship between the creation of man and the earth, citing how Yahweh made "man" (Hebrew: *adam*) out of the "dust of the ground" (*'adamah*) to "till the earth" ("Adam"). According to Oelschlaeger: "Man of the *adamah* means literally 'man of the ground,' or farmer, as in the story of Noah, 'a man of the soil' (Gen. 9: 20). This Adam—the paradigmatic human being—is the cultivator, the tiller of the soil. *'Adamah* can also mean the inhabited land and especially the arable land as distinct from wilderness (Hebrew *midbar*)" (52). Thus, man is firmly rooted to the ground, and to the exploitation of this ground. The word "man" itself contains its own destruction, its eventual return to this ground, to decay and become fertilizer for the next generation of those who must till the land. To the section of III.2 concerning Jaun's plan for improving the city of Dublin, Joyce adds, "compost liffe in Dufblin by Pierce Egan with the baugh in Banghkley of Fino Ralli" (BL 47487-30, JJA 62: 59, FW 447.22–24). The discovery of all the cultural artifacts either in the river or along the shore is part of the "compost" of the Liffey ("liffe") and, on a larger level, of life ("liffe"). All human endeavors and creations become compost, fertilizer for the next generation of lives, legible in the remains buried in the ground.

In this first chapter, the theme of the landscape's legibility has been demonstrated in a variety of contexts. Overall, the natural world in *Finnegans Wake* is inextricably linked to narrative; it records narratives itself (through the bogs, stone monuments, and rituals, for example), is reflected in etymology, is a subject of art (such as the Breton cave paintings), is a component of language (the Ogham alphabet), or is used to create art (*The Book of Kells*). The early sketches introduce landscape's legibility through mythology, language, history, and religion, laying the foundation for the subsequent developments of this legibility in I.4, I.5, and III.3. The emergence of book III out of "The Delivery of the Letter" (drafted December 1923 to January 1924) was a result of the developing theme of the interdependence of history, language, and landscape. Sullivan's *The Book of Kells* provided Joyce with alternative ways of "reading" a text (translated to the *Wake* in terms of the hen's scratchings, the tea stain, the grass and turf remaining on the letter, etc.). These alternative ways of "reading" suggested the legibility of other "texts," of which the landscape was undeniably one.

2

City versus Country

Finnegans Wake is exemplary as a subject for ecocritical inquiry because of the way in which it addresses the interaction and interdependence between city and country. Modernization began to strain the relationship between city and country and cause tension between the two both culturally and socially, despite enduring economic and geographic interconnectedness. I argue for an ecological modernism that focuses on urban ecology—one that does not entirely reject the trope of modernism as metropolitan nor one that wholly embraces the idea of a pastoral modernism, but one that allows for the uncovering of the complex debates over modernity and nature taking place during this period, from the ways in which humanity was understanding the impact of modernization on the land, the ways in which nature was being politicized, to the ways in which agriculture, transportation, leisure, and domestic life were being redefined.

To begin this discussion, I look to the first sentence of I.1, drafted in 1926, and to Joyce's use of the word "environs." In criticism of *Finnegans Wake*, much has been made of the importance of "Eve and Adam's," of "Howth," of the "commodious vicus of recirculation," and of "riverrun," but what of "environs?" Most critics and readers seem to assume that this word simply refers to the general area around Howth, and it most certainly does, but what else can be made of "environs"? David Mazel, in a seminal ecocritical essay, returns to the subject of ecocritical inquiry and examines the very word "environment." Looking up the term in the *Oxford English Dictionary*, Mazel writes how he "was not wholly surprised to discover that performance is originary to the word itself," elaborating:

A root verb plus a suffix, *environment* once denoted "the act of environing," that is, surrounding. But with the obsolescence of the verb *environ*, this active sense has been lost, so that we no longer hear it in the way we do in words such as *judge*ment and *govern*ment—words that still echo with the full senses of the actions and the actors upon which they necessarily follow. What remains of our sense of environment, by contrast, is not any action but a thing; thanks to a nominalising process that effaces both act and actor, we no longer speak of what *environs* us, but of what our environment *is*. (138–39)

This idea of what "environs" is constant through the *Wake*, and each element of the text is part of a larger context, or contained within a larger whole. For example, descriptions of ALP are almost always in conjunction with the riverbanks, the sea, and the city of Dublin, and Dublin itself is always part of the larger country of Ireland, and Dublin and its environment are inseparable. There is a restoration of the act of environing in the *Wake*, a reinstatement of that which surrounds and contextualizes.

This second chapter focuses on the relationship between city and country, and the spaces in between (suburbs, parks, harbors, etc.). It begins with a discussion of the "Anna Livia Plurabelle" chapter, I.8, and moves to explore the expanding importance of the Liffey in the *Wake* before moving on to drafts of I.6, III.3, III.4, and IV. The first section addresses the 1924 drafts and subsequent expansions of I.8 and the figure of ALP as the Liffey, focusing closely on the ways in which Joyce expands the Liffey's relationship with Dublin city as HCE. Overall, this chapter asserts the necessity of reexamining the "country" in modernist literature, and of inserting the "city" into ecocriticism, and argues for the importance of *Finnegans Wake* in closing these gaps.

An Life: The Life of the Liffey in I.8

The first chapter to be discussed here is I.8, "Anna Livia Plurabelle," which expands the importance of Dublin city's natural setting to the *Wake*. In 1924 letters to Weaver concerning I.8, Joyce explained that he viewed the draft of this chapter as largely about the *actual* River Liffey (I stress the word *actual* because of the critical focus on metaphors of flow discussed earlier; this is not to say that this metaphor is not important, but only to say that the physical river itself is just as, if not more, important) and its relationship with Dublin city. The first draft of this chapter presents the river as a structuring force for language and narrative: it is the medium across which dialogue travels, it is the origin of the city's name, and it gives its rhythms to the text itself.

Throughout the *Wake*, the relationship between city and country, Dublin city and its environs, is often represented in terms of the relationship between the male and the female, HCE and ALP (though HCE is also the landscape at times as well). In early drafts of I.8, Joyce recounts ALP's union with HCE, beginning with a focus on ALP and her preparations for courtship. The character of the river and the available flora along the riverbank define ALP at her toilette:

> She first let her hair fall and down to her heels it flowed and then mothernaked she washed herself from crown to sole with bogwater and mudsoap and greased her keel with butterscotch and multiplied moles all over little mary, and then she wove a garland for her hair and pleated it and plaited it of meadowgrass & riverflags and bulrushes & waterweeds & leaves of weeping willow and then she made her bracelets and her anklets and her armlets and her necklet amulet of cobbles and pebbles and rich gems & rare ones & rhinestones & watermarbles. (BL 47471b-77, JJA 48: 9, FDV 126.7–15, FW 206.29–207.7)

Her hair "flowed" like water, and she washes with the brown mud and turf-filled Liffey water. She styles her hair by weaving grasses and leaves into it, and bejewels herself with gemstones and pebbles of the riverbed. The meeting she prepares for is with the city of Dublin (as HCE), and in her youth, she does not yet recognize what awaits her.

Joyce once said to Frank Budgen that the Liffey was as important as Christianity to Dublin's development, and this sentiment can be observed in Joyce's attention to the specific geography of the Liffey and the land through which it flows.[1] The first drafts of I.8 were slightly more concerned with the Liffey as a symbol, but as the *Wake* progressed, the Liffey (and rivers in general) takes on a leading role in Joyce's presentation of history. June and July 1925 brought the second and third typescripts for I.8, containing many additions of world rivers to demonstrate the connection between civilizations and their relationships to water. To these typescripts, Joyce not surprisingly incorporates many of the Metchnikoff notes from VI.B.1 and also focuses on padding the chapter with the names of other rivers and riverine terms. The second typescript gains: "Oronoko! What's the trouble?" (BL 47474-165, JJA 48: 96, FW 214.10), "backwater," "wave," "thames" (BL 47474-160, JJA 48: 85, FW 199.1), "short Brittas bed," "ambushore" (BL 47474-147, JJA 58: 87, FW 201.20), "dneepers," "gangres" (BL 47474-142, JJA 48: 82, FW 196.18), and several other additions related to bodies of water, their contexts, and their ecology.

The third typescript (July 1925) exhibits small changes and additions to the river material, such as "her peakload of rivers" (BL 47474-145, JJA 48: 102, FW 199.23), "about in Ow and Ovoca?" (BL 47474-148, JJA 48: 105, FW 203.14–15), "Tell me the sound of the shorthorn's name. And drip me why," "^nubilee^ letters" (BL 47474-150, JJA 48: 107, FW 205.7), "Southfolk's place but howmulty ^plurators^, "Are you suir?" (BL 47474-172–73, JJA 48: 123, FW 203.9), and "Garonne! Garonne!" (BL 47474-175, JJA 48: 125, FW 205.15) (to replace "Go on! Go on!"). The rivers added at this draft level vary in location, size, and cultural or historical "importance": the Garonne, in southwest France and northern Spain, is a fairly small river, especially when compared to the Orinoco (the second longest river in South America), the Dnieper (the fourth longest river in Europe), or the Ganges (roughly 2,500 km in length and sacred to the Hindu faith). In line with the work of Metchnikoff, Joyce composes a portrait of the Liffey as part of a larger network of waterways that have dictated the shape and culture of their respective nations and civilizations.

This third typescript of I.8 introduces more transitional, riparian spaces with Joyce changing "backside" to "bankside" and adding "shores," "shoal" (BL 47474-173, JJA 48: 123, FW 202.5), and "peats be with them" (BL 47474-173, JJA 48: 123, FW 202.30), all to the same page. "Bankside" and "shores" embody the spaces between the ordered land and the chaotic water; they are the unpredictable liminal spaces, the ecotones.[2] A sand or gravel bar that extends into the water, a shoal is composed of sand, silt, or small pebbles and develops where a stream or ocean current deposits such sedimentary material.[3] A shoal can be glacial (a shoal moraine), and, like peat, it can record the traces of previous geological eras. It is appropriate that these transitional additions are to the section telling the story of ALP and her passage from youth to maturity: "She must have been a gadabout in her day, so she must, more than most. Shoal she was, you bet!" (BL 47474-173, JJA 48: 123, FW 202.4–5).

Another source to turn to concerning Joyce's usage of rivers is W. K. Magee's (more commonly known by his pseudonym, John Eglinton)

Pebbles from a Brook (a text of which Joyce once said that he "knew a great many sentences and ends of sentences by heart" [qtd. in Kain 358]). Magee uses the word "shoal" in a paragraph beginning, "Nature abhors perfection," arguing that anything seeming to have reached "perfection" is only in "some backwater or shoal out of the eternal currents, where life has ceased to circulate" (45). He continues:

> The course of time is fringed with perfections but bears them not upon its bosom. The river goes to the sea, time to eternity, and we mortals desire perfection, but unable to repose in the universal purpose and find satisfaction in fullest action, we cling to the banks and the limits of the stream, and where a temple is mirrored in quiet waters of a philosophy opens a secure cove, we drift in to reflect beauty and wisdom, and hear the great floods outside pour ever onward. (45)

Magee's use of the terms "shoal," "currents," "river," "sea," "banks," and so forth is in a context that lends a great deal to how Joyce uses these terms at this draft level. The shoal and the banks are spaces outside the flow of life; they are safe havens for those fearing failure. The natural course is that of the river flowing "to the sea," as this mimics the flow of time into "eternity." Believing that art and knowledge will lead to the attainment of eternity is a falsehood. ALP's movement is the "correct" path in the *Wake*, and the trappings of civilization are only these "secure coves" wherein humankind hides while the "great floods" of time press on, eventually wearing away at these very coves.

In the "ryewye rhyme" (BL 47474-172, JJA 48: 122, FW 200.33) (later the "wyerye rima," evoking the River Wye of Wordsworth's "Tintern Abbey"), the epistemological aspects of Magee's argument merge with a specific focus on Dublin's geography and the natural history of the Liffey. The "rhyme" of ALP in the first draft of I.8 is from the perspective of the Liffey/ALP long after she has been tarnished by the demands put upon her by the city of Dublin. Though her life before Dublin was not exactly virginal ("Two lads in their breeches went through her before that, Barefoot Byrne and Billy Wade," and she was "licked by a hound while doing her pee"),[4] this life is looked back upon fondly and romanticized, much in the way nature is romanticized in the earlier "Tristan and Isolde" sketch.

The young girl who had labored over her hair and her jewelry has now been demoralized by the city, and the rhyme ends with the river's thinking of a different fate. ALP expresses a longing for a different outcome for her life; she wishes that she took a different course, literally, rather than flowing through Dublin. She covets a new "bankside" because that which she has now is a "putty affair" and is "wore out" (BL 47471b-74v, JJA 58: 4, FW 201.7). A woman already advanced in age, she wishes her husband— her "old Dane hodder dodderer" (BL 47471b-74v, JJA 58: 4, FW 201.8), composed of the Dane and Dodder rivers (the Dodder being a tributary of the Liffey [Warner 106])—would wake up and cavort with her, satisfying her desire for the renewal of her banks. She thinks about leaving HCE/ Dublin, dreams of a "lord of the manor" or a "knight of the shire" coming to whisk her away (though both of these terms suggest she will not escape, as both roles are dependent on a similar domination of landscape). "Only for my bed is as warm as it smells it's up I'd leap & off with me to the Bull of Clontarf to get the kind air of Dublin bay & the race of the seawind up my hole,"[5] she thinks (BL 47471b-74v, JJA 48: 4, FDV 124.37–39, FW 201.19–21). She longs for the "Bull of Clontarf" (the North Bull Wall, now Bull Island [built from 1819 to 1824 to protect ships coming into the port]), and after the North Bull Wall, the Liffey opens out into Dublin Bay and then to the sea, a freedom of which the walled-in ALP can only dream.

She ultimately remains where she is, however, for her (river)bed in Dublin city is comfortable; it is "as warm as it smells." The river does not try to change its course, but remains confined within its walls in Dublin; the wife does not in the end seek a new lover, but because of the comfort offered by the familiar old husband, remains. The Liffey's position in Dublin city—walled, dammed, channeled, and polluted as it may be—is painless; like Bloom and Molly at the end of *Ulysses*, the river stays in its pairing with the city because it is easy. The renewal ALP desires, the journey out to Dublin Bay, is simultaneously a longing for a death; without Dublin city, the Liffey is no longer special, but just another stream of water dissolving into the larger oceans. The "environs" of both Dublin city and of the River Liffey itself are integral here to the way in which the text develops. In the same manner that the sea in "Proteus" demarcates the boundary between life and death, these concurrent expansions of the wetlands are here to remind us of the transitional space between land and water, city and nature.

The gossiping washerwomen try to discern who was the first to wade in ALP's waters, and one of them proposes: "She was a young thin pale slip of a thing then & he was heavy lurching Carraghman as strong as the oaks there used to be that time in killing Kildare that first fell across her" (BL 47471b-75, JJA 58: 5, FDV 125.10–13, FW 202.26–32). This hypothesis is wrong, "corribly wrong" (BL 47474-173, JJA 58: 123, FW 202.35), alluding to Lough Corrib in Counties Galway and Mayo, and the terminology Joyce uses demonstrates this fallacy. In the first draft, "killing Kildare" alone tells us this is incorrect, as the Liffey rises by Mt. Kippure and Tonduff in the Liffey Head Bog in County Wicklow (Warner 9–10). In subsequent drafts, Joyce adds "dykes" before "killing Kildare," and "peats be with them" after "oaks." The effect of these additions is to evoke the restrictive quality of Kildare's landscape: the Liffey does not flow freely there. After descending from the gentle hills and comparable wilderness of the Wicklow Mountains, the river, when it enters Kildare, encounters both man-made and geological restrictions such as dikes, weirs, canals, irrigation ditches, flat peat lands, dams, industries, manors, and houses.[6]

In subsequent drafts, Joyce changes "Carraghman" to "Curraghman" (BL 47471b-75, JJA 48: 5, FW 202.9) (to which he then later adds, "making his hay for whose" [FW 202.29]), to strengthen this theme of the Liffey/ALP's physical restriction. The Curragh, the Central Limestone Plain of Ireland, supports the Pollardstown Fen in County Kildare by delivering nutrient-rich water from the gravel in the Curragh aquifer. The Curragh is also the location of Ireland's equine industry (the limestone provides nutrients that strengthen the horse's bones), and the upkeep of the stables and racecourses requires considerable amounts of water. Thus, when the Liffey reaches County Kildare, its flow is restricted by both the geology of this region and its human inhabitants. The Curragh has been the historic center of aristocratic horse racing since the seventeenth century (Warner 48), and additionally, because of the fertility of the Curragh plain itself and because of the Liffey, this area made a prime spot to construct army barracks (Warner 52). In these contexts, the reference to HCE as "Curraghman" also implicates imperialism in ALP's restriction in "killing Kildare." After this, the second washerwoman corrects the story (a young, wild river/girl like ALP cannot have had her origins in a place like Kildare), and tells of the Liffey's origin in "Wicklow, the garden of Erin." In short, the portrayal of ALP in I.8 is as a body of water inextricably linked to its history as the river of a city, and the existence of Dublin city is portrayed as inextricably linked to its river. Together with the developments of the ecological framework provided by VI.B.14, this portrayal leads to a strengthening of the river's importance throughout the *Wake* during 1924 and 1925.

Dalway, Dorghk, and Nublid: I.6

This next section continues with the theme of the city's dependence on the river, expanding to the dependence of all Irish cities upon their proximity to water in I.6. Following revisions of I.5 for *transition,* Joyce composed the first draft of I.6 in the summer of 1927, to, in a sense, recap the progress made with the *Wake* up to that point. I.6 is largely a series of questions that Shem puts to Shaun, with the first two concerning the various roles of HCE and ALP. The first question of the first draft of I.6 revisits the many forms HCE has embodied in the *Wake* up through the summer of 1927, beginning: "What secondtonone myther rector & bridgemaker was the first to rise taller through his beanstale than the bluegum baobabbaum or the giganteous Wellingtonia Sequoia, went nudiboots into a liffeyette when she was barely in her tricklies, was well known to clout a conciliationcap on the esker of his hooth" (BL 47473-117, JJA 47: 5, FDV 92.12–17, FW 126.10–15). The question ends: "and though he had all the baked bricks of bould Babylon to his lusting placys he'd be lost for the want of an ould wubblin wall?" (BL 47473-120, JJA 46: 11, FDV 93.9, FW 139.11–13). HCE is a "myth erector," a storyteller, a builder of bridges and walls (a theme that dominates the next section of this present chapter concerning III.3), a Celtic king, an army general, a magnificent tree, a conqueror of new lands, a progenitor of a new race. During this same period of composition, HCE also becomes the Scandinavian tree of life, the "Yggdrasselmann" (BL 47472-376, JJA 46: 170, FW 88.23)[7] in I.4, which also appears in book III.

The beginning of this first question concerns the figure of I.1, the giant, Finn, embedded in the landscape. He is the giant of Jack and the Beanstalk ("beanstale") and is larger than the largest trees (the blue gum, the baobab, and the sequoia). The "myther rector" and "beanstale," in relation to Jack and the Beanstalk, also suggest an untrustworthy narrative, as in "a hill of beans" or a "tall tale" (such "tall tales" are what, after all, indicts HCE). The subject of the question is a man of civic life, the "bridgemaker," the builder of "Babylon," but he is also a man of the mountains; he is the Yawn figure on the esker ridge of III.3, and he "waded" in the Liffey "when she was barely in her tricklies," all the way up in the Wicklow Mountains.[8]

The second question, preceded in the manuscript by "Δ," turns its focus to ALP, asking: "Does your mutter know your mike?" (BL 47473-120,

JJA 46: 11, FDV 93.11, FW 139.15). The first draft of Shaun's answer is in the form of a song to his mother and is in clear contrast to the urban HCE:

> When I turn me optics
> From such urban prospects
> Tis my filial bosom's
>   Doth behold with pride
> That pontificator
> And circumvallator with his dam so garrulous
>   All by his side.
> Annealive, the lisp of her
> Would make mountains whisper her
> And the bergs of Iceland
>   Melt in waves of fire
> And her spoon me spondees and her drickle-me
>   yondees
> Make the rageous Ossean kneel
> And quaff a lyre.
> If Dann's plane Ann's purty, if he's fane she's flirty, if he's dane she's dirty with her auburn streams and her coy cajoleries and her dabblin drolleries, for to rouse his rudderup or to drench his dreams. If hot Hammurabi and cowld Clesiastes could espy her panklettes, they're break bounds again, and renounce their ruings, and denounce their doings for river and river, and a night. Amen! (BL 47473-121, JJA 46: 13, FDV 93.12–35, FW 139.16–28)[9]

Looking away from the "urban prospects," Shaun finds his inspiration in nature; his response speaks of the influence of nature on writing—that is, on the creation of "spondees" and through the words of Ossian. As his response comes to an end, Shaun also tells of how law ("Hammurabi") and religion ("Clesiastes") are challenged by nature's own structures ("her panklettes," like the anklets ALP donned in I.8), and the "Amen!" signals the end of Shaun's hymn to nature/his mother.

The answers to questions one and two display two different types of creative powers through both their content and their form. The first answer is stereotypical masculine speech: short, concise, and sparse. The second answer is stereotypical *l'écriture féminine* (though obviously this term would not have been known to Joyce): poetic, rhythmic, and fluid. ALP is HCE's "garrulous" dame ("dam"), and her speech possesses creative abilities; she can make mountains talk (the Viconian "mountainy mots") and icebergs melt. The flowing of a river can be mistaken for a human voice on a quiet mountain, and a river's warmth will melt ice. This creative power is likened to poetry, as supported by the "spondee," the "lyre," and the reference to Ossian.[10] With "dam," there is also the physical dam of HCE/Dublin as suppressor (echoing I.8). The words flow out in this "garrulous" manner because she is not allowed to speak, not allowed to flow as she is meant.

Questions three and four return to the city of Dublin, to the "urban prospects." The third question asks for the Dublin city motto (*Obedientia Civium Urbis Felicitas*: The Citizens' Obedience Is the City's Happiness), presented in this first draft as "Thine obesity, O civilian, hits the felicitude of our orb!" (BL 47473-123, JJA 46: 17, FDV 94.14–15, FW 140.6–7). With the fourth question, Shem asks Shaun for a particular Irish city: "What Irish capitol city (ah dea o dea) with a deltic origin and a nunous end (a dust to dust!) of two syllables can boast of having a) the most expensive brewing industry in the world b) the most expansive public thoroughfare in the world c) the most extensive people's park in the world d) the most phillohippuc theobibbus paupulation in the world?" (BL 47473-123, JJA 46: 17, FDV 94.16–21, FW 140.8–13). The "deltic origin" and the "nunous end" refer to the Greek letter "d," delta, and the Irish letter for "n," *nuin*. The "deltic origin," is, of course, the "delta" of ALP, the maternalized representation of the Liffey, represented by Joyce with the Greek Δ. The delta of ALP as mother is the origin of Shem and Shaun, and the delta of the Liffey is the origin of Dublin itself. "Nunous," in addition to referring to the Irish letter "n," also refers to the Hebrew letter "n," *nun*. Bringing this back to the Ogham alphabet, Godfrey Higgins explains that both the Irish *nuin* and the Hebrew *nun* refer to the ash tree (25). The opening of the fourth question in I.6 serves three other purposes: it links three ancient cultures—the Greeks, the Hebrews, and the Celts; it links the development of alphabets directly to nature; and it defines Dublin geographically, not just orthographically—from the "deltic origin" (the Liffey Delta) to the "nunous end" (the ash trees of the Phoenix Park and of the Wicklow forests).

Three of the four characteristics of the city in question are related to economics, engineering, and city planning: the brewing industry harnesses the Liffey's water for human use; the "most expansive public thoroughfare" is Sackville Street (now O'Connell Street), laid out by the Wide Streets

Commission of the 1750s; and the "most extensive people's park" is Europe's largest city park, Dublin's Phoenix Park.[11]

For this question, the respondent is not just Shaun, but the four historians, Mamalujo, who each provide a separate answer to the question for their respective provinces of Ireland. The first answer is "Delfas," given by Mark, written in over a crossed-through "Belfast" (for the province of Ulster). The beginning of this answer contains words and phrases such as "ribs," "floxy loss," "tenderbolts of my riverts," and "hommers" (which implies "hammers," but is also the French for "lobster," *homard*) and concludes with the line: "You with yer orange garland and me with my conny cordial, down the greaseways of rollicking into the waters of wetted life" (BL 47473-124, 125, JJA 46: 18–19, FDV 94.26–28, FW 140.15–21). Referenced in this first answer are Belfast's shipbuilding and linen industries, both of which existed because of Belfast's seaside location, as indicated by the play on "wetted" and "wedded." The economy is "wedded" ("wetted") to the water, and the answer concludes with a completed ship heading out to sea.

The second answer is "Dorhqk" (Cork), for the province of Munster: "And sure where can you have such good old chimes anywhere, and leave you, and how I'd be engaging you with my plovery soft accents and descanting on the scene below me of the loose vines of your hairafall with my two loving loofs braceliting the slims of your ankles and your mouth's flower rosy and bobbing round the soapstone of speech" (BL 47473-125, JJA 46: 19, FDV 94.28–33, FW 140.21–27). This answer, infused with a Cork accent and cadences, introduces the plover, a wetland bird commonly found in Irish marshlands. Cork's Irish name, roughly pronounced "Cork" but spelled *Corcaigh*, means "marsh" and relates to the feats of civil engineering undertaken to build Cork city on a small, marshy, island in the River Lee's estuary.

The third answer is "Nublid" (Dublin) for Leinster (and I have bolded relevant terms): "Isha, why wouldn't be happy avourneen, on the **mills** money he'll soon be leaving you when I've my owned **streamy** Georgian mansion lawn to recruit upon by Dr. Cheek's special orders with my panful of **soybeans & Irish in my east hand and an james's gate in my west**, after all the errears & erroriboose of embattled history, with yourself **churning over the newleaved butter** (*more* power to you!) the best and the cheapest from Atlanta to **Oconee** whilst I'll be drowsing in the garden" (BL 47473-125, 126, JJA 46: 19–20, FDV 95.7–8, FW 140.28–36). This answer is constructed around staples of Dublin's river- and sea-based economy through mills, agriculture, brewing, and dairy, from the Irish Sea to the Guinness Brewery, located along the Liffey at Dublin's St. James's Gate. In this passage, the River Liffey/ALP asks about the money made from her and the fact that it allowed for the emigration and subsequent success of many Dubliners in America. The "Georgian mansion" is a play on both the architectural style popular in the eighteenth century but also the town of Dublin, Georgia, on the Oconee River.

The fourth and final answer is "Dalway" (Galway), for the province of Connacht (BL 47473-126, JJA 46: 20, FDV 94.8, FW 140.36), and contains the line: "Holy eel and sainted salmon chuck chubb and duckin dace, I never saw *your* aequal! says she, leppin half the lane" (BL 47473-127, JJA 46: 21, FDV 94.11–13, FW 140.36–141.4). The city's Spanish Arch, the Shandon Cathedral bells, the major cities and the counties of the province (Sligo, Tuam, Mayo, and Galway), and the region's Atlantic fish characterize the answer. The idiomatic expressions used in Joyce's version of Galwegian speech in this answer derive from the region's proximity to the sea and its economic dependence upon the fishing industry.[12]

Thus, the question that asks the name of the "Irish capitol city" with a "deltic origin" is met with a four-part answer: the city is a universal Irish city composed of "Delfas," "Dorhqk," "Nublid," and "Dalway," representing all four provinces, and defined by its economic and linguistic relationship to the sea, as all are defined by their "deltic origin." Thematically, this section of I.6 exhibits Joyce's balancing of the city with its geography and environment, examining how cities are often constructed through the manipulation and exploitation of their natural resources, and how, as a result, the existence of cities is contingent upon their relationships with their environments.

Dublin and Environs: VI.B.29

In the book *Dublin Bay*, archaeologist Brian Lalor emphasizes that the geography of Dublin Bay itself is of highest importance to the origin, development, and character of Dublin city and its surroundings (8). Drafts of III.3 and III.4 during this stage of composition are closely related to the role of the relationship between nature and the feminine from drafts of I.8. Keeping ALP's depiction in I.8 in mind, one sees how III.3 functions as a complement through its depiction of HCE as city. From both perspectives, the two are dependent on the other for their existence, endurance, and prominence. Continuing with the idea of environing, much of III.3 concerns the development of cities and their relationships to the environments upon which they are built and which surround them. The chapter also deals with the Viconian establishment of villages and of community on the path toward the birth of the modern city. The *Wake*'s narrative moves toward the development of community around FW 506.34, with Joyce describing HCE, his family, and their home (which in Vico would be the "hut" phase). As Joyce revised this section of III.3, the narrative becomes increasingly focused on HCE as city and ALP as nature, as Joyce presents, extending from I.8, the development of civilization as the marriage of the urban and the rural, the city and the country. This section also demonstrates the different methods of Joyce's note-taking from source texts and how such material appears in drafts of the *Wake*.

The relationship between the urban and the nonurban through a shared history, mythology, environment, and language is demonstrated from December 1928 to January 1929, as Joyce was working on the typescript of III.3§A–B (BL 47484a-156–247v, JJA 58: 307–413, FW 474.01–554), including "Haveth Childers Everywhere" (FW 532.06–554). The "Haveth Childers Everywhere" sketch (first drafted in 1924) focuses on the development of civilizations and the building of cities, with HCE stereotypically representing the urban and the patriarchal. This sketch, and the rest of III.3 surrounding it, underwent substantial expansions and revisions during this period of composition; on the 1929 and 1930 drafts, Joyce crowded the section with references to nature, crystallizing and expanding the tension between country and city. Jean Michel Rabaté, in an essay on III.3, addresses the urban themes of this chapter and provides a theory for the development of this tension. Although he does not go further with this point, Rabaté explains that some of the additions may be "a wry allusion to the city built by Cain after his murder and flight 'East of Eden'" (HJW 399). Drawing upon the theory that the tension between Cain and Abel is an allegory for the supplanting of shepherding by agriculture (discussed further in chapter 4 of this study), it is appropriate that on the 1929 typescript of III.3§A–B, many of the additions engage this tension by demonstrating the move away from the countryside and from agriculture and into the cities (also parallel to the Viconian movement from the forests to the villages to the cities).

On a structural and philosophical level, the contraries involved in the balancing of I.8 and III.3 contribute to the larger idea of history's cyclical movements, the "*Courser, Recourser*" (FW 481.2) from Joyce's "zigzag v spiral corsi ricorsi Vico" (VI.B.1: 29). This note derives from the first chapter of Metchnikoff's book, *Le progrés*, which critiques, not surprisingly, modern ideas of "progress." Using Vico's cyclical history and Darwin's theories of evolution, Metchnikoff argues that "progress" is a subjective term and "dans l'histoire, comme dans la nature, l'évolution ne suit jamais une marche rectiligne" (4).[13] He argues that this idea of "progress" has actually just served "ouvrir des abîmes entre la nature et l'homme" (10).[14] The "zigzag v spiral corsi ricorsi" note provides a visualization of Metchnikoff's nonlinear conceptions of history, nature, and civilization. These notes, with their articulation of the split between nature and man, and emphasis on the nonlinear (like the course of a river), may explain the philosophical origins of Metchnikoff's pursuit of the relationship between rivers and civilizations, and may also explain additions Joyce makes to the 1929 typescript of III.3§A–B that relate to this critique of progress by collapsing the binary of city and country.

Joyce articulates this binary with the addition, "I have your tristich now. It recurs in three times the same differently. And speaking of this same famous site of yours, Mr. Tupling Towns, would be reoccur now in city or country if you know the difference" (BL 47484a-251–51v, JJA 58: 319–20, FW 481.10). The "tristich," "three," and "Tupling" refer to three different periods of settlement in Dublin (Celtic, Viking, Anglo-Norman) as well as to Vico's three ages. The layering of these tripartite structures (spatially and temporally) represents Vico's idea of history in which one civilization rises, "progresses," then falls, initiating the beginning of another cycle. Each individual event may have a seemingly linear movement, but when looked at in a wider context, all of these movements are absorbed by larger structures (the cycle, or spiral). The dissolution of the boundary between country and city presages the coming "corsi ricorsi" and also attempts to close this *abîme* between nature and man.

The second typescript of "Haveth Childers Everywhere," from August 1929, relies heavily on notes from VI.B.24.[15] This notebook contains several topic clusters geared toward an expansion of HCE as "city man," toward the various stages of human institutions, toward the development of community, and toward the development of civilization at the expense of the environment (there are notes on Americanisms, Carthage, Spain and Portugal, New York, Vienna, Islam, drink, Oslo and Norway, Russian religious rites, trade guilds and crafts, Ibsen, Holland, erotic texts, Irish names, saints' names, and the ceremony of the "equatorial crossing"). Within these topic clusters, there are also approximately three dozen ecologically themed notes, most of them crossed through, signaling a pointed gathering of such material for this late 1929 to early 1930 phase of the *Wake*.

A few notes in VI.B.24 support this hypothesis by referring to hydro-engineering, a quintessential example of how nature is harnessed (and one that has also existed for centuries):[16] "Δ flow uphill" (VI.B.24: 9, FW 546.32), "Δ rolling logs/from sawmill" (VI.B.24: 102, FW 580.4), "conduict" (FW 537.14), "viaduct," "acqueducked" (VI.B.24: 198), "*mae d'agua*" and "sewage" (VI.B.24: 199). Together, these notes concern the manipulation of nature in the establishment of cities and their economies. But other notes—like "Humidia," "Riverside Drive" (VI.B.24: 206), "Gramercy Park" (VI.B.24: 206), "Coney Island" (VI.B.24: 206), "Hudson Terminal" (VI.B.24: 206), "Slutspark" (VI.B.24: 227), and "water of Liffey" (VI.B.24: 279)—show the interconnectedness of civilizations with the nature they may assume they have subdued. In earlier drafts of I.8, there is discussion of the Liffey "turning back," referring to the Liffey's tidal nature, and here, in conjunction with the other hydro-engineering terms and its appearance with "congested districts" (FW 580.30), the "Δ flow uphill" refers to Dublin Corporation's management of the Liffey's flow (through channelization, walling, damming, etc.) and its proposed plan in the beginning of the twentieth century to change the direction of the river's flow into Dublin Bay.

Subsequent typescripts of "Haveth Childers Everywhere" see the expansion of the engineering themes that appeared in the August 1929 second typescript. In modernist literature the privileging of city over country and man over nature is often represented in terms of technology and mechanization, and the exploitation of nature through engineering is one of Joyce's ways to explore this theme. For example, there are several more additions relating to hydro-engineering at the 1930 draft level of "Haveth Childers Everywhere": "canal grand, my lighters" (BL 47484b-383, JJA 59: 104, FW 551.23), "pons for aquaducks" (BL 47484b-385, JJA 59: 106, FW 553.21), "He walked in by North Strand with his towel in his hand" (BL 47484b-359, JJA 59: 108, FW 534.27), and "water gas telegraph telephone/pneu all running inside the sewers" (BL 47484b-413, JJA 59: 137, FW 542.4–7).

On the next draft level for III.3§B, from April 1930, Joyce adds even more engineering-related terms: "water tap / W tap" (BL 47484b-459, JJA 59: 206, FW 544.16), "never saw the sea" (BL 47484b-460, JJA 59: 207, FW 544.31), "precipitation works" (BL 47484b-454, JJA 59: 197, FW 551.18), and "watertap 200 yards off" (BL 47484b-459, JJA 59: 206, FW 544.16–17).

In 1930, Joyce was working on book III, chapter 3, and relying heavily on material recorded in VI.B.29. Both III.3 and VI.B.29 have almost exclusively been described as intended to write the story of the "city-building male" to balance the already composed chapter of the female river. However, a closer examination of the notebook and a reassessment of the source materials indicate that what Joyce is interested in at this phase of composition is, again, the interdependence of the city and its environs, and more specifically, the dependence of Dublin city upon the River Liffey and Dublin Bay.

ALP's connection to nature, the fluidity of her rhythms, and fertility all uphold the "Mother Earth" stereotype, the Gaia-Tellus image from *Ulysses*. Yet Joyce begins to engage with the complexities of this imagery, permitting the ALP figure more depth and more agency. As Deane, Ferrer, and Lernout explain of VI.B.29, the notebook does show how "Joyce had determined that after his watery female 'Anna Livia' he would write a male city-building parallel in the second part of III.3" (4). Though this statement is true, VI.B.29 also figures in the collapse of these binaries, focusing on the ways in which cities are inescapably bound to nature, and the idea of the subjugation of the "watery female" by the "city-building" male is actually critiqued in VI.B.29 and the related drafts.

I start with a source text for VI.B.29, from which Joyce had also recorded notes in an earlier notebook (VI.B.7), Charles Haliday's *The Scandinavian Kingdom of Dublin*, an 1881 study of Dublin as a Scandinavian seaport. Haliday's study begins with a lengthy introduction by John Prendergast, who asserts that Haliday actually began this book to "write a history of the port and harbour of Dublin, with a view to trace the progress of improvement in the navigable channel of the Liffey" (cv). Clearly much more interested in the "seaport" aspect of Haliday's work than the "Scandinavian," Prendergast focuses much of his introduction on the engineering projects that turned the River Liffey and Dublin Bay into safely navigable channels. One VI.B.29 note, "Ballast office / Ball" (VI.B.29: 44), is recorded from Prendergast's introduction. This note refers to the Ballast Office, the headquarters for the supervision of Dublin harbor, the ball that adorns this building, and likely also to Sir Robert Ball, the astronomer associated with Dublin's Dunsink Observatory. Dunsink determined Ireland's official time, 25 minutes behind Greenwich Mean Time, and the ball on top of the Ballast Office dropped every day at 1:00 p.m. GMT so that ships could check their chronometers.

Prendergast's introduction provides a history of the New Channel and the walling in of the Liffey and recounts the 1707 establishment of the Ballast Office, responsible for the first phases of the engineering project. Prendergast's introduction contains detailed records from Ballast Office committee reports explaining the problems with silting in Dublin Bay and assessing possible solutions. The Great South Wall of Dublin Bay, a breakwater extending far out into the bay, was begun in 1717 and is also known as the Ballast Office Wall. Prendergast then details the importance of three maps related to Haliday's project that show the early history of the Liffey, Dublin Bay, and Dublin Port: a 1673 map of Dublin port and harbor by Sir Bernard de Gomme, Petty Down's 1655 map, and Captain John Perry's map of 1728. Prendergast then explains the history of Dublin port and harbor through these maps, recounting Perry's plan for a new entrance to Dublin harbor and how "the canal was to be carried through the sands of the North Bull, parrallel [sic] with the north shore of Dublin Bay" (cvii). Prendergast explains that with these maps and the information collected by Haliday, "a good conception can be formed of the extraordinary changes effected in the channel of the Liffey in the course of 200 years" (cix).

These details inform the present section of *Finnegans Wake* (III.3), with the "North Strand" addition coming from Prendergast's explanation of how, on De Gomme's map, the "northern shore of the bay is now represented by the line of Amiens-street and the North-strand, the latter still preserving the original denomination" (cix–cx). Joyce's interest in names and words preserving traces of other cultures, languages, and, in this case, geographies surfaces here, as the topographical North Strand no longer exists but remains only in the name of the road itself. Prendergast explains how the river emptied into the bay before "the commencement of the eighteenth century, when the Ballast Board was erected in 1708" (cx), and from their foundation, the Ballast Board and the corporation began to work on the construction of a new channel and the walling-in of the Liffey so as to ensure smooth passage for commercial shipping. The Ballast Board and Ballast Office considered themselves to own "the river and strand" (cxii), and these facts from Haliday, when compared to the simultaneous engineering additions at this draft level, contribute to Joyce's inclusion of the Ballast Office at this particular draft level.

When Joyce finishes with Prendergast's introduction and begins taking notes from Haliday's actual text, he records other notes that speak to the material Prendergast presented, such as "Swell of the Liffey / Δ" (VI.B.29: 45).[17] When Joyce leaves Haliday behind and turns to other source texts with different topics, he continues taking notes that relate to Dublin Bay, such as, "It borrows its name from the river that slides by it," regarding the origin of the name of Galway, "Δ," and to "the Bay Limesoiled" (VI.B.29: 77), from the *Encyclopaedia Britannica*, referring to the limestone in the mountains around Dublin. More notes include "Swan Water" and "New Holland" (VI.B.29: 94), from a passage in Weston St. John Joyce's *The Neighbourhood of Dublin*: "When the delta or slobland formed at the confluence of the Swan Water, the Dodder and the Liffey was embanked and reclaimed in 1792, it became known by the name of New Holland, possibly on account of the desperadoes resorting there, the original New Holland having been a convict colony" (23).

The development of the Liffey and Dublin Bay were integral to the way in which Dublin developed as a capital city in *Finnegans Wake*. This relationship is further demonstrated as VI.B.29 continues, wherein Joyce takes notes from the *Encyclopaedia Britannica* on the way in which another national capital, Washington, D.C., was developed through the reclamation and channeling of the Potomac (bolded terms will be discussed below):

[M]uch of the land surrounding the Capitol was a marsh; there were no streets worthy of the name, the roads were very bad and the members of Congress were obliged to lodge in Georgetown. For many years such characterizations as "Wilderness City," "Capital of Miserable Hutts," **"City of Streets without Houses," "City of Magnificent Distances"** and "**a Mudhole almost Equal to the Great Serbonian Bog**" were common. Resolutions were frequently offered by some disgusted member of Congress for the removal of the capital.[18]

Joyce records these notes on VI.B.29: 57:

city of streets without
houses city of magnifi-
cent distances

a mudhole almost
Equal to the great
serbonian bog
(VI.B.29: 57)

On a page of Joyce's revisions to a February 1930 typescript of III.3, there appears, "Fort Dunlip, then-on-sea hole of Serbonian bog, now city of magnificent distances, good & walled" (BL 47484b-109, JJA 59: 133, FW 539.24). Joyce's additions here include the old nicknames for D.C., another VI.B.29 note, "good & walled," and a play on the naming of seaside towns (such as Bexhill-on-Sea, etc.). The "good & walled," in its original source context, refers not only to the Liffey but to Dublin's old city walls in general. However, on this typescript, Joyce combines it with D.C.'s reclamation from the marshy lands of the Potomac and the shifting coastline of Dublin caused by the channeling and walling of the Liffey and Dublin Bay, resulting in the "then-on-sea." Dublin's city wall becomes conflated with the Liffey wall and the breakwaters extending into the bay, and Dublin becomes conflated with Washington, D.C. Thus, this addition to III.3, when viewed in light of the avant-texte, implies that the emergence of Dublin as a capital city was dependent upon the engineering projects that alter the layout and course of the city's water sources.

This theme continues with another note from the same notebook relating to the Viconian cycle: "Wilderness city capital / of miserable hutts" (VI.B.29: 56). This note, too, belongs to the Washington, D.C., cluster. Several of Joyce's notes on D.C. concern the layout of the city and derive from a section in the *Encyclopaedia Britannica* that addresses the planning that went on behind the city's design. For example, the note "Lenfant" (VI.B.29: 52) refers to Pierre Charles L'Enfant, appointed by President George Washington in 1791 to design the layout of America's new capital city. Joyce notes "beautification" and "park like" (VI.B.29: 52), both of which derive from a line describing the appointment of a commission later in 1901 that was "to prepare plans for the beautification of the city" and had "submitted a design for a park-like treatment" of much of the area (qtd. in VI.B.29 51). The note "reclaim" (VI.B.29: 53) refers to Potomac Park, which "has already been reclaimed from the Potomac river" (VI.B.29 51). Only through reclamation, dredging, channeling, damming, and walling bodies of water and manipulating natural resources did the modern city emerge. Several other notes in VI.B.29 relate to this topic, like "Boullawards" (VI.B.29: 81), referring to the land reclamation involved in the improvement of the waterfront in Rio de Janeiro (VI.B.29 79). The notes "wilderness city capital" and "of miserable hutts," though not incorporated at this draft level, provide an extra example of Vico's forest-to-hut formulation and also provide another example of the tendency to divide "wilderness" from "civilization."

These thematic interpenetrations can also be observed through four other additions on the August 1929 second typescript: "Seven ills havd I habt" (BL 47484a-291, JJA 58: 404, FW 541.1), "And I raided a dome on the bog" (BL 47484a-290, JJA 58: 403, FW 541.5), "my carpets of guerdon city" (BL 47484a-246, JJA 58: 411, FW 553.8), and "Atlantic City" (BL 47484a-170, JJA 58: 415, FW 482.9).[19] These additions are representative of the changes being made at this draft level and pave the way for the more substantial additions made from VI.B.29 to III.3 in 1930. "Guerdon city" ("Garden City") and "Atlantic City" are inserted at the same time, pointing to a source text discussing American urban development. The later addition of "lecheworked lawn,"[20] alluding to Letchworth, the English Garden City founded in 1903 by Sir Ebenezer Howard, also suggests a larger interest in urban planning and utopian communities. Responding to the increasing pollution in industrial, urban areas, Howard's planning concept of the "Garden City" (articulated in his 1898 *To-morrow: A Peaceful Path towards Real Reform*) provided a utopian vision of self-sufficient communities living harmoniously with both industry and environment. Garden cities, in Howard's own explanation, would be a "group of slumless, smokeless cities" (qtd. in Ward 4), and would be completely integrated with the natural world, as presented in contemporary advertisements for "Garden Cities" such as Welwyn (founded 1920). Joyce's "guerdon city," from the earliest drafts of III.3, is specifically furnished with "selvage mats" and "carpet gardens" (FW 553.8). These are textiles of sorts, but "selvage" (VI.B.1: 126) also implies *silva*, Latin for "woodland." The mats and carpets are made from the trees and the flowers, reminding one of a suburban home that has brought nature indoors with its floral carpeting and pine mats. The suburbs, the transitional space between city and country, and these "selvage mats," are the nature that has been domesticated, tamed, and appropriated for interior decorating. However, according to Vico, all developed from the forests, and all will eventually return to them. These suburban homes, the civilizations that have chopped down the trees and named streets after them, will one day be overrun by the forests again, their carpets growing flowers, their mats being grown through by trees.

As mentioned above, the suburban location of Chapelizod and the Phoenix Park in the outskirts of Dublin city is crucial to understanding the larger themes, tensions, conflicts, and patterns of change that appear throughout the *Wake*. The suburb is a transitional space, both culturally and geographically, and the primary definition of "suburb" in the *Oxford English Dictionary* actually dates as far back as the fourteenth century: "The country lying immediately outside a town or city; more particularly, those residential parts belonging to a town or city that lie immediately outside and adjacent to its walls or boundaries."[21] The earliest definition, dating from approximately 1387, relates to the suburbs of Rome, and Robert Harrison argues: "[T]he ancient city of Rome, whose destiny so preoccupied and fascinated Vico, was eventually reclaimed by the forests, first by analogy, then in the form of forest-peoples from the north, and finally by the vegetation belt itself. The Forum became wild pasture land for Dark Age cattle. Wilderness overgrew the roads that led to Rome. The work of history fell to the ground it had tried to surmount under the auspices of god" (13). The "Seven ills havd I habt" addition refers to the founding of Rome by Romulus, a descendant of Silvius (according to book 6 of *The Aeneid*). Romulus's heroic founding of the great city of Rome was accomplished through the construction of a wall around the "seven hills," a wall that separated city from forest. As a descendent of Silvius, of the forests, Romulus severed himself from his own origins by building the wall, codifying the separation of culture and nature in the mythology of Western civilization.

Descending from this founding of Rome, cities have been traditionally understood in terms of this dichotomy between outside the wall or inside the wall, and it is no coincidence that HCE as builder of walls is a major theme of his presence in the *Wake* or that the suburban locations of Chapelizod and the Phoenix Park play a formative role in the text. HCE is Humpty Dumpty, "Balbus,"[22] Ibsen's "Master-Builder," and Gilgamesh, the "builder of the walls of Uruk," the Sumerian city. Harrison argues further, concerning this point, "Walls, no less than writing, define civilization. They are monuments of resistance against time, like writing itself, and Gilgamesh is remembered by them. Walls protect, divide, distinguish; above all, they *abstract*. The basic activities that sustain life—agriculture and stock breeding, for instance—take place beyond the walls [. . .] Gilgamesh is the builder of such walls that divide history from prehistory, culture from nature, sky from earth, life from death, memory from oblivion" (14–15). HCE, as a Gilgamesh figure, believes himself builder of these walls and in possession of power over nature. The construction of the wall is a physical articulation of the separation of the civilized world from the uncivilized world, of the institutionalization of civil society.

Extending this image of HCE as Gilgamesh figure, Deane, Ferrer, and Lernout characterize the sources for VI.B.29 as relating to "cities and citybuilders" (VI.B.29 4). Sources for this notebook include James Hardiman's *The History of the Town and County of Galway* (originally published in 1820 and reprinted in 1926 by the *Connacht Tribune*); A. Peter's *Dublin Fragments* (which contains material on Dublin customs, parks, streets, theaters, and houses); James Collins's *Life in Old Dublin*, described as "a long guided tour of Dublin, revealing the many layers of history hidden beneath the surface of the modern city" (VI.B.29 6); John Warburton, James Whitelaw, and Roger Walsh's *History of the City of Dublin* (1818); Samuel A. Ossory Fitzpatrick's *Dublin: A Historical and Topographical Account of the City*; Weston St. John Joyce's *The Neighbourhood of Dublin*; D. A. Chart's *The Story of Dublin*; Dillon Cosgrave's *North Dublin: City and Environs*, a 1928 *Official Guide to the City of Dublin*; *Thom's Directory*; B. Seebohm Rowntree's *Poverty: A Study of Town Life*; and Washington Irving's *A History of New York*. It is important to note that while Dublin is the major theme of these VI.B.29 sources, the texts are not strictly urban by the common definition: one of the histories is *topographical*; one is about Dublin *and environs*; another is the *town and county of Galway*; and yet another is a study on *town* life.

With VI.B.29, Joyce continues the move toward *Finnegans Wake* as presenting images of the relationship between urbanization and the natural world in the twentieth century. In *Finnegans Wake*, the city and the country are *not* radically separate from one another but are deeply interrelated communities that depend on each other for their existence and survival. The "back-to-the-land" ideology, popular during the early and mid-1900s (and again in the 1960s and 1970s and, to an extent, today), largely rejects civilization and its so-called trappings, but Joyce understands the inescapability (and this is not to say that he does desire such escape), as well as the futility, in urbanites rejecting their rural counterparts. To support this assertion, I now turn to the specific notes taken from sources for VI.B.29.

While accounting for each individual note in VI.B.29 is outside the scope of this study, a few notes can be highlighted as examples of Joyce's conception of the relationship of a city to its environment. The first notes from *The History of the Town and County of Galway* (which even the editors of VI.B.29 shorten to *History of Galway*, ignoring the "Town and County" part) are "Galliv," "Iren for Galliv," and "It borrows its name from the river that slides by it" (VI.B.29: 58). These notes all derive from a passage linking the name "Galway" to the name of the river: "*Galvia*, or *Galiva* [. . .] seems to have given name to the town" (qtd. in VI.B.29 56). Building upon this idea, the introductory exhibit in the Galway City Museum endorses a claim set forth by Mary Kavanagh's *Galway-Gaillimh: A Bibliography of the City and County* that the name "Galway" itself derives from the Irish for "stony river" (103).

Taking notes from *Life in Old Dublin*, Joyce continues with the wilderness/city motif, noting "wood of Selcock" (VI.B.29: 69), the eighteenth-century name for the area now occupied by the North Circular Road (VI.B.29 68). This note, in a manner similar to the Haliday notes, shows the geographical history of the city of Dublin. On VI.B.29: 75–76, Joyce lists several suburbs of Dublin whose names derive directly from their geography: "Conra's ridge / -dram" (Drumcondra), "Farnham's rath" (Rathfarnham), "Still of Lorcan" (Stillorgan), "Meadow of Dalkin" (Clondalkin), and "Inchicore = Island / of Berries." Clondalkin, *Cluain Dealgáin* (O Hehir 284), "meadow of Dalkin" (BL 47484b-356, JJA 59: 86, FW 532.13), appears in the text with "Farnum's rath or Condra's ridge, or, the meadows of Dalkin of Monkish tunshep" (BL 47484b-356, JJA 59: 86, FW 532.12–13). O Hehir suggests the origin is *Fearannan*, or "landholder" (284), while *rath* is "fort." Consequently, this idea presents another image of HCE "walled" in his Chapelizod homestead: a landholder's fort. "Clondalkin" is also found on VI.B.29: 45, from a passage in Haliday concerning what constituted "Dyflinarskidi," the Norse name for the territory around the city of Dublin (VI.B.29 43). Two notes on the next page, "the Bay Limesoiled" and "Greater Dublin" (VI.B.29: 77), now from the *Encyclopaedia Britannica* entry on Dublin, continue this trend. "The Bay Limesoiled," mentioned briefly above, again relates to Dublin's location on Ireland's central limestone plain and to the runoff from the limestone into the groundwater and into Dublin Bay.

"Dyflinarskidi" had appeared in another form back in 1925, added to drafts of III.4, and was associated with the same country-versus-city theme as it is four years later in the context of VI.B.29. In III.4, to emphasize the inevitability of history's repetition, the invasions of Ireland are suggested with "Dyfflinsborg" (BL 47482a-21, JJA 60: 39, FDV 263.16–17, FW 582.21–22), "Europe's the prey!" (BL 47482a-21, JJA 60: 39, FDV 263.25, FW 582.31–32), and "Kingsdown" (BL 47482a-21, JJA 60: 39, FDV 263.29, FW 582.35). Both "Dyfflinsborg" and "Kingsdown" refer not only to the renaming of Irish places by colonizers, but also to the development of the railroad in Ireland: "Kingsdown for his orb's extension" (BL 47482a-22, JJA 60: 39, FDV 263.29, FW 582.35–36), or the connection of Dublin and Dún Laoghaire by rail for the "orb's" (*urb*, "city" and "borg" as *burg*) expansion. In addition to the railroad casting HCE as an imperialist and a developer, this addition also presents the invaders of Ireland as if they are on a train. Upon reaching Ireland, everyone gets off, except for the Romans, who famously never reached Ireland: "change here for Looterstown. Onlyromans, keep your seats!" (BL 47482a-21, JJA 60: 39, FDV 263.26–27, FW 582.33–34).

Disease, Famine, Housing

By the early twentieth century, increasing urbanization had led to major problems in terms of, among many things, public health and public housing, and new solutions were needed to respond to these new ills. VI.B.29, in addition to city planning, also addresses engineering for the purpose of alleviating urban poverty and disease. In addition to the engineering of rivers from VI.B.24, VI.B.29 exhibits a concurrent interest in nature's own versions of "engineering." Two additions, one relating to the Roundwood Reservoir, a preoccupation for Joyce since *Ulysses* (U 17.164–228), refer to "tubers": "I collected the rain's riches in my bathytub of roundwood and I conveyed it with cheers and cables through my longertubes of elm" (BL 47484b-393, JJA 59: 119, FW 542.6–7) and "tuberclerosies I reized up from the spudplants & berriberries from the great" (BL 47484b-393, JJA 59: 119, FW 541.36). The former addition corresponds to the note "elm wood conduit pipes" (VI.B.29: 109) from the following passage in D. A. Chart's *The Story of Dublin*: "In 1308 Dublin obtained its first public water supply. A three-mile conduit was constructed from the Dodder [. . .] into the city, where it flowed like an ordinary brook down the main street [. . .]. At first the pipes laid by the Corporation to supply the side streets were of lead, but in the seventeenth century, on the plea of economy, these were replaced by wooden ones made of elm, which existed until some eighty years ago" (28–29).

Elms, like all trees, have their own form of botanical "plumbing" that enables nutrients and water to move throughout their bodies. Here, the trees are put to use doing what they are already designed to do; the art of industrial plumbing collapses when the original inspiration, the transport systems existent within plants, is uncovered because of economic necessity. The "tubes" come from the combination of this function of the elm trees with "tuberclerosies" and "spudplants," as potatoes are, in fact, stem tubers. The "reized spudfully" of FW 542.1 also refers to rhizomes, which, before becoming a favored term of Gilles Deleuze, were simply horizontal plant stems able to grow roots and shoots from various nodes. Tubers and rhizomes are their own forms of engineering, storing and carrying nutrients for the plant and being the location for asexual reproduction ("reized" may also include the German verb for travel or journey, *reisen*).

This joining of plant ecology with the city and engineering is not dissimilar to the arguments set forth by Ernest Burgess, Roderick McKenzie, and Robert Park in their formative 1925 work of urban ecology, *The City*: "The plant ecologist is aware of the effect of the struggle for space, food, and light upon the nature of a plant formation, but the sociologist has failed to recognize that the same processes of competition and accommodation are at work determining the size and ecology organization of the human community" (64). This conception of the modern city-dweller as subject to the same laws that dictate the survival of plants provides a superb metaphor for understanding the relationship that develops between the city, famine, disease, overpopulation, and ecology in the *Wake*.

In the context of VI.B.29, the notes "tubercolrosis," "potatoeplant," and "berries berries / berriberries" (VI.B.29: 81–82) derive from an *Encyclopaedia Britannica* article on Rio de Janeiro. These notes relate specifically to issues of public health in the modern city responsible for many of the major civil engineering projects of the late nineteenth and early twentieth centuries, such as the walling of the Thames and the institution of sewage systems.[23] The abovementioned notes "Swan Water" (a now-buried river in the Rathmines area of Dublin) and "New Holland" (VI.B.29: 94) concern the 1792 embankment and reclamation of the "delta" or "slobland" formed at the "confluence of the Swan Water, the Dodder and the Liffey" (W. Joyce 23) that was called "New Holland."[24]

City versus Country · 109

The notes "Thames," "The Lea," "lagoon," "estuarine character" (VI.B.29: 119), "Pimlico / Moor-gate," "Fleet (river)," "Tributary," "Kentish town," "King's Cross," "Hollow: Hole-bourne: Holborn," "a navigable creek," "pebble beds of Blackheath and Woolwich," "Croydon," "Battersea" (VI.B.29: 120), "suburban railway," "Walthamstown," "fourteen road bridges," "Serpentine river (lake)" (VI.B.29: 121), and "288 miles of sewers" (VI.B.29: 122) all come from the *Encyclopaedia Britannica* entry on London. These notes describe public works projects involving water, town names derived from their proximity to water, towns situated because of their proximity to water, or simply names of bodies of water. The entry "embankment" (VI.B.29: 177), later in the notebook, certainly also applies to London and the Thames embankment, as well as to the embankment undertaken in Dublin. Some of these notes appear in the context of HCE's "conquering" the Liffey while representing issues of public health in urban spaces: "the crown to my eastuarine munipicence?" (BL 47484b-418, JJA 59: 151, FW 549.20), "Rivierside and drive" (BL 47484b-378, JJA 59: 144, FW 547.19), and "embankment large" (BL 47484b-418, JJA 59: 151, FW 549.19). The former is from the note "estuarine character" (VI.B.29: 119) and is directly from the *Encyclopaedia Britannica* entry explaining the original geography of the area that is now London: "The low ground between the slight hills flanking the Thames valley [. . .] was originally occupied by a shallow lagoon of estuarine character, tidal, and interspersed with marshy tracts and certain islets of relatively firm land" (qtd. in VI.B.29 118).

Based on the notes on the founding of both London and New York City, it appears Joyce is interested in linking Dublin's "estuarine character" with that of London and New York, as well as demonstrating the uninhabitable land upon which many of the world's major cities were constructed. "Rivierside Drive" is New York City's Riverside Drive, along the Hudson River, and "rivier" is Dutch for river. Since New York was originally a Dutch colony, the "rivier" implies both linguistic and territorial colonization by the Dutch.[25] The note "sycamore"[26] (VI.B.29: 201), taken from Washington Irving's *A History of New York*, discusses the "founder" of New York City, Peter Stuyvesant, and the overrunning of New York City by plants:

[Stuyvesant] fortified the city, too, with pickets and palisadoes, extending across the island from river to river; and above all, cast up

> mud batteries or redoubts on the point of the island, where it divided the beautiful bosom of the bay. These latter redoubts, in process of time, came to be pleasantly overrun by a carpet of grass and clover, and overshadowed by wide-spreading elms and sycamores; among the branches of which the birds would build their nests and rejoice the ear with their melodious notes. (240–41)

When European settlers first colonized the land that now hosts New York City, it was a lush and fertile area, and there was (and still is) a sense of the environment constantly fighting back against its occupants.

The note "embankment large" refers to the Thames embankment project undertaken in the late nineteenth century, largely because of devastating outbreaks of water-borne illnesses cholera and typhoid. Metropolitan engineer Sir Joseph Bazalgette constructed London's underground sewers and the embankments of the Thames as a way to control the city's waste and prevent the stagnation of Thames water that led to the spread of disease. Charles Dickens, in his *Dictionary of the Thames*, wrote: "[F]ew London improvements have been more conductive to health and comfort. The substitution of the beautiful curve of the embankment, majestic in its simplicity, with its massive granite walls, flourishing trees, and trim gardens, is an unspeakable improvement on the squalid foreshore, and tumbledown wharves, and backs of dingy houses which formerly abutted the river" (qtd. in Hanson 34). Other plans during this period related to the crisis in public health included the transplanting of the urban poor to the outskirts of town, and the note "cottage green," also from the *Encyclopaedia Britannica*, refers to "an extensive scheme taken up in 1904" for the housing of the poor that "included the provision of cottage dwellings in the suburbs" (VI.B.29 77).[27]

The paradox of moving the city's poor onto lands once traditionally associated with the aristocracy merges with several other notes from VI.B.29 that reinforce the Anglo-Irish relationship with the countryside and the suburbs. Notes relating to another part of "Greater Dublin" (VI.B.29: 77), the Phoenix Park, appear again with the notes "demesne," "magazine," "Fifteen acres" (VI.B.29: 75), and "Queen's Garden at the Phoenix" (VI.B.29: 113), from Cosgrave's *North Dublin: City and Environs*. "[S]uburban Viceroy" (VI.B.29: 124) displays the relationship between English imperialism, the suburbs, and, specifically, the "suburban" Phoenix Park, home of the Viceregal Lodge. "Dolly Monnroe" (VI.B.29: 95), from *The*

Neighbourhood of Dublin, refers to the origin of the name "Dollymount," describing a house that was originally "built as a hunting residence" (W. Joyce 121–22), akin to the Viceregal Lodge in the Phoenix Park. These notes tie together the urban poor and the Anglo-Irish aristocracy through their relationship to the land.

The next source used in VI.B.29 is Rowntree's *Poverty: A Study of Town Life*.[28] The previous notes on public health and housing continue in VI.B.29 with "dying by houserows," "condemned," "Jerrybill," "yardless," and "W tap" (VI.B.29: 138). "Yardless" is in direct contrast to the "demesnes" and "hunting lodges" referenced above, and later notes like "house lost in dirt," "nightsoil has to be removed through house" (VI.B.29: 146), and "Drip coming through ceiling" (VI.B.29: 150) connect the impoverished to nature, but in a drastically different way than the upper classes relate to it. "W tap" and "Labourer at plant" (VI.B.29: 140) place the narrative at the period in the history of the city when the class of urban working poor was expanding greatly, especially in Ireland, because of the post-famine decline in agriculture and rural life and the subsequent shift into the city's factories and slums. When viewed in the context of the urban working poor and related social issues, the "city versus country" tension presents another location of conflict between the Irish and the Anglo-Irish. The clash between the "demesnes" of the Anglo-Irish and the "yardless" homes of the urban poor adds weight to issues of the Irish environment and its appropriation by social and political forces (to be discussed further in the next chapter of this study).

In 1925, the addition of "in Urbs in Rure" (BL 47484a-120, JJA 58: 202, FW 551.24)—a confusion of *Rus in Urbe*,[29] Latin for "Country in the City"—to the first typescript of III.3 supplies another concrete reference for this opposition. The motto *Rus in Urbe* appears on Dublin's Aldborough House (1793), one of the last great mansions built in the city in the eighteenth century. Chart wrote that the house was "'a sermon in stone' on the extravagance which ruined the Irish nobility" (326). A large parcel of land accompanied Aldborough House, like many other eighteenth-century mansions, thus creating the effect of *Rus in Urbe* and imitating the rule of the earls in the countryside. The Phoenix Park is also implicated in the desire for *Rus in Urbe* through the idea of providing an organized version of nature within the space of the city.

The relationship between the Anglo-Irish and environmental conservation was briefly discussed in the introduction, and the theme of *Rus in*

Urbe provides a valuable image to accompany the fact that in the twenty-first century "nature conservation is still largely identified with an Anglo-Irish culture" (Viney, *Smithsonian* 307–8). John Feehan's discussion of how the romantic movement impacted Ireland only "within the walls of the demesnes" (583) is also relevant to this section and draft level of the *Wake*. The frequent alignment of HCE with an Anglo-Irish landlord is a locus for Joyce's examination of the politics of landownership and tenancy, and of what such politically inscribed land has meant for the Irish and their relationship to the physical land.

One characteristic that sets *Finnegans Wake*'s treatment of land apart from many of the popular works associated with the Irish literary revival is its portrayal of the relationship between ideas of landownership and agriculture, issues that led almost directly to the growth of the Home Rule movement in the post-famine years. HCE's landlordism becomes associated with Irish famine (including, but not limited to, the Great Famine). For example, in I.3, HCE, in the position of landlord, exists "behind faminebuilt walls,"[30] bringing the theme of the walled city to other binaries created by physical walls. It is important to note that the Great Famine is not the only Irish famine present in the *Wake*, but only one in a cycle of plenty and scarcity. For example, "her turlyhyde I plumped with potatums" (FW 549.31) refers to an account in Chart's *The Story of Dublin* that explains how the wars of the fourteenth century "produced a famine over the whole country" (33). This famine, however, was "providentially relieved by the stranding of a whole school of whales at the mouth of the Dodder at Ringsend. The chronicler calls them 'Turlehydes'" (33). While the whales provided a temporary source of food for Dublin, Chart explains, the city was "only to find, later on, that the terrible famine had bred the still more terrible pestilence. Every few years it descended on the cramped, refuse-strewn streets of the mediaeval town and carried off thousands of victims" (33).

One note from the 1928 *Thom's Directory* following immediately from the Rowntree text is "Two-toothed locust worms" (VI.B.29: 156), which derives from a passage in *Thom's* concerning a plague of "strange worms," "supposed to have been locusts," that descended upon Ireland and "devoured everything green in the land" (qtd. in VI.B.29 155). The line to which this note was added reads, "famine with Englisch sweat and oppedemics the twotoothed dragon worms with allsort serpents" (BL 47484b-438, JJA 59: 179, FW 539.36–540.1) at this draft level. According to the

Encyclopaedia Britannica, this "English sweat" refers to "a pestilential disease appearing in England in the fifteenth century that spread to other parts of Europe, including Dublin, in 1528 ("Sweating Sickness").[31] "Oppedemics" combines the Latin *oppidum*, "town," with "epidemics," creating a specifically urban disease.

Clive Ponting's *A New Green History of the World* is a reading of world history through world resources, and Ponting discusses Ireland's agricultural practices in the context of its recurring famines (listing, in addition to the Great Famine, famines of 1318, 1594–97, 1739–41, and 1816–17). He devotes most of the discussion, justifiably, to the Great Famine, and explains the agricultural conditions from the preceding decades that led to the extensive devastation of this famine in particular. Ponting asserts that the Great Famine did not arise unexpectedly, but that "by the 1830s poor harvests were becoming the norm" (103), and that even with a good crop, a large number of the population was at risk for starvation. Ponting includes all of the popularly acknowledged causes of the famine in his account (overpopulation, poor climate, economic disparity, trade regulations, and land politics), but he also focuses on two crucial and often overlooked causes of the famine: the potato itself and the devastation of both land and community caused by monocrop agriculture. The potato, though suited to the "need to provide food from tiny plots of land," is low in nutritional value, and "not well adapted to growing in the wet climate of Ireland" (103). Joyce records "Hawkins-Spud" (VI.B.29: 156) from *Thom's*, referring to John Hawkins, one of the three men (along with Sir Walter Raleigh and Sir Francis Drake) who have been credited with introducing the potato to Ireland. The line "froren black patata" (FW 495.10) is "frozen black potato," with *patata* being the Spanish for "potato." Potatoes originally came from South America and were imported to Europe in the sixteenth century, and thus calling them "patata" here inscribes the potatoes with their origins in the European colonies. The "frozen black" may refer to a potato specimen preserved for germination in Europe and to the potato blight itself (the acute cause of the Great Famine), which turned potato crops black.

Conscious of the role the potato has played in Ireland's history and culture, Joyce refers to the crop at least one hundred times in the *Wake*, with Fweet (the online *Finnegans Wake Extensible Elucidation Treasury*) producing no fewer than eighty-four elucidations for "potato" and another thirty-five for "spud." The VI.B.3 note discussed earlier, "child (found chalice in potatofield)" (VI.B.3: 11), from Flood's *Ireland: Its Saints and Scholars*, shows that the unearthing of Ireland's history depends also on the potato; cultivating the crop has shaped much of the Irish landscape, has been responsible for the discovery of some of Ireland's most valuable artifacts, has changed the makeup of the Irish population, and has, at least for the last century and a half, greatly shaped the collective consciousness and memory of Ireland. The relationship between the land and language in *Finnegans Wake* reaches a crux when faced with the issue of the Great Famine. Stuart John McLean, in *The Event and Its Terrors: Ireland, Famine, Modernity*, agrees with Angela Bourke's argument that in addition to the lives lost, the 1840s were a period of real "cultural loss" for Ireland, "marking the disappearance not only of specific practices and idioms, but of an entire corpus of orally transmitted knowledge and belief actualized through the lived relationship between people and landscape" (5). In short, who is left to carry on the names of the places, the history of these names, the stories associated with the topography?

In addition to the colonial implications and the way in which famine redefines a culture's connection to its landscape, famines may have been of particular interest to Joyce at this stage of *Finnegans Wake* because they are one of the first instances of conflict arising between humanity and nature. In "Environmental Crises—Past and Present," A. S. Boughey identifies famine as the first "environmental crisis," citing both the Old Testament story of Joseph and his interpretation of Pharaoh's dreams and "written records of famine in China over a period of 2,000 years" (10). One of the most visible effects of human dependence on the environment, famine has recurred across all continents for as long as heterotrophic organisms have needed to eat. The causes of famine vary but generally include crop failure, either as a result of uncooperative weather or of populations that require more food than the land can sustain (or both). With Ireland integrated into the English market economy, those who once farmed for subsistence now saw their product become a tradable commodity, and basic laws of supply and demand led to the exacerbation of any food shortages. Food prices would rise and become too high for those dependent on potatoes for their survival, while other goods from Ireland continued to be exported to England.[32] In Ireland, discussion of the Great Famine often centered on issues concerning British control of the land and the economy and the resultant poverty of the Irish people, and Ponting explains that leading up to the famine, there were "about 650,000 landless labourers living in permanent destitution and most of the rural population lived in squalid, one-room cabins" (105). At this point, there was little difference between the urban and the rural poor.

Overall, one of the primary themes Joyce explores during the composition of the *Wake* is the relationship between city and country, urban and rural, man and nature. While not new themes by any stretch of the imagination, the way in which Joyce depicted them in the *Wake* was certainly new, especially in terms of literary modernism. Not engaging with modernist utopian approaches to the natural world, Joyce demonstrates the folly of seeing society, particularly modern urban society, as separate from nature, and he argues against this harmful belief by thoroughly linking these supposed binary oppositions through language, economics, culture, and history. The transitional images of riverbank, seashore, suburb, park, and so forth serve to complicate the boundaries established by the historical walling off of nature from civilization. Though this interdependence of city upon environment would not be questioned now, it is odd that modernist studies still shy away from discussions of the environment in this context. Examining a text like *Finnegans Wake*, with its simultaneous thematic and stylistic interweaving of city and country, begins to undo this tendency.

Chapelizod and the City

As Joyce progresses with *Finnegans Wake* into the mid-1930s, he returns to interests from the first stages of the *Wake* and expands them, incorporating them into the current material. One such early interest that also extends the suburb theme from the prior section is the specific placement of the Earwicker household in Chapelizod. The establishment and growth of cities, continuing from "Haveth Childers Everywhere," is a central theme in the first draft of II.1§6A, and Joyce combines this theme with Chapelizod as well as with the second reference to Quinet's quotation. Together, the resulting passage combines the passing of (seasonal) time with the plant thyme with the development of cities:

> Since the days of Roamaloose and Rehmoose the pavanos have been strident through their struts of Chapelldiseut, the vaulsies have meed and youdled through the purly ooze of Ballybough, many a mismy cloudy has tripped taintily along that hercourt strayed reelway and

the rigadoons have helf ragtimes revels on the platauplain of Grangegorman; and, though since then sterlings and guineas have been replaced by brooks and lions and some progress has been made on stilts and the races have come and gone and Thyme, that chef of seasoners, has made his usual astewte use of endadjustables and whatnot willbe isnor was, those danceadeils and cancanzanies have come stimmering down for our begayment through the bedeafdom of po's taeorns, the obcecity of pa's teapucs, as lithe and limbfree limber as when momie mummed at ma. (BL 47477-21, JJA 51: 29, FW 236.19–32)

This passage contains another version of the Dublin city motto with "obcecity" (*Obedientia Civium Urbis Felicitas*, or Citizens' Obedience is City's Happiness [also notably present in I.6]), and there are also Romulus and Remus, as "Roamaloose and Rehmoose," who have founded Dublin, beginning with Chapelizod ("Chapelldiseut"). Joyce inserts the Harcourt Street Railway as "hercourt strayed reelway," feminizing the city for Isolde of "Chapelldiseut." The girl also has pearls, of sorts; the "purly ooze" of Ballybough is the reclaimed land just north of the Liffey mouth and the slimy Royal canal that defines this neighborhood of the city. This passage echoes ALP in many ways, particularly in terms of the "stimmering" and the "momie mummed at ma," and when combined with the allusions to the Quinet passage, it serves as a way of expressing the growth of the young girl and the growth of Dublin city. The "platauplain" of Grangegorman reminds readers of the Liffey plain again, but is instead referring to the neighborhood of Grangegorman (considerably higher than the Liffey), and combined with Ballybough, this reference perhaps traces the North Circular Road.

The final lines of the passage evoke the flowers from Quinet. In "A Wake in Chapelizod," Sam Slote examines the changes Joyce made here to Quinet's quotation, explaining that the flowers "have become dances" and that such a dance "endures through decay and entropy" (49). "Furthermore," Slote continues, "in this particular variation on Quinet's theme, Joyce substitutes Chapelldiseut for Quinet's 'les Gaules,' thereby returning, in this game, Isolde back to Ireland from France. In so doing, he places Chapelizod at the centre of the myth of historical continuity and change" (49). A long section of the first draft of II.1§6 (early 1932) concerns itself with describing Chapelizod. Joyce relied heavily on a *Thom's Directory* "Chapelizod" entry for much of this passage, though that is indiscernible when reading the final text of the *Wake*.[33] A trend concerning the *Thom's* transfers is that Joyce uses the names of at least one dozen houses, pubs, or streets in the neighborhood whose name relates, in some way, to the natural world (terms directly from *Thom's* are italicized):

> In these places sojournamous. By this *riverside*, on this *sunnybank* how buona the vista, by Santa Rosa! *Afield of May*, the very *vale of spring*. *Orchards here are lodged*: sainted laurels evremberried: you have *view ashgroves, aglen or marrons and of thorns*: Glannaulinn, Ardeevin, purty glint and plaising hoyt. This Norman court at boundary of the ville, yon ivied tower of a church of Ereland with our king's house of stone, *belgroved* of *mulbrey*, all is for the retrospectioner. Sweet as auburn cometh up as a flower that fragolance of the *fraisey beds*: the phoenix, his pyre, is still flaming away with true Pratt spirit: *the wren, his nest*, is niedelig, as the turrises of the Sabines are televisible. There is the cottage and the bungalow for the cobbeler and the brandnewburgher but Isolde, her gardens are for the fairhaired daughter of Aengus. All out of two barreny old perishers and one inn, one tap and one tavern and only two million two hundred and eightythousand nine hundred and sixty lines to the wuestworts of a general poet's office. (BL 47478-127, 128, JJA 52: 10–11, FDV 146.5–19, FW 264.15–265.28)

The opening, "In these places sojournamous," is similar to the opening of the III.4 description of the Phoenix Park as it sets the stage for a passage that will function primarily as a survey of a particular location. Most of the italicized terms (like "riverside" and "sunnybank") refer to the names of houses along the Liffey in Chapelizod and on the road toward Lucan. "Saint Lucan's" points toward the town of Lucan, upstream from Chapelizod, and the importance of this oft-mentioned village in the *Wake* may stem partially from its being the point where the Liffey is met by its tributary, the Griffeen River (Warner 74). Some of the names refer to vegetation that grows in the region, like "Orchard Lodge," "Mulberry Hill," or "Strawberry Beds," referring to the apple trees, strawberry plants, and mulberry bushes found in the Liffey Valley. Much like the aforementioned "selvage mats" (associated with the Garden City) to describe the relationship between suburbanization and the environment, the house known as Orchard Lodge would have likely required the clearing of a substantial portion of that eponymous orchard for its construction.

Then, the line "This Norman court at boundary of the ville, yon ivied tower of a church of Ereland with our king's house of stone" suggests that another source Joyce used for this Chapelizod passage is Francis Elrington Ball's six-volume *A History of the County Dublin* (1902–1920). Chapelizod as a "Norman court at boundary of the ville" with the "king's house of stone" refers, according to Ball, to the Anglo-Norman claim on the lands of Chapelizod and to the house of King William III that was located on a bank by the river (4: 163). Last, the "boundary of the ville" once again reinforces the suburban location of Chapelizod and its location outside the city walls.[34]

"The wren, his nest" refers to the Wren's Nest weir (by the Strawberry Beds ["fraisey beds"]), used to power various industries since the eighteenth century (W. Joyce 348).[35] The Liffey Valley Park Alliance explains that the other weir near Palmerstown, also known as the Glenaulin weir, was used "to provide a water supply and to generate electricity for the Guinness estates."[36] The inclusion of both the Wren's Nest weir and the Glenaulin weir, both located along the Liffey before it reaches Chapelizod, provides another image of the subjugating of nature and the female (the Liffey as ALP). The importance of the Liffey for Guinness, and, consequently, of Guinness for Dublin, is included at this draft level as another example of economic dependence on natural resources. In his portrait of the Liffey, Dick Warner discusses the important role played by Liffey mills in the growth of the Irish economy and emphasizes just how important "water power was to industry in this country before the introduction of the steam engine" (56), citing the "nearly two hundred mill sites [. . .] identified on the Liffey and its tributaries" (58). Warner also explains just how old this technology really is, tracing the harnessing of waterpower back to the ancient Greeks in the first century BC and to the Chinese Han Dynasty (56). In Ireland, Warner continues, "there were small water mills associated with monastic sites in the Early Christian Period and some massive ones associated with the medieval monasteries of the great continental religious orders" (56).[37] At this stage of the *Wake*, the prevalence of waterpower over centuries and across cultures would have provided Joyce with a way to connect disparate sections of the text. The relationship between waterpower and the development of Christianity in Ireland would also have appealed because of Joyce's imminent return to both the Saint Kevin and Saint Patrick sketches.

In the II.1§6 "Chapelizod" passage under examination, the distance provided, "two million two hundred and eightythousand nine hundred and sixty lines," is the number of twelfths of inches in three miles (Senn 12), which is the distance, according to the 1928 *Thom's Directory* (253), from Chapelizod to the General Post Office. In Dublin, distance had been traditionally based on the General Post Office, demonstrating the colonial authority over even spatial matters.[38] This relationship is also conveyed through the landscape, extending to marginalia on the right of the Chapelizod passage in the manuscript, added to the fair copy of II.2§1–3: "The localisation of legend leading to the legalisation of latifundism" (BL 47478-166, JJA 52: 58, FW 264.R6–R13). The "localisation of legend" comes from the Latin "locus" (meaning "place"), rooting "legend" (story, tale, myth, history) firmly in place (and the story of HCE in Chapelizod). To Campbell and Robinson, the reference to the "latifundia" is also evidence of the development of "patriarchal landed estates" (168). Chapelizod and many of its townlands were originally laid out as these types of "landed estates," and Joyce's use of the term "latifundia," from the Latin *latus* (broad/spacious) and *fundus* (estate/farm),[39] but now typically associated with Latin America, universalizes the organization and management of land.

Further along in II.2, Shem's marginalia refers to the Irish Gavelkind ("Old Gavelkind the Gamper and he's as daff as you're erse," FW 268. L4), a practice of land inheritance from Brehon Law. According to William Ernest Montgomery's *The History of Land Tenure in Ireland*, the term "gavelkind" comes from the Irish *gabhail-cine*, meaning, "accepted from the tribe." It refers to the process in which, following a death, the deceased's lands do not pass to the next male heir, but are passed to the entire "sept," or community/tribe (6, 2n). This democratic acquisition of land is in stark contrast to the Anglo-Norman and Anglo-Irish policies of private ownership. On the 1934 typescript of this section of II.2, Joyce adds "Yeomansland," which appears in conjunction with "the loftleaved elm Lefanunian abovemansioned" (BL 47478-189, JJA 52: 91, FW 265.4–5). This juxtaposition sets the small landholders against the Big House estate. Together, "latifundia," "gavelkind," "Norman court," "bungalow," "mansion" and "Yeomansland" present the general history of landownership in Chapelizod and in Ireland: passing from communally owned space, to ascendancy mansion, to private residential home.

These "Chapelizod" sections also engage with the village's history from past to present, from its associations with Brian Boru and the Norman court to its modern designation as "ribbon development" (BL 47478-141, JJA 52: 36, FW 265.24) (added to the 1934 typescript). On the December 1938 galley proofs for book IV, ALP refers to the Phoenix Park as HCE's "green belt": "With your brandnew big green belt and all" (BL 47488-217v, JJA 63: 318, FW 620.2). A "green belt" is "an officially designated belt of open countryside in which all development is severely restricted, usually enclosing a built-up area and designed to check its further growth,"[40] and was popularized in the 1920s and 1930s as fears of urban sprawl grew. This fear was more prevalent in Britain, but also extended to Ireland. In 1910, a public meeting in Clontarf called for a "Garden City" at Marino (McManus 182), and the Lord Lieutenant of Ireland launched "an international competition to plan the restoration and development of Dublin" in 1914 (Anne Power 326). Patrick Abercrombie, who "proposed a green belt, satellite towns, and a newly planned national capital, which fitted, according to his perception, with the spirit of the Irish independence movement and with what Abercrombie had seen (and liked) of Haussman's Paris" (Anne Power 326), won the competition. While Abercrombie's plan ("Dublin of the Future") did not come to fruition because of the Easter Rising, Anglo-Irish War, and Irish Civil War, these early inroads into planning led to the development in the 1920s and 1930s of suburbs modeled on Ebenezer Howard's "garden city" idea (such as Marino, Drumcondra, and Crumlin) and a general move to suburbanize the working classes of the inner-city (McManus 182–94). One of the Joyce family residences, Millbourne Avenue, was at the heart of the "Drumcondra Scheme" development, and many of the family residences would have been at the center of this development (in Fairview, Phibsboro, Drumcondra).

In short, the Dublin suburbs are integral to the *Wake*. Ruth McManus explains how "Dublin's physical area grew extensively during the early twentieth century [. . .] as low-density suburbs were built around the city" (21). In the early stages of composition for *Finnegans Wake*, it seems Joyce chose Chapelizod for its association with Tristan and Isolde. However, as the text developed, Chapelizod and the Phoenix Park became a way for Joyce to explore the changing perceptions and roles of cities, suburbs, and countryside during the first decades of the twentieth century. From the Liffey's weirs to the list of houses in the village, to the Norman castle and Chapelizod's modern "ribbon development," this section of II.1 localizes the legend of Tristan and Isolde, HCE and ALP, firmly in early-twentieth-century Chapelizod. Joyce's detailed portrait of the one village throughout the years allows that village to serve as a metonym for all communities. The sections of *Finnegans Wake* drafted earlier focus on a more historical or mythological relationship with the land, but as Joyce continued reading (both his source texts and his own already drafted work), land became increasingly politicized and plays a major role in the *Wake*'s discussion of the politics of nation, nation-building, nationality, and nationalism. Landscape, along with language, is a decisive factor in the *Wake*'s depiction of culture, history, and identity.

This chapter has proved the importance of the "environs" in *Finnegans Wake*: from the specifics of Irish geography in I.8 to the interdependence of Irish cities and their natural resources, to the focus on urban planning and the attention to urban spaces, *Finnegans Wake* is exemplary in its display of the inextricability of country and city and its articulation of an urban ecology.

3

The Politics of Nature

Joyce employed the motifs of rain, cloud, and storm throughout the *Wake* for a variety of reasons, but Joyce's 1936 trip to Denmark revealed a political reason behind these motifs. Ellmann records an anecdote of Joyce's that concerns his dislike for umbrellas: "I think the umbrella is a royal instrument. I know a young lord of Cambodia who lives in Paris; because of his high rank his father has the right to carry seven umbrellas, and my noble friend himself walks with six umbrellas, suspended one over the other. Yes, the umbrella is a mark of distinction" (JJ 694). While this anecdote, like many attributed to Joyce, may be apocryphal, it suggests that Joyce understood the mark of royalty and privilege to be an estrangement from the forces of nature. Here, the ability to avoid the weather is associated with class. An umbrella is not just a way to shield from rain; it is a "royal instrument."

Throughout the *Wake*, Joyce also includes weather in the question of the relationship between geography and identity (both individual and national). This association can be traced to a seemingly innocuous note from VI.B.10: "a wintry" (VI.B.10: 28). This note was taken from a piece in the 11 November 1922 *Leader* that reads: "A certain muddling on the part of the Provisional Government has helped to make many Irish-Irelanders adopt a wintry attitude towards those who sit in high places" (qtd. in VI.B.10 44). Surrounding entries—"MM the govt," "Irish tinge," and "Mick Collins"—suggest that the entry is transferred to VI.B.10 in its context, and "wintry" stands out as an adjective for describing the tense relationship between the "Irish-Irelanders" and the new government. Mere coldness in attitude has become temporal, a season of political upheaval that implies another insurrection ("Mick Collins"). Such rebellions and treasons are a large part of Ireland's history, and another note on VI.B.10: 40 reminds us of this implication: "cycles of hist. W. Tone Childers." The association of the cyclicality of history with the change of seasons is supported by another note in VI.B.10, the opening words of *Richard III*: "Now is the winter—" (VI.B.10: 57). The word "winter" appears a few pages later in the notebook, in conjunction with the title of an article in the *Irish Times*: "Winter turned leaves of book of nature" (VI.B.10: 47). On this page there are several conceptual notes, and the pages that follow continue with the aforesaid Anglo-Irish Treaty theme: "Move up Mick, Make room for Dick" and "the boys (I.R.A.)." This section of VI.B.10 also contains a few notes relating to "Cyclops," appropriate to this cluster of notes on Irish politics.

The relationship between weather and nationality also appears with one note from VI.B.24, "Humidia" (VI.B.24: 7, FW 48.5), from a cluster about Carthage. The note was added to the beginning of I.3 to duplicates on the *transition* 3 pages in 1936 (BL 47475-111v, JJA 45: 301, FW 48.5) and accomplishes three primary things. First, it is a reference to "Numidia," an ancient African kingdom (third century BC).[1] Joyce likely chose this reference because of the potential pun on "humid," which would bring Metchnikoff's theories about successful civilizations depending upon climate back into the text. Second, the "humid" is another reference to Ireland's climate, and the opening of I.3 is heavily focused on the foggy, cloudy, damp conditions that prevent the reader from seeing, in both a literal and metaphorical sense. Third, because of Ireland's climate, the name "Humidia" is a pun on the Roman name for Ireland, *Hibernia*, which, of course, contains the Latin *hibernus*, "wintry." Thus, the name given to the country is intrinsically linked with its climate.

In this chapter, I build on these themes of the relationship between nationalism, identity, climate, and landscape. From the first section, dealing with the establishment of the Phoenix Park as hunting ground, to subsequent sections concerning imperialism and territory, Irish Free State energy policy and the trope of self-sufficiency, and the relationship between war and the environment, this chapter argues that in *Finnegans Wake*, landscape is always political.

Phoenix Park and the Hunt

The Phoenix Park has already been discussed in terms of its role as a transitional space in the *Wake*, but Joyce also uses it as a politicized space through the role of hunting (primarily in English and Anglo-Irish culture). The foundation of the Phoenix Park as a hunting ground, as the space in first drafts of III.4 with the "pretty deers" that are "caught inside" (BL 47482a-35v, 36v, 37v, JJA 60: 68, 70, 72, FDV 253.33–254.15, FW 564–65), is particularly crucial to the way in which the role of the Phoenix Park develops and unites central political themes of landscape in the *Wake*. Though contrary to our current conception of a park, the *Oxford English Dictionary* presents the primary definition of "park" as a space reserved for hunting: "An enclosed tract of land held by royal grant or prescription and reserved for keeping and hunting deer and other game. Now hist. exc. in the names of areas which were formerly legal parks, esp. Windsor Great Park."[2] In this definition, a park is inherently associated with monarchy and authority. Prior to its formal establishment as hunting ground by Ormonde in the seventeenth century, the Phoenix Park originated as an Anglo-Norman hunting ground (on lands that were part of a grant made by Strongbow in 1174) (McCullen, *Illustrated History* 71). In the *Wake*, Phoenix Park is often metonymic of English control over Irish land, an association resulting from this early designation. The regulation of lands for hunting grounds was usually an imperial project; the enclosure of these lands, to ensure that prey could not escape and that predators and poachers could not enter, mimics the exercising of authority over subjects and territories.

The threat of violence in this exercise of control over "wild" space appears in the earliest sketches of the *Wake* to problematize the political relationship between power and nature. The park is established as an isolated, separate space for the preservation and maintenance of the hunter's prey. Stocked (in this case, artificially) with game, the hunting grounds simulate the dynamic present in an uncontrolled natural space; a recreation of the king's taming of his kingdom, an illusion maintained for the upholding of power. A clear example of this relationship is the Forest Laws, originally introduced by William the Conqueror (who appears in I.2), whose zeal for hunting altered the English landscape through the establishment of the New Forest in the late eleventh century (Young 64). In his history of England, David Hume pays particular attention to the ways in which the king established this forest and to the violence enacted in this space, not just upon the hunted but also upon any threat to his hunt:

> There was one pleasure, to which William, as well as all the Normans, and ancient Saxons, was extremely addicted; and that was hunting: But this pleasure he indulged more at the expense of his unhappy subjects, whose interests he always disregarded, than to the loss or diminution of his own revenue. Not contented with those large forests, which the former kings possessed in all parts of England; he resolved to make a new forest near Winchester [. . .]. At the same time, he enacted new laws, by which he prohibited all his subjects from hunting any of his forests, and rendered the penalties much more severe than ever had been inflicted for such offenses. The killing of a deer or boar, or even of a hare, was punished with the loss of the delinquent's eyes. (Hume 241)

Hume presents William I and the Forest Laws in a manner implying a clear relationship between the king's treatment of his subjects, the landscape, and the animals of that landscape. The importance of hunting to the ruling classes is that it reinforces their authority in all venues, as the killing of artificially stocked prey (as well as the ability to obtain such artificially stocked prey and maintain it in an artificially created space) is intended to convey the threat of violence to the subjects.

In the *Wake*, hunting, the land set aside for its undertaking, and the birth of forestry associated with this land, are emblematic of England's authority over Ireland. The VI.C notebooks also provide a couple of forestry references, with "deforestation" (VI.C.3: 8) and "timber ceased 1765 / deforesting the military" (VI.C.7: 224), both of which were eventually transferred to later drafts. Though Ireland's deforestation began in the Stone Age with the clearing of land for agriculture, England's policies often tended to exaggerate the problem. Much of Ireland's remaining woodlands were cut down to build the British naval fleet, and by the end of the nineteenth century, Ireland was the most deforested land in Europe (McCracken 95). The establishment of the Forestry Commission from the 1919 Forestry Act (UK) was primarily caused by the timber shortage during World War I; thus, some of Ireland's early environmental policies were enacted because England exhausted the timber in its colony and needed to ensure the sustainability of woodland resources for national and economic security.[3] In the early twentieth century, the Irish government made a decision to take direct action in reforesting Ireland, a project inherited from the British government that was turned into a nationalist cause. The relationship between forestry and empire, present also with both William the Conqueror and his Forest Laws and the Duke of Ormonde and the rangers for the Phoenix Park, also appeared in VI.B.1, with the notes "John II of Lichtenstein / owns forests de partout," "holding down throne," and "1st draw (hunt)" (VI.B.1: 8). Hunting and forestry provide illustrations of English dominion over Irish land, and this theme becomes a significant point of departure for Joyce's inclusion of the politics of land in the Wake.

In pre-twentieth-century Ireland hunting was largely associated with Anglo-Norman culture (though the *fian* warriors were also mythical hunters). In *A History of Nature Conservation in Britain*, David Evans explains that hunting became an increasingly popular pastime during the reign of King John (1199–1216), shortly after the Norman invasion of Ireland. Hunting later became a favorite pastime of the Ascendancy, and as demonstrated by Hume's passage, hunting was not only the way in which mankind asserted its dominance over the natural world, but also a way in which the ruling classes asserted their dominance over the other classes.

In *The Country and the City*, Raymond Williams argues for the similarity between the establishment of parks and the actions of landlords: both attempt to make "nature move to an arranged design" (124). The land around Anglo-Irish estates was also ordered and governed, domesticated and civilized, reproducing the way in which the estate's inhabitants assumed and maintained their authority. These parks and demesnes also kept the landed gentry separate from their tenants and from the peasantry, and their imposition of order upon nature symbolized their power over those individuals. In Williams's discourse, the landlord reinforces his or her power over the designated space and the tenant through economic coercion, a modern redefinition of the relationship embodied by the ritual of the hunt. This intersection of landlordism, the Ascendancy, and the hunt is important for understanding the way in which imperialism and nature interact in the Wake.

The first appearances of hunting in the avant-texte of the Wake arose by chance from a piece on "Reynard the Fox" from a 1922 issue of the *Quarterly Review*. Joyce obtained this particular issue of the *Quarterly Review* because of its critical article on *Ulysses* by Shane Leslie, who, as Geert Lernout explains, was himself the son of an Anglo-Irish landlord ("Rev. of Shane Leslie: Sublime Failure" 164), and this connection may contribute to the *Wake*'s alignment of hunting and landlords with criticism. From these connections, and from the placement of the hunting terms in the early drafts, it is possible that the VI.B.10 hunting notes derived from this article relate to Joyce's sense of himself, or of the artist figure on a more general level, as a hunted animal.[4]

The image of the hunted fox appears throughout the *Wake* as a way to articulate and explore the paradoxical intersections of violence and nature and the continual reversal of established order. The name "Reynard," the red fox anthropomorphized as a trickster figure, is the French for "fox," *renard*, but likely derives from both the French and the Germanic words for "to reign," *régner* and *regieren*,[5] etymologically linking the fox with monarchy and disturbing the established hierarchy. This association presents another way in which to understand the relationship between the king and foxhunt, and it is no surprise that Joyce has recorded "William the Conk," creator of the Forest Laws, on page 21 of VI.B.10, the first extant *Finnegans Wake* notebook.

Many of the several dozen instances wherein terminology relating to hunting surfaces in the *Wake* appear in conjunction with accusations against HCE (such as in I.4) and in the context of the warring brothers (such as in I.6's "The Mookse and the Gripes," a revision of Aesop's "The Fox and the Grapes"). In the first question of I.6, "hounded become haunter, hunter become fox" (FW 132.16–17), referring to the HCE/Finn MacCool figure, and showing the speed at which allegiances and polarities can shift. Such reversal becomes important for Joyce's presentation of Parnell and for his presentation of HCE's rise and fall. The Phoenix Park's "rushy hollow," the spot where HCE committed his unknown crime, appears on VI.B.10: 79 and is transferred to first drafts of I.2 ("maidservants in the rushy hollow whither nature as they alleged had spontaneously & at the same time sent them both" [BL 47472-97v, JJA 45: 3, FW 34.20]) alongside several of the hunting notes that become associated with King William I and King George IV. Additionally, in this same section of I.2, Joyce writes, "Hesitency was clearly to be evitated" (FW 35.20), referring to Richard Pigott's forgery of a letter attempting to link Parnell to the Phoenix Park murders (S. Clark 338). Parnell, who referred to himself in code as "Mr Fox" during his affair with Katherine O'Shea, later saw this name used against him by his opponents following the divorce scandal (Callanan, *Parnell* 67). An entire section in I.4 related to hunting contains the lines, "Gundogs of all breeds were beagling with renouned urbiandorbic bugles, hot to run him, given law, on a scent breasthigh" (FW 96.36–97.1) and "a deaf fuchser's volponism hid him close in covert" (FW 97.13–14). Then, this section ends with another allusion to this misspelling: "But the spoil of hesitants, the spell of hesitency" (FW 97.25). Combined with the use of "hesitency" in I.2, this reference in I.4 aligns the hunted fox with the persecuted Parnell and the Phoenix Park murders.

In VI.B.10, there are two full pages (totaling seventeen entries) from the October 1922 "Reynard" article.[6] There are a handful of other hunt-themed entries across the notebook, such as "heard a fox" (VI.B.10: 122), from a *Daily Mail* piece titled "Hunting Onlookers," and "hounds find / scent is breasthigh" (VI.B.10: 39), from a 1922 *Daily Mail* piece titled "Missing the Hunt." The issues of the *Daily Mail* from which these entries originate are from November 1922, suggesting that Joyce continued to be interested in the theme of hunting after the initial chance encounter in the *Quarterly Review* and thus recorded some tangentially related terms or phrases from this later newspaper.[7] Additionally, a letter to Harriet Shaw Weaver from Paris dated 17 October 1923 shows also that hunting was on Joyce's mind in more abstract contexts; Joyce writes, "The wild hunt still continues in the Paris jungle" (LI 205) in reference to flat-hunting. Then in VI.B.1, from an article in the *Irish Independent,* Joyce recorded "timber topper (chase)" (VI.B.1: 68). Additionally, in VI.B.5, Joyce took three pages of notes from a story by Chateaubriand called *"Les Chasseurs,"* or "The Hunters" (VI.B.5: 135–38).

The hunt intersects with the Phoenix Park and with the monarchy in the first drafts of I.2, from September 1923, wherein King George IV and his hunting party arrive in Dublin and pass HCE's home on their way to the Phoenix Park. The king encounters HCE tending his garden, complains about the potholes in the road, and then gives HCE his name. In keeping with a theme discussed earlier, Robert Harrison argues, "The hunt ritualizes and reaffirms the king's ancient nature as civilizer and conqueror of the land. His forests are sanctuaries where the royal chase may reenact, in a purely symbolic way, the historic conquest of the wilderness" (74). The class division present in I.2 reinforces this idea and also appears in the first revisions of the "Tristan and Isolde" sketch (April to October 1923). The relationships between the three central figures in the Tristan and Isolde story can also be characterized by a hunt or a pursuit. A seemingly simple addition of "from the Curragh" (BL 47481-30, JJA 56: 72, FW 387.1), referring to the famous center for horse racing in County Kildare, introduces class into this sketch. A seventeenth-century account of Kildare, from the Ordnance Survey papers now held at the Royal Irish Academy, describes the Curragh as a place where all "the nobility and gentry of the kingdome" came for "hawking and hunting" ("Proceedings" 353). On this same topic, Joyce alludes to Oscar Wilde's *A Woman of No Importance* at least three times throughout the *Wake* (FW 150.27, FW 153.26, FW 181.22), with Lord Illingworth's line in act 1 describing an English gentleman out hunting: "the unspeakable in full pursuit of the uneatable" (173). In this sense, the foxhunt is a sterile act of violence, as the prey is killed not for food, but only for sport, signaling the wastefulness and irrationality of the English gentry, and the arrival of the king in I.2, combined with the "Curragh" addition in "Tristan and Isolde," develops the theme of class in terms of the enjoyment of the natural world and the coopting of its resources.

In the first draft of "Here Comes Everybody" (September 1923), the hunt is united with Adam's naming of the creatures in Genesis. In the first drafts of this sketch (the first draft and the first two fair copies), a king—a composite of King George IV; the "sailor king" (FW 31.11) William IV; and William the Conqueror, the initial progenitor of the English Forest Laws—arrives with his "royal hunting party" (BL 47472-98r, JJA 45: 4, FDV 62.14–15, FW 31.2) in Chapelizod, embodying the relationships between the park, the king, and the hunt. This composite king confronts HCE, "the G.O.G. (grand old gardener)" (BL 47472-97, JJA 45: 2, FW 30.13),[8] who was out "following his plough for rootles in the rear garden" (BL 47472-98r, JJA 45: 5, FDV 62.6–7, FW 30.15–16). HCE's surname derives from his response to the king, who asks him if he "had been engaged in lobstertrapping." HCE replies: "No, my liege, I was only a cotching of them bluggyearwigs" (BL 47472-97, JJA 45: 2, FDV 62.18–19, FW 31.7–11), resulting in the king's assignment of the name "Earwicker."

The rear garden of the Earwicker household extends to the Phoenix Park, and this reenactment of Adam's naming of the creatures in the first chapter of Genesis further suggests that the Phoenix Park was intended to be a modern Edenic space in the *Wake* from its earliest stages of composition. At an ecocritical level, Adam's naming of all the earthly creatures has often been blamed as the source of many of the world's evils; Karla Armbruster (developing themes of Ursula LeGuin's "She Unnames Them") refers to this biblical story as "one of the dominant myths grounding Western culture's anthropocentrism" (119n15). Jacques Derrida also describes this "naming" in *The Animal That Therefore I Am* as a kind of sacrifice, relating this story to that of Cain and Abel. For Derrida, Abel's animal sacrifice derives from God's granting Adam the freedom to name the animals, and this idea transfers to the rhetoric of Cain being "hunted," "tracked," or "persecuted" after he commits the "second original sin" (42–43). Accordingly in I.2, HCE is both namer and named. However, he also assumes the Adamic role as his name derives from a suppression of nature (the ridding of earwigs from his attempt at maintaining an ordered natural space, his garden—supported, also, by his designation as "grand old gardener" [FW 30.13] or "Grant, old gartener" [FW 336.21]). Conversely, the king's naming of HCE has placed HCE in the same position as the game that the king is entering the park to hunt.

This scene of HCE's naming and the king's hunting party also connects to the first draft of III.4. Following the long description of HCE's bottom, as metonym for the Phoenix Park, the first draft of III.4 continues, and the narrators talk of the king's impending hunting visit to the Phoenix Park.[9] The narrators enquire, "Do you not have heard that the king shall come tomorrow?," and a reply comes that he "shall come for hunting on our ilcome fuxes" (BL 47482a-37v, JJA 60: 72, FDV 256.3–4, FW 367.24–25). Finding themselves lost in the king's hunting grounds, the narrators venture to map their location: "I fear lest we have lost ours respecting these wild parts. All now appears quite shaggy and beastful" (BL 47482a-38v, JJA 60: 74, FDV 255.25–26, FW 566.33).

They are lost in a Dante-esque forest, *una selva oscura*, until they come to a signpost: "[T]o the point, 1 yard, to Sara's bridge, 600 yds, to the Wellington Memorial, 800 yards, to the General Posting Office 2 miles, to Dunleary Obelisk, via the Rock, 8 miles" (BL 47482a-38v, JJA 60: 74, FDV 255.29–32, FW 556.31–567.04). The locations of which the distance from the "point" in the Phoenix Park is given share one thing in common: their relationship to the English crown. "Sara's Bridge" was named, in the late eighteenth century, after the wife of the Lord Lieutenant of Ireland and was renamed "Island Bridge" in 1922 (Mink 175). The Wellington Monument, in honor of the Duke of Wellington, is, in the *Wake*, England's power manifested as a large phallic monument in the center of the Phoenix Park (as demonstrated by John Bishop's interpretation of the giant superimposed upon Dublin in *Joyce's Book of the Dark* [34–35]). The General Post Office was the symbolic location for the staging of the 1916 Easter Rising, but based on Joyce's placement of the GPO here, it again represents England's attempted control over Ireland's space and time. As mentioned above, distance in Dublin was traditionally based on the General Post Office, demonstrating the colonial domination over Irish perceptions of space.[10]

The "Dunleary Obelisk" is the 1821 obelisk built in commemoration of King George IV's visit. Dún Laoghaire itself was renamed "Kingstown" because of King George's arrival there in 1821, recalling the king's bestowal of HCE's agnomen in I.2. This detail suggests that the king arriving for his hunt in the Phoenix Park is indeed King George IV in 1821. At the end of a draft of III.2, from summer 1925, Shaun's departure is narrated with dramatic nationalist rhetoric and Yeatsian imagery; his departure is lamented with the "foggy dews" and the "barleywind" (BL 47483-52, JJA 57: 176, FW 428.11–13), but his return will be a glorious one wherein he will take part in revolutionary actions that will return the land of Ireland to the Irish. His return will ensure that "Don Leary gets his own back from old grog Georges Quartos" (BL 47487-17v, JJA 62: 32, FW 428.18–19), a line Joyce adds to the galleys of book III. Hence, Dún Laoghaire will no longer be "Kingstown"; it will no longer directly bear the colonial inscription. King George's presence suggests that the issue at hand here is the English control of the land; the English king comes to Ireland to hunt, to murder native species for his own pleasure. The English king has the power to invade the sacred landscape of the Phoenix Park and to use it in any way he wishes. He also holds the power to change the way in which people relate to the landscape by changing the very name by which a particular space is known.

Self-Sufficiency: Irish Energy, Irish Materials

The question of self-sufficiency appears in the *Wake* to explore economic and cultural issues of an independent Ireland. In this section, I examine the relationship between Irish art, Irish artistic materials, and Shem's self-generated writing. Within I.7, Joyce also refers to issues of energy self-sufficiency in the Irish Free State, which is aligned with Shem's production of self-sufficient art. At other points in the *Wake*, Joyce engages Sinn Féin's inward-looking policies, the Irish Free State's focus on energy self-sufficiency, and the Free State's trade-off between modernization and environmental conservation. This section also returns to some themes from the first chapter of this study, using images of decomposition to explore the ways in which Joyce uses peat in the *Wake*.

Joyce was working on first drafts of the Shem chapter (I.7) while continuing to revise sections of I.5 in January 1924. The two sketches are intertwined at this draft level through the relationship between Irish flora and fauna, Irish artistic subjects, and self-reliant Irish art. In addition to the ink from the berries of Irish trees that were used for *The Book of Kells* discussed in the first chapter of this study, Sullivan explains that "the early Irish pens were the quills of swans, geese, crows, and other birds" (34), and "[g]oats, sheep, and calves supplied the skins" (35) for the vellum. Accordingly, the most famous work of Irish art is created from and using material bodies of animals, along with Irish trees. As a result, Shem's apparent grotesqueness in I.7, his writing upon his own body with his own excrement, thus places him in line with the finest scholars of Irish Christianity.

Hilary Clark connects the emphasis on the materiality of writing to Shem's consumption, arguing that in the *Wake* language is something consumable, both in terms of the individual writer and in terms of cultures and languages on the whole. In this sense, languages, cultures, and artwork are forms of decomposers, feeding off the remnants of the past. Though she does not use the term "decomposer" herself, Clark explains that Shem "eats spoiled food [. . .] the scraps and leavings of other writers from alien cultures [. . .] linguistic compost" (463). This description is an image for Joyce's vision of cultural accumulation and connects to the continued articulation of a sedimented language, introduced in chapter 1 of this study.

The attention of I.7 then shifts to Shem's compulsive food consumption. He is a connoisseur of a certain type of seafood: "Lazenby's teatime salmon tinned, as inexpensive as pleasing, to the plumpest roeheavy lax or friskiest troutlet that ever was gaffed between Leixlip & Island Bridge" (BL 47471b-50, JJA 47: 331, FDV 113.26–28, FW 170.27–29).[11] The food that Shem eats here is very earthy; the salmon that Shem eats is from the Liffey (his mother, ALP), and the gravy he likes is also described in terms of the land: it is "bogbrown" (BL 47471b-55, JJA 47: 341, FDV 114.1, FW 171.1).[12] The Liffey-derived fish and fish eggs and the "bogbrown" gravy are examples of Shem's harmful acts against Ireland, and the fact he eats eggs from the Liffey also suggests he is consuming a form of himself. On the one hand, Shem's self-generated, self-sufficient artwork is similar to Joyce's own focus on Irish subjects in his own work and is also in line with Free State self-sufficiency and domestic production rhetoric. But, on the other hand, it is also another form of Ireland as the "old sow that eats her farrow" designation of Ireland from *Portrait* (171), and in this context, Shem's consumption is harmful to the future of Ireland.

This sense of Shem as a threat to Ireland continues in the second part of I.7 (FW 187–95), wherein Joyce drafts the charges Shaun brings against Shem. Shem's penultimate sin (which also connects to the fable of "The Ondt and the Gracehoper") is failing to save and put away for "our predictable rainy day" (BL 47471b-66v, JJA 47: 378, FDV 121.32, FW 192.33), and his final sin is his rejection of his mother, ALP:

> Pariah, Cannibal Cain, you oathily forswore the womb that bore you & the paps you sometime sucked and ever since you have been one black mass of jigs & jimjams, haunted by a sense of having been or not being all you might be or might have been: and so, thank God from the innermost depths of your heart, it is to you blacksheep, to you, pick of the waste paper basket, *ay*, to you, unseen blusher of an obscene coalhole, that your coalblack ^turfbrown^ mummy is acoming, little oldfashioned mummy, little wonderful —— running with her tidings, all the news of the greatbig world, bellhopping the weirs, ducking under bridges, rapidshooting round the corners, by the hills of Tallaght & the Pool of the phooka & places called Blessington & Sallynoggin, babbling, bubbling, chattering to herself, giddygaddy grandmamma, gossipaceous, Anna Livia. (BL 47471b-72, JJA 47: 389, FDV 121.35–122.8, FW 193.32–195.4)

In this passage, Shaun (as embodiment of the Irish Free State ethos/Irish nationalism) criticizes his brother for not loving Ireland enough and not in the proper way. Additionally, Joyce has changed "coal" to "turf" on this draft, and together with the already existing "coalhole," this change creates a politicized opposition between foreign and domestic, aligned with Shaun's own binaristic vision of nationalism. By this, I mean that the native Irish turf is set against the imported coal, and such energy politics were of utmost concern to the new Irish Free State. Consequently, Shem has forsworn the "womb" that bore him, which, in this case, is the River Liffey, as well as the land of Ireland (represented by the turf). Shem is thus also a threat to Irish nationalism, and Shaun chastises him for his lack of patriotism, shown here by his failure to promote Irish resources and Irish culture. Shaun also claims he has forsworn the mother's milk, the "paps," which are also the "Paps of Ana," the mountains in County Kerry (which are supposedly shaped liked breasts).[13] Shaun questions Shem's connection with the land (the shepherd, Abel, herding the "blacksheep" of Shem/Cain), and the objects of Shem's forswearing become not just his mother, but also his mother country (the land of Ireland). However, Shem's self-generated art, his focus on Irish materials for Irish art, and his "bogbrown" and "turfbrown" colors also suggest an alternative nationalism. Shem's nationalism is one rooted in the materiality of Ireland and focused on processes of detritus, decomposition, and decay.

In I.7, Shem feeds off and creates from detritus, and Joyce expands this process of formation to show the growth of languages, cultures, and nations. To further explain this, I look to Merleau-Ponty, who discusses the idea of cultural "sedimentation" and a "sedimented" language (10), which is, in part, a geological metaphor for what Ferdinand de Saussure referred to as the "diachronic." In this present chapter, the idea of linguistic sedimentation expands to include cultural sedimentation, and thus provide Shem with an alternative vision to Shaun's nationalist politics.

The Irish Free State, Bogs, and Why Buckley Shot the Russian General

Such sedimentation, is, in this chapter, the settling and layering of language, culture, and land, and with this concept in mind, I turn here to specifically address the political role of bogs, the dominant feature of the Irish landscape, in the *Wake*. Bogs (used interchangeably with both "turf" and "peat" here, though the bog actually is the area composed of the turf/peat) are elements of the physical landscape that exemplify sedimentation in the *Wake*. Both highly politicized and aestheticized throughout Irish history, bogs are integral in the *Wake* for addressing the way in which the Irish Free State dealt with environmental policy and for further conveying the relationship between land, identity, and nationhood. *Finnegans Wake* was in dialogue with concerns about bogs and the politicization of landscape, and looking back to the concerns articulated in this 1939 text establishes continuity with our present environmental concerns, such as turf cutting.

Bogs are neither land nor water, solid nor liquid; they occupy a transitional space, both geographically and culturally. As Barbara Hurd describes in *Stirring the Mud: On Swamps, Bogs, and Human Imagination*, they are a margin where "there is only constant and languid saturation" (5). The *Oxford English Dictionary* defines a bog as follows: "A piece of wet spongy ground, consisting chiefly of decayed or decaying moss and other vegetable matter, too soft to bear the weight of any heavy body upon its surface; a morass or moss."[14] In ancient Ireland, the locations of the bogs determined the political and economic climate of Ireland; trade routes and patterns of settlement aligned with the bogs (for example, with the aforementioned *Eiscir Riada* [Esker Ridge], the line of debris deposited by receding glaciers that formed a pathway through the bogs in the Irish midlands and became the primary land route through the bogs [Feehan and McElveen 116]). Clonmacnoise, one of Ireland's most celebrated monastic sites, was famously established at the place where the Esker Ridge crossed the Shannon River. Thus, even the placement of major sites of Irish Christianity was dependent upon bog geography. Aalen, Stout, and Whelan argue for the inextricable relationship between Ireland's inhabitants and its bog lands: "Whilst boglands have strongly influenced rural economy and culture, settlement distribution and communications, they are themselves deeply humanised landscapes which have evolved, indeed sometimes originated, in close association with land use systems. The bog has been etched as deeply into the human as into the physical record in Ireland, to an extent unrivalled elsewhere in Europe" (106). Bogs have shaped Ireland's history by determining early political divisions in the country, dictating the pattern of settlements through the availability of stable land, and shaping consciousness through the landscape's liminality.

Moreover, as mentioned in the context of I.7, bogs have been an important source of income and fuel for centuries (Edwards 52). Peat became a popular source of fuel because of its ubiquity in the country; bog covers "one-sixth of the total land area" of Ireland (Aalen, Stout, and Whelan 106). Because of both natural causes and deforestation (begun in the middle ages, not just because of English rule, as is often the popular belief), Ireland has very little tree cover. Bogs, instead of trees, are how carbon is fixed. Peter Foss and Catherine O'Connell, in "Bogland: Study and Utilization," explain how bogs form: "Waterlogging first reduces oxygen levels and slows the decay of dead vegetation, which settles and gradually becomes peat, a precursor of coal" (184). This characteristic makes peat a cheap and popular form of heat, but also makes this peat particularly damaging both to the environment and to health because of the high concentration of carbon. Current debates about its use are particularly impassioned because of the tension between its role in traditional rural Irish culture and its high environmental impact.

Bogs are becoming more of a popular topic in Irish studies and ecocriticism because of their relationship to Irish culture and because of the controversy surrounding the decimation of Ireland's bogs, both in terms of development (the draining of bogs) and through the continued practice of turf cutting. In addition to the role of the bog as a carbon sink, a bog's ecology is very delicate, and once the ecology of a bog (particularly raised bogs) has been disturbed, it is impossible to right it again (though plans of rewetting drained bogs to act as carbon sinks surfaced in a July 2012 Dublin meeting of experts from the IPCC [Intergovernmental Panel on Climate Change]).[15] Bogs are crucial to Ireland's environmental health because of the amount of water they hold and the amount of carbon they fix, and the degradation of these bogs will most certainly have serious negative consequences for the country in the future, particularly in terms of flooding and air quality. The IPCC has also suggested that the rewetting of drained industrial bogs could be a significant factor in Ireland's ability to offset its greenhouse gases.[16] In recent years, the emphasis on biodiversity in Ireland has impacted the way in which bogs are treated, as bogs are critical to Ireland's biodiversity, particularly in areas where significant land is used for agriculture. So many of Ireland's species rely on these wetlands that continued exploitation of bogs would greatly reduce Ireland's already very low biodiversity. Though the commercial cutting of peat continues, Bord na Móna (in control of 80,000 hectares of bog, of which 60,000 hectares are "severely degraded" because of drainage and peat extraction) has made and continues to make a concerted effort to work with ecologists (such as the IPCC) to draft plans conscious of the country's environmental heritage.[17]

The ubiquity of bog land, the lack of other energy sources, and the cultural role occupied by bogs in Ireland combine to help to account for the endurance of turf cutting, especially in rural Ireland. Additionally, the need for the Irish Free State to produce its own energy—and energy from a distinctly Irish source—meant that the drive to modernize transformed this traditional practice into an industrialized one (peat also fuelled power plants and trains, though the peat-fired train was not very efficient). Howarth, back in 1911, had described how it would "seem possible that Ireland may possess great undeveloped wealth in peat" (193), presaging the Irish Free State's promotion of extensive turf cutting as a way to increase energy independence (Feehan and McElveen 114–17). With the foundation of the Free State, peat was valued as an explicitly Irish resource that could lead to energy independence, and turf cutting was championed by both Éamon de Valera and Sean Lemass. One of de Valera's many speeches focuses on the importance of turf for Ireland's energy and industry, and the 1934 creation of the Turf Development Board (now Bord na Móna) sent exploratory committees to Russia and Germany to learn the most efficient methods of turf cutting and drying (MacManus 267). According to biographer M. J. MacManus, de Valera's goal of industrializing Ireland strongly depended upon the energy from turf, and the industrial-scale turf cutting and drying that began during this period was to make Ireland "largely independent of imported coal" (267). Mary E. Daly's *Industrial Development and Irish National Identity, 1922–1939* argues thus: "It is not surprising that one of the earliest initiatives by the Dail Eireann was the establishment of a Commission on Industrial Resources" (4). John Feehan, an environmental resources lecturer at University College Dublin, also explains how "mechanical exploitation" of bogs was "regarded as a triumph of the newly independent Free State, ranking alongside the taming of the Shannon and the Liffey" (584). In short, a focus on modernization and industrialization was to be expected for the new Irish Free State as it had felt itself repressed, for centuries, under foreign rule. The problem always arises in developing countries and economies when the balance is lost between modernization and environmental conservation, and this problem in terms of Ireland's bogs began with the Free State and continues to the present.

In *Finnegans Wake*, bogs are not merely present as decorative aspects of the Irish landscape but are crucial points of intersection between history, politics, human beings, and landscape and are representative of the exploitation of nature. In III.2, Joyce summons Free State energy discourse and combines the idea of turf/bogs as metonyms for Ireland with the presence of the Liffey, because of their role in the construction of Irish identity in the early years of the Irish Free State. Jaun, in III.2, presents a lengthy plan for improving Dublin city, where he will "clean out the hogshole and generally ginger things up" (FW 447.2). Alluding to Jonathan Swift's "Proposal for the Universal Use of Irish Manufacture" (1720), Joyce writes: "Burn only what's Irish accepting their coals. You will soothe the cokeblack bile that's Anglia's and touch Armourican's iron core" (FW 447.4–6). In Jaun's plan, the products of Irish soil (the coals) are to be cast aside for England's coke and America's iron (which also echoes Shaun's criticism of Shem in I.7).

Such a relationship between bogs and Irish nationalism can also be found in the II.3 addition: "Shinfine deed in the myrtle of the bog twinfainmain stod up to slog" (BL 47480-2, JJA 55: 3, FDV 183.28–29, FW 346.27–28). "Shinfine" refers to Sinn Féin, ascribing the weight of nationalism to the turf. Furthermore, on the 1938 galley proofs for book III, Joyce adds: "The racist to the racy, rosy. The soil is for the self alone. Be own kind" (BL 47487-43v, JJA 62: 84, FW 465.28–36). This reference to Sinn Féin,[18] whose name, of course, translates to "ourselves alone," comments on the fine line between xenophobia ("racist") and nationalism. Here, the "soil" itself, the land, is only for the Irish people ("racy," as in "racy of the soil"), their "own kind."

Sinn Féin employed rhetoric concerning the Irish environment in much of their early politics (for example, with that of the Irish National Foresters), as Joyce demonstrates earlier in "Cyclops" (U 12: 1268). The narrator of "Cyclops" begins with the recounting of an incident "at the corner of Arbour Hill" (12: 1). Arbour Hill is the name of an area of Dublin but also the name of a prison and of the cemetery where fourteen of the Easter Rising leaders executed at Kilmainham Jail are buried. Arbour Hill, last, is also an arbor, not only because of the trees that already populated the area, but also because trees were planted for each of the executed Rising leaders. The conversation in "Cyclops" shortly turns to the ways Ireland and its resources have been exploited over the centuries:

> And the beds of the Barrow and Shannon they won't deepen with millions of acres of marsh and bog to make us all die of consumption.
> —As treeless as Portugal we'll be soon, says John Wyse, or Heligoland with its one tree if something is not done to reafforest the land. Larches, firs, all the trees of the conifer family are going fast. I was reading a report of lord Castletown's . . .
> —Save them, says the citizen, the giant ash of Galway and the chieftain elm of Kildare with a fortyfoot bole and an acre of foliage. Save the trees of Ireland for the future men of Ireland on the fair hills of Eire, O. (U 12: 1256–64)

This early example from *Ulysses*, ironized though the scene may be, illuminates how the assault on a nation's landscape is inseparable from an assault upon the nation's identity in *Finnegans Wake*.[19]

In terms of the *Wake*, the sketch that most clearly demonstrates the relationship between bogs, Ireland, and national identity is one of the last sketches to be drafted for the text, "How Buckley Shot the Russian General" (drafted from late 1936 to early 1937). Continuing with the discussion of Shem and his forswearing of the land of Ireland in I.7, and with the role of the landscape in Irish Free State and Sinn Féin rhetoric, the Buckley story further develops the relationship between territory and nation. The "original" Buckley story, told by Frederick A. Buckley, a rates collector along with John Stanislaus Joyce, concerned a soldier and a Russian general in the Crimean War (Costello and Jackson, "Rifleman Buckley"). In the story, as told by Joyce's father, the soldier Buckley had planned to shoot a Russian general but took pity upon him as he was attempting to defecate, but Buckley finally decides to shoot the Russian general when the general "prepared to finish the operation with a piece of grassy turf" (JJ 398). Ellmann argues that Joyce was convinced this story "was somehow archetypal" and that Joyce labored to find a suitable place for it in *Finnegans Wake*, refusing to leave it out. When Joyce posed the problem of where to situate this piece to Samuel Beckett, Beckett commented that the story was "[a]nother insult to Ireland" (qtd. in JJ 398n), referring to the piece of turf. Commenting on how Joyce does integrate the Buckley story into the *Wake*, Ellmann also argues, "Joyce saw Buckley in his own role of the ordinary Irishman in combat with imperial authority" (JJ 399n). With the late addition of this sketch to the *Wake*, the themes of war, land, and nationhood find a common denominator. Buckley's decision to shoot the Russian general is thus a result of the general's insult to the physical *land* of Ireland, embodied in the small piece of turf.

Butt and Taff broadcast the story of Buckley and the Russian general, and the first description of Taff is as "a smart boy, of the peet freers" (FW 338.5), which brings the piece of turf (as peat) to the forefront from the very beginning. Turf also appears in conjunction with its exploitation in simultaneous revisions of III.3, as the "fender" described in relationship to Cain also appears in a piece of extradraft material as "fender, a product of Hostages / Co. Engineers" (BL 47486a-222, JJA 61: 296, FW 518.15–16). HCE's presence in "Hostages / Co. Engineers" describes him again, clearly, as an engineer, often used throughout the *Wake* as a figure capable of manipulating nature. The "fender" of I.3 also specifically becomes a "turfing iron," a spade-like device used for turf cutting: "The illegallooking range or fender, alias turfing iron, a product of Hostages and Co., Engineers" (FW 518.15–16).

Shortly after the Buckley sketch was drafted, Joyce adds several additions relating to both "turf" and "Clontarf" (i.e., Battle of Clontarf) to the book I galley proofs in 1938. The simultaneity and proximity of these additions demonstrate the intended connection between these two sections. For example, to the end of I.3, Joyce adds, "Thunder and Turf married into Clandorf" (BL 47476a-44v, JJA 49: 94, FW 71.33) to the list of names HCE is called, alluding to the marriage of Sitric Silkbeard, leader of the Vikings ("Thunder"), to the daughter of Brian Boru ("Turf"). Additionally, to the section in I.4 concerning Festy King's trial, Joyce changes "any luvia o'er his face" to "any luvia peatsmoore over his face" (BL 47476-52v, JJA 49: 114, FW 86.9), and also adds "by the plain of Ir" (BL 47476-52v, JJA 49: 114, FW 86.9) to the already existing "clanetourf." This same line also notes that Festy King was "once known as Melechy" (FW 86.08), referring to Malachy II, who succeeded Brian Boru following his death at Clontarf. "Turf" appears again in the third typescript of IV§5 (BL 47488-152v–60, JJA 63: 234–43), in reference to the Battle of Clontarf: "Snf? Only turf, wick dear. Clane turf. You've never forgotten, batt on tarf" (BL 47488-158v, JJA 63: 240, FW 625.17–18). This addition derives from a note in one of the last notebooks for *Finnegans Wake*, VI.B.47: "broin burroo You've never fogodden batt on tarf? Snf? Only turf. Clanetourf too. why" (VI.B.47: 24). This identification of Brian Boru with turf is because of Clontarf, but both turf and Clontarf serve as metonyms, respectively, for Ireland's historically charged landscape. As I have argued, bogs play a similar metonymic role, and in the beginning of II.4, Joyce adds "Bog carse ond dam neat, sar!" (BL 47480-2, JJA 55:3, FDV 183.28–29, FW 339.6) to a section detailing the history of the Viking and Norman invasions of Ireland.

Because of the relationship between warfare and land in the Buckley sketch, it is not surprising that "Clontarf" is punned upon here and that the sections relating to Clontarf from I.1 are revised in I.3 and I.4 as well. In the same way that the Battle of Clontarf was a decisive battle in the history of Dublin and Ireland as a whole, turf is central to the way in which Irish cultural geography, agriculture, and culture have developed. Bogs are integral to understanding the way in which Ireland's political identity has been so frequently tied to its landscape, and bogs, like languages and cultures, bear the traces of battles waged. Thus, Buckley shoots the Russian general because his use of the piece of turf to clean himself represents the disrespect with which Irish landscape has been treated.

War and Nature

Another significant way in which Joyce merges nature with the political is through war (and on a larger scale, through conflict in general), as is demonstrated above through the discussion of the Buckley sketch and the Battle of Clontarf. Although, as Greg Winston explains, "Joyce's literary response to the military presence is often subtle, entrenched, and difficult to detect at first glance" (*Joyce and Militarism* 11), *Finnegans Wake* is, in fact, quite riddled with allusions to war. The contemporaneous escalating of conflict in Europe likely influenced the inclusion of a war-themed sketch such as "Buckley" (and of several war-related additions during these final revisions). As Joyce is writing the Buckley sketch during the lead-up to World War II, the additions relating to Sinn Féin are in part comments on the dangers of nationalism. On 12 March 1938, Hitler annexed Austria into the Third Reich, and this annexation was the first of many campaigns to regain the German-speaking territories lost after World War I. The Sinn Féin party (founded in 1905 by Arthur Griffith) had split in 1926, with Éamon de Valera forming his own Fianna Fáil party, and the former party's beliefs concerning the territorial rights of the Irish can be conflated with the reasoning behind Germany's annexation of Austria. Ursula Heise, in her study of conceptions of the global and the local, identifies "the most extreme" example of this type of thinking: the Nationalist Socialist Party's "rhetoric of Germans' natural connectedness to 'blood and soil' (Blut und Boden), which helped legitimate fascist political structures, military expansion of the 'life space' (Lebensraum), and unprecedented violence both within and outside what was claimed to be Germans' legitimate space of domination in the 1920s and 1940s" (47). The nationalist ideologies present in "Cyclops," combined with the rhetoric of the years leading up to World War II, influence the Sinn Féin references in late drafts of the *Wake* and communicate the relationship between Irish nationalism, the Irish landscape, war, and xenophobia.

One such Sinn Féin reference appears in 1938, in the second typescript of IV§1, with Joyce inserting another line linking the environment to Sinn Féin (and also back to "Cyclops"): "The smog is sonne feine, somme foehn avant!" (BL 47488-15–22, JJA 63: 19–32, FW 593.8–9). The *foehn* (or *föhn*) is a type of wind that occurs in the lee side of the mountain range, with which Joyce would have been very familiar from living in Switzerland (whose warm temperatures can be attributed to this *foehn* wind from the

Alps). The links between Sinn Féin, the Battle of the Somme (which took place across the banks of the Somme River in 1916), and the *foehn* develop Joyce's associations between war, climate, and politics, connecting back to the VI.B.10 notes (such as "a wintry") and the VI.B.24 "Humidia" note discussed at the beginning of the present chapter. The addition "behold the residuance of a delugion: the foggy doze still going strong, the old thalassocrats, maskersof the waterworld [. . .] blowing great" (BL 47480-206, JJA 55: 359, FW 367.24–36) plays a similar role, with "foggy doze" referring to the song "The Foggy Dew." The *foehn* is revisited with "blowing great," suggesting a storm, or a flood; the "thalassocrats" (*Thalassa*, the Greek goddess of the Sea) "delugion" of the "waterworld."

The song "The Foggy Dew" has several versions, two of which are directly applicable to this section and stage of composition of *Finnegans Wake*. The song was originally a ballad from the early nineteenth century and recounts the story of a man who woos a young woman to protect her from the "foggy, foggy dew." A second version of the song is from the Easter Rising period and urges Irishmen to fight for Ireland (not for England) in World War I. The song's nationalist message is articulated through the evocation of the soldier's relation to the landscape, both in Ireland and on the battlefields of World War I (such as at the Battle of the Somme). Paul Fussell identifies this motif in *The Great War and Modern Memory*, explaining: "If the opposite of war is peace, the opposite of experiencing moments of war is proposing moments of pastoral. Since war takes place outdoors and always within nature, its symbolic status is that of the ultimate anti-pastoral" (231). The imagery of dew, spring, and Easter in conjunction with that of a soldier's death (glorious if for Ireland, in vain if for England) falls into place with the conclusion of the *Wake* and its themes of rebirth and renewal, even though the song's message is a naïve, idealistic one, akin to that of early Georgian World War I poems (such as Rupert Brooke's "The Soldier").

Along these lines, Jespersen explains that the origin of the English word "Easter" derives from the Old English *eastron*, which was "the name of an old pagan spring festival, called after Austro, a goddess of spring" (44).[20] The "foggy dew" itself is the calm after the storm, after the "leaden rain" of British weaponry in the Easter Rising. The "foggy dew," the "glen," and "the plains of Royal Meath" are all summoned in the song to create a portrait of Ireland, with the dew itself becoming a metonym for the Irish character through the climate. The climate of Ireland, though often unpleasant and always unpredictable, is closely aligned with the Irish character, and its embodiment in the "foggy, foggy dew" represents the bittersweet struggle for Irish independence.

Other additions to this section that merge nature and war largely revolve around trees, such as the additions "weepon, weeponder, song of sorrowmon," and "like a solidery sap" (BL 47480-117v, JJA 55: 212, FW 344.2). The trees, the weeping willows, weep for the soldiers; felled like trees, their blood flows like sap. Joyce also adds "yewleaved" (BL 47480-40v, JJA 55: 76, FW 339.28) a few lines earlier, and, along with the willow, the yew is one of the letters of the Ogham alphabet. In keeping with the Easter theme, willows are said to usher in springtime, and with "their quick growing nature and habit of growing next to water," the willow is also "a symbol of fertility and life" (Mac Coitir 40). Miranda Green, in her *Dictionary of Celtic Myth and Legend*, believes that the willow may "represent the Tree of Life that is periodically cut down at winter and reborn at spring" (qtd. in Mac Coitir 44), further supporting the themes of war and regeneration.[21] In the second set of galley proofs,[22] Joyce continues expanding this connection, adding to the second page of the *Wake*: "verdous catapulting the camibalistics" and "boomeringstroms" (BL 47476a-133, JJA 49: 290, FW 4.4–6). "Verdous" refers to *vert*, tree felling, as well as to Verdun. Catapults and ballistics ("camibalistics") are weaponry, with "boom" being their sound, and "cannibalism" a comment on the grotesqueness of war. "Boomeringstroms" contains the Dutch *boom* (tree), the Czech *strom* (tree), the German *Sturm* (storm), and the German *Strom* (stream). The "boom" and storm also suggest thunder, and with the "boomerang" as "boomering," there is the ever-present Viconian thunder and *ricorso*.

The typescript of II.3§4, 6 (ca. 1936–1937) continues to align trees with soldiers by referring to them as "felled." At the Battle of Clontarf, legend has it that when Brian Boru was ambushed and killed by Brodir, Bromerleaudir said: "Now let man tell man that Brodir felled Brian" (O'Hanlon 437). Joyce then adds "The field of karnags and that bloasted tree" (BL 47480-40v, JJA 55: 76, FW 340.7–9) before "Forget not the felled! For the lomondations of Oughrem!" to the typescript of II.3§4. These references reprise the tree/stone motif, referring to soldiers as "felled" trees, and also revisit the megaliths of Carnac ("karnags"). In addition to forestry and fallen soldiers (and the fallen Brian Boru), "Forget not the felled" also alludes to a Thomas Moore melody about the Battle of Aughrim, "Forget Not the Field." In addition to the effect that a high number of casualties would have upon the soil, the terrain itself becomes altered when hosting continuous warfare. However, a quiet form of narrative is stored within the landscape through these alterations as the layers of sediment preserve the history of these ecological changes. Perhaps this record of change is why "Aughrim" becomes "Oughrem" (again referring to the tree-based Ogham alphabet), which also connects language and landscape, like the addition of "langdwage" (BL 47480-2, JJA 55: 3, FDV 182.18, FW 338.5–14). To make these relationships even clearer, Joyce adds to the 1938 galley proofs of I.4: "The war is in words and the wood is the world. Maply me, willowy me, hickory he and yew yourselves. Howforhim chirrupeth evereachbird. From golddawn glory to glowworm gleam" (BL 47476a-59v, JJA 49: 132, FW 98.34–99.1). War, words, wood, and world are connected, all storing their own distinct versions of historical narrative.

In some of the first revisions of the "Butt and Taff" sketch, Joyce continues to work with the relationship between climate and nationality. Again, this relationship is particularly noteworthy in Ireland, wherein the country's Latin name, *Hibernia*, refers to its cold climate, and wherein the country's identity throughout the world is synonymous with its wet weather. The revision of one of Butt's passages gains four more additions relating to weather and landscape, with the play on time/weather (*temps*) incorporated as well. Furthermore, with the introduction of Russian vocabulary, these relationships become increasingly connected to the Crimean War: "whatik of wraimy wetter!" (BL 47480-48v, JJA 55: 96, FW 347.7), "blodiens and godinats of them" (BL 47480-49v, JJA 55: 96, FW 347.6), "Krzerszonese" (BL 47480-49v, JJA 55: 98, FW 347.9), and "in the Bok of Alam" (the Bog of Allen) (BL 47480-49v, JJA 55: 98, FW 347.20–21). *Vreme*, in Bulgarian, means both "weather" and "time" (like *temps*), and *wetter* is German for "weather," as well as, obviously, the state of being more wet. *Veter* is also Russian for "wind," and *godina*, in Bulgarian, means "year." "Chersonese" is the name of the peninsula upon which Sevastopol is located, incorporating the Crimean War context of the Buckley sketch. "Karkonosze," or Krkonose, is a Polish and Czech mountain range that once formed the border between Silesia and Bohemia. Following "Krzerszonese" in the *Wake*, there is "Milesians," referring to the Milesians of both Ireland and Silesia. The mention of the Krkonose

Mountains contributes to the dialogue concerning national borders, as this region was constantly undergoing a shift in territorial boundaries during this period (and would only continue to do so as World War II began with Hitler's invasion of Poland on 1 September 1939).

In short, war is closely related to nature in the *Wake*, and particularly in the later sketches and drafts that were written in the lead-up to World War II, because of the role land itself plays in being the cause of conflict and in determining national identity. Last, Joyce uses warfare and conflict to further express the ways in which cultures and languages blend over time, the way land can bear the scars of conflict, and the way humans return to the earth.

What's Left? Polar Exploration

Continuing with the relationship between land and national identity, I now move toward the theme of exploration and focus particularly on how polar exploration appears in the *Wake* to engage themes of imperialism and progress. In the late twentieth century, there was little uncharted territory left on earth. Most exploration had ended well before the twentieth century began, with the exception of two vast, uncharted regions: the Arctic and the Antarctic. In *Finnegans Wake*, Joyce uses polar exploration and polar explorers to query the need for humankind to assert its dominance through the conquest of territory and the urge to map and survey. This section provides contextual information for the importance of polar exploration to the late Victorian era and reviews Joyce's possible knowledge of polar exploration, his early use of an "arctic beast" in one of his "Epiphanies," and the way in which polar exploration is incorporated into the *Wake*.

"[N]ansense" (FW 326.21), from II.3 of the *Wake*, alludes to Fridtjof Nansen, the Norwegian explorer and key figure of the "Heroic Age" of polar exploration (the 1890s to the 1920s, roughly). Nansen became an international figure after two significant achievements: in 1888 Nansen led the first team to cross Greenland, and then his North Pole expedition of 1893–1896 reached a record northern latitude (86° 14') ("Dr. Nansen's Journey"). Chronicling both of his journeys in two popular books, *The First Crossing of Greenland* (1890) and *Farthest North: Being a Record of a Voyage of Exploration of the Ship* Fram, *1893–1896, and of a Fifteen Months' Sleigh Journey* (1897), Nansen exhibited bravery and heroism that appealed to a wide audience. In addition to his scientific, navigational, and exploratory achievements, the excitement and danger of his travelogues inspired a generation of polar explorers.

In July 1895, the Sixth International Geographical Congress was held in London and was closely linked to the Royal Geographical Society (RGS, founded 1830),[23] though delegates from more than a dozen other nations were in attendance. During this period, the definition of geography as a discipline was being debated, and the imperial aims of much early geography, particularly in terms of mapping and surveying, were made clear.[24] The polar regions were of greatest concern to the Geographical Congress, and one of the primary talks of the congress was on the subject of "Arctic and Antarctic Exploration" ("Sixth International" 232). Introduced by Georg von Neumayer (director of the German Maritime Observatory at Hamburg) and Clements Markham (president of the RGS), this session at the congress decided that Antarctic exploration must be undertaken by the end of the century and must also be the result of international cooperation (Lüdecke 127). Despite good intentions and the assertion by Neumayer that some rivalry would "stimulate the competition on a field ennobling the human race" (qtd. in Lüdecke 129), the next congress, held in Berlin in 1889, revealed national rivalries (particularly between England and Germany) and led to the division of the field between several nations (Fütterer et al. 7).

Gradually, the necessity for cooperation for the purpose of scientific progress gave way to the necessity for national pride, and accordingly the endeavor became the "race for the pole" that it is now called. David Mountfield argues in *A History of Polar Exploration* that behind the "sudden burst" of polar exploration in the last decade of the nineteenth century were two main motives: "scientific curiosity and individual, or nationalistic, rivalry" (139). On one level, exploration simply provided another platform for individuals and nations to compete. Coupled with new developments in science and technology and the mystique of the polar regions, the politics of polar exploration ensured that the "Heroic Age" would be characterized by competition over modernization and technological competence of individual nations.

Though its existence had been posited since the classical period, no record exists of any person seeing Antarctica until 1820. It would be almost another one hundred years until the Norwegian explorer Roald Amundsen reached the South Pole on 14 December 1911. While reaching the poles might no longer seem remarkable in a culture where it is possible to take Arctic cruises, it is important to recognize that the efforts of polar explorers such as Nansen and Amundsen in the late nineteenth century signified that there was no longer any unmapped space in the world.

In addition to this radical new conception of the earth (one not unlike, for example, the way in which the earth was viewed after the "Earth Rise" photos emerged from the Apollo space missions), this turn-of-the-century polar exploration was intensely political and nationalistic. In the scramble for the South Pole, Amundsen was in close competition with the British explorer Robert Scott. At a time when England's almost supreme world dominance was beginning to fade, the failure of the British contender to reach the South Pole first was not very popular in Britain. For example, an article in the *Guardian* from 9 March 1912 titled "The Conquest of the South Pole" reads: "It is a great exploit, and Englishmen, who have had so great a share in the exploration of the South Polar regions, will heartily congratulate him and his countrymen on the distinction they have gained. Whether Amundsen was the first to reach the South Pole remains, of course, to be seen; no word has yet come of Captain Scott, and until we know whether he reached the Pole, and, if so, when, the question who is the victor in the race remains uncertain" (6).

In addition to the national competition inspired by the polar regions, the mystique of the *terra incognita* and the *terra nullis* of the polar regions redefined territorial expansionism. Prior to the exploration of the Arctic and Antarctic, such expeditions were usually undertaken for material gain (for spices, slaves, crops, etc.). However, the barren lands around the poles would not be lucrative in this sense, and their exploration was more of a competition *of* resources than *for* resources. This idea of a barren land, an already negated *terra nullis*, also disrupted human logic, laying the groundwork for our current fascination with these locales and for narrativizing them.

Joyce's life closely paralleled this age of polar exploration, and there is little possibility that these polar expeditions could have escaped the attention of a young man raised as a citizen of the British Empire. A cursory search through the primary Irish newspapers of the period (the *Freeman's Journal* and the *Irish Times*) returns dozens of articles on the subject every year between 1890 and 1925. Nansen would have been a very well-known name, and a 7 December 1906 letter to Stanislaus, wherein Joyce confuses Nansen's name with that of [Knut] Hamsun, suggests the level of fame achieved by the explorer during this period.[25]

While there is no direct evidence (i.e., there is unfortunately no letter wherein Joyce exclaims to Nora about his excitement over polar exploration) that the polar regions interested Joyce in his youth, number 16 of the "Epiphanies" refers to an "arctic beast," which at least suggests a familiarity with literature about the region (either in nonfiction, fiction, or mythical accounts) and possibly even with Nansen's writings, as some of the most famous passages concern encounters with polar bears. Joyce writes: "A white mist is falling in slow flakes. The path leads me down to an obscure pool. Something is moving in the pool; it is an arctic beast with a rough yellow coat. I thrust in my stick and as he rises out of the water I see that his back slopes towards the croup and that he is very sluggish. I am not afraid but, thrusting at him often with my stick drive him before me. He moves his paws heavily and mutters words of some language which I do not understand" (PSW 176). In Joyce criticism, little has been made of this epiphany, or any of the individual epiphanies (though much, obviously, has been made of the term itself). Jay B. Losey's article "Dream-Epiphanies in *Finnegans Wake*" interprets the above epiphany in a manner that could be explored differently, particularly when taking into account the final sentence of the epiphany. Losey argues that this epiphany "reveals Joyce's belief that the artist should lead his people and contribute to their literary culture through art. Despite the stark imagery of the epiphany, Joyce refuses to become paralyzed and instead reacts decisively ('thrusting at him often with my stick') when the beast rises out of the water" (614).

Losey relates this incident to "Proteus" and to Stephen's encounter with the dog on Sandymount strand. "Joyce probably recognized the 'arctic beast' in his dream as another manifestation of Proteus," Losey continues, seemingly because of the presence of the stick (Stephen's ashplant) (Losey 614). The fact that the narrator concludes with the way that the animal "moves his paws heavily and mutters words of some language which I do not understand" suggests that there is a barrier to communication. What seems important about this epiphany (if the connection to "Proteus" is to be accepted) is that the authorial figure is struggling with the inability to connect to the artistic material. In one possible interpretation of Stephen's ashplant in *Ulysses*, the ashplant is read as a tool of self-defense, much like the stick in this epiphany. It is also what keeps the artist at a distance from the subject he desires to represent and is consequently closely related to Stephen's artistic failures.

The "arctic beast" itself is likely a polar bear because of its "yellow" coat (technically, a polar bear's fur is clear, though it is often characterized as being white while actually appearing yellow). Despite the fact that polar bears had been known of since at least the late sixteenth century (A. Dalton 32) (though they were not recognized as a separate species until 1774),[26] the Victorian fascination with exotic animals and the popularity of zoological gardens, coupled with the emphasis on exploration of the polar regions, meant that these bears became much more common in popular culture.[27] Joyce would have seen polar bears in the Dublin Zoo (Ellmann explains that Joyce compared the zoo in Zurich to the Dublin Zoo [JJ 743]),[28] and the novelty of the polar bear—a displaced representative of the barren, inhospitable, and unconquerable Arctic regions—may have influenced its inclusion in this "arctic beast" epiphany because of its radical otherness.[29]

In addition to the "arctic beast" epiphany, the "Ithaca" episode of *Ulysses* refers to this *terra nullis* quality of the polar regions. Included in the many reasons Bloom lists for his admiration of water is water's "sterility in the circumpolar icecaps, arctic and Antarctic: its climatic and commercial significance: its preponderance of 3 to 1 over the dry land of the globe" (U 17.191–93). In addition to Bloom's appreciation of the lack of life forms present in the (solid) water at the poles ("sterility"), Bloom then thinks of his wife as a region to be "explored," like the "land of the midnight sun," in this same episode. The question "In what final satisfaction did these antagonistic sentiments and reflections, reduced to their simplest forms, converge?" (U 17.2227–28) is answered: "Satisfaction at the ubiquity in eastern and western terrestrial hemispheres, in all habitable lands and islands explored or unexplored (the land of the midnight sun, the islands of the blessed, the isles of Greek, the land of promise), of adipose anterior and posterior female hemisphere" (17.2229–36). Molly's backside, here, is thus described as two sections of "melonous hemisphere" (17.2242), much like the later association of ALP's anatomy and the earth in *Finnegans Wake* ("geometer" FW 297.1). "[T]he land of the midnight sun" is, of course, the polar regions (where the sun never sets for a portion of the year because of the latitude). Though these regions are "unexplored" (in 1904, but not in 1922), the analogy between the female body and the earth, and the mysteries both still hold, comforts Bloom; he enjoys this space that exists beyond his comprehension. It is perhaps for this reason that under the "Penelope" heading on the British Library notesheets, the note "<LB Shackleton>" (515) appears.[30] The note, tagged with "LB," may relate to Bloom as explorer of Molly's "unexplored" regions as Ernest Shackleton was one of the explorers of "the land of the midnight sun."

Following this appearance in *Ulysses*, polar exploration appears in Joyce's work again a few years into work on the *Wake*. Though a large portion of the material relating to polar exploration does appear in the "Norwegian Captain" sketch, quite a few other references appear throughout the *Wake*'s composition history. For example, drafts of III.3§B (1929), the section dealing with the establishment of cities, incorporate polar explorers to convey the impulse to conquer and to order (relating back to the above discussion of the imperial aims of mapping and geography). Robert Scott's ship, the *Terra Nova*, appears in this section. (Captain Scott's *Terra Nova* expedition reached the pole on 17 January 1912, a mere thirty-three days after Amundsen's, but unfortunately, Scott's entire team perished on the return trip.) Though "Terra Nova" is a term not limited to Captain Scott, the appearance of the "Nova Tara" in conjunction with HCE's role as conqueror of lands in III.3, the Scandinavian references in this section (such as "Wodin," "Noreway," and "Bygmester" [Ibsen's *The Master Builder*]), plus "Ibscenest nansence!" and "lowest basement in hystry!" invoke Scott and the Norwegian Nansen.

Furthermore, in VI.B.29 (one of the primary notebooks used at this draft level) the notes "reshackle ~" (VI.B.29: 132) and "basement basemeant" (VI.B.29: 150) seem to have nothing to do with polar exploration, but the additions of which they are a part contain references to both Shackleton and Nansen. The addition "^+Lowest basemeant in hystry!+ ^ Ibscenest nansence. ^+nansence!+ ^" (BL 47484b-431, JJA 59: 171, FW 535.18) and the revision "I schicked ^+wegschicked+ ^ Duke Wellinghof to shockle ^+reshockle+ ^ Roy Shackleton" (BL 47484b-441, JJA 59: 181, FW 541.21) were both made in March 1930, to the draft level Deane, Ferrer, and Lernout designate as III§3B.14 (VI.B.29 9). The "lowest basement in history" is the South Pole, and because of the spelling of "history" with "hy," it is also the female genitalia (leading back to Bloom's alignment of Molly's bottom with the hemispheres and with unexplored lands). In this example, the explorations of the polar regions are aligned with an exploration of the female body.

The "Shackleton" references indicate Ernest Shackleton, who might have been a particularly interesting figure for Joyce. Not only was he knighted by Edward VII after reaching the farthest point south in January 1909 on his *Nimrod* expedition, but Britain's famous explorer was actually born in Ireland, in County Kildare, to an Anglo-Irish family (Barczewski 10–11). Joyce adds a Shackleton reference to late drafts of II.4 with "Shackleton's brown loaf," one of three references to Shackleton that appear within just five pages (FW 392.33, FW 393.01, FW 397.17). "Shackleton's brown loaf" refers, on the one hand, to the Liffey's Shackleton's weir, named as such because the adjacent mills were operated by George Shackleton. Shackleton's, also known as the Anna Livia Weir, has been the site of a mill since the end of the eighteenth century.[31] On the other hand, the addition also refers to Ernest Shackleton, captain of the *Endurance*, who had been a member of Captain Scott's first expedition, *Discovery*, in 1901–1904 (and who was related to George Shackleton). Shackleton's weir is located not very far from the Dublin/Kildare borders, so the mill, the weir, and the polar explorer—the Anglo-Irish, knighted polar explorer—are joined together as three versions of power over the natural world.

Shackleton's weir was likely added to the above section of III.3 because of this dual implication of the name—the weir as a subduer of the Liffey and the explorer as a conqueror of land. To these drafts of III.3, Joyce adds another reference to Shackleton's weir with "shekleton's" (BL 47486b-467, JJA 61: 469, FW 512.28), and he also adds "Fletter O'Ford, that, honey, I hurdley chew you" (BL 47486b-467, JJA 61: 469, FW 512.31) to the same line. This second addition contains the translation of one of the names for Dublin, *Baile Átha Cliath* (as "Town of the Ford of the Hurdles"), which refers to the first "ford" of the River Liffey that led to the development of the city of Dublin.[32] The ford of the Liffey led to the first phase of Dublin's existence, and the mills and weirs later ushered in another phase. The fact that "Shackleton's" is the weir Joyce often comes back to implies that he viewed both George Shackleton's weir and mills and Ernest Shackleton's exploration as different instruments in the same imperial or economic project.

Other Joyce critics have also remarked upon the presence of polar explorers and polar exploration in Joyce. In *The Books at the Wake*, J. S. Atherton asserts that Joyce "had certainly read the articles of 'Polar Exploration'" in the eleventh edition of the *Encyclopaedia Britannica*, though Atherton unfortunately provides no reasons for why he believes this (84). B. J. Tysdahl, in "Joyce's Use of Norwegian Writers" (1969), identifies Fridtjof Nansen as one of the "conspicuously present" Norwegian writers in *Finnegans Wake* (1).[33] Tysdahl explains, "Joyce probably liked the Norwegian scientist, explorer, diplomat, and writer Fridtjof Nansen. As an ambassador of the Norwegian government of 1905 Nansen went to England to secure British recognition of a free Norway. Joyce hoped for a similar development in Ireland" (11). Tysdahl also quotes Joyce's famous line from his 1 September 1905 letter to Stanislaus about Dublin becoming a capital just as "Christiania" (Oslo) has become (LII 205). Citing Joyce's pacifism, Tysdahl continues his reasons for Joyce's appreciation of Nansen with a discussion of Nansen's humanitarian work after World War I and of Nansen's involvement with the League of Nations (both of which earned Nansen a Nobel Prize in 1922).

Joyce takes a few notes from an obituary notice for Nansen (who died on 13 May 1930) in VI.B.32, begun May 1930 (VI.B.32 28). These notes were not used in 1930, but were transferred to the Madame Raphael VI.C notebooks to be used in the middle of the 1930s. Taken from the purported obituary notice are the notes "Nansen,"[34] "ravens on ice,"[35] "driftwood,"[36] "Fram Groenlands / [isey morn]" (VI.B.32: 12), and "Ammundsen" (VI.B.32: 14). "Fram" is the famous ship Nansen used on his North Pole expedition, and "Groenlands" refers to his crossing of the Greenland interior.

Nansen believed that there had to be a passage between the seas east of Greenland and the seas north of Asia, and he proposed the existence of a current between the North Pole and Franz Josef Land that originated somewhere in the Arctic Ocean above Siberia and moved toward Greenland. Nansen believed he would reach the North Pole by following this current, a branch of the Gulf Stream, or "gulpstroom" (FW 319.27), which appears later in the "Norwegian Captain" sketch, as well as in Nansen's *Farthest North*.[37] However, the only way to follow this current was to allow a ship to become lodged in the winter pack ice. The *Fram* (which appears in the original title of Nansen's *Farthest North* [*Met Fram over Polhavet*]) was the purpose-built ship for this expedition, and it was a remarkable ship because of its ability to withstand the pressure of being moored in pack ice for several months. Nansen's plan did not work out as well as he had hoped, and he and another team member decided to try to reach the pole on foot after he concluded the *Fram* would not drift to more than 85° N. They never did reach the North Pole and wintered on Franz Joseph Land, but not before reaching the farthest north any human had ever reached before, 86° 14' N.

Several geographical locations from the *Fram* expeditions appear throughout the *Wake*, particularly in "The Norwegian Captain." One of the last sections of the *Wake* to be drafted (early 1935), "The Norwegian Captain" sketch appears in book II, chapter 3 (II.3§1A, C) (BL 47479-2v–22, JJA 54: 2–42, FW 309–331.36). The *Fram* also appears in the first draft of this sketch: "And aweigh he yankered on the Norgean run so that seven sailend sonnenrounders was he breastbare to the brinabath, where bottoms out has fatthoms full, fram Franz José Land" (BL 47479-5, JJA 54: 8, FDV 169.19, FW 312.5–8).[38] In this part of the sketch, the captain is ordering his suit and preparing to embark on another voyage. The language is melodramatic, echoing Ariel's "full fathom five" from *The Tempest* and evoking the length of his journey with references to the rising and setting of the sun ("sonnenrounders"). The Norwegian captain will be going far, far away, as far as Nansen went with his *Fram* toward Franz Joseph Land and toward Spitsbergen (the largest island of Norway's Svalbard archipelago ("sputsbargain" [FW 317.25]).

"Franz José Land" (BL 47479-5, JJA 54: 8, FDV 169.19, FW 312.7–8) is thus Franz Joseph Land, an archipelago close to the North Pole, "arguably discovered" in 1865 by Norwegians (Mills 305), who called it "Fridtjof Nansen Land" (though its present name comes from that given by Austro-Hungarian explorers in 1873 [Mills 286]). The fact that it is Franz *José* Land in the *Wake* and not Franz Josef/Joseph Land conflates the classical period of exploration (when the primary explorers were of Spanish and Portuguese patronage) with exploration in the nineteenth and early twentieth centuries. On one level, this reference suggests that political power comes and goes and that land claimed by one country will inevitably be claimed by another country at another time. In the classical period, the goal was usually circumnavigation for the identification of safe trade routes, whereas in the nineteenth and twentieth centuries, the goal was reaching the poles. On a practical level in terms of the *Wake*'s composition, Franz Joseph Land was in the news throughout the mid-1930s because a group of Russian sailors (the USSR had annexed the territory in 1926 [Mills 305]) completed a circuit of the islands "long regarded as impossible" ("Small Boat" 359), but feasible in 1932 because of a shift in climate that had melted some of the polar ice. Many aspects of Joyce's "Franz José Land" are important for the *Wake*: the intrusiveness of exploration, the audacity of claiming territory for another nation, the squabbles that ensue between nations over territorial claims, the politics associated with such claims, the oddity of naming land for a person, and, finally, the inevitable rise and fall of global powers.

When the Norwegian captain returns to Ireland, the *Fram* appears again as the ship's husband ("shop's housebound") speaks of the captain's return to Ireland. "He was as deep as the north star," the ship's husband explains of the captain's voyage, and then concludes with "Afram" (FW 317.9) before describing his return. Then, the ship's husband turns on the captain, accusing him of attempting to invade and take over Ireland just as "Shackleton Sulten" (FW 317.15), referring, again, to Ernest Shackleton. The tailor alludes to two more of the areas associated with Nansen's *Fram* voyage: "zembliance," and "mansk" (as in "under its zembliance of mardal mansk" [FW 317.33–34]). "земпи" ("zemly") is the Russian for "land," and in addition to Nova Zemlya (an archipelago north of Siberia in the Arctic Ocean that appears in Nansen's *The First Crossing of Greenland* [456]), this term refers to any of the Arctic territories with "Zembla" or "Zemlya" in their name. "Zembla" is the Dutch for "land," and Nova Zemlya is also sometimes referred to as "Nova Zembla." Either way, the translation of either of these terms to "New Land" is relevant for the Norwegian captain as polar explorer and for the politics of exploration, joined through Scott's *Terra Nova*. Additionally, "Mansk" refers to Murmansk, the Russian city above the Arctic Circle founded during World War I with origins as a railway terminus. Together with the terminology throughout this passage that constructs the Norwegian captain as a trespasser, "zembliance" and "mansk" cast the captain/HCE figure as an explorer of the unconquered polar regions.

Moreover, after the captain orders his suit, he will travel (roughly) from pole to pole, from "godthaab" (BL 47479-6, JJA 54: 9, FDV 169.26, FW 312.19) (the Danish name for Greenland's capital, Nuuq) down to the Cape of Good Hope. The Cape of Good *Hope*, however, becomes the Cape of Good *Howthe*, translating the southernmost point of his journey (first rounded by Bartolomeu Diaz in 1488) to Ireland: "Loritz off his Cape of Good Howthe and his trippertrice" (BL 47479-5v, JJA 54: 8, FDV 169.26–27, FW 312.18–20). The translation of this exploration to Ireland continues with references to Irish coastal locations in II.3: "skibber breezed in" (BL 47479-9, JJA 54: 15, FDV 172.6, FW 315.13–14) and "Skibberen" (BL 47479-9, JJA 54: 15, FDV 172.14, FW 315.34) (Skibbereen, in West Cork), "skerries" (BL 47479-10, JJA 54: 17, FDV 172.25, FW 316.12), and "dalkey" (BL 47479-11, JJA 54: 19, FDV 173.2, FW 317.5).

To make the connection between exploring the Arctic and exploring Ireland clearer, Joyce adds "greeny land" (BL 47478-276, JJA 52: 185) to a II.2§4 typescript during this period, combining the Nansen/polar explorer theme with an Irish setting. While these elements were being added to the first draft of II.3, Joyce was also revising the "Mamalujo" section, so such thematic echoes are not surprising.

As II.3 continues, the weather forecast section contains the addition of the VI.B.32 "Ammundsen" (VI.B.32: 14) note: "Aestmand Addmundson you, you're iron slides and so hompety domp" (FW 325.22–23). Katarzyna Bazarnik makes the point that Joyce first wrote "Estmand Edmanson" but "later changed it into a more explicit 'Aestmand Addmundson' as if he wanted the reader not to miss or misunderstand the clue" (170). Instead of "Edmanson," "Addmundson" not only more directly points to Roald Amundsen, but the "add" and "mund" also, quite literally, paint Amundsen as a figure who added to our understanding of the world ("mund" is the Anglo-Norman for "world," derived from the Latin *mundus*).

In Joyce's work, polar exploration serves as a vehicle for representing the territorial aims of imperialism and for demonstrating the radical otherness of these barren areas of the globe. Looking back to the "arctic beast" epiphany and to the "<LB Shackleton>" note from the *Ulysses* note sheets (Herring 515) suggests that the polar regions spurred Joyce's imagination at an early stage.[39] These early references, in conjunction with the appearances in *Finnegans Wake*, also pose the question of what is left to imagine when we have seen everything, and what is left to explore when we have been everywhere on earth.

Development versus Conservation

In the nineteenth century, in parallel with the Home Rule Bills of 1886 and 1893, there was significant emphasis on the need to develop Irish manufacturing and energy production in Irish nationalist politics. Even before this, the 1850s had witnessed interest in redeveloping Galway as a transatlantic port and had also brought the first plans to harness the Shannon River (later realized in the 1920s Ardnacrusha dam outside of Limerick city). Both of these plans for exploiting Ireland's watercourses resulted partially from an awareness of the factors that led to the Great Famine. In *British Democracy and Irish Nationalism, 1876–1906* Eugenio Biagini explains, "The question of taxation—and, implicitly, free trade and protection of Irish industry—was an issue on which Nationalist opposition focused. The 'revival of Irish industries' had long been one of Parnell's most cherished dreams" (125). The question that arose, again, was how Ireland could modernize while still maintaining its culture, traditions, and natural heritage. Earlier in Joyce's work, such as in his short 1912 piece on the transatlantic harbor proposed for Galway, "The Mirage of the Fisherman of Aran," or Bloom's utopian hymn to plumbing in "Ithaca," there was a distinct faith in the aesthetic possibilities of infrastructure, but as the Irish Free State matured, Joyce became cautious of the trade-offs between modernization and conservation.

While "environmentalism," as we currently understand the term, is often thought of as a recent development, reactions to plans to dam the Liffey exhibited similar anxieties over the effects of human intervention into the natural world. While the Poulaphouca Dam was not constructed until the late 1930s (1938–1940), there was a discussion about the Poulaphouca Reservoir as early as 1925, as it appears in an *Irish Times* article from 7 May of that year. Before the idea of harnessing the Shannon appeared, there were three different plans to harness power from the Liffey (as presented, for example, in a Saturday, 19 January 1924, issue of the *Freeman's Journal* [7]). One plan was put forth by the Anna Livia Development Co. and would have included the creation of six reservoirs along the Liffey. All three schemes, however, did include the creation of the Poulaphouca Reservoir. These mid-1920s proposals to electrify the Liffey were not well thought out and were met with harsh criticism by the public, and, ultimately, the concerns about the problems of damming the Liffey in this manner were too significant to proceed at that point in time. Concerns about the loss of cultural heritage, natural heritage, and economic livelihoods of those living in the impacted area dominated this debate in terms of the destruction of Leixlip Castle, the flooding of the famous "Salmon Beds" of Leixlip (which would mean the removal of valuable spawning beds for fish), the problem of how to power County Kildare, and the destruction of the jobs for fishermen who fish near the mouth of the river (*Freeman's Journal* 12 March 1924).

Consequently, an alternative solution would be needed, and the earlier plan of damming the Shannon, from the 1850s, was revisited. This time, it would become the "Siemens-Shuckert" scheme (which becomes the Ardnacrusha Dam). In this manifestation the scheme first appeared in an *Irish Times* article on 20 December 1924, in the transcript of a statement made by the Minister for Commerce. An article from 24 December 1924 displays a headline emphasizing the relationship between the hydroelectric power and Irish nationalism: "Free State Power / Continental Experts Favor the Shannon Scheme." "Ardnacrusha" itself appears in the *Wake* as "Erdnacrusha" (FW 262.15), making this hydroelectric scheme a literal "earth-crusher," and thus questioning the actions of the Irish Free State.

On FW 307.9, Joyce explicitly writes of "The Kettle-Griffith-Moynihan Scheme for a New Electricity Supply." The three figures listed were all involved with these various schemes for electrifying the Liffey—Kettle was the chief engineer, Griffith was the consulting-engineer, and Moynihan was the borough-engineer. Joyce likely kept these names intact because they also allude to Thomas Kettle, the supporter of the Third Home Rule Bill (1912), and Arthur Griffith, the founder of Sinn Féin. Hence, the references to the Shannon hydroelectric plant are closely tied to nationalist rhetoric in the *Wake*.

An example from drafts of book III also evokes this opposition between modernization and conservation. While working on early drafts of III.4 in 1925, Joyce lists seven possible disasters that could befall man (HCE): sickness, fire, flood, storm, burglary, encroachment, and explosion.[40] With the exception of encroachment, each disaster made its way into III.4 in 1925. "Encroachment" finally appears in the drafts in the late 1930s, close in temporal proximity to the drafting of the Buckley sketch. The word is added to the beginning of III.3 in the context of a proposed plan by Dublin City Council to form a marina at Dollymount called "Blue Lagoon." A 1929 opinion piece in the *Irish Times* describes the plan as "the formation of a salt-water lake at Dollymount by the enclosure of the area between the Bull and the mainland with sluice-gates."[41] The "Blue Lagoon Scheme," as it came to be known, would have been devastating for the ecology of Bull Island, as well as for the newly established (July 1931) bird sanctuary that provided protection for the many species of birds who rest or winter on the unique tidal mudflats and marshes of Bull Island. In a 1949 article titled "Violation of Sanctuary," though published a decade after the *Wake*'s publication, P. G. Kennedy explains that the "Blue Lagoon" would have "provided for a dam at both ends connecting the island with the mainland and forming a permanent lake" (43).

While the source for Joyce's information for the III.3 additions is not known, it is clear what he is referencing: "Encroachment spells erosion. Dunlin and turnstone augur us where, how and when best as to burial of carcass, fuselage dump and committal of nuisance. But, since you invocate austers for the trailing of vixens, I would like to send a cormorant around this blue lagoon" (BL 47486b-502, JJA 61: 629, FW 479.18–22). "Encroachment spells erosion" refers to the way in which the encroachment of development upon Bull Island will result in the erosion of the island's sand and soil, gradually destroying its fragile ecosystem. A project such as the Blue Lagoon would be a textbook example of how urban development leads to erosion. The "Blue Lagoon Scheme," as well as the establishment of the bird sanctuary on Bull Island, were politically motivated projects, with the former a perceived move forward for the Irish Free State, while the bird sanctuary was perceived by many as an obstruction to "progress." In this manner, Michael Viney explains how Seán Lemass opposed the Free State's Protection of Wild Birds Act of 1930, arguing: "If the economic situation becomes better, we can then afford to indulge in luxury legislation of this kind, but we must put the necessities of human beings before those of wild birds" (qtd. in Viney *Smithsonian* 307).

In Ireland, where activities such as bird-watching and hill walking had been typically associated with the English, this privileging of "progress" and financial gain over nature happened easily, and the same reckless privileging of development (often unchecked) occurred again during the Celtic Tiger. In turbulent times, the natural environment is often overlooked for more immediate and quantifiable gain. Joyce continues this section of III.3 with another reference to the grave of the Parthalonians, near Howth, and in conjunction with the "burial of carcass" and "fuselage dump," it seems the birds will lead the human to the location of burials (as the pecking hen discovers the letter). Joyce has again brought the action to the seashore, and the specific birds he references, the dunlin and the turnstone, can be found on Bull Island. They are waders with long, thin beaks designed to scavenge through detritus on the shore and plunge into the sand. The developers who wish to destroy the habitat of these birds become the carcasses that provide their food, and the technology (represented by "fuselage") employed will also be buried in the sands. The birds neglected by politicians like Lemass will have the final tweet.

Land is almost always political in *Finnegans Wake*; this is a substantial claim to make about a writer who is so often referred to as both metropolitan and apolitical. Landscape is a key factor in the formation of cultural and political identities, and struggles over land have so often resulted in violence. The environment is often exploited for political gain and national security; the presence of turf cutting in *Finnegans Wake*, along with other uses of nature (such as weirs, hydroelectric schemes, dams, public health and housing, cloud seeding, bird sanctuaries, and forestry), are part of a deep concern for the enduring interdependence of the human and nonhuman world. Such uses in the *Wake* are nearly always paired with the political ideologies from which such ideas of progress stem. Joyce's attention to the exploitation of turf, to hydroelectric schemes of the 1920s and 1930s, and to urban planning in the Free State is an extension of earlier optimism concerning the exploitation of natural resources present in *Ulysses*, such as with Leopold Bloom's hope for devising a hydroelectric scheme and his praises of water in "Ithaca." In the *Wake*, however, and especially in later drafts, this hope is balanced by a measured skepticism concerning the difficult trade-offs that occur when nature stands in the way of modernization.

4

Religion and Ecology

In *Conversations with James Joyce*, Arthur Power recalls an exchange wherein Joyce queries the relationship between religion, nature, and modernity: "The parable of the lillies [sic] of the field touches on a deeper note, but one wonders why that parable was not taken further, and why the great subconscious life of Nature was ignored, a life which without effort reaches to such great perfection. Nowadays the churches regard the worship of God through nature as a sin" (48). When Joyce says "nowadays," he is referring to our modern era and to the interpretation of Judeo-Christian belief that presupposes human supremacy over and separation from this "subconscious life of Nature." In this chapter, I examine the ways in which Joyce explores the intersections of religion and nature through Christian imagery and iconography, fertility myths, holidays and traditions, divination and prophecy, and the concept of providence.

A critical detail to note here is that Joyce does not necessarily fall into the trap of idealistically linking "primitive" cultures to an earth-focused spirituality. While this idea is certainly present in the *Wake*, Joyce seems to agree with Jacques Derrida's later critique of Claude Lévi-Strauss, arguing against the belief that any one structure of beliefs is in any way superior to another. Though many contemporary ecotheologians oppose the primitivization of any religion, it is important to mention that even some prominent ecotheologians like Thomas Berry still adhere to this idea of "native peoples" being close to a so-called "gospel of the earth" (xiii–xiv).[1] In the introduction to their collection *Deep Ecology and World Religions*, David Barnhill and Roger Gottlieb provide an overview of what religion "is" and how it functions, and provide a picture of a new "spiritual deep ecology" that applies to all religions and "challenges the (now) conventional notion that human beings are essentially different than, separate from, and superior to the natural world" (18). Though Barnhill and Gottlieb do also tend toward the idealization of Buddhism, wilderness, and Native American spirituality, all of which fall roughly into this category of primitivism, they do attempt to locate a common ground in the human relationship with the environment for all world religions. *Finnegans Wake* also links the world religions through their biocentric mythologies and presents an image of all religions growing, like language, from the earliest human responses to natural phenomena.

Divination, Providence, and Meteorology

The theme of divination that developed throughout the *Wake*'s composition closely relates to the relationship between nature and spirituality, as well as to theological anxieties that the sciences provoked during the late nineteenth and early twentieth centuries. Divination, an important topic for VI.B.33, is an alternative to the belief that the human has no control over nature, but also presents a Christianity and a spirituality wherein the human is more concerned with its relationship to nature.[2] The popularity of mysticism and of the occult during the Victorian era and the early decades of the twentieth century are indicative of a desire to return to a pre-Christian, animist order and realign the human position in the universe.

The role of prophecy in the *Wake* also derives from the thunder of Vico, for whom divination and prophecy were deemed the first languages. Robert Harrison argues that Vico "insists that the celestial auspices—signs in the sky, such as the lightning or the flight of birds—were the first of all languages, preceding even human phonetic language" (5). Throughout the *Wake*, divination and prophecy play an important role in developing the relationship between language, nature, and religion. In his study of Vico and *Finnegans Wake*, Donald Phillip Verene argues for the expanded role of providence in Joyce's use of Vico, explaining that Joyce transforms Vico's tripartite structure into a fourfold structure with the addition of "providence" (8). Verene argues that "Vico's providence" is Joyce's "golden bough," and that "providence," here, is defined as "the divine perceived or heard within history" (8). I argue that, through the symbol of the thunder, the workings of nature become a twentieth-century substitute for "providence" as the *Wake* develops. The vicissitudes of the weather become a determinant of events and their outcomes. Verene is not remotely concerned with the environment in his study, but in his discussion of providence and "ideal eternal history" he presents a useful argument for an environmentally focused reading of Joyce: "History begins in the thunderous sky, in Jove's appearance to the gentile giants. The descendants of Noah, roaming the great trackless forests of the earth for generations after the flood, without language, customs, or cities, without religion, marriage, or burial, suddenly experience the sky full of thunder and lightning. They hear and see for the first time a thing of a different order, because until now the atmosphere has not been dry enough for the occurrence of such a 'phonemanon'" (Verene 191–92, FW 258.22). In summation, what causes the thunder is the fact that the waters of the flood have finally evaporated. "Providence" is replaced by meteorology.

The occult-related sources consulted for VI.B.33 color the revisions to the II.1 pages for *transition* 22, and Glugg's attempt to guess the color "heliotrope" becomes an exercise in divination and the black arts. The dominance of the sun and flowers in II.1 influences the addition of "Meteoromancy" (BL 47477-102, JJA 51: 192, FW 228.20–21), as the "divination" of "heliotrope" includes weather patterns. The note "meteorom-" (VI.B.33: 62) is from Arthur Edward Waite's *The Occult Sciences*, deriving from a passage that reads: "Aeromancy. This is the art which, sometimes under an alternative appellation, Meteoromancy, is concerned with the prediction of things to come by the observation of atmospheric variations and the different phenomena of the air, particularly those of thunder, lightning, and fiery meteors" (123). The primary definition for "divination" in the *Oxford English Dictionary* is "the foretelling of future events or discovery of what is hidden or obscure by supernatural or magical means" ("Divination," def. 1a). Divination was once considered a sin because it was seen as an affront to God's design. However, in *Finnegans Wake*, God's design, providence, is often manifested in the weather. "Meteoromancy" and "aeromancy" become ideal arts for inquiring into the unpredictable natural world, and accordingly influence Joyce's change of "weather permitting" to "weather prophetting" (BL 47486b-451, JJA 61: 433, FW 480.7–8) in III.3. "Weather permitting" implies that the human action is dependent upon the will of nature, but "weather prophetting" gives agency to the human.

Joyce's inclusion of divination through nature was part of a larger modernist fascination with the primitive and the premodern. One of the primary texts that defined these things as an interest in the early twentieth century was James Frazer's *The Golden Bough*, which appears in the background of many *Wake* sections. For example, relating to the topic of weather, Frazer explains that in many cultures, magicians became kings because of their assumed power over nature (this idea relates back to the earliest drafts of "Roderick O'Conor"). This assumed power was largely embodied, according to Frazer, in their ability to "make rain" (85). Toward the end of the II.1 *transition* 22 revisions, Joyce adds "A fork of hazel o'er the field" (BL 47477-94, JJA 51: 178, FW 250.23), referring to hazel twigs "used by diviners or dowsers to seek water or hidden veins of metal" (Mac Coitir 74).[3]

In addition to divination through nature, the inclusion of the hazel is linked with the ideas of kingship through the introduction of Finn Mac-Cool at this same draft level. Mac Coitir, in *Irish Trees: Myths, Legends, and Folklore*, explains the many roles played by the hazel tree in Celtic lore: "The hazel, with its nourishing nuts and habit of growing near water, is a symbol of fertility, wisdom, kingship, poetic inspiration and mystical knowledge" (74). He continues, explaining that the "Salmon of Knowledge," from which "Finn Mac Cumhaill" acquired his wisdom, initially gained this wisdom because it fed off hazelnuts (75–77).[4] Mac Coitir links the hazel and Finn by explaining how "the English name hazel itself derives from an Anglo-Saxon word meaning 'authority or kingship' while the Irish word *Coll* also had the meaning of a chieftain" (79). This information provides an explanation for the addition "Hetman MacCumhal foots the funeral" (BL 47477-110, JJA 51: 169, FW 243.14), with "MacCumhal" also linking to meteoromancy with "Cumhal" implying (among other things) "cumulus."[5] Possessing power over nature (or at least being believed to have this power) was once crucial to establishing a sense of order and control over a group of people. The hazel provides a way for Joyce to unite themes of kingship, religion, and nature through the figure of Finn MacCool.

The specific link between trees and prophecy occasionally heralds the downfall of certain individuals, philosophies, or civilizations in the *Wake*. Staying at the draft level, Joyce adds an allusion to *Macbeth* in II.1 that blends prophecy and divination with religion, kingship, and cosmic order: "For a burning woould is come to dance inane" (BL 47477-101, JJA 51: 198, FW 250.16). The prophecy itself, "Fear not Till Birnam Wood / Do Come to Dunsinane" (*Macbeth* 5.5.42–43), refers to the disturbance of nature, of the "natural" order by Macbeth. Discussions of *Macbeth* have seldom focused on the peculiar fact that in the prophecy, the "wood" itself is to come to Dunsinane. Extending from earlier sections in the *Wake*, Joyce's literal interpretation of the witch's prophecy addresses historical issues of the relationship between kingship and forest. In the *Wake*, the control of the forest by the monarchy is apparent through the treatment of the Phoenix Park, the demesnes of the Anglo-Irish Big House, and the land of the tenant farmer. Such control over landscape often serves for Joyce as metonym for the imperialist project, much like the discussion of the Norwegian captain and polar exploration in the previous chapter of this study.

Robert Harrison argues that Shakespeare's use of forests is related to the deforestation of England's woodlands (well under way before the eleventh century and continuing into Tudor and Stuart times), and that this issue is a primary reason for their inclusion in *Macbeth*. He also links this deforestation to Lady Macbeth's sterility, her "barrenness" (100–102); in the case of oft-feminized Ireland, such a prophecy implies that the Irish landscape will recover from (English) deforestation.[6] Shakespeare inverts the traditional iconography of the forest: "the savagery that once traditionally belonged to the forests now lurks in the hearts of men—civic men" (Harrison 100). Harrison argues of the final act of *Macbeth*: "The soldiers of the opposing army advance toward the castle camouflaged behind boughs cut from the trees of this forest [. . .] The lawlessness that Vico associated with the 'nefarious forests' has here found haven in Macbeth's civic barbarism, but by the end of the play the moving forest of Birnam comes to symbolize the forces of natural law mobilizing its justice against the moral wasteland of Macbeth's nature" (104). The addition of this prophecy from *Macbeth*, in conjunction with the VI.B.33 divination notes and the "meteoromancy" additions, integrates ideas of nature, origins of kingship, and the genealogy of religions.

The idea of weather as providence actually appears quite early in the composition process of the *Wake*. A quotation from the early "Tristan and Isolde" sketch exhibits the alignment of the feminine and the natural, with the waves now a major focus of the narrative: "The sea looked awfully pretty at that twilight hour so lovely with such wellmannered waves. It was just too gorgeous sensation he being exactly the right man in the right place and weather conditions could not possibly have been improved on. Her role was to roll on the darkblue ocean roll that rolled on round the round roll Robert Roly rolled round. She gazed while from an altitude of 1 yard 11½ inches his deepsea peepers gazed O gazed Odazedcrazedgazed into her darkblue rolling ocean orbs" (BL 47481-94r, JJA 56: 2, FW 385–86). Isolde's relationship to the sea is both Byronic and Wagnerian, but with the emphasis on "both together in the most fashionable weather" (BL 47481-94r, JJA 56: 2, FW 396.25), a more complex role for the sea is introduced, one analogous to the narrative of the "Four Waves of Erin" in the first version of "Tristan and Isolde."[7] The weather possesses a certain agency as well as an alliance with Isolde, suggesting, in conjunction with the "Roderick O'Conor" sketch, a pagan magical belief in nature's manipulability. Conversely, this belief is also in line with the Celtic pre-Christian view of nature that, according to John Wilson Foster, is one wherein nature is "vital, autonomous" and "at times inhospitable" ("Encountering Traditions" 33). Isolde's belief that the natural world is sympathetic to her may be Joyce's setting the stage both for Isolde's edification and for the indifference of nature.

The fact that the weather "could not possibly have been improved upon" and is "most fashionable" is a traditional narrative technique, as the reader knows that this beautiful weather will eventually become stormy again (here indicating the tragedy that will befall Tristan and Isolde). In Bakhtinian terminology, such phrasing establishes the sea as a chronotope in "adventure-time," and Bakhtin points to the use of storms in such narratives as phenomena required to move the plot forward (93). The weather then is an active agent in this *Wake* sketch, assuming providential power over the fate of the two lovers. The outcome of this specific event largely depends upon unseen, unknowable forces of the environment and on the "author"—that is, on chance, on the serendipitous arrangements of time, place, character, weather, setting, and so forth (the "right man in the right place"). As Bakhtin argues, in "adventure-time" the moments "are controlled by one force—*chance*," and this "chance time" is the specific time during which irrational forces intervene in human life: "the intervention of Fate [Tyche], gods, demons, sorcerers" (94). In this context, the weather in "Tristan and Isolde" becomes a substitute for "fate" and is also a twentieth-century modernization of the Viconian "providence" that effected order, civilization, nations, and laws (Vico 87).

As briefly mentioned in chapter 1, one primary element of the letter's composition, attempted delivery, and discovery is the weather conditions around these three events. The focus on the weather develops in the first drafts of I.5. The sketch known as "The Revered Letter" (I.5§2), ALP's letter defending the character of HCE, was the first section of I.5 to be drafted (December 1923). In this section, the chronotope concept from the discussion of "Tristan and Isolde" also appears with the merging of time and weather. In the first draft, Joyce ends the letter in the same fog that pervades I.3: "Hoping the clouds will soon dissipate you will enjoy perusal and completely" (BL 47471b-33, JJA 46: 259, FDV 83.6–7, FW 453.30–31). With the composition of I.5§1, 3, and 4 shortly following I.5§2, this cloudy atmosphere remains, and the weather conditions surrounding the letter and its composition take precedence. Key examples of this emphasis include the fact that the letter may have been written while being "rained upon or blown around, by a regular racer from the soil" (BL 47471b-17, JJA 46: 5, FDV 84.25–26, FW 108.5), as well as an addition of another "cloudy" to the line, "Has anyone, it might be with profit some ^cloudy^ evening be quietly suggested, ever looked sufficiently longly upon a stamped addressed envelope?" (BL 47471b-29v, JJA 46: 232, FDV 85.17–19, FW 109.1–8). Developing from the "cloud" of witnesses obfuscating the story of HCE (I.3) and the "winds" carrying Hosty's ballad (I.2),[8] the letter's composition during meteorological recalcitrance is appropriate.

On the second draft of I.5§2, Joyce adds one more "cloud" addition, "we think of him looking at us yet as if to pass away in a cloud," as well as another addition linking writing with weather: "once you are balladproof you are unpercable to haily, icy and missilethroes" (BL 47471b-37, JJA 46: 263, FDV 281.30–31, FW.615.22; FDV 282.28–29, FW 616.31–33). Here, ballads and treacherous weather are equally harmful. In summary, clouds are invoked as a universal way of confounding visibility and understanding, and the other weather elements (rain, hail, ice, wind) create an unstable atmosphere that conceals the validity of any information surrounding the letter. In addition to these implications for Joyce's use of weather, the coldness throughout the passages relating to the letter's composition, transmission, transportation, burial, and discovery may refer to the coldness of the universe before creation, before the sun. This astral view provides a necessary macrocosm for the everyday weather patterns Joyce uses in this section of the *Wake*.

Toward the end of the second draft of I.5§4, one reads of the many holes in the letter that were actually "provoked by the fork of a professor at the breakfast table, professionally piqued to introduce time into a plane surface by making holes in space" (BL 47471b-48v, JJA 46: 312, FDV 89.11–14, FW 124.8–12).[9] On the 1924 fair copy, Joyce changes "time" to "tempo," which is "time" in Italian, but also "weather" (this is also the same in Spanish, *tiempo*, and in French, *temps*, as the Latin is *tempus*). Joyce himself notes this strange correlation in a notebook dating from this period: *"temps* = weather" (VI.B.5: 127). In French, the definition of *temps* in the meteorological sense stresses that it is the "État *de l'atmosphère a un moment donné,*" the atmospheric condition at a particular moment.[10] This "tempo" line is located toward the end of the draft and draws the sketch together, as "time" is placed here to balance "space," and "temps" as "weather" helps to reaffirm the importance of the atmospheric conditions in which the letter was delivered and discovered. The play on "time" and "weather" also serves to link the unpredictability of the weather with the ambiguity of historical narratives, the watery history of Mamalujo, and Viconian providence.[11]

Weather again takes a starring role in drafts of III.4 that come later in the *Wake*'s composition. "They're coming back, down the scales, the way they went up, sweetheartedly, hot and cold and electrickery with autumn lounge and porter free" (BL 47482a-15, JJA 60: 27, FDV 260.33–261.2, FW 579.1–7) introduces the various cycles present in this draft of III.4. As the storm approaches, the atmospheric pressure is dropping (thunderstorms can occur when a mass of cold air meets a mass of hot air), and "electrickery" is the lightning, an electrical discharge between regions of opposite charge (either in the same cloud, between two different clouds, or between a cloud and the ground) (Allaby 98). The storm is coming, "in spite of all that science could boot & art could skill" (BL 47482a-15v, JJA 60: 28, FDV 261.1–2, FW 579.7–8)—that is, our advancements in knowledge cannot overcome the weather, cannot overcome the larger forces that lead to our own demise. The storm moves closer; "Close the gate" is immediately changed to "Bolt the gate" (BL 47482a-15v, JJA 60: 28, FDV 261.2, FW 579.8) (evoking thunderbolts, which are also part of the Finn MacCool/Giant's Causeway story), and all that is left to turn to is religion, the first language: "Practise preaching. By faith alone" (BL 47482a-15v, JJA 60: 28, FDV 261.4, FW 579.22–23). Then comes the "(l)ovely weather," the calm eye of the storm that precedes the destruction of Sodom and Gomorrah: "Gomorrn. Solong" (BL 47482a-15v, JJA 60: 28, FDV 261.4–5,

FW 579.23–24).¹² On the next draft, "Lovely weather" is changed to "season's weather" (BL 47482a-30, JJA 60: 217, FW 579.23–24), presaging the *ricorso*.

Then, there is a quick recap of a life in Viconian terms:

> For they met & mated & wed & buckled & got & gave & reared & raised & planned & plundered & pawned their souls & pillaged our bodies & fought & feigned & strained relations & broke the bank & hated the sight of one another & bequeathed their ills & turned their coats & belied their origins & never learned the first day's lesson & tried to mingle & managed to save & feathered some nests & fouled their own & escaped from drowning by the skin of their teeth & were responsible for congested districts & took to drink & published their privates & tramped over the world to the court of pye poudre & were cuffed by their customers & bit the dust & went as they came and yet they come back, lamp in hand & shirt on high, peekabooing. (BL 47482a-16, 18, JJA 60: 31, 33, FDV 261.6–15, FW 579.27–580.12)

HCE and ALP assume, in addition to the roles of husband and wife, father and mother, the roles of invaders, soldiers, traitors, civic developers,¹³ travelers, and businessmen. HCE and ALP, like all couples, have been through a lot, but their relationship endured. Just before this section of III.4, the wind begins to come up outside, preparing for the *ricorso*, for the great storm and the return to calm. The historian, Mark, ignores this procession of events (and of time): "Stop! Did he stir? No, he's fast. So he is. Come to bed. It's merely the wind on the road outside to wake all shivering shanks from snoring" (BL 47482a-4, JJA 60: 6, FDV 260.12–13, FW 578.1–2). The historian ignores the warnings provided by history. Thus, the civilization present at this point in the *Wake*, represented by the family of HCE, will fall victim to the same threats that have toppled all earlier civilizations, but will also proceed with the same hope. Much happens to individuals and to civilizations in their short lives, and in the end, they do return to where they began.

Throughout the *Wake*, with the female as the watery element and the male as the land element, the unification of the two (often through storms and floods) provides renewal and new life through the fertility of the land. Such associations of the feminine with weather and the change of the seasons have been present throughout the *Wake* as early as the first drafts of "Tristan and Isolde," but in the final draft levels of the "Norwegian

Captain" sketch, for example, themes of exploration, colonization, and conquest are balanced by the presence of the uncontrollable forces of nature embodied in the feminized unpredictability of the weather. As the tale of the Norwegian captain continues in HCE's pub, it is continually interrupted by radio announcements including advertisements, news, and a weather forecast. The weather obviously affects sailors and dictates their trajectories, and the successes (and failures) of the polar explorers referenced in II.2§3 were also almost direct results of changes in the weather. Additionally, weather forecasts are modern divinations, or as such forecasts are presented elsewhere in the *Wake*, "meteoromancy" (FW 228.21–22), and thus belong to the second Viconian stage of auspices and marriage (appropriate, then, for the Norwegian captain's story of marriage).

In addition to the role weather plays in the fate of the Norwegian captain and his bride-to-be, the weather forecast is important to these late drafts of the *Wake* as it both sets the stage for the end of the book and aids in resolving the role weather has played throughout the *Wake*. The importance of the weather forecast to these late drafts of *Finnegans Wake* can clearly be observed by the numerous pointed weather additions and by the contexts of these additions. The weather, as well as being a symbol of renewal and rebirth (a theme obviously important to the "end" of the *Wake*), is also a natural phenomenon not yet entirely under human control (in VI.B.47, notes on "cloud seeding" do appear [VI.B.47: 9]). Weather forecasts are a way for Joyce to connect twentieth-century science and technology with ancient religious traditions concerning the weather and its prediction.

Joyce incorporates "orege forment" (BL 47476a-77v, JJA 49: 174, FW 132.9) and "isobaric patties" (BL 47476a-77v, JJA 49: 174, FW 133.4) to III.3 in 1937 (in addition to the concurrent weather forecast of II.2§3), referring to a storm (*orage*, French for storm) fomenting and to isobars (lines representing atmospheric pressure that are used to predict weather patterns). These two additions introduce weather forecasting into III.3, serving to both foreshadow III.4 and IV and expand the weather forecast of II.3, of which the first draft reads: "Welter focuseed. The allexpected depression is over Schiumdinebbia, harolded by faugh sicknells and umwalloped in an unusable suite of clouds, having filthered trough the same gorgers' kennel on its wage wealthwards and incursioned a sotten retch of low pleasure, missed in some ports but with lucal drizzles, the outlook for tomarry (Streamstress Mandig) beamed brider, his ability good" (BL 47479-18v, 19, 20, JJA 54: 34, 35, 37, FDV 176.33–39, FW 324.24–34).

To emphasize the relationship between weather forecasting and prophecy, Joyce later adds a reference to Columba with "Colunnfiller predicted" (FW 324.26), alluding to the saint's spurious prophecies.

To emphasize the Scandinavian provenance of the captain, Joyce also adds in another reference to *The Master Builder* after "Schiumdinebbia" with "a bygger muster" (FW 324.27–28), where *byge* is Danish for "shower." The report tells the patrons in HCE's pub that a band of low pressure is moving in from the east ("depression" / "a sotten retch of low pleasure") and that there is considerable fog ("faugh sicknells"), cloud, and drizzle. This ridge of low pressure is coming in from the east, from Scandinavia and Saint George's Channel ("Schiumdinebba" and "same gorgers' kennel," respectively). Joyce adds to the typescript of the weather report another example of Scandinavian seafaring: "Wind from the nordth. Warmer towards muffinbell, Lull" (BL 47479-35v, JJA 54: 80, FW 324.25). *Nord* is "north" in Scandinavian, and the merging of "north" and "nord" into "nordth" again comments on the influence of Scandinavian languages upon the English language, as well as invokes the provenance of the Vikings. The "faugh sicknells" are fog signals, navigational warnings for ships during periods of low visibility. In conjunction with the "incursion" of this low-pressure trough, the weather itself becomes another of Ireland's marauders (but also one of its protectors).

When Joyce returns to this section of III.4 in 1936, he expands the presence of the weather, incorporating two additions to the description of the Phoenix Park that continue to develop the link between weather, land, marriage, and colonization: "blue and buff of Beaufort" (BL 47486a-121v, JJA 61: 98, FW 567.25) and "from fury of the gales" (BL 47486a-179, JJA 61: 252, FW 567.14). Blue and buff are the colors of the Whig party in the United States (blue and orange for the United Kingdom Whigs), and blue and white were the colors of the Duke of Beaufort (whose name is associated with the Badminton Hunt, also known as the Beaufort Hunt, a famous event that dates back to the seventeenth century [Dale 214]). During George IV's visit to Dublin Castle (during his 1821 visit), those on horseback were made to wear the Beaufort colors. The "from fury of the gales" is added to a line describing why the queen remained in England during George IV's visit (the first attempt by the royal party to cross the Irish Sea was thwarted by high winds), and Joyce translates this to "fury of the gales," also implying fury of the *Gaels*—that is, the visit is unwanted by

Ireland. The wind itself is colluding with the Irish to repel the royal party, playing a providential role in determining the course of Irish history.[14]

The weather plays a curious role all throughout the *Wake*, including when Joyce is working on the final stages of his text. On the first galley proofs for book IV, after the first main paragraph, Joyce adds the line: "A hand from the cloud emerges, holding a chart expanded" (BL 47488-199v, JJA 63: 286, FW 593.13). Then after "Advert" (FW 599.24), he adds an entire "cloudy" passage, deriving largely from notes in VI.B.47. The sources for VI.B.47 are highly directed, with Joyce knowing precisely what information he required. The notes include information from a history of Howth, notes relating to the rain cycle, and notes "from some article or brochure on meteorology" that "include a classification of clouds, mention of sun spots, presumably for their influence on the weather, a definition of 'fog' as a 'cloud in which we are,' as well as the mention of stiger guns; cannons that were used in Italy to protect vineyards from hailstones" (VI.B.47: 9). Many of these notes are incorporated into the revision of the "Saint Kevin" sketch and serve to unite the sections of book IV.

Most of the last additions to the galley proofs can be found in VI.B.47, with "Cirrhonimbus / Cirrhocumuls," "pallium [Cirrus]," and "Cirrhonimbus / storms / cumulonimbus" on VI.B.47: 60, and the influence of earlier themes reverberating with "my cold father" (VI.B.47: 40), "ponds secret water poplar" (VI.B.47: 62), "cold front" (VI.B.47: 63), "fog = cloud in which we are" (VI.B.47: 63), "⊞ highly charged with electrons" (VI.B.47: 79), "fog = W round dust" (VI.B.47: 79), "⊏ writes sizes of the 2 Irelands" (VI.B.47: 91), and "sudden dew" (VI.B.47: 91), among others. These notes are translated into the following passage:

> Where. Cumulonubulocirrhonimbant heaven electing, the dart of desire has gored the heart of secret waters and the poplarest wood in the entire district is being grown at present, eminently adapted for the requirements of panicstricken humanity and, between all the goings up and comings down and the fog of the cloud in which we toil and the cloud of the fog under which we labour, bomb the thing's to be domb about it so that, beyond indicating the locality, it is felt that one cannot with advantage add a very great deal to the aforegoing by what, such as it is to be, follows, just mentioning however that the old man of the sea and the old woman of the sky if they don't say

nothings about it they don't tell us lie, the ghist of the phantomime, from cannibal king to the property horse, being slumply and slopely to remind us how, in this drury world of ours, Father Times and Mother Spacies boil their kettle with their crutch. Which every lad and lass in the lane knows. Hence. (BL 47488-203v, JJA 63: 292, FW 599.25–600.4)

The clouds are present at each stage of humanity, through all the ups and downs and the toil. Despite the fact that all will always remain in a "fog" (i.e., the big questions will never be known), all still continues as if this fog will someday permanently clear. However, the cloud always returns, just in a different shape: cumulus, cumulonimbus, cirrocumulus, or nimbostratus. Likewise, from "cannibal king" to "property horse," from cannibalistic tribes to individual private property owners, all people are the same, too, just in different forms.

Like the boiling of the kettle for the preparation of the tea in I.5 that evokes all four basic elements, here the boiling of the kettle is a microcosm for the hydrologic cycle, the changing of state from liquid to gas. Finally, the economy Joyce presents here is indeed very "drury," as "Father Times and Mother Spacies boil their kettle with their crutch." In addition to evoking the life of Dublin's less fortunate (those with whom Joyce, who grew up largely in Dublin's north inner city, would be well acquainted), the designation of the parents as time and space, in conjunction with the process of boiling water for tea, suggests that the world and its phenomena are being regulated by the decrepit couple of time and space.

Agri/culture: Fertility Myths and Civilization

Continuing with the importance of weather, but returning to the discussion of *The Golden Bough*, I argue in this section that a significant portion of the *Wake*'s engagement with the relationship between nature and spirituality is explored through fertility myths. Fertility rites also connect nature with the female body and provide a basis for the organizational structures of societies. In *Staying Alive: Women, Ecology, and Development*, Vandana Shiva argues that ideas of "development" have brought extraordinary damage to both women and to nature, and that "new images of mastery and domination functioned as cultural sanctions for the denudation of nature" (28). Throughout the final years of work on *Finnegans Wake*, Joyce continues to engage fertility myths by linking them to issues of agriculture's historical importance to civilization and to the political alignment of domesticated land, crops, and animals with the domestication of the female body. The *Wake*'s presentation of ALP as a Mother Earth figure is sometimes at odds with the text's fascination with the human exploitation of the environment, but farmland and agriculture exist in the *Wake* at the crossroads of this tension to articulate the intersection of culture and nature.

The first fertility myth to discuss regarding the *Wake* is the story of Cain and Abel. Joyce famously explained to Weaver in a 16 January 1924 letter that chapter I.7 would be a "description of Shem-Ham-Cain-Esau etc and his penmanship" (LI 208). This characterization indicts writing (specifically, Shem's writing of ALP's letter) as a betrayal, a crime, a violation of nature and of God's will. In her essay on the composition of I.7, Ingeborg Landuyt points to the line "the arbutus fruitflowerleaf of the cainapple" (FW 121.10–11) as being "a clear precursor of this chapter [I.7]" (HJW 143), focusing primarily on the reference to Cain. Landuyt is right to focus on the figure of Cain, but a more comprehensive examination of the cross-cultural transformations and implications of this myth, as well as an explication of the plants Joyce chooses, further illuminate Joyce's equation of Shem and Cain.

According to comparative religion scholar Samuel H. Hooke, the story of Cain and Abel was cribbed from the traditions of other cultures and grafted onto the Adam and Eve story (122). Hooke provides evidence that the biblical story of Cain and Abel actually stems from three separate stories. The first of these three stories "reflects the ancient feud between the desert and the sown land, between the settled tiller of the soil and the pastoral nomad" (123), and is based upon the Sumerian myth of Dumuzi and Enkimdu. The second story relates to the ritual of sacrifice (and to recurring themes in *From Ritual to Romance*): "The rejection of the agriculturist's offering implies a failure of crops, and this calls for some sort of expiatory ritual" (Hooke 123). Hooke continues, explaining that in the Septuagint, the killing takes place *in* the field, in "the tilled soil, whose infertility has brought about the situation, that the slaying of the shepherd takes place" and thus, that the killing was in fact a "ritual killing intended to fertilize the soil by drenching it with the blood of the victim" (124).[15] Hooke highlights the theme of ritual killing followed by flight as present in all three of these stories, and this theme relates directly to Shem's actions and his self-imposed exile.

Arguing that the "original form" of the Cain and Abel story "was probably a ritual myth depicting a ritual slaying intended to secure fertility for the crops," Hooke concludes that "the slaying was followed by the flight of the slayer, who was protected by a mark which indicated his sacred character" (126). With this complex textual history of the Cain and Abel tale in mind, the emphasis on the cold weather in I.5 and I.7, with their focus on the letter and on Shem, may also refer to the infertility of the ground. In the contexts of both the genealogy of the Cain and Abel story and the role of Shem in the *Wake*, the "ritual killing" is aligned with the act of writing. Both become sacrificial acts that return fertility to the land, ensuring the continuity of the species (though also, paradoxically, introducing greater evil into the world). The myth of Cain and Abel/Dumuzi and Enkimdu also echoes the perpetual existence of violence in nature in the *Wake*, as discussed regarding the Phoenix Park in chapter 3 of this study.

The themes of infertility and sacrifice, as well as the theme of flight (also cited by Derrida in his reading of Cain and Abel in *The Animal That Therefore I Am* [42–44]), infuse much of the Shem chapter and color his attempted "exile." In addition, the specific plants Joyce implicates with Shem/Cain, the "cainapple," or "arbutus," and also the crabapple, are carefully chosen to develop the theme at hand. After an initial physical description of Shem in I.7, Joyce writes: "in the very dawn of history even Shem himself seeing himself, when playing with words in his garden nursery asked of his brethren & sisters the first riddle of the universe: When is a man not a man?: offering a prize of a crabapple to the winner" (BL 47471b-54, JJA 47: 339, FDV 113.11–14, FW 170.3–8). In *The Idea of Wilderness*, Max Oelschlaeger also argues that the sacrificial aspects of the Cain and Abel story "are characteristic of ancient fertility religions" (51), an inspiration behind Joyce's choice of the crabapple. The prize of a crabapple, specifically, is tied to the apple's ability to self-pollinate and to help with cross-pollination of other plants because of its large production of flowers. Like a tree, Shem is raised in a "garden nursery," which is also a version of Eden, and he is currently unable to pollinate on his own. Thus, the prize of a crabapple would solve Shem's inability to "pollinate." The "cainapple" or "arbutus" is discussed in more depth in chapter 1 (the arbutus tree is also known as the "Strawberry Tree" but sometimes also as the "cainapple"; its Irish name is *Caithne*, and its Latin name is *Arbutus unedo*). Furthermore, *unedo* translates to "I eat only one," developing Shem's self-consumption and production in I.7 (Jahn 80). And finally, the colloquial name "cainapple," according to Alice Coats, derives from the belief that the berries of the tree were drops of Cain's blood (Coats 19). The link of "crabapple" to "cainapple" directly connects these choices of tree to the Cain and Abel myth and the infertility of the land.

The shift to agriculture is widely regarded as a key development in the history of civilization, so it is not surprising that fertility rites would take a front seat in terms of governing festivals, traditions, structures, and faith of any given culture. In the introduction to *New Science*, Vico explains the development of cities from the countryside through recourse to the image of the plough on the book's frontispiece. The moldboard, the curved blade of the plough, is *urbs* in Latin, and in the frontispiece: "The mouldboard is hidden to signify that the first cities, *urbes*, which were all founded in cultivated fields, arose only after families had spent many years withdrawn and hidden deep amid the sacred terrors of their hallowed groves" (Vico 11). This statement clearly connects to the change from nomadic shepherding to settled agriculture and continues to foreground the importance of natural resources in the growth of civilizations.

Sections of I.3 turn to the domestication of animals and crops as a hallmark of civilization through the stories of Cain and Abel and Jacob and Esau. Earlier, in VI.B.5, Joyce recorded, "⊏ seedsman" (VI.B.5: 7), which, tagged with the Shem sigla, relates to the discussion of the Cain and Abel story. Shem/Cain's relationship to agriculture further appears with the line, "[T]he worryld had been uncained. Then, while it is odrous comparisoning to the sprangflowers of his burstday which was a viridable goddinpotty for the reinworms" (BL 47476a-175v, JJA 49: 372, FW 59.10–13). The switch to arable land with its bursting flower gardens is a "veritable garden party." Worms come out when it rains, and the "reinworms," playing on both "rain" and "reign," relate to the above discussion of kingship and the control of nature. In I.3, there is also "Kane" with his "fender" (which also appears in III.3, discussed above) or Cain with his spade, digging a "patch" on the previously "blank face" of the land: "Patch's blank face beyond recognition, pointedly asked with gaeilish gall wodkar blizzard's business Thornton had with that Kane's fender" (FW 63.5–7).[16] Abel and Esau, the "Edomite" (FW 72.11), were the old order, the nomadic shepherds and hunters, and their supplanting by their brothers (Cain and Jacob) is representative of the dominance of the new order of tillage and agriculture and its settled, stationary life.

In another illustration of the themes of Weston's *From Ritual to Ro-*

mance and the focus on arable land, HCE is linked with King Arthur at the end of I.3. He is "Azava Arthur," who "skall wake from earthsleep, haught crested elmer, in his valle of briers" (FW 73.36–74.2). According to legend, King Arthur will awaken and return to earth when his "mighty horn" (FW 74.4) is blown, and the "haught crested elmer" also returns HCE to his earlier role as a tree being uprooted from the earth. Joyce's inclusion of "O Truiga, when thy green woods went dry" (FW 74.9–10)—alluding to "taiga" (the "swampy coniferous forest area of Siberia; also, the zone of temperate coniferous forest stretching across Europe and North America")[17]—presents even more infertile land. As HCE falls asleep, the land becomes increasingly less abundant, and as the rain stops, the land is temporarily laid waste.

In revisions of I.1, the references to the Egyptian *Book of the Dead* are also connected to the land's fertility and its role in a civilization's prosperity. A note in VI.B.32, "wheat = Osiris" (168), comments on the body of Osiris, the Wheat-god, being eaten "daily" by the "beatified" (Budge 31). This reference also ties in with the *Wake*'s evocations of religion as deriving from responses to the environmental conditions that dictate survival. The line to which this note is added becomes: "So may the priest of seven worms and scalding tayboil, Papa Vestray, come never anear you as your hair grower wheater beside the Liffey that's in heaven! Hep, hep, hurrah there!" (BL 47475-269, JJA 44: 285, FW 26.09). This line incorporates "Hep," the Egyptian celestial river,[18] and also ALP's advancing age (the hair growing "wheater," or whiter). ALP's "aging," as the Liffey, is the progression through the water cycle, with the rain bringing more "wheat" as her hairs grow "whiter." The "new life" of the Liffey comes as rain from "heaven" (from clouds). Rain brings new life, and decay brings new life: the worms are necessary for decomposition, and decomposition provides the minerals that aid in the growth of new crops.

Composed in close temporal proximity to I.7, 1924 drafts of III.3 continue to work with fertility myths and the choice of specific plants to ground these myths in history and tradition. The section under examination here is that of Mamalujo interrogating Yawn about the who, what, where, when, why (and specific weather conditions) of the event in question. On the second draft of the "Upfellbown" passage from this section (BL 47482b-85v, JJA 58: 46, FDV 240.22–241.7, FW 503.8–505.29),[19] Joyce defines the tree as a "maypole" (BL 47482b-97, JJA 58:65, FW 503.33–34) tree specifically ("rub / maypole" [VI.B.14: 232]). Combined with the bonfires that also appear in this section of III.3, this reference carries the implication of May Day celebrations, developing links between the origins and significances of festivals and how they derived from responses to the physical environment. The maypole addition implies that the bonfires mentioned earlier in the passage ("—There were fires on every bald hill in holy Ireland that night? / —You may say they were. Bonfires, no less! [. . .]") (BL 47482b-84v, 85, JJA 58: 44–45, FW 501.34–502.12) are the bonfires of 12 July, the day of the Battle of the Boyne, and those of the 1 May Bealtaine festival.

The festival of "Beltane" ("May Day") is described in *The Golden Bough* as that "which ushered in summer" (Frazer 622), which means that the chilly weather may also be there to establish winter before signaling the change to spring and summer:[20]

—Was there rain by any chance?
—Plenty.
—There was a fall of snow too, was there?
—The nicest of all.
—Did it not blow some wind as well?
—Out of all jokes it did. (BL 47482b-84v, 85, JJA 58: 44–45, FW 501.34–502.12)

Finn Fordham also discusses the addition of the maypole, but from a slightly different angle: "It was a 'maypole,' emphasising again the fact of it being a human construct, not a purely organic form independent of humans, but a tool for social ritual, and for organising social space. The representatively natural form has become a folkloric focus. But as much a maypole—a static and non-growing form—it also takes the human—or superhuman—form of a giant" (HJS 1, chart 3).[21] In his article comparing textual growth and arboreal growth, Fordham argues that Joyce "plays off the extent to which the tree is a human construction: literally planted and symbolically structured" (HJS 1, chart 2). This point enters into the broader debate between post-structuralism and ecocriticism, but carefully separates the two realms; the tree does physically exist and is something with which humans have always physically engaged, but the attribution of symbolic meanings to such an object is also unavoidable and part of its total existence.

Joyce may not exclusively be focusing on the tree in and of itself but rather may be using the tree to explore the way in which objects have been appropriated by human culture. Charles Darwin wrote, "The affinities of all the beings of the same class have sometimes been represented by a great tree" (146), uniting the material tree with the symbolic tree in the *Origin of Species*. The material tree has provided models for alphabets, for artistic creation, for explaining familial relationships, for explaining the introduction of evil into the world, for explaining the structure of the cosmos; but underneath all of this, the tree is an indispensable part of human life. The symbolic weight attached to the tree cannot undermine its primary importance as a giver of life through its provisions of food and its production of oxygen as a by-product of photosynthesis, and throughout the *Wake*, trees come to represent the struggle and symbiosis between the material and the ideal.

Thus, Fordham is correct that Joyce is using the maypole as a human construct, but his explanation is limiting. In conjunction with the other religious rituals, ceremonies, and festivals at this draft level all related to environmental factors (e.g., seasonal changes, agricultural productivity, and lunar cycles), it appears Joyce is just as concerned with presenting cultural traditions with clear origins in the observations of nature and dependence on its patterns as he is with the presentation of metaphors built from nature.

Joyce's addition of "mistletoe" (BL 47482b-97v, JJA 58: 66, FW 504.35) to an alternate version of the second draft of III.3 also illustrates the above argument, closely linking specific flora to specific rituals and traditions. In VI.B.14, Joyce recorded "Pliny, mistletoe" (VI.B.14: 29), "gui de l'an neuf" (VI.B.14: 29), "mistletoe. golden sickle / 6th moon. powdered" (VI.B.14: 29), and "gui caught in white apron / golden sickle" (VI.B.14: 47, with "gui" being the French word for "mistletoe").[22] The first note derives from the second volume of Pliny's *Natural History*, from a passage discussing how the druids held "nothing more sacred than mistletoe and the tree on which it grows, provided that it is an oak. Groves of oak are chosen even for their own sake, and the magicians perform no rites without using the foliage of these trees" (qtd. in VI.B.14 62). The mistletoe connects the "Upfellbown" passage of III.3 to the Nordic and Celtic May Day traditions and, especially in light of the Druidic context offered by Pliny, to customs surrounding Celtic kingship. Furthermore, Odin's son Balder—the Nordic god associated with light, spring, and renewal—was killed by mistletoe (Frazer 608). *The Golden Bough* gives significant attention to this event, depicting it as the first event in the progression leading toward Ragnarök.

The power of the mistletoe, Frazer believes, derives from its position on the oak, "growing not from the ground but from the trunk or branches of the tree" (701). Thus, the mistletoe's location is an analogue to the belief that kings inhabited a spiritual plane between the earth and the heavens. Pliny also explains that, in Druidic tradition, the mistletoe is revered because "anything growing on oak trees they think to have been sent down from heaven" (qtd. in VI.B.14 62). Frazer continues by syllogistically demonstrating how "the priest of the Arician grove—the King of the Wood—personified the tree on which grew the Golden Bough" (703), linking mistletoe, kingship, trees, and May Day.[23] The varied meanings of the mistletoe are culturally determined, but they do originate from specific properties and characteristics of the plant itself. Therefore, the mistletoe could not be simply interchangeable with another plant.

Two other inclusions, in addition to the existing "triliteral roots and his acorns" (alluding to the Yggdrasil),[24] give the tree life and the dynamism associated with Shem in the tree/stone motif: "pinecorns" (BL 47484a-45, JJA 59: 185, FW 505.5) and "resin" (BL 47484a-45, JJA 59: 185, FW 505.1). "Pinecorns" is a combination of both "pinecones" and "acorns," two structures that play vital roles in the continuity of their associated species. Pinecones are structures that contain the reproductive systems of coniferous plants and that store seeds and pollen, while acorns are the nuts that store the seed for an oak (Masueth 731–35). Resin is a secretion primarily of such coniferous plants that, like the formation of the cone itself, also protects the plant and its seeds to help ensure their continuity (Masueth 731–32). The incorporation of these three botanical structures serves to counter arguments that the tree is present in the *Wake* merely for its symbolic weight, and is in line with the larger themes of fertility, rebirth, and renewal associated with May Day and the grounding of religious tradition in specifics of the environment.

W. J. Perry's *The Origin of Magic and Religion* (a source for VI.B.14) considers the relationship between the development of art and religion and the sources of food for a particular society. Perry explains that "rites connected with the fertility of cattle and with the procuring of crops" (3) have been the two foundational elements of almost all systems of belief. With regard to the stage of the *Wake* wherein Perry was read, the most influential notes taken from his text relate to fertility rites and ALP, as much of the first and second chapters of Perry's book concern the ancient concept of the "Great Mother." The relationship between fertility, civilization, nature, and the female already present in the *Wake* is reinforced by material found in Perry.

In the beginning of his second chapter, Perry continues to foreground the importance of humanity's relationship to nature and to the modes of food acquisition in the development of religion, arguing that "gods do not seem to make their entry on the scene until the step had been taken from the food-gathering to the food-producing stage of culture" (25). The context of this note from Perry reads: "The early civilizations of Egypt, Elam and Sumer were founded on irrigation, certainly the earliest form of food production known to man, for tillage of the soil for dry cultivation was later than irrigation in all parts of the world" (25–26). Perry goes on to explain how the Nile naturally undergoes cycles of irrigation, a natural occurrence that happens nowhere else on earth (26). Consequently, Joyce's recording of "⊏ irrigation" (VI.B.14: 138) hints at an interest in how Egyptians and other cultures in the region imitated the cycles of the Nile to ensure a stable food supply. Deane, Ferrer, and Lernout point out that the "⊏ irrigation" note is connected by a line to a note below that reads "Tammuz" (VI.B.14: 138), whom Perry explains to be "the son of the Great Mother" (29) in Sumerian mythology. Joyce connected the two notes because of Perry's account that the figure of the Mother Goddess was usually accompanied by her "son and lover," who was "connected intimately with irrigation, and with agriculture and vegetation generally" (28).[25] Shem's "earthy" qualities of I.7 are given more substance with VI.B.14's characterization of Shem as a Tammuz-like figure and as an initiator of irrigation.

The relationship between agriculture and the emergence of accompanying gods and goddesses extends again to the relationship between agriculture and kingship, which Perry explains as leading to the relationship between the practice of maintaining a calendar and the authority of the king to determine this calendar. The note "lunar calendar (flood)" (VI.B.14: 138) continues Joyce's interest in the human "creation" and management of time, a point also made by Deane, Ferrer, and Lernout in their discussion of the hagiographical note clusters in VI.B.14 (8).[26] The notes "drowned and revived" (VI.B.14: 138) and "1st ruling family" (VI.B.14: 138) surrounding the "lunar calendar (flood)" note also relate kingship to nature through Osiris-like cycles of flooding, drowning, and revival. Tammuz (associated with Shem in VI.B.14) had been associated with a "prehistoric king" (29), and his participation in myths of agricultural decay and bounty (a myth also discussed at length in Frazer) is the basis for the note "drowned and revived."[27]

Themes of fertility and renewal are often embodied in the *Wake* through the family structure. In the "Norwegian Captain" sketch, the relationship between the land and its cultivator is illustrated through marriage. The first draft of section II.3§2 (mid-1936) tells of how marriage tamed the wandering seafarer, a tale akin to how domestication of animals and crops tamed the wandering shepherds. This first draft of the sketch contains a lengthy passage concerning such issues in assorted contexts. The references to channeled Dublin rivers, to the Nile, and to the geographical entities of suburb and demesne expand marital domestication and relate it to the nature/culture duality:

> Such was the act of goth stepping the tolk of Doolin, testies Touchwood and Shenstone (incooperated), the chal and his chi, their roammerin over. Kaemper Daemper to Jetty de Waarfft, him that grand old man to be that haard of hearing and her the petty tondur with the fix in her changeable eye. Me lord, me lad, he goes with blowbierd. Then was a little incident that hoppy go lumpy Junuary morn, at Inverliffey (matingpoint of the engagement) synnbildising graters and things O nilly not all, here's the first Cataraction! As if even she cared an assuan damn about her harpoons sticking all out of him between the phenian and his psourdonome. Sdrats ye, Gus Paudheen! Kenny's thaw to ye, Dinny Oozle. While the cit was leaking asphalt like a suburbiaurealis. In his rure was tucking to him like old booths, booths, booths, booths. (BL 47479-185, JJA 54: 303, FDV 179.1–13, FW 332.10–35)

The "grand old man" is Prime Minister William Gladstone, relating this passage to Home Rule (also supported by the "Inverliffey," using a version of the Latin name for Ireland, *Hibernia*). It also refers to HCE's characterization as the "Grant, old gartener" ("Grand Old Gardener") of II.3§3, cultivator of the land (BL 47479-206, JJA 54: 338, FW 336.21).

The "first cataraction" is the first cataract of the Nile, but in Christopher Moriarty's guide to the Dublin and Wicklow area, he also describes the spot in the Dodder River past the Beaver Row footbridge as the "First Cataract," which "is caused by an outcrop of limestone and where a millstream once began" (16). The "assuan damn" refers to the Nile's Aswan Dam (built at the First Cataract), and "*nil*" (as in "O nilly") is French for

Nile, further suggested by the "O" preceding it, which usually refers to ALP. "Inverliffey" is also the Irish "*Inbhear Life*," the Liffey estuary. "Tondur" seems to be a combination of two of the peaks located at the Liffey's source: Tonduff and Kippure.[28] The "Inverliffey" is the "matingpoint of the engagement," and thus, the "domestication" of the Norwegian captain is portrayed as the act of entering Dublin Bay. The greater domestication of people (the birth of civilizations, the move away from a nomadic lifestyle, represented here by the captain's continual journeys) is represented through the compounding of the references to the Liffey and to the Nile.

The "cit leaking into suburbiaurealis" is the city slowly engulfing the countryside ("his rure"); it is Chapelizod, the transition point between Dublin city proper and the country. "Suburbiaurealis" also contains the Latin *Rus in Urbe*, and in 1937, on a fair copy of II.3§6, Joyce adds "of a townside up the countrylife" (BL 47480-164v, JJA 55: 288, FW 356.34) to further suggest this image. The transition from the pastoral to the agricultural led to the first established communities, which led gradually to the development of cities, which led to the establishment of the suburb.

When preparing book III for the printer of *Finnegans Wake*, Joyce returned to revisions begun earlier in the 1930s, and the final set was completed and dated 1 July 1936. Many additions to these pages of *transition*, *Tales Told of Shem and Shaun*, and *Haveth Childers Everywhere* relate to the imminent approach of dawn and the calm after the storm, as well as to the numerous cycles relating to rebirth, renewal, and regeneration. The addition, "After suns and moons, dews and wettings, thunders and fires, comes sabotag" (BL 47486a-73v, JJA 61: 7, FW 409.29), lists the days of the week, and "suns" (Sunday) contains a pun on the looming usurpation of the father by the *son* and the moon by the *sun*. The "thunders"/Thundersday/Thursday linking has appeared throughout the *Wake*, but in this particular reference, it is accompanied by Vico's other institutions (with "dews and wettings" as weds/weddings), presenting the calm that comes after rain (the "dews and wettings") and the thunder and lightning (the "thunders and fires"). In terms of fertility, "wettings" as rain again bring new life in terms of both crops and of the sustenance of all life, and "wettings" as weddings bring forth new children.

On the second typescript of II.3§2 (approximately December 1936), the importance of riverbanks and floodplains for the fertility of the land and the subsequent development of a civilization continues in conjunction with the dependence of language on nature and the relationship between the female and fertility of the land. Joyce adds two previously discussed notes from VI.B.12's index of Michelet's Vico: "moutainy mots" and "plain language." The missing term from this group of three is "littoral sense," but the way Joyce transfers these notes into the text incorporates the third term as well: "to mountainy mots in her amnest plein language" (BL 47479-190v, JJA 54: 310, FW 333.26–27, VI.C.6: 4), with *amnis* being Latin for "river" and *plein* implying "full" or "at flood stage" in French. As intercourse is also represented as "flooding" throughout the *Wake* (particularly in I.8), "fertility" takes on both meanings here: the fertility of the female and the subsequent production of children and the fertility of the land to ensure the sustenance of these future generations.

At the end of the third typescript of II.3§6, Joyce adds: "He beached the bark of his tale; and set to husband and vine: and the harpermaster told all the living conservancy how that win a gain was in again" (BL 47480-246v, JJA 55: 378, FW 358.17–19). The word "husband" (both the noun and the verb) comes from the Old Norse *bóndi*, meaning "peasant owning his house and land." The word was originally the present participle of *búa* or *bóa*, meaning "to dwell" or "to have a household";[29] to "dwell" implied to cultivate land, to till the ground, to have a wife. To the galley proofs of book III, Joyce adds "seed and nursery man" (BL 47487-63v, JJA 62: 122, FW 496.12) to a description of HCE, further strengthening this bond between land ownership, tillage of land, and the establishment of families, communities, and civilizations.

Seasons, Springtime, and Spirituality

In addition to the focus on fertility rites, *Finnegans Wake* contains several examples of other religious festivals, beliefs, and traditions that developed in close connection with observations of nature. This section continues in the same manner as the previous section on fertility myths, but expands to discuss other holidays and traditions. In 1927, on the galley proofs for the *transition* pages of I.4,[30] Joyce changes "by the wrath of God" to "by the wrath of Bog" (BL 47472-295, JJA 46: 132, FW 76.31). "Bog" means "God" in Russian, but it also just means "bog" (like "sod" in "Whose thunder and weddin and soddin [FW 56.33], which implies "sodden," as in waterlogged, like a bog).[31] This line is added to a section concerning HCE's burial, aligning HCE's burial in the ground and subsequent return to the soil with the decomposition of matter in bogs. Because of the Christ-like nature of his burial behind a "stone slab" and the designation of the "spring offensive" (BL 47471b-8, JJA 46: 4, FDV 65.12, FW 78.15), the "Bog" also evokes the "Böög," the sacrificial snowman of Zürich's Sechseläuten, the festival of fertility and spring awakening. Death, burial, fertility, and renewal are all united through the conflation of "God" and "Bog." Last, this replacement of "God" with "bog" suggests a conception of divinity in which Joyce bestows upon the earth the supreme powers of order and creation.

On the *transition* 3 pages,[32] Joyce adds a passage linking Noah and the flood with the flower girls, botanical life cycles, and springtime: "Noah Beery weighed stone thousand one when Hazel was a hen. Now her fat's falling fast. Therefore, chatbags, why not yours? There are 29 sweet reasons why blossomtime's the best. Elders fall for green almonds when they're raised on bruised stone root ginger though it winters on their heads as if auctumned round their waistbands" (BL 47475-203, JJA 45: 323, FW 64.33–65.2). Her "fat's falling fast" refers to the storage of fat for hibernation; as spring approaches, the reserves have almost been used up, whereas in "auctumn," there was a bit of excess around "their waistbands." The "29 sweet reasons" refers to the flower girls/leap year girls, and to the days in February in a leap year. February, in Ireland, is when the first flowers (usually daffodils, followed by crocus) begin to appear. The "Elders" are older men, but also the elder tree, which symbolized mischief in Irish folklore. "Young" almonds on the tree are usually green. The "strong root ginger" is a rhizome, the underground part of the plant that assists in reproduction. Surviving on root ginger all winter, the new products of spring (whether they are young crops or young girls) are alluring.

To revisions of III.1, Joyce also adds seasonal references, with "till its rusty October in this bleak forest" (BL 47486a-74, JJA 61: 8, FW 410.9), "Prost bitten!" (BL 47486a-79, JJA 61: 21, FW 424.9), and "When the natural morning of your nocturne blankmerges into the national morning of golden sunup" (BL 47486a-80v, JJA 61: 23, FW 428.17–18). October is "rusty" because of the colors of the leaves, but in combination with the "*bleak* forest" (italics mine) and the "Prost bitten" ("frost bitten"), it also alludes to a tertiary definition for "rusty," which refers to plants "affected with rust or mildew."[33] Together, these additions refer to the changing of the seasons, the passage through autumn and winter to the reawakening of spring, the life-giving waters of the river, and the fertility of the soil.

The passage of time and of the seasons is also a theme in VI.B.14 notes from Perry's *The Origin of Magic and Religion*, wherein he discusses the creation of calendars for agriculture:

> In Egypt, with the annual flood of the Nile, it must have been difficult for the agriculturalist, without some method of counting time, to know exactly when to begin operations. The day of the beginning of the flood was of great importance to him, for his work must cease once the water had begun to flow over the land. Thus it is that the day of the flood was the beginning of the Egyptian year. The Egyptians measured all their time from that date. The calculation of the recurrence of such a day as that of the Nile flood is not easy. It involves the use of a calendar based on the movements of some heavenly body. The Egyptians used, in the first instance, the lunar calendar in order to calculate this important date. (30–31)[34]

"Time," in the way it is understood today, is another cultural construct born out of biological and ecological necessity. In a biblical analogue, time also begins with the flood, which, continuing the discussion of ALP and the flood, further ascribes an ontological role to ALP. Perry also makes another important point (echoing themes of kingship and nature in the *Wake*) by asserting that early ruling families and calendars were inextricably linked (31). Following a few notes on Egypt and on early burial chambers ("mastaba," "ziggurat," and "pyramid" [VI.B.14: 138]),[35] Joyce skips quite a bit ahead in Perry, and though he takes a couple of notes at random, his note-taking ceases shortly thereafter, suggesting that the information concerning fertility, agriculture, kingship, calendars, Egypt, and Sumer fit the purpose.[36]

On VI.B.14: 197, Joyce then begins taking notes from Stephen Langdon's *Enuma Elish: The Babylonian Epic of Creation*, the latest edition "of an Akkadian text reconstructed from cuneiform inscriptions on seven tablets found in 1850 in the ruins of the palace of Ashurbanipal in Nineveh" (VI.B.14 12). This epic attracted considerable attention when it was discovered because, as Deane, Ferrer, and Lernout explain, it bore many "linguistic, conceptual and narrative similarities" to the Hebrew version of Genesis, and thus, it was claimed that the Hebrew Genesis "was a derivative of this Sumerian myth" (VI.B.14 12). These theories bridging cultures and religions through similarities in mythological narratives support Joyce's bridging of Celtic custom, folklore, religion, and monuments through a shared geography and through Saint Patrick.

Hooke's *Middle Eastern Mythology* also addresses such shared histories, identifying two "controlling myths" that appear throughout numerous cultures. The first controlling myth is the myth that explains the changing of the seasons and the ensuing productivity of the land, and the second is the myth of creation (23). Deane, Ferrer, and Lernout argue, "If Joyce did not believe in the purity of origins, he was most curious about the various stories invented by mankind to account for its beginnings" (VI.B.14 12). One note recorded from Langdon's book on the *Enuma Elish* is "dragon" (VI.B.14: 197), taken from the original text that reads: "the chief significance of the Epic and the ritual of the spring equinox consisted in the return of the sun from the regions of winter darkness, the victory of light over the dragon of storm and night [. . .] The myth, and the ritual to which it gave form, was probably inspired more or less by the ancient cult of Tammuz, the young god of vegetation, who died yearly, sojourned in the lower world, and returned to the upper world" (32–33). Joyce may also have been thinking here of Stefan Czarnowski's belief (in *Le culte des héros et ses conditions sociales: Saint Patrick, héros national de l'Irlande*) that the date of Saint Patrick's death, 17 March, "is seen to correspond with the spring equinox" (VI.B.14 11). The *Enuma Elish*, according to Hooke, was the poem or chant associated with the Babylonian New Year festival, Akitu, and is a ritual myth concerning the death and resurrection of a god (41–46). The combination of this theme of resurrection with the passage of the seasons supports Hooke's theory of the two "controlling myths" of civilization and also demonstrates Joyce's interest in the links between these two myths.[37]

In *The White Goddess*, Robert Graves studied the Ogham tree alphabet extensively and put forward the theory that the early Celtic peoples used a lunar tree calendar to keep time. In *Irish Trees*, Niall Mac Coitir explains that while his theory has not been substantiated, Graves "deserves credit for being the first in modern times to realise the Ogham alphabet was based on a seasonal cycle of trees" (184), and this seasonal quality also links the Ogham alphabet to Joyce's notes from Perry on the lunar calendar. On their own, Joyce's notes concerning stones (see chapter 1 of this study) and his additions referring to trees may seem inconsequential, but when considered together during one specific phase of his work on *Finnegans Wake*, they construct a much different narrative. In the context of the Perry notes, the VI.B.14 notes concerning Breton culture and monuments, the notes from the *Enuma Elish*, and the "Upfellbowm" passage mentioned earlier, these notes and additions become meaningful signposts for the primacy of natural history within Joyce's universal history. History before humans, and before writing developed, must be read through the earth, through "the testament of the rocks" (FW 73.32–33). As evidenced from the Ordovician rocks to the megalithic stones at Carnac and the dolmens and Ogham stones of Ireland, nature was the only place to turn for communication and for art. Without any preexisting "culture," culture was born out of the human interaction with nature, from the imagination's interactions with the objects that structured everyday life. As with the Tammuz and Ishtar myth explaining the passing of the seasons, the presence of trees in myths concerning cycles of death and rebirth becomes an important facet of Joyce's presentation of Celtic spirituality and ritual in subsequent sections of the *Wake*.

Drafts of sections of II.1 weave together tides, moon, sun, and trees with religious customs. On an early 1931 typescript of II.1 §4 (BL 47477-74v–75, JJA 51: 94–95), Joyce adds a passage regarding the affinity between Jewish ceremonies and the moon, referencing "Neomenia" (the Jewish festival of the new moon) and "Seder" (the Jewish feast commemorating Exodus, made possible because of a full moon) (BL 47477-74v, JJA 51: 94, FW 244.3–12). "Seder" is spelled like the cedar tree, as "Ceder," and is linked also to "pire" (BL 47477-74v, JJA 51: 94, FW 244.3), "lolave branches" (BL 47477-77, JJA 51: 101, FW 244.4), and "log foyer" (BL 47477-77, JJA 51: 101, FW 244.12).

The moon continues to appear throughout notebooks and drafts of this period, with VI.B.35 containing, "HCE sol / ALP luna (her phases)/ 2 Easters (P.S. & E.S.)" (VI.B.35: 23) and "rhythm of sea / tide transgression / 1 / 4 ½ / 9 / 18 / 111" (VI.B.35: 27). These notes signal an association of the tides with the phases of the moon, and a "transgression," in geological terms, is a period denoting a shift in sea level that alters the shoreline, results in flooding, and can be induced by isostatic changes, orogenies, or climatic change (Goudie 2: 1060). In the context of Joyce's notes, it seems the interest lies in the way in which human cycles (in this case, holidays and the female menstrual cycle) align with nonhuman cycles of the moon and the tides, which are themselves part of a larger cycle of geological transgression and regression. The note "2 Easters (P.S. & E.S.)" (VI.B.35: 23) concerns the AD 325 fixing of the Easter date (the first Sunday after the first full moon on or following the vernal equinox), decreed by the Council of Nicaea, which bestowed the task of calculating the date of Easter upon the Church of Alexandria. What once began as a pagan holiday, wherein the date was aligned with the seasons, became a Christian holiday with a carefully calculated occurrence.[38] With the establishment of the calculation of Easter, the Church standardized the phases of the moon, and the understanding of time was forced to align with church doctrine.

Selva Oscura: Christianity, Forests, Birds

Initiated with the early sketches of "St. Kevin" and "St. Patrick and the Druid," Joyce continually revisits the relationship between Irish Christianity and Celtic nature-worship throughout the composition of the *Wake*. From VI.B.3, Joyce introduced the theme of Christianity's authority over the land of Ireland with the "woods of Fogloot" addition, from the note "(Focluth [wood of])" (VI.B.3: 9).[39] From J. M. Flood's *Ireland: Its Saints and Scholars* (11), this note concerns how Saint Patrick was first brought to Ireland as a slave, but then later returned to the island to introduce Christianity to its inhabitants. From Patrick's *Confessions*, Flood summarizes the saint's account of the events that occurred after his departure from Ireland: "After six years' captivity Patrick escaped from Ireland to France and made his way to Tours, where he stayed for four years receiving instructions from St. Martin" (11). Then, after further time in Auxerre and Rome, "[t]he Saint's thoughts often turned towards the people amongst whom he had spent the years of his captivity, and he was finally induced to undertake the conversion of Ireland by a vision" (11):

> I saw in the visions of the night a person coming from Ireland with innumerable letters, and he gave me one of them, and I read in the beginning of the letter "The voice of the people of Ireland," and I thought at that very moment that I heard the voice of those who were near the wood of Focluth, which is adjoining to the Western Sea, and they cried out, as it were with one voice, "We entreat thee, holy youth, to come and walk still amongst us," and I was very much pricked to the heart, and could read no further, and so I awoke. (Qtd. in Flood 12)

The details that these voices call out to Patrick from a *wood* and that these messages are delivered in a *letter* are of greatest importance to the *Wake*. Historically, woods and forests have been the spaces of disorder and anarchy; they were often seen as the unmapped spaces opposed to civilization where irrationality and immorality reigned. In Ireland specifically, during the Cromwellian period, the 1798 rebellion, and the Anglo-Irish War, the "woods" were the places where the Irish (the "woodkerne") could hide, and the woods were seen as frightening, menacing spaces in need of eradication.

This alignment between the Irish people and the "wild" landscape appears throughout the *Wake*'s composition. In VI.B.29, the note "Greater Dublin" comes from a passage in the *Encyclopaedia Britannica* describing the proximity of Dublin to the wilderness: "Mountains practically touch the confines of Greater Dublin" (qtd. in VI.B.29 74). Then, Joyce takes two notes from Samuel A. Fitzpatrick's *Dublin: A Historical and Topographical Account of the City* that continue this theme, but add political weight with "bushments" and "underwoods" (VI.B.29: 89). These notes originate in a passage from the *Holinshed Chronicles* concerning Sir Arthur Grey's failed attempt to fight the Irish troops who had retreated to the Wicklow mountains: "the sides are full of great and mightie trees upon the sides of the hills, and full of bushments and underwoods" (qtd. in VI.B.29 86).

This association between the native Irish and the wild Irish landscape is a common colonizer/colonized trope (such as with the North American colonists' description of Native Americans, for example), which also relates back to the passages about the establishment of Washington, D.C., from VI.B.29 and III.3. In a 1689 *History of Ireland*, Richard Cox provides an example of the way in which woodlands were aligned with the Irish and subsequently denigrated and feared by the English: "The rebels being well acquainted with these woods, laid their ambushes so cunningly that the English could neither fight in that devilish place, nor retire out of it; courage could but little avail them, whilst being mired in the bogs, they were forced to stand still like butts to be shot at. Discipline or conduct were of no use in that place, where it could not be practised; in short, the English were defeated, and the whole company slain" (170). The Irish landscape is a "devilish" place, one that seems to try to trap the English soldiers in its bogs. The land itself is "unruly," like the Irish themselves, and basic goodness, order, and law were valid for neither the place nor its inhabitants. These notes are not transferred to drafts until those for II.1§6 in 1931 or 1932, but their presence in the notebook at this time is nonetheless significant.

Prior to independence, the English belief that the Irish people were more in touch with nature even extended to the level of policy. In the late nineteenth century, then Prime Minister William Gladstone wanted to plant three million acres of Ireland with new trees, believing that this could somehow "restore peace and quietness to that country" (qtd. in Burke 22). To Gladstone, the reforestation of Ireland would somehow cheer the Irish people by giving them back their natural landscape and thus make them forget their desire for Home Rule. The attitude presented by Cox in the above passage endured until Irish independence and contributed to the correspondence between woodlands and nationalism during the late nineteenth and early twentieth centuries.

Thus, reading Saint Patrick's vision as Christian allegory, it is possible that the "wood" may refer to an actual wood, but it likely refers to pagan Ireland and its "uncivilized" worship of nature deities. As an example of this trope, Robert Harrison describes how Dante's forest in the first canto of the *Inferno* represents the non-Christian world. Therefore, the voices are the people calling to Patrick to help them out of the dark, chaotic, formless forested landscape, the Dantean *selva oscura*. The forests are the *foris*, the "outside": they exist in a space detached from laws and from society. As Jeremy Tambling explains in *Dante and Difference*, the origin of the term *selva oscura* in Dante, the Latin *selva*, is closely related to the Greek *hyle* that signifies the chaotic, primal matter (72). The designation of the "woods" of Focluth signifies the existence of a Christian imperative behind the domination of Ireland, its people, and its wild landscape.

The "(Focluth [wood of])" (VI.B.3: 9) note appears in drafts of III.3. Yawn, asked by the inquisitors as to why he is shivering and if he wants his mother, responds: "The woods of Fogloot! Omis padredge!" (BL 47484a-248, JJA 58: 316, FW 478.34). In addition to evoking Saint Patrick's dream, Yawn's "padredge" is a blend of "Patrick," *padre* (Spanish for "father"), *mis padres* (Spanish for "ancestors"), and "partridge." Without recourse to the mythological and theological implications of the partridge, these three connotations of "padredge" create an image of birds as genealogically linked to humans, blurring the boundary between the human and the nonhuman. Looking to the roles played by nonhuman figures in mythology and ancient religions (two topic clusters in the notebooks during this period) provides a precedent for this interpretation, and the fact that these themes are invoked in conjunction with Saint Patrick articulates (and consequently undermines) the authority of anthropocentric interpretations of Christian doctrine.

Examining the symbolic implications of the choice of the partridge reveals possible ramifications of rivalry, falsity, and infidelity. The merging of *padre*, "father," and "partridge" derives from the Latin name for "partridge," *Perdix perdix*. In Greek mythology, Perdix was the name of Daedalus's nephew, and Daedalus became jealous as Perdix was proving to be a better craftsman than he (Perdix invented the saw, the compass, and the potter's wheel). Enraged by a potential usurpation, Daedalus threw his nephew off of the Acropolis and into the sea, but Perdix was rescued by Athena and turned into a partridge (Werness 318). In III.3 Shem (the Daedalus figure) rebukes his brother, Yawn (who is therefore in the role of the partridge Perdix). In Brewer's *Dictionary of Phrase and Fable*, the partridge is also aligned with sex, as the phrase "*Perdrix, toujours perdrix*" refers to a French king teaching a lesson about monogamy to his confessor (699). In the early Christian period, the partridge also stood for the devil because the bird steals and incubates eggs that are not its own (699), and it was believed that the devil stole children and indoctrinated them. Shaun, in the role of Patrick/partridge, looks upon the Irish people as birds that have ended up in the wrong nest and thus in need of the Christianity he will bring to their land.

Birds have often played curious roles in theology. In the *Wake*, the bird's transitional role between nature and culture also appears as Johnny MacDougal interrupts with an anecdote including three more bird types added to the *transition* 15 pages:[40] "greyleg" (graylag, European goose), "duck," and "plover" (BL 47486b-451, JJA 61: 433, FW 478.35–36). "Duck" is not a particularly specific term, but breeds of ducks, along with the plover and the graylag goose, are migratory water birds for which Ireland is an important wintering habitat. The pre-Linnaean name for the graylag goose, the "Wild Goose," also alludes to the "Wild Geese," the Jacobins who fled Ireland after the Williamite Wars (D'Alton, *History* 4: 492). Johnny specifically addresses Yawn as "greyleg." He warns, "that duck is rising and you'll wake that stand of plover" (BL 47486b-451, JJA 61: 433, FW 478.35–36), before describing his own relationship with the "woods of Focluth," which are historically situated in County Mayo (in Johnny's section of the country).

Joyce also adds "Tir-non-Ogre" (BL 47484a-249, JJA 58: 317, FW 479.2) (*Tír-na-nóg*, which translates from the Irish to "Land of the Young") to the description of Mayo here, locating the "woods of Focluth" in the Irish equivalent of Eden, Valhalla, or Elysium. *Tír-na-nóg* also appears here because of its association with Irish myth and with the figure of Oisín and the *Tuatha Dé Danaan*, but also because of its atemporality and its defiance of spatial positioning (legend has it that *Tír-na-nóg* was not able to be located on any map and existed only "far, far, west"). The addition of "zoedone of the zephyros" (BL 47484a-249, JJA 58: 317, FW 479.8), the land of the zephyr, the West Wind, is therefore also related to the addition of *Tír-na-nóg*.[41]

An alteration of the "woods of fogloot" addition also introduces Irish wolves, extinct in Ireland since at least 1786 (Hickey 14). Yawn as Patrick/Parnell senses that Johnny's story about *Tír-na-nóg* is merely a way to trick him, and Yawn changes the "woods of fogloot" to the "wolves of Fochlut!" (BL 47484a-8, JJA 58: 109, FW 479.13) and pleads that he not be flung "to the twolves" (FW 479.14). The change from "fogloot" to "Fochlut" brings in the Irish for wolf, *faolchú*, which translates roughly to "evil hound." This etymological link between "evil" and "wolf," "*faol*" and "*faolchú*," provides context for the myth surrounding Saint Patrick, the wolf, and the lamb, and also explains the recurring presence of the wolf in *The Book of Kells* as a symbol of evil. Also containing the German for "twelve," *zwolf*, "twelve" becomes the twelve apostles, and the Yawn figure's plea to Johnny becomes a plea against betrayal, linking the figure back to Parnell.

There are also several "bird" additions to early drafts of III.3 and to contemporaneous drafts of I.6§3. One such addition to III.3 contains the infamous Sweeney, the Danish word for "bird" (*fugle*), the German word for "goose" (*Gans*), a play on "flamingo," and a play on "Phoenix" ("flaming"): "and bird flamingans sweenyswinging fugelwards on the tipmast and Orania epples playing hopptociel bommptaterre" (BL 47484a-205, JJA 58: 356, FW 504.23–24). The Irish story of *Buile Shuibhne* tells of "mad" King Sweeney and his "birdlike" behavior, the "sweenysinging." The Sweeney story is often seen as an example of the confluence of the Christian and the Celtic and has been interpreted as arising from "the monastic tradition of settlement" having felt "itself threatened by the dynamics of nature" (Foster, "Encountering" 33). In the story, the Ulster King Sweeney is "turned into a bird-man by a curse from a saint whom he insults and is driven in madness to the tree canopies where he makes mad beautiful verse" (Foster

32–33). The story also provides superb documentation of the landscape of twelfth-century Ulster, cataloguing all of the Irish trees and shrubs inhabited by Sweeney.

Despite the story's leafiness, however, John Wilson Foster explains that the overall purpose of the story is to show that "spirit is separate from, and finally triumphs over, nature" (33). Sweeney's occupancy of this transitional space, physically, mentally, and spiritually, is echoed with *ciel* and *terre* (French for "sky" and "earth," respectively). Birds also occupy this space, hovering between earth and sky, and for this quality they are given importance in the *Wake* in terms of their behavior, habitats, symbolism, role in augury, and prevalence in mythology. Even without knowledge of the theology behind the Sweeney tale, the relationship between the earth/sky binary and the importance of birds in the *Wake* is still visible. Birds serve to unite these two realms, as birds, accompanied only by certain insects, inhabit both.

The sheer ability of birds to fly, to inhabit both of these worlds, contributes to their importance in early religions and mythologies as well as to the association of the Holy Spirit with a bird in the Christian tradition. Joyce adds "Umpidgeon" (BL 47484a-178, JJA 58: 421, FW 485.20) and "hagion pneuma" (VI.B.27: 4)[42] (Greek for "Holy Spirit") to III.3 and I.6§3, respectively. There is also another possible reference to the "Umpidgeon" embedded in a Christ addition: "Ichthyan! Hegvat! Tosser!" (BL 47484a-177, JJA 58: 420, FW 485.11). The "Icthyan," *Ichthyus*, echoes the "Itch dean" a few lines before (FW 485.3), which is the motto of Yawn's crest and means, "I serve" ("Ich dean"). Yawn's crest is composed of three feathers, and in this context is likely an allusion to the Holy Spirit as bird.

The next addition, "Your bard's highview, avis on valley!" (BL 47484a-205, JJA 58: 356, FW 504.16), evokes the famed image of the God-artist figure "paring his fingernails"[43] from *Portrait*, but through the bird as "bard" and the Latin for "bird," *avis*, the bird is given creative agency. It is no coincidence that the hen then plays such a central role in the understanding of the letter. The hen, in addition to being a Greek term for "one," and *poule* being French slang for "prostitute," is also used because of certain characteristics of poultry, such as their proclivity toward scavenging. Chickens/hens inhabit another transitional role because of their status as semiflightless or as "reluctant fliers" (Roots 129).[44] The "avis" with the "bard's eyeview" in the *Wake* is the hen, the creative force that exists between earth and sky, matter and spirit.

In *Variation of Plants and Animals under Domestication*, Darwin dedicated the seventh chapter entirely to fowls, and he believed that studying domesticated species was the best way to observe evolutionary patterns. Clive Roots explains that "the unnatural loss of flight has occurred in several domesticated birds like the chicken and turkey, which have very inactive lives compared to their wild ancestors" (ix). On these same III.3 pages for *transition*, Joyce adds "ouragan of spaces," which Finn Fordham argues serves to again problematize the question of origins. The phrasing "ouragan of spaces" contains the French word for "hurricane," *ouragan*, attributing our origin to the sky (and, again, placing our fate in the hands of the weather or nature), but it also provides the evolutionary angle (as well as the "chicken or the egg" question). These questions are all innately linked to the question of creativity's origins and of the origins of language and writing, but they could not be articulated as clearly without this recourse to specific biological detail. The "chicken or the egg" question is made clear by Joyce's addition of "eggdrazzles" (BL 47484a-205, JJA 58: 356, FW 504.35) at this draft level, returning to another explanation for the world's origin, the Yggdrasil. The Yggdrasil also inhabits both earth and sky; the roots are dug deep into the earth, while the branches reach toward the sky. Thus, on this draft level, the "tree stuck up" of the first draft of III.3 has become both the Norse Yggdrasil and Darwin's tree of life from *On the Origin of Species*.

Science versus Religion

Another significant theme in the *Wake* is the tension between science and religion; throughout the text, both are presented as possible interpretations of the world, with neither being necessarily more valid than the other. From the focus on Darwin and its juxtaposition with religious and mythological references to the directed recording of notes on topics relating to science, Joyce evidently intended to incorporate developments in the sciences in the *Wake* to suggest that one era's truth can quickly become another era's superstition.

This pitting of religion against science is demonstrated through legend and fable with the Yggdrasil, the Garden of Eden, Darwin, and physics. This debate is also apparent with the several additions and notes relating to technology and physics from contemporaneous notebooks: VI.B.4 contains clusters on mathematics, and VI.B.23 contains notes on radio and radio waves, roads, cities, and electricity. The notes from VI.B.4 and VI.B.23 prepare to temporarily shift the perspective toward urban civilization and modern technology, constructing a thematic parallel between the "natural" and "technological" elements Joyce is working with at this stage.

In III.3, as the interrogators continue to question Yawn, they switch their tactics, moving from the time of the event to the place of the event, attempting to pinpoint its exact location. One possible location is the Garden of Eden, and on this draft level, Joyce continues to decouple the story from its Christian context through recourse to Darwin. The initial references to Darwin appear on the fair copy of the revised typescript of this section, with Joyce adding "origin of spices and charlotte darlings with silkblue askmes chattering in dissent to them" (BL 47484a-1, JJA 58: 1, FW 504.28–29) and "their unnatural refection" (BL 47484a-1, JJA 58: 1, FW 504.33), punning on Darwin's name, on his *Origin of Species*, and on his *Descent of Man*. At this draft level, Joyce adds another Darwin reference, "Remounting a liftle towards the ouragan of spaces" (BL 47484a-205, JJA 58: 356, FW 504.14), in conjunction with "Orania epples" (BL 47484a-207, JJA 58: 357, FW 504.24), placing three decidedly non-Christian elements—the *Origin of Species*, Newton's apple, and Emania of the Apples (Emania, the locale to which Manannán MacLir, the Celtic sea-god, fled to escape Christianity)—into the story of Eden. Fordham contends that Darwin's presence here is largely because of the tree of life and the larger metaphor of the tree of knowledge and the place of science on this latter tree. Fordham continues, arguing that Joyce juxtaposes Frazer with Darwin, and later with quantum mechanics, to show the larger *subjectivity* of science and align it with other forms of "superstition" (HJS 1: par. 24). This view may also contribute to the addition of "Let's hear what science has to say" (BL 47484a-208, JJA 58: 358, FW 505.27) on this same draft level, again presenting science as just another point of view, no more valid than any other outlook.

Specific scientific terminology appears throughout the *Wake* and the *Wake* notebooks. For example, in VI.B.27 (in use from approximately May through July 1929),[45] Joyce lists: "quantum," "protons" (VI.B.27: 141), "finite space," and "nebulae spiral" (VI.B.27: 142). Earlier, in VI.B.23, Joyce recorded, "Avogadro," "Athomic weight" (VI.B.23: 116), "ampere," "coulomb," "electron," "proton," "volt," and "a nod to cathode" (VI.B.23: 119). One of these notes appears in the addition to III.3, "Coloumba mea, frimosa mea" (BL 47484a-294, JJA 58: 409, FW 549.14), which joins the chemistry and physics terms with the Holy Spirit. The phrase is from Song of Solomon 2:10 and translates to "My dove, my beautiful one" (with *columba* meaning "dove" in Latin). The Coulomb is also the SI unit for electric charge and is paired with the addition "Volted ampire" (BL 47484a-294, JJA 58: 409, FW 549.16) ("volt" and "ampere" are the SI units for electrical potential energy and electric current). This is also the kingdom of heaven as the "vaulted empire." Joyce also adds "from anodes to cathodes" (BL 47484a-294, JJA 58: 409, FW 549.17) to the same line in III.3, echoing from "alpha to omega." The juxtaposition of terms from physics with references to the Holy Spirit also suggests again that in many ways, science becomes a contemporary form of religion.

"The Ondt and the Gracehoper" updates the time versus space dichotomy to include modern technology, and the animals in the fable are also updated to include contemporary entomology. In VI.B.4, VI.B.27, and VI.B.21, Joyce records detailed notes on entomology (e.g., "arachnid," "mandible," "Siphonaptera" [VI.B.4: 229], "ocellus" [VI.B.4: 242], and "pygydium" [VI.B.4: 246]), demonstrating an attention to accurate representations of the insects themselves, as well as an emphasis on connecting nature and language through "entymology" (VI.B.21: 183) (entomology + etymology = entymology). Clive Hart, writing in "His Good Smetterling of Entymology," argues, "Apart from the names of insects, Joyce includes, in several languages, many other terms from natural history, with a strong bias towards bees and butterflies" (57), further linking entomology and etymology.

There were several popular works of entomology during the late nineteenth and early twentieth centuries that would have made this a familiar topic, but additionally, the sheer number of insects (estimated at around ten million different species, and, in terms of number of individual insects, the ratio of insects to humans is 200 million to 1) decenters the human presence on the earth, making the human only one species in a vast world of insect dominion. Entomology during Joyce's lifetime focused on the behavior of insects, demonstrating that insects can have behavioral patterns and social structures as complex as any mammal. Aside from this general familiarity with entomology from popular science, Joyce may also have been drawn to insects because of their historically polarized representations. Culturally, insects have often served two opposing roles: in the first, insects are curses from above, sent to bring famine and misery to all forms of life, and in the second role, they are deities, worshipped for their association with rebirth and renewal.

In *The Golden Bough*, insects present themselves in several belief systems as curses of infertility, particularly infertility of the land. Biblically, insects (often presented as locusts) are curses from God, sent to destroy the land of Egypt. In Deuteronomy 28, if the commandments are obeyed, "Blessed shalt thou be in thy city, and blessed shalt thou be in the field" (Deut. 28:3); the earth will be fertile to provide for its citizens, and the citizens will be fertile to provide for the earth. But if the commandments are not obeyed, "cursed shall be the fruit of thy body, and the fruit of thy land" (Deut. 28:18); the earth will become "iron" (Deut. 28:23), and all the seeds and "all thy trees and fruit of thy land shall the locust consume" (Deut. 28:38, 42). Generally, insects appear in the Bible as signs of God's fury, consuming crops, laying the land waste, and subsequently, starving the disobedient society. Insects ravage fields and bring suffering, representing a bond between the gods and the fertility of the land that endures throughout history. In the second role, insects are deified (as the scarab beetle has been in many religions ranging from Ancient Egyptian to Buddhist).

Hart explains that Joyce approaches entomological terms in "The Ondt and the Gracehoper" in a way similar to his layering of the names of rivers into I.8 and of roads into III.4, but that the biological terms here are perhaps more significant: "As insects have always been closely associated with superstition and with primitive gods, Joyce raises earwigs, beetles, and other small creatures to divine status" (57).[46] Joyce uses insects to set modern faith in the sciences against religion (and for this reason may use the Latin names of particular species). Returning to the introduction of this study, I point to the fact that one of Lawrence Buell's criteria for an ecological text is that "The nonhuman environment is present not merely as a framing device but as a presence that begins to suggest that human history is implicated in natural history" (7–8), and the use of fables and myths in the *Wake* works with this criterion, allowing Joyce to merge traditional and classical narratives with contemporary ideas of the nonhuman world.[47]

Another addition to III.3 at this draft level re-creates the Viconian cycle, beginning with pre-Christian cosmology and moving through religion, science, democracy, and universities: "did not I festfix my unniversires, wholly national [. . .] rosetted on two stelas of littleegypt [. . .] democritas" (BL 47484a-294v, JJA 58: 410, FW 551.28). In another example of the control HCE believes he has, he has here "fixed" the universe. This fixing of the universe is also the goal of mythology, of religion, of science; on some levels, it can be understand as the goal of all human institutions and customs. The "national" and "democritas," particularly when placed alongside "littleegypt," are nation and democracy, with "democritas" also being "Democritus." The latter appears here because of Ancient Greece's democracy and because of Democritus's pre-Christian perspective and atomic cosmology: Democritus, too, was an early "fixer" of the universe. In Vico's conception, the universities are the final stage of human civilization before *ricorso* occurs, before all crumbles and returns to the forest to begin anew. This short line from III.3 thus presents the history of the world from the universe to the institutionalization of the universe—the university—and also suggests the continual revisions of both science and religion in our history.

The abovementioned addition, when placed in its larger context of III.3, recounts HCE relating all that he has done for ALP. He has brought civilization to nature (as ALP); he has taught her about the world and about culture, and he has taught her to speak properly. On the macrocosmic level, this passage is also culture telling nature what it has done for it through the founding of universities and the creation of language. HCE is the creator, claiming to have constructed the universe, the stars, language ("rosetted," referring to the Rosetta Stone), and democracy. The physics references such as "Volted ampire" and "from anodes to cathodes" were added to this draft shortly before this passage, and, alongside the Rosetta Stone and Democritus, they all serve here to undercut HCE's boastings of his accomplishments. Democritus was one of the primary developers of atomic theory; positing a materialist explanation of the universe, he proposed that there were numerous possible worlds, each with an explicit beginning and end. Democritus's theory did not involve questions concerning a *primum mobile* or a "final cause," but it was a precursor to the Newtonian mechanism of the Enlightenment. In Democritus's cosmology, the only governing force is natural law. In the context in which they were added to the drafts, the references to physics from VI.B.27 are specifically applied to the descriptions of light and electricity being introduced to cities, but when placed alongside this concurrent addition referring to Democritus, the "natural laws" of physics suggest also a larger ordering force, returning again to the desire to find structure in the universe, the common root of both science and religion.

Throughout this chapter, I have argued that the *Wake*'s engagements with religious topics are often presented in terms of their relationship to the natural world. Like language, history, and economies, religion in the *Wake* is also clearly derived from a response to the environment. Vico's Providence is updated as the unpredictability of the weather; it is a force that cannot be understood by human reason. Weather forecasting in the *Wake* is a form of divination, an inquiry into the unknown workings of nature. Early religions and myths developed as responses to the necessities of survival, as demonstrated by the *Wake*'s focus on fertility myths and festivals celebrating the harvest. Civilizations organized themselves around their agriculture, and the founding myths of many cultures revolve around themes of infertility of the land. Holidays developed in response to observations of natural cycles, from the changing of seasons to the arrival of the yearly floods. Early Christianity in Ireland was closely linked to natural imagery, particularly in terms of Saint Patrick and his summons back to Ireland. Joyce also engages topics in contemporary science—from evolution, electricity, physics, chemistry, entomology, and ecology—to suggest both the existence of a higher unknown governing force and that the sciences and religion are equally subjective in their descriptions of the world, both dependent upon cultural constructions and the creation of specific discourses.

5

Growing Things

When Joyce was visiting Denmark in 1936, the journalist Ole Vinding asked, "Do you like flowers, Mr Joyce?" to which Joyce replied, "No. I love plants, green growing things, trees and grass. Flowers annoy me" (JJ 694). In this final chapter, I examine Joyce's love for "growing things," presenting this growth in several different contexts that include the growth of plants but also range from the growth of a language to the growth of young girls to the growth of civilizations.

Coming of Age: ALP, Issy, the Flower Girls, and Heliotrope

One of the main points of the "Anna Livia Plurabelle" chapter is the conflation of a woman's coming of age with the movement of a river from its mountain source to the sea. "To understand this chapter," Epstein writes of I.8, "it would be helpful to consult a contemporary account of the river" (91). This is indeed helpful, as doing so does help one to understand a couple of specifics about the Liffey, but also, it alerts one to the fact that Joyce is, perhaps unintentionally, referring to the course of the Vartry (another river with its origin in County Wicklow) at some points. Many notes concerning the Liffey and rivers in general are found in VI.B.6, and three key examples are used to describe Anna Livia's youth and her move from the mountains to the city: "garden of Erin = Wicklow mountains," "Luggelaw" (VI.B.6: 147), and "Liffey's detour / devil's glen" (VI.B.6: 73).[1]

When transferred into the drafts, the first note becomes: "It was ages & miles before that in the county Wicklow, the garden of Erin, before she ever thought **dreamt** she'd end in *the [barleyfields &] pennylands* of Humphreystown & she lie with a landleaper, well on the wane. Was it, was it? Are you sure? Where in Wicklow? Tell me where, the very first time! I will if you listen" (BL 47471b-75, 76, JJA 48: 5–6, FDV 125.13–18, FW 202.35–203.17).[2] The first option presented is in "the glen there near Luggelaw" (BL 47471b-76, JJA 48: 7, FDV 125.19, FW 203.17), which, in addition to being an air of Thomas Moore's, is another name for Wicklow's Lough Tay that drains into Lough Dan and eventually terminates in the Avonmore. The other referent may be Luggala, another name for the Wicklow peak also known as "Fancy Mountain." The Liffey begins in "the garden of Erin before she ever dreamt she'd end in the barleyfields & pennylands of Humphreystown & lie with a landleaper" (BL 47471b-75, JJA 48: 5, FDV 125.16, FW 203.7), again referring to the economic utility of the river. In summation, the Liffey, which starts in the beautiful Wicklow Mountains near Glendalough, never thought it would end up in the filth of Dublin. This repression, the inhibition of the natural flow of the Liffey, is the fate ALP dreams of leaving behind but cannot.

On the fair copy of I.8, from March 1924, Joyce adds to the passage concerning "Barefoot Byrne and Billy Wade" (BL 47471b-84, JJA 48: 25, FDV 125.26–31, FW 204.6–18): "she found her stride ^and lay^ and wriggled ^in all the stagnant black rain pools^" (BL 47474-120, JJA 48: 45, FDV 125.26–31, FW 204.17–18). This line seems to refer not to the Liffey but to the River Vartry, which, according to the River Vartry Protection Society, runs from the "Wicklow Mountains at Sally Gap to the Broadlough Bird Sanctuary at the Irish Sea" near Wicklow town. "Devil's Glen," which also appears in this passage, is a gorge near the Sally Gap through which the River Vartry falls into the "Devil's Punchbowl."[3] Therefore, the washerwomen present two incorrect courses of the Liffey: that of the Avoca and that of the Vartry. These incorrect courses are a form of gossip and are here to represent the girlish experiments of ALP, who eventually, in maturity, finds "her stride" and descends to the "stagnant black rain pools" of Dublin, *dubh linn* ("black pool").

Children in the *Wake* typically represent growth and the processes of growth: the growth of children into adults, the growth of languages, the growth of flora and fauna, the growth of civilizations, and the evolutionary growth of species and of individuals. Also, children are often represented as natural elements: the girls are represented as flowers, and Shem and Shaun are a tree and a stone, respectively. In addition to the course of the Liffey's representing ALP's transition into sexual maturity, Issy's growth is figured through images of flora, which also connects to later drafts of book

II. In the first draft of III.4, Issy is no longer associated with the river or the clouds but with the woods and the flowers. She is asleep in her room: "a barleycandy whistle on her counterpane, wildwood's eyes, and primarose hair, quietly, all the woods so wild in mauves of moss and daphnedews, now all so still she lay, like a happy lost leaf, like any flower stilled" (BL 47482a-10, JJA 60: 17, FDV 248.15–19, FW 556.15–22). The designation of "barley" for the type of candy is tied in with ALP's ending up in the "barleyfields" of Dublin's brewing industries. Issy, embodying the new modern woman, has easily and unknowingly embraced the changes that had been so alienating to her parents' generation. The fact that she dreams of wild woods, flowers, and moss suggests she is dreaming of her mother's source in the wild fields and upland bogs (covered in sphagnum moss or peat moss) of Wicklow (Foss and O'Connell 185). Though she has never known this freedom herself, this desire to return to the forests, to a place of origin, is implanted in a sort of collective unconscious. This alignment between Issy's growth and the primroses, moss, dew, and the "flower stilled" is integral to understanding how Joyce depicts "growing things" in the *Wake*.

The revisions of I.8 lead into the first draft of II.2§8, "The Triangle."[4] Completed in July 1926 in a copybook that also contains drafts of III.4 and I.1, the first draft of II.2§8 connects to these other two chapters and to I.8 in ways critical to the progression of the *Wake*. Luca Crispi, in his essay on the composition of II.2§8, argues that "once Joyce arrived at the seminal idea that Shem and Shaun will perform a geometry lesson by investigating their mother's element, the end of the river, the delta, the composition appears to have advanced relatively quickly and easily" (HJW 219). Crispi asserts that here ALP "is the figure of forbidden knowledge that initiates the boys into the most enigmatic realms: both the realm of abstract mathematics and that of basic feminine, maternal physiology" (HJW 220). As is typical in most Joyce criticism, the river Liffey, its estuary, and Dublin Bay are ignored and treated as mere vehicles for the conveyance of another idea. However, the language used in II.2§8 and the section's subsequent relationship to I.1 establish that Joyce had more in mind for the role of Dublin's wetlands than merely being a symbolic presence; the fact that the boys attempt to return to their mother, the river, through mathematics and cartography is part of the larger commentary on science as emblematic of "the fall." The "realm of abstract mathematics" is certainly not what the boys are truly seeking here; ALP is the "figure of forbidden knowledge," a knowledge of nature and of the world rendered incomprehensible to the fallen.

The task set by Shem, extracted from Euclid's *Elements* (to describe an equilateral triangle on a given finite straight line), is initially to "[c]onstruct an equilateral triangle" but is changed quickly to an "equilittoral" triangle. "Littoral," a term referring to the aquatic zone in closest proximity to the shore,[5] is used to maintain ALP's association with ecotones and wetlands from I.8. Accordingly, Shem and Shaun try to find the third point on the triangle—*their* origin—the Liffey delta, as the Liffey's origin is, of course, in Wicklow (with the entire triangle also being the delta). This measuring of the earth ("*geo*-metry") also relates ALP to the letter through its geodetic quality. Joyce had noted that the Nile delta was named as such because of its shape, triangular like the Greek delta, and in Joyce's shorthand in his notebooks and drafts, the delta (Δ) stands, of course, for ALP.

The way to begin this geometrical construction, Shem says, is to take a "mugful of mud" and "dump it at a given point of coast to be called *a* but pronounced olfa" (BL 47482a-67, JJA 53: 4, FDV 160.20–24, FW 286.31–287.15). Shem continues to give directions until the triangle has been inscribed, and says, "Now I'll show you whom your geometer was," and the resulting construction is a slightly obscene interpretation of a Venn diagram, revealed by the following lines: "We carefully lift up by her hem the muddy ^apron^ of our A.L.P. Kearfully until its nether apex is where a navel is bounds to be. Waaaa. Tch! And there's your muddy delta for you the first of all equilittoral ^equiliteral triangles^" (BL 47482a-67v, JJA 53: 5, FDV 165.11–15, FW 297.7–27). William York Tindall sees the landscape itself as being intrinsically important to this sketch: "Plainly the discovery of her [ALP's] Omega involves local geography: muddy, prismic delta, Howth, and Dublin Bay" (*Reader's Guide* 177). When the diagram Joyce has drawn in the manuscript is compared with a photograph of Dublin Bay, the image of a vagina becomes quite clear; Dublin Bay is the birth canal through which Shem and Shaun traveled. In VI.B.6, Joyce noted, "Sea animal to land / animal (Thyroid)" (VI.B.6: 59), to which the editors provided the gloss: "It is believed by biologists that the thyroid has played a prominent part in the change of sea creatures into land animals (migrating from an iodine rich to an iodine poor environment)" (VI.B.6 43). The origins also point to the aquatic origin of *all* life: the slow, careful process of our evolution from anaerobic, single-celled aquatic organisms. This connection between the geological and the individual is important for understanding Joyce's layering of varied forms of growth throughout the *Wake* because it conflates the particular with the universal.

Joyce's expressed distaste for flowers in the Vinding quotation that opens this present chapter is not, however, in agreement with the ways in which flowers are used in Joyce's texts. Flowers are almost always "growing things" themselves in the *Wake*, responsible for the hope of new life and the endurance of life in general (especially through the images of the "flower girls" and through the references to Quinet's flower-infused review of culture's impermanence). In this section I focus on the relationship between growth and questions of botanical agency and, more specifically, between sexual reproduction and flowers. An examination of Joyce's incorporation of floral and botanical images, characteristics, and metaphors into the *Wake* reveals an alignment between growth in nature, language, text, and the individual. Starting with a discussion of one particular reference in *Ulysses*, this section then moves to discuss two sections of book II.

In the beginning of *Ulysses*'s "Ithaca" episode, as Stephen and Bloom are heading toward 7 Eccles Street in the early hours of the morning, the reader is faced with the question, "Of what did the duumvirate deliberate during their itinerary?" (U 17.11). The answer is given as follows:

> Music, literature, Ireland, Dublin, Paris, friendship, woman, prostitution, diet, **the influence of gaslight or the light of arc and glowlamps on the growth of adjoining paraheliotropic trees**, exposed corporation emergency dustbuckets, the Roman catholic church, ecclesiastical celibacy, the Irish nation, jesuit education, careers, the study of medicine, the past day, the maleficent influence of the presabbath, Stephen's collapse. (U 17.12–18)

The line I have bolded above is the topic under investigation here. The term "paraheliotropic" is often glossed over by critics as akin to "phototropic," which relates to the movement of a plant toward (or away from) a light source. In Gifford's Ulysses *Annotated*, for example, readers are told: "In botany: 'of leaves that turn their edges toward brilliant antecedent light.' Paraheliotropism is the inhibition of leaf abcission due to light; a common example is a tree's retention of the leaves close to a streetlight (suggested by Roland McHugh)" (556). In relation to "Ithaca," this annotation is misleading. In fact, the annotation is not just misleading; it is not correct, and it is important to clarify this point because of Joyce's specific reliance on the botanical term in *Ulysses*.

The term "paraheliotropism" appeared in an 1881 issue of the journal *Nature*, in a letter to the editor titled "Movement of Plants," written by a Mr. Charles Darwin. Darwin describes his observations of the various rotations of plants in reaction to the direction of the light source: "The leaves of some plants, when brightly illuminated, direct their edges toward the light, and this remarkable movement I have called paraheliotropism" (409). In the *Oxford English Dictionary*, the term is defined as "A type of tropism in which a plant's leaves move to reduce injuriously intense illumination, usually by keeping their blades parallel to the light rays."[6] This term, then, describes the movement of the individual leaves and describes a self-defense mechanism of sorts that is demonstrated by some plants. For example, one plant that clearly exhibits paraheliotropism is the Tedera, common to the southwestern United States, which, during points of the day with the most intense sunlight, rolls up its leaves to prevent transpiration (which makes the plant valuable in this region because of its resistance to drought).

The discussion at hand in *Ulysses* in relation to paraheliotropism is related closely to another phenomenon, photoperiodism, defined as "The phenomenon whereby certain physiological processes in animals and plants are influenced by the length of daily exposure to light."[7] W. W. Garner and H. A. Allard first defined photoperiodism in a 1920 paper in the *Journal of Agricultural Research*. The ability of plants to have *reactions* and to *move* was quite a hot topic in this field, and one specific debate about this subject concerned the effect of artificial light (and particularly electric streetlights) on the growth of plants. In 1904, electric streetlamps were still new in Dublin—while the first appeared in 1881, electric streetlights were not widespread in Dublin until 1903, when the Pigeon House generating station opened. What this reference shows is Joyce's attention to current developments in technology and to scientific trends (he would have been working on "Ithaca" not long after the 1920 photoperiodism paper was published) and that his use of botany is not ornamental, nor can it be reduced to banalities about love and women as his use of flowers typically have been.

This reference to paraheliotropism in *Ulysses* reinforces Bloom's interest in popular science, but it also suggests that Bloom's wanderings throughout the day—a very sunny day, by Dublin standards—was a kind of self-defense (as critics largely agree it was; Bloom continues wandering throughout the city to avoid returning home to face the fact of his wife's adultery, and to avoid thinking about it). For a very different reason, the same can be said for Stephen Dedalus, who, like leaves curling up to protect themselves from the sun, protects himself by hiding his vulnerable side.

Additionally, it is important to note that the reference to paraheliotropism applies to both Stephen and Bloom (both largely ineffectual in *Ulysses*) and that this term is discussed at nighttime. The impact on the trees in question here is in terms of their growth, and like the plants under the artificial light, Stephen and Bloom can be seen as stunted characters. Joyce's specific use of paraheliotropism relates to the sexual failures of both Bloom and Stephen, to the self-defense mechanisms of Bloom, and to the stunted growth and maturity of Stephen Dedalus.

In *Finnegans Wake*, and particularly in II.1 and II.2, such botanical terms are used in equally specific ways and are used to articulate questions of growth in terms of sexuality, maturity, and progress. The children's games section of II.1 (drafted in 1930, after much of book I and book III had already been drafted) employs botanical imagery combined with the treatment of these games as metonyms for larger themes of growth and maturity that pervade the *Wake*.

The botanical imagery in these sections is combined with notes and topics from Joyce's reading in linguistic theory, particularly that of Marcel Jousse, Sir Richard Paget, and Vico.[8] Notebook VI.B.32 (1930) contains notes both from Richard Paget's *Human Speech: Some Observations, Experiments, and Conclusions as to the Nature, Origin, Purpose, and Possible Improvement of Human Speech* and from *Babel, or, The Past, Present, and Future of Human Speech* (both also 1930). The notes taken from Paget can be traced primarily to drafts of I.6, but the influence of Paget in book II is undeniable. Joyce integrates the ways in which language develops and grows for these theorists into other systems of growth, and in several places throughout the *Wake*, linguistic roots merge with botanical roots (e.g., "triliteral roots and his acorns" [FW 505.4]). In terms of the translation of the Paget material to the *Wake*, the seven "roots" of Indo-European language ("ad," "an," "da," "rup," "tan," "sa," "su"), when transferred to the drafts, are placed alongside fruits and seeds integral to plant growth and reproduction: "A1 an the highest but Roh re his root; filled fanned of heckleberries whenas all was tuck and toss up for him as a yangster to fall fou of hockinbechers wherein he had gauged the use of raisin; ads aliments, das doles, raps rustics, tams turmoil; sas seed enough for a semination but sues skivvies on the sly" (FW 130.13–18). In addition to the transfers made when VI.B.32 was in use, the Raphael transcriptions of unused Paget notes from VI.B.32 (found in VI.C.8: 4–11) make their way into II.3, again combining language, speech, and flowers (FW 360.3–7).

To provide some specific examples, Paget argues in *Babel* that "human speech [. . .] has grown up by a process of evolution" (12). Overall, Paget's text provides a Darwinian reading of language and speech. Moreover, Deane, Ferrer, and Lernout argue that in this text, "Paget states the theory that the development of the child recapitulates the evolution of the species" (VI.B.32 9). They refer to Paget's suggestion that children can be likened to "primitive man" (37, 57) in their capacity for linguistic ingenuity, for the creation new words, and even for the genesis of new systems of communication.

Laurent Milesi argues that the "heliotrope" riddle and its phonetic description can be closely tied to Jousse's gestural theories ("Supplementing" no page), and he carefully examines Joyce's notes from Paget in VI.B.32, though he does not highlight the role of botany in these sections (despite "heliotrope" being a specific flower). In addition to the discussion of linguistic roots, the correlation between botanical growth and linguistics can be found in the source texts themselves, thus making Joyce's own alignment of the two perfectly comprehensible. In the Darwinian-influenced *Babel, or, The Past, Present and Future of Human Speech* Paget argues, "Human speech is a wild growth, even our finest flowers of speech are but wild flowers" (8). In Paget's 1930 *Human Speech* he also writes of pollination in the chapter titled "Origin and Development of Speech." Here, in support of his belief that gestures are "the essential element of speech" (126), Paget provides some examples of "animal gesture in connection with the courtship rituals of insects and of birds" (126). For example, he describes two boastful "dances" that bees perform upon finding either good nectar or good pollen and the female acceptance of nesting material from the male in bird species such as the Grasshopper Warbler and the Louisiana Heron (136).

In II.1, the game played is one wherein one child must guess the color thought of by the girls, which Joyce famously defined as being called "Colours or Angels and Devils" (LI: 295). Glugg has the task of guessing the color "heliotrope," which, as Sam Slote explains, is ambiguous in and of itself because it is not only a color but also "a stone, a flower, and an orientation (*heliotropos*: turning toward the sun). Variants of the word 'heliotrope' pervade this chapter from the first draft" (HJW 189). The designation of "heliotrope" as the color in II.1 may also serve to contrast the worldviews of the two brothers in terms of mechanism and organicism. From the first draft, Chuff is associated with light ("Chuffy was a nangel then and his soard fleshed light like lightening" [BL 47477-6, JJA 51: 14, FDV 130.6, FW 222.22–23]), as opposed to Shem, who, like Bloom and Stephen of "Ithaca," is in darkness, unable to awaken the female energies. Typically, it is Shaun whom all the women in the *Wake* desire, and his association with sunshine extends this to a botanical interpretation and makes "heliotropical," as John Bishop explains, a moving toward the sun and a "resurrection, and the rebirth of consciousness" (FW xxii).

Dirk Van Hulle argues that after Glugg fails to answer the riddle for a second time, "the rainbow or flower girls dance and sing in praise of their sun hero Chuff" (*Textual* 103). Then, in the first draft of II.3 (FW 236.33–240.4),[9] the flower girls expose themselves to the sun (Chuff); they "tournasoled" (BL 47477-33, JJA 51: 74, FDV 135.10, FW 236.36) or turned toward the sun, the "sol," which Van Hulle calls "heliolatry." The girls are then described as "yenng frilles-in-pleyurs" (BL 47477-9, JJA 51: 9, FDV 131.11–12, FW 224.22–24), a reference to the second volume of Proust's *A la recherche du temps perdu*, *A l'ombre des jeunes filles en fleurs*, often translated as "In the shadow of young girls in flower" (Grieve). In the context of this chapter concerning growth, this Proustian reference asserts Joyce's linking of the coming of age of the female with the growth of flowers. A focus on leaves also appears in Joyce's addition to II.3§6, "and they leaved the most leavely of leaftimes and the most foliagenous till the come the marrer of nirth" (BL 47480-222v, JJA 55: 388, FW 361.26–33), a section concerning the loss of sexual innocence of the girls, the appearance of buds on their leaves akin to the allusion to Proust's *jeunes filles en fleurs*.

To support this alignment, the reproductive parts of a flower are presented in this 1930 draft in quite sensual terms:

> Just so styled are their petals each of all has a stalk unto herself love and all of all of their understamens is as open as he can posably she and tournasoled straightout or sidewaist according to the courses of things feminite towooerds him, their lord & stigmatiser, that they may catchup in these calyzettes those parryshoots from his

muscalone pistil, (O my goodmiss! O my greatness! O my pricelestly preshoes!) while dewyfally as dumbelles they allisten to his elixir.

Enchainted, sweet dear Stainusless, dearest dearest, we herehear aboutabuds thee salutant Pattren of our unschooled, deliverer of softmissives, send us a wise and letters play of all you canceive of from your holy post. Sweetstaker, we toutes were drawpaits so want lotteries of ticklets. Will bee all buzzy one another again minmie for you are pollen yourself. (BL 47477-33, 34, JJA 51: 74–75, FDV 135.8–21, FW 236.33–238.35)

Flowers themselves are useful for understanding evolution, as they have evolved in terms of color, fragrance, and texture to become more appealing to insects and animals for pollination purposes. Pollination, the reproductive "act" of flowers, is the movement of pollen (which contains the sperm) from the anther (part of the stamen, the male reproductive organ) to the stigma (part of the pistil, the female reproductive organ). Once the pollen reaches the stigma, the ovule is fertilized, and the seeds of the next generation are produced; thus, the girls bare themselves to Chuff, wishing for pollination (Wilmer 3–4).

The fair copy of this section alters the flower parts line slightly, changing it to: "Just so styled with the nattes are their flowerheads now and each of all has a lovestalk" (BL 47477-38, JJA 51: 78, FW 236.33–34). The addition of "nattes" points toward "night," contrasting with Chuff's sun and providing the necessary change in temperature many plants require for flowers to blossom. Gnats are an insect conducive to pollination (Wilmer 533), and "lovestalk" instead of just "stalk" clears this passage up for anyone not well versed in flower reproduction.

Some of the botanical imagery in the *Wake* likely relates back to the technology of the period, particularly to time-lapse photography and to cinema of the period. Christina Alt, in the introduction to *Virginia Woolf and the Study of Nature*, recounts the prevalence of short nature documentaries preceding feature films throughout the 1910s, 1920s, and 1930s and their extreme popularity with cinemagoers. Alt quotes film historian Laura Marcus, who observes that "the fascination with films which speeded up natural processes, as in the growth and unfolding of a flower, and with filmic slow-motion" arose from a "sense that film could show the very workings of nature, opening up entirely new dimensions of the visible, and the invisible, world" (qtd. in Alt 59). John McCourt, writing of the "cinematic" qualities of *Ulysses* in the introduction to *Roll Away the Reel World: James Joyce and Cinema*, quotes Jean Epstein, who also describes this type of nature film described by Laura Marcus. Epstein writes of how "a documentary shot describing in a few minutes twelve months in the life of a plant [. . .] seems to free us of terrestrial, i.e. solar time, of the rhythm to which we seem ineluctably bound" (qtd. in McCourt 9). The popularity of these types of films in the 1920s and 1930s indicates that Joyce would have been familiar with such cinematic portrayals of botanical growth and that they would have influenced how Joyce incorporated this material into II.1.[10]

As mentioned previously, the question of the agency of plants was a major debate in natural science during this period. The publication of Darwin's 1880 *The Power of Movement in Plants*—a study of phototropism—was met with great excitement, and the first fifteen hundred copies sold out quickly (F. Darwin 502–10). In addition, the debates over photoperiodism, paraheliotropism (exaggerated, also, by the Great Depression), and "sensitive plants" (first identified by Darwin in his 1875 *Insectivorous Plants*) furthered discussions about the effect of external stimuli on plants.

On the topic of "sensitive plants," the first draft of II.2 contains the line, "Mimosa multimimetica, the miming of miming (or is it an ash sapling)" (BL 47478-286, JJA 52: 14, FDV 142.10, FW 267.2–3). "Mimosa" is a genus of plant whose name derives from the Greek "mimic." According to the *Oxford English Dictionary*, "The name alludes to the movements of the leaves ('mimicking' animal life) shown by many plants of this type,"[11] which are called "sensitive plants," meaning that the leaves of these plants fold up in response to touch. Joyce's selection of mimosa carefully entwines the botanical specificity of the flower reproduction in II.1 with the behavior of the "flower girls," and the mime/mim in both words refers to the "Mime of Mick, Nick and the Maggies." In this sense, the children's game not only, as J. S. Atherton asserts, "re-enact[s] the history of their race" ("Sport" 58), but it also imitates the behavior of nature. The flower girls turn their petals inward, protecting their reproductive organs, just as the mimosa flower shies away from touch.

The garden is a space wherein nature is arranged into an externally determined pattern, and it provides another plane for the joining of women and nature. References to gardening continue in the first draft of II.2. One such reference, "Eire, Eire, clane cuntrary, how does your girdle grow?

Eat earthy earthapples. Leap the law. Wide hiss, we're wizening. Hoots fromm, we're globing" (BL 47478-121, JJA 52: 20, FDV 143.18–20, FW 272.1–8), begins with the nursery rhyme "Mary, Mary quite contrary, how does your garden grow?" and moves on toward the story of Adam and Eve with the "earthapples" and the "hiss" of the serpent. Replacing "Mary" with "Eire" turns Ireland into a gardener, watching over her plants and waiting for them to mature. "Clane" is Clane, County Kildare, mentioned because it is both by the Liffey and the location of Clongowes. Because of Clane's proximity to the Liffey, "Leap the law" is likely another reference to Leixlip, in addition to its referring to the betrayal of God's edict. The theme of gardening is related to the fertility associated with riverbanks, and the reference to Clongowes links the education of the children with their growth. The "seeds" of knowledge are, if you will, "planted," and will be harvested like a potato, or *Erdäpfel* in German. "Earthapple," in addition to *Erdäpfel*, is also "apple," providing a relationship between knowledge, growth, and sin and bringing the references to gardening back to the Garden of Eden.[12]

The second reference demonstrates that the motifs of gardening and planting are directly linked to the progression of history and the development of children: "Dark ages clasp the daisy roots. Stop if you a sally of the allies, hot on naval actiums pitched engagements banks of oars & lightlicked estudis are a B. C. minding missy, please do" (BL 47478-121, JJA 52: 20, FDV 144.1–3, FW 272.9–14). In French, daisy is *marguerite*, one of the flowers used by Quinet, but it is also related to the previously discussed "margaritomancy." The children studying their "ABCs" ("estudis are a B. C.") are the *marguerites*, the Maggies, advancing toward maturity and sexual knowledge. The "dark ages" are in contrast to illumination (required for the growth of the daisies, the maturity of the girls, and the advancement of all human civilizations out of the Dark Ages). The lines following "daisy roots" all relate to war, with "sally" meaning either "sallyport" or "sally forth," "allies," "naval Actium" (the Battle of Actium [Octavius against Antony and Cleopatra]), and "oars" referring to Viking oarsmen. Like the poppies that refer to the war dead in Flanders Fields, history reveals itself here through the "daisy roots."

The representation of botanical growth and agency through the sexual maturation of young girls, the evolution of language, and the procession of history provides a richer understanding of how Joyce addresses the theme of growth through the *Wake*. Through the genetic examination of this subject, it is evident that Joyce also wove the growth of his text into the growth of children, adults, plants, civilizations, and language. In this sense, Joyce's love of "growing things" is made clear, and the composition of *Finnegans Wake*, on some levels, mirrors the natural processes of life.

Marriage and Trees

In II.1, the themes of maturity and growth continue with the introduction of several phrases relating to gardening, planting, and roots, helping to strengthen the link between adolescent sexuality, flora, and history. One line of the II.1 drafts, "The mar of murmury mermers to the mind's ear, uncharted rock, evasive weed" (BL 47477-105, JJA 51: 196, FW 254.18–19), echoes ALP with its dynamic "murmury mermers" (with *mer* and *mère*, the French for "sea" and "mother," respectively) and with the rock and weed relating to HCE, the static male figure. The "evasive," or invasive, weed suggests a foreign object planting itself on foreign soil: either HCE as the land copulating with ALP as the river or HCE as city attempting to subjugate ALP as nature. The "uncharted" rock also suggests unknown female regions, connecting again to "The Triangle" sketch.

Additionally, the "Norwegian Captain" sketch addresses the relationship between invasive and native, figuring this polarization in terms of marriage, which is often used to articulate the relationship between HCE and ALP, culture and nature, city and country throughout the *Wake*. Marriage throughout the *Wake* is sometimes a symbol for the conquest of nature by civilization (personified in nature's frequent alignment with the female, though HCE is sometimes the mountain, too), but perhaps because Joyce himself had recently married (Joyce and Nora married in 1931), marriage also becomes a metaphor for the way in which Joyce represents growth and resolution. The marriage of the Norwegian captain to the tailor's daughter in II.3 is also the marriage of the seafarer and the land, the colonizer and the colonized, and man and woman, and also extends to Joyce's interest in the influence of migration on both land and language. The collision of these opposing forces ends positively: marriage brings children and a new family; the blending of different tongues produces a new language.

Philip McCann told the basic narrative of the Norwegian captain, of "a hunchbacked Norwegian captain who ordered a suit from a Dublin tailor, J. H. Kerse of 34 Upper Sackville Street," to John Joyce: "The finished suit did not fit him, and the captain berated the tailor for being unable to sew, whereupon the irate tailor denounced him for being impossible to fit. The subject was not promising, but it became, by the time John Joyce had retold it, wonderful farce, and it is among the native and outlander tales, humorous but full of acrid repartee, that found their way into *Finnegans Wake*" (JJ 111). In the version of the story that appears in the *Wake*, the captain eventually gives up after three tries to fit the suit and marries the tailor's daughter instead. Most accounts of the story as it appears in the *Wake* focus on the farce aspect of the tale, but few focus on what as early a critic as Ellmann has identified as one of the "parables of native and outlander." This story of marriage has much larger political and colonial implications, functioning also as an image of the "marriage" of human and nature, the figuring of "conquest" of nature or landscape as female, and a parable of the founding of both a family and a city (which also connects this sketch to III.3§B).

The Norwegian captain wishes for a suit of clothing, but also attempts to be the sui*tor* to the tailor's daughter, characterized (like Issy) by watery elements (specifically "dew" in this section, which also emphasizes her role as flower girl and connects her particularly to the Issy of I.6 and III.4). In the larger context of this passage, the line "Floodlift, her ancient of rights regaining, so yester yidd, even remenbrance," which likely refers to the Nile's (or really any river's) life-giving floods, intimates Issy's/the tailor's daughter's sexual initiation (implying fertility on both levels). This feminized image of natural renewal follows the seasonal cycles from earlier in the sketch. The renewal provided by the flood is in line with Rose and O'Hanlon's explanation that Issy (embodied in the figure of the tailor's daughter) is akin to a flower awaiting spring. Issy/the tailor's daughter, they argue, "has been lying in her truckle-bed all winter long, thinking romantic thoughts and praying for the bad weather to come to an end and wanting the primroses to spring up again and all the leaves to appear on the bare boughs in the wood" (170). The passage of the seasons and the cyclical weather patterns mirror the young girl's dreams of love and of her growth into sexual maturity. The pending marriage of the sailor with the tailor's daughter is depicted as the imminent arrival of springtime, returning to the alignment of botanical growth and blossoming sexuality present in II.1 and II.2, and also looking forward to the "flood" at the end of book IV (which is also responsible for growth).

The sexual maturation of girls presented in parallel with botanic growth also appears in drafts of III.4. In the chapter, there is another account of the rise and fall of HCE, his development, his role as civic leader, his wealth, and his children. Instead of flowers this time, trees are used in the story. The capital is made "out of landed selfinterest" (BL 47482a-9v, JJA 60: 16, FDV 268.4, FW 589.8–9), and HCE's womanizing is described as "running a girl in Goatstown, harbouring fallen women & felling the pines" (BL 47482a-7v, JJA 60: 12, FDV 268.9–10, not in FW). Again, civilization develops at the expense of nature, and the land is feminized, exploited, and betrayed. However, the daughter, who was seen on her way "to the oakroom fancy ball" (BL 47482a-7v, JJA 60: 12, FDV 268.12, not in FW), is a "picture queen" (BL 47482a-7v, JJA 60: 12, FDV 268.11, not in FW) and is a ray of light and hope. The trees in III.4 become a symbol of decay and of hope, of death and of creation.

The comparison between "fallen women" and "felling the pines" is integral to one section of II.1. To the 1932 fair copy of II.1 §4–5, Joyce adds, "Artho is the name is on the hero, Capellisato, shoehanded tree murderer" (BL 47477-91, JJA 51: 173, FW 254.36–255.2), which is then later changed to "shoehanded slaughterer of the shader of our leaves." The designation "tree murderer" is from "tree murderer = woodsman" (VI.B.3: 107), a note taken from O. Henry's story "An Adjustment of Nature" in *The Four Million*. The story is largely focused on a waitress named Milly who is couched in imagery of "Evehood" and "motherhood" and spoken of as the "Goddess" of a down-home diner. The narrator and his friend, a painter believing in the "Unerring Artistic Adjustment of Nature," imagine what may become of Milly: "Milly, like some vast virgin stretch of pine woods, was made to catch the lumberman's eye" (106). The two then find displeasure in their own image of Milly as a "virgin stretch of pine woods," envisioning her marriage to a "tree murderer" (105).[13] In O. Henry's story, the "tree murderer" destroys the "virgin stretch of pine woods" just as the husband despoils the wife.

This idea of the "tree murderer" appears at other points in the *Wake*, too, and one example from I.2 puts this image in the context of early forestry laws, such as those set by William the Conqueror. Three specific terms relating to the historical management of forests and parkland can be found in I.2, with the inclusion of "woodwards," "regarders," and "vert" (FW 34.25). The term "woodward" originated in the eleventh century and described the office of managing woodland and growing timber. A "regarder" was also an officer responsible for the management of forestland, but this term was Anglo-Norman.[14] In their context in I.2, these terms are associated with the Phoenix Park and with original sin; HCE's "impropriety" was "advanced by some woodwards or regarders" (FW 34.15). Joyce continues, describing HCE's transgression in front of the "dainty maidservants" in "the rushy hollow wither," and refers to this as "a first offence in vert or venison" (FW 34.20–25). "Vert" is either "green vegetation growing in a wood or forest and capable of serving as cover for deer"[15] or "the right to cut green trees or shrubs in a forest."[16]

In conjunction with the presence of "woodwards," "regarder," and "vert" in I.2 (not to mention the discussions of forestry in terms of the Phoenix Park and the Irish National Foresters), the addition to II.1 of the "tree murderer" note from O. Henry (and also in conjunction with *Capellisato*, which alludes to Chapelizod) refers to the management of the woodlands and to the domestication of both nature and women. As mentioned above, the VI.C notebooks contain "deforestation" (VI.C.3: 8) and "timber ceased 1765 / deforesting the military" (VI.C.7: 224), which actually also appear in the "Cyclops" British Library note sheets:

B <deforesting for military reasons>
B <1765 timber ceased>
timber a crop must be cut. (204.77–79)

Both VI.C notes are crossed in the notebooks, indicating that they were transferred to drafts in the mid-1930s.[17]

This relationship between female sexuality and trees is also evident in the first draft of II.2 with, "who once under the branches of the elms, their shoes as yet unshent by the stoniness of the way, went, arms enlacing along by fancied banks of blooms & rambler roses, thinking about it, the It with the itch in it, the business we were born for" (BL 47478-118, JJA 52: 16, FDV 143.4–7, FW 267.25–268.6). The tree/stone motif retains the dynamic/static parallel but also adopts the female/male duality. The youthful, virginal female ("shoes as yet unshent by the stoniness") is placed under the elm tree, but the moving branches of the elm presage sexual maturity ("the business we were born for"), as does the association with the ALP-like language of "arms enlacing by fancied bank of blooms."

During these final years of the *Wake*, the association between sexuality, botany, and history becomes a leading structural device for the expansion of book II. The interrelation between the vicissitudes of nature and the growth of civilizations continues to be a key theme as Joyce progresses with work on II.1. In line with Rome's translation to Chapelizod in the tree murderer passage, two other lines added at the II.1§6A draft level reinforce the return to Ireland as Joyce reintroduces Tara and as Isolde merges with the figure of Grainne. The additions of "Look sharp, she's signalling again from the asters. Turn again wishfulton loud mere of Doubtluin. Arise, land under wave" (BL 47477-116, JJA 51: 114, FW 248.8) and "even though mode grow mannerish and the Tarara boom decay" (BL 47477-121, JJA 51: 119, FW 247.28) convey the birth of modern Ireland, starting with the mythical Tara and "Land-Under-Wave," the kingdom wherein the king's daughter was a lover of the mythical Diarmaid (of Diarmaid and Grainne). The "boom" is also *baum* (German for "tree"), and when juxtaposed with "decay," the rise and fall of civilizations (such as the one centered around the Hill of Tara) is illustrated with an image of the growth and decay of trees.

When Joyce composed II.2§6, the lengthy footnote of FW 279 continues to connect marriage and sexuality with the earth's fertility: "Wait till spring has sprung in spickness and prigs begin to pry" (BL 47478-306, JJA 52: 232, FW 279.42). "Nature tells everybody about it," Joyce continues, referring, like the "the business we were born for," to the instincts of reproduction. Through such instincts, "nature" is again given its own agency. As Joyce continued to align the human figures with flowers, trees, and water, these relationships, so often imaged as marriages, grew to be inseparable from the "universal history" in the *Wake*. The image of marriage to convey the inescapable bond between nature and culture is used so readily because of its connection with Vico's human institutions, its position in terms of both religion and the formation of the nuclear family, and its ability to produce new life (as well as its more contractual aspects).

Evolutions: Fossils, Rocks, and Rivers

Another important aspect of "growth" that appears throughout the *Wake* is the way in which evolution functions on levels extending from the individual to the geological. In the late proofs for *Finnegans Wake*, Joyce develops the links between evolution, nature, and language. Following the passage in II.3 that revisits the story of Grannuaile from I.1, Joyce writes: "And aye far he fared from Afferik Arena and yea near he night till Blowland Bearring. And the sea shoaled and the saw squalled. And, soaking scupper, didn't he drain!" (BL 47479-15, JJA 54: 25, FDV 175.1–4, FW 320.27–320.31). In the Norse sagas (fitting for the context of the

"Norwegian Captain" sketch) "blueland" or "Blaaland" is the old name for Africa, hence "Blowland." Here, the Scandinavians have again taken to the seas ("fared," "sea shoaled," "squalled," "soaking scupper"), traveling from Africa to the Bering Strait. The "Bearring" is the Bering Strait (see also FW 602.30, "polar bearing"), named after Danish explorer Vitius Bering (Glasheen 750).

In the late nineteenth century, the theory of the Bering Strait land bridge was first popularized, proposing the previous unification of Alaska and Russia and providing a hypothesis for the migration of peoples. From the 1880s to the 1930s, the question of the Bering Strait as once being a land bridge joining what is now Alaska and Siberia was hotly debated. In 1894, G. M. Dawson asserted that the shallow seas around the Bering Strait must "physiographically" belong to the continental plateau and not the ocean basin. He argued that "in later geologic times more than once and perhaps during prolonged periods [there existed] a wide terrestrial plain connecting North American and Asia" (qtd. in Hopkins 2). D. M. Hopkins explains that this theory was supported by the findings of several "fossil mammoth remains on the Unalaska and Pribilof Islands, cited by Stanley Brown (1892) and by Dall and Harris (1892)," which "lent conviction to the notion that much of the Bering continental shelf had indeed once been dry land connecting these remote islands with the Alaskan and Siberian mainland" (2). One of the most significant developments came in 1934, when Reginald Daly published *The Changing World of the Ice Age*, which argued that sea levels fluctuated in response to changes in glaciers during the Ice Ages. The presence of the Bering Strait here in the *Wake* is directly connected both to the polar exploration discussed in chapter 3 and to contemporary issues in archaeology and anthropology.

In the term "Afferik Arena," *Affe* is "ape" in German, *Afer* is "African" in Latin, *rik* is Danish for "realm," and *arena* is Latin for "sand." This term merges the two separate regions linguistically to underline the Bering Strait migration hypothesis and to emphasize the effects of exploration on the understanding of geography. Influenced of course by Darwin, the late nineteenth and early twentieth centuries brought passionate interest in the study of human evolution. The discovery of early human fossils during these decades dramatically altered perceptions of humanity's place in creation, and they were, unsurprisingly, a popular subject and a common topic in the news (for example, a 1925 issue of *Popular Science* contained the large headline, "The 'Missing Link' at Last?: Discovery of ape man's skull may prove theory that Africa is the birthplace of man" [50]). After two major finds, the first being an 1891 discovery of a human fossil on the island of Java by Eugene Dubois and the second the 1907 discovery of the "Heidelberg Man" in Germany, most attention was turned to Africa, believed by Darwin to be the cradle of humanity. In 1924, Raymond Dart discovered a small child's skull in a quarry near Tuang in South Africa and named it *Australopithecus africanus*, meaning "Southern Ape from Africa" (Rice 107). Dart's success in Africa led to other crucial discoveries during the 1920s and 1930s, particularly by the Scottish archaeologist Robert Broom, who found the first adult fossils of an *Australopithecus africanus* in 1936. In 1935, Mary Leakey also began her work at the Olduvai Gorge in Tanzania that led to Donald Johanson's 1974 discovery of "Lucy."[18] "Afferik Arena" likely refers to these discoveries, and with *Affe* ("ape"), this sketch also contains the Greek *anthrôpos* (FW 318.5), the Latin *homo* (FW 318.6), and the German *Mensch* (FW 318.27). The name by which we refer to man evolves in the same way the physical man does.

In addition to those in II.3, Joyce also adds references to prehistoric humans and Neanderthals to the 1936 *transition* pages of I.1. The addition "Heidenburgh in the days when Head-in-Clouds walked the earth" (BL 47475-10v, JJA 44: 246, FW 18.23) refers, on the one hand, to religion in Vico's *New Science*, implying both giants (with their heads in the clouds) and the pagan belief in deities' embodiment in nature. On the other hand, this addition also refers to the "Heidelberg man," the early human posited from the 1907 discovery of one fossilized jawbone in Germany (and perhaps the source of "fassilwise" of FW 13.32). H. G. Wells, in *A Short History of the World* (1921), discusses the impact of the discovery of the Heidelberg man upon our understanding of ourselves. When Wells first mentions the Heidelberg man, he writes of the "single quasi-human jawbone" that was "absolutely chinless, far heavier than a true human jawbone and narrower, so that it is improbable the creature's tongue could have moved about for articulate speech" (25). Consequently, biological evolution was necessary to the development of speech, an idea that would have appealed to Joyce's interest in theories of gestural language from Jousse, Paget, and Vico.

Additionally, the discovery of these early humans queried hierarchies organized around race and religion. Joyce's description in I.4 of "the same man (or a different and younger him of the same ham) asked in the vermicular with a very oggly chew-chin-grin" (FW 82.12), with its mention of the vernacular ("vermicular"), appears in conjunction with a reference to the 1843 Slave Trade Act (the acts known as 6&7 Victoria, or, in the *Wake*, "Was six victolios fifteen" [FW 82.12–13], *International Labour Organization*). The "different and younger" refers to an ancestor of modern man, and "of the same ham" refers to Noah's son Ham, both suggesting common ancestry for all humankind. Joyce's juxtaposition of human ancestry with the modern slave trade becomes an argument for the equality of all beings and against the artificial hierarchies that resulted in such an abominable economic practice in the first place. The "chin-grin" accompanying the "vermicular" also demonstrates the same relationship between speech and physiology implied by Wells.

Wells writes that seeing the jawbone of the Heidelberg man is "like looking through a defective glass into the past and catching just one blurred and tantalizing glimpse of this Thing, shambling through the bleak wilderness, clambering to avoid the sabre-tooth tiger, watching the wooly rhinoceros in the woods" (24). Wells's focus on the "wilderness" and the "woods" is characteristic of the rhetoric of the period as feelings of threat were common concerning the idea that the rational human descended from something that seems so alien and so animalistic in its physical appearance (i.e., the feeling that these fossilized remains could not be precursors of us; they are heathens, animals that lived in the chaos of the wilderness and the woods). By placing this "Thing" in the "bleak wilderness," Wells reduces the Heidelberg man to a plane with the "sabre-tooth tiger" and the "wooly rhinoceros." This equation of the human and the animal, or rather, this rehabilitation of the human to its proper category of "animal," is one of the most important ideas of the late nineteenth and early twentieth centuries, and Joyce's inclusion of nonhuman animals and prehistoric humans is representative of these changes.

In addition to human fossils, several other "rocks" appear throughout the *Wake*, often in conjunction with themes of language, cultural exchange, and evolution. On the *transition* pages of I.1, Sir Tristram is also "violer d'amores," and he has "rearrived" from "Armorica." "Armorica" is usually glossed as either "America" or "Armorica/Aremorica," the latter being an ancient name for an area of present-day Brittany. "Armorican," like "Ordovican," is also a name for a geologic time period, linguistically representing the once-united landmasses of Ireland and Brittany. According to Pliny's *Natural History*, the name "Armorica" was Celtic in origin, denoting, as Charles Anthon explains, "a region bordering on the sea, and derived from the Celtic words ar mor, 'on the sea'" (2: 115–16).[19]

The final passage of I.3 is laden with geological terms and references, returning to early human history and to early natural history with some of nature's oldest artifacts: rocks. Joyce includes "build rocks over him" (BL 47472-191, JJA 45: 218, FW 73.9), "with rochelly exetur" (BL 47476a-185, JJA 49: 392, FW 73.23), "chambered cairns" (BL 47472-155v, JJA 45: 198, FW 73.29), "eolithostroton" (BL 47472-155v, JJA 45: 198, FW 73.30), "the evoluation of human society and a testament of the rocks from all the dead unto some the living" (BL 47475-120, JJA 45: 332–33, FW 73.32–33),[20] and "skatterlings of a stone" (BL 47475-31, JJA 45: 298, FW 73.34). Believed to have been naturally created by geological processes, the "eolith," or "eolithostroton," is an ancient stone instrument from the Pleistocene era. At the end of I.3, the references to rocks, cuneiform ("langwedge" [FW 73.1]), ancient burial techniques, and so on also provide a narrative of cultural evolution. The combination of these images, of the "Oxmanswold" and the "chambered cairns," points, on a microcosmic level, toward HCE's retiring to sleep, but on a macrocosmic level, they point toward HCE's death and toward the even larger cultural and geological processes continuing in the world while one is asleep.[21]

Conclusion

New Boundaries of Ecocriticism

Joyce's Ecotaph

In "A Preliminary Stratigraphy of *Scribbledehobble*," John Barger argues: "If one chooses to push the limits of the geological metaphor for Joyce's *Finnegans Wake* notetaking, the physical notebooks may be seen as a series of riverbeds into which notes, like sedimentary pebbles, have been deposited over a period of months or years" (127). This description is quite appropriate; a genetic reading of any theme or section of the *Wake* reveals that much of what Joyce ended up writing developed out of the words already present and that the process was cumulative. The aesthetic of the bog and the midden heap throughout the *Wake* is important for understanding Joyce's attitudes toward language and toward the composition of his work. Bogs do not provide the graceful model of growth that the traditional image of the tree does; bogs provide a model of growth dependent on decay, detritus, and accumulation. Midden heaps, likewise, are the repositories of a culture's waste; they are the objects that are left behind. The way in which Joyce composed *Finnegans Wake* relied upon the detritus of others' words and the scatterings of dozens of source texts. Over time, the fragments of text became part of one another, creating layer upon layer of text for the *Wake*. Evolution states that genes mutate over time in response to external factors, and in *Finnegans Wake*, language does the same. Over time, a word becomes detached from its original context but enters into another system, gaining a new context that nonetheless contains its etymological trace.

This section presents some final examples of Joyce's environmental themes in the *Wake*, uniting themes from each of the preceding five chapters. In the "Mutt and Jute" dialogue of I.1 (first drafted in 1926), an account of Dublin's foundation is embedded within the presentation of how various wars and invasions contributed to the language spoken in Ireland. Joyce uses specifics of Dublin's waterways to again demonstrate the link between history, geography, and nation:

> Walk a dun blink roundward this albutisle and you skull see how olde ye plaine of my Eltershunfree and ours, where wone to wail whimbrel to peewee o'er the saltings, where wilbycitie by law of isthmon, where by a droit of signory, icefloe was from his Inn the Byggning to whose FinishtherePunct. Let erehimruhmuhrmuhr. Mearmerge two races swete and brack. Morthering rue. Hither, crachingeastuards, they are in surgence: hence, cool at ebb, they requiesce. Countlessness of livestories have netherfallen by this plage, flick as flowflakes, litters from aloft, like a waastwizzard all of whirlworlds. Now are all tombed to the mounf, isges to isges, erde from erde. (BL 47472-34, JJA 44: 122, FW 17.17–30)

In this passage, the city of Dublin is inextricably bound to the Liffey, and its own history is implicated with the changes in the river's landscape. The city is bound by the isthmus ("isthmon") of Sutton to the north, its "Byggning" (which also alludes to its Scandinavian heritage), and it extends from the sea to the point where it "finishes," the "Finishthere Punct" (*Punkt*, the German for "point," and also the Phoenix Park). Memory is linked again with water; Thomas Moore's "Let Erin remember the days of old" merges with German's *Errinerung* ("memory"). The "two races" merge as does the fresh water with the saltwater, the "swete and brack." The Liffey's tidal quality is conveyed with "hither, crashing eastuards," its eastward movement toward the sea, and "eastuards" is also "estuary," a tidal inlet of the sea that can include fjords, lagoons, bays, and river mouths. The merging of the two races with the "swete and brack" water of the tidal estuary is also mirrored by the merging of the languages as demonstrated by the numerous Danish, Norse, Greek, Latin, French, Italian, Irish, and Dutch words.

This merging of fresh and saltwater with the tidal nature of estuaries and their sedimentary properties is linked with the recording of histories, the "countlessness of livestories" etched into the beach and washed away by tides. Ecologically, an estuary is important because of its function as a transitional space; the quality of being between land and sea contributes to estuarial regions' high levels of biodiversity. Because of this, estuaries have also played significant roles in world history, dictating the rises and falls of civilizations, determining cultural traditions, and preserving artifacts of what occurred there, creating layers of narrative that include the human, the natural, and the national. In the *Wake*, these layers of history are stratified and continually shifting. The final line of the paragraph above from I.1 evokes the fairly clichéd notion of creation as dependent on destruction with its tombs and burial mounds and its "isges to isges, erde from erde" (ashes to ashes, dust to dust). The return to the dust, the earth (*erde*), also includes bacterial decomposition, with "erde" not being far from the French for "shit," *merde*.

More than a decade later, this mixing of language and nature also pervades the end of the *Wake*. In book IV, as ALP prepares for her return into the hydrological cycle, she becomes increasingly anxious about the future of her relationship with HCE (as Dublin city/the landscape): "You will always call me Leafy, won't you?" Obviously a pun on "Liffey," this line also suggests that the river will someday no longer be *leafy*—that is, will no longer be young, beautiful, and fertile. Because of the leaf-drop that occurs (for most plants) as autumn approaches, ALP worries she will lose some of her external beauty as she ages (referring both to the trees along the Liffey and to the Liffey itself). As the section continues, ALP is guiding HCE from Chapelizod, and they reach the weir at Islandbridge just before the river becomes channeled. After they pass over this weir, she ceases. The city has momentarily stifled nature's voice with the channeling and damming of the Liffey, but ALP assures, "I'll begin again in a jiffy."

Joyce adds to the beginning of the first typescript of IV§5 (BL 47488-134v–37), "No wind, no word. Only a leaf, just a leaf and then leaves" (BL 47488-135, JJA 63: 213, FW 619.22). Throughout the entire composition of *Finnegans Wake*, Joyce has been working with this relationship between nature and language, and this line provides a fitting conclusion to the query. As is demonstrated by an addition to the second typescript of this section that merges language, the flow of the river, and flowers, "in the langua of flows" (BL 47488-145, JJA 63: 227, FW 621.22), our language derives from the environment in which we live, and the rhythms of our speech and our writing mimic the natural world (the line implies a language of flowers as well). Dirk Van Hulle, drawing upon Mauthner and Jespersen source texts, argues that this "langua of flows" line demonstrates how "ALP seems to become the personification of language itself" (HJW 452) with her simultaneous consistency (*langue*) and instability (*parole*).

Adding to the dependence of speech on nature, "no wind, no word" likely also refers to the descent of the Holy Spirit in Acts: "And suddenly from heaven there came a sound like the rush of a mighty wind, and it filled the entire house where they were sitting. Divided tongues, as of fire, appeared among them. All of them were filled with the Holy Spirit and began to speak in other languages, as the Spirit gave them ability" (Acts 2:2–4). Book IV's "bearing down on me now under whitespread winds like he'd come from Arkangels" (FW 628.10) also contains this reference to "winds" coming from above; here, the winds are bearing messages like those of the archangels. The divine origin of the winds is juxtaposed with Vico's thunder, and together, "no wind, no word" further supports the *Wake*'s alignment of weather with providence.

ALP's voice begins to blend into the trees as she prepares to nourish their roots as rain again: "Lsp! I am leafy speafing. Lpf!" (FW 619.20–21). She continues, "The woods are fond always. As were we their babes in" (FW 619.23–24),[1] returning to the woods (Wicklow) in which she was born (cf. I.8). ALP attempts to rouse HCE (as the city, the landscape, culture, and civilization), begging him to accompany her and attempting to persuade him with arboreal compliments: "I want to see you looking fine for me. With your brandnew big green belt and all. Blooming in the very lotust and second to nill, Budd!" (FW 620.1–3). She tells him, "I could lead you there and I still by you in bed" (FW 622.19–20), trying to convince him to come with her back to from whence she came.

When trying to persuade HCE to join her, she also recounts the times in which HCE had been victimized, and the "wood" also returns to the recurring motif of the hunt with an addition to the fourth typescript of IV§5: "Or the Wald Unicorns Master, Bugley Captain, from the Naul, drawls up by the door with the HonourableWhilp, and the Reverend Poynter and the two Lady Pagets of Tallyhaugh, Ballyhuntus, in their riddletight raiding hats for to lift a hereshealth to their robost, the Stag, evers the Carlton hart" (BL 47488-162, JJA 63: 263, FW 622.24–29). "Carlton hart" is County Kildare's Carlton House, with its expansive hunting grounds dating back to the Norman invasion of Ireland. This passage also includes pointers ("Poynter"), the dogs used in hunting, but as "Reverends," uniting religious persecution with hunting.

In VI.B.47, Joyce recorded "the Wards' Master" (VI.B.47: 17), referring to the master of the hunt for the Ward Union Staghounds, established in 1830 (and based in County Meath).[2] The change from "Ward" to "Wald" brings in the German word for "forest" (*Wald*) and continues the emphasis on trees and woodlands and the return to this "wood." The "Whilp" is also the "whip," "A huntsman's assistant who keeps the hounds from straying by driving them back with the whip into the main body of the pack."³ ALP brings up this memory of being hunted to rouse her husband, insinuating that HCE ("evers the Carlton Hart") will again become a victimized figure. "Ballyhuntus" (*Baile* [Irish "town," such as in *BaileÀthaCliath*] hunt us) suggests that the city itself will be hunted, or that the city itself will do the hunting. Either way, this word suggests that the tensions and violence embodied in the motif of the hunt are inescapable truths of life and that the existences of such tensions are what creates continuity.

At the end of book IV, ALP abandons the attempt to persuade HCE to come with her and accepts that she will be facing her end alone. She looks back on her life, how she established an existence on the soggy, marshy land on which Dublin is built: "On limpidy marge I've made me hoom. Park and a pub for me" (FW 624.15–16). Comforting herself by reviewing her life with HCE, she thinks that the city itself will one day crumble into the river, too: "But it's by this route he'll come some morrow" (FW 625.14). As the wind comes up, signifying rain, she begins her goodbyes: "Sea, sea! Here, weir, reach, island, bridge. Where you meet I" (FW 626.7–8).

On the fourth typescript of this section, Joyce adds a line that develops "Where you meet I" and echoes the mixing in I.1 of the "swete" and "brack" waters in the tidal estuary of Dublin Bay: "I wisht I had better glances to peer to you through this baylight's growing. But you're changing, acoolsha, you're changing from me, I can feel. Or is it me is? I'm getting mixed. Brightening up and tightening down. Yes, you're changing, sonhusband, and you're turning. I can feel you, for a daughterwife from the hills again. And she is coming. Swimming in my hindmoist" (BL 47488-174v, JJA 63: 258, FW 626.36–27.3). "[Y]ou're turning" refers to both Shem and HCE's designation as tree throughout the *Wake* (the leaves turning autumn colors) and to the usurping of the father by the son. The "brightening up" is the growth of the tree thanks to the sun (son), and the "tightening down" is the digging of the roots further into the earth as the tree grows. The tree provides an appropriate image for the "sonhusband"; the tree itself continues to live, but only through the shedding of its leaves. The autumnal falling of leaves signifies one death for the tree, though the leaves will grow again the following spring. The deciduous tree is its own father and son,

HCE and Shem, at the same time. The "daughterwife from the hills" is the new water of the Liffey descending from Wicklow, as well as Issy growing into adulthood, both moving in to take ALP's place.[4]

The image of the wood, the forest, and the accompanying trees pervades the *Wake* throughout its entire composition. Through Vico's argument that all human institutions are eventually reclaimed by the forest, to the role of such wooded spaces in theology, mythology, and literature, forests provide Joyce with a wide-ranging way to explore the relationship between the nonhuman and human worlds. The materiality of writing and of writing materials also lends itself to parallels with the structure of trees, and *Finnegans Wake* continually reminds itself of the provenance of the paper upon which it is drafted, revised, and eventually printed.

The *Wake* acknowledges the genesis of the stories it contains, attempting to account for the narratives that continually recur in world history through their reenactment by a seemingly simple family living by Dublin's Phoenix Park. With the Phoenix Park, Dante's *selva oscura* becomes a *selvaantica*, the "ancient forest" that appears in Dante's earthly paradise. Robert Harrison argues in *Forests* that "thanks to the purgatorial process, this forest has ceased to be a wilderness and has become a municipal park under the jurisdiction of the City of God," and, that "[i]n Christianity's vision of redemption, the entire earth and all of its nature become precisely such a park, or artificial garden" (85–86). In the *Wake*, this is what nature often becomes; the fallen natural world is always-already inscribed, culturally and linguistically. However, in the *Wake*, the fallen natural world is also responsible for many of the ways in which culture performs this inscription; it is intimately bound up with the genesis of art, language, religion, culture, and society. Sam Slote explains, "With the Phoenix Park, 'the most extensive public park in the world' (FW 140.12–13), Chapelizod takes on the status of a kind of pastoral Hibernian Eden in *Finnegans Wake*, but it is an Eden that has not been abandoned, an Eden that has also grown and evolved" ("A Wake" 49). The Phoenix Park (as Eden) may be the site of the intersection between violence and the natural world, but it is also a site of hope and resolution. The *Wake* articulates problems that occur when culture and nature clash, but also demonstrates the many ways in which we are defined by the interactions between the two, and through these interactions it suggests the redemptive powers of nature.

A 1936 addition to III.4 reads, "We shall too downlook on that ford where Sylvanus Sanctus washed but hurdley those tips of his anointeds"

(BL 47486a-122, JJA 61: 99, FW 570.31–33). The founding of Dublin city, the "town of the ford of the hurdles," which in itself implies an invasion of nature, required the existence of the sacred wood, the "Sylvanus Sanctus" as a space set apart from the city but still within its boundaries, a space reserved for the hunt, the reenactment of civilization's imposition of order. The leaves from this "Sylvanus Sanctus" are the world's stories. ALP carries these fallen leaves into the sea, and the remaining leaf is the letter, the story, the organic material that returns to the earth and initiates the cycle all over again. Leaves (both of trees and of paper), love, life, and the Liffey all unite at the end of the *Wake*: "My leaves have drifted from me. All. But one clings still. I'll bear it on me. To remind me of. Lff!" (BL 47488-174v, JJA 63: 258, FW 628.6–7).

Giambattista Vico recorded in his *New Science* the "order of human institutions" as "first the forests, after that the huts, then the villages, next the cities, and finally the academies" (98). After the academies are established, the cycle begins again, and all returns to the initial cover of the forest. The "forest" in Vico and in Joyce, signifies many things; it is both the barbaric, non-Christian forest of Dante and the sacred, Edenic *silva*. It is the primeval chaos out of which the universe was created and a protective shelter for all of creation. It is also the material forest, the one comprised of trees, rocks, soil, and animals. In the *Wake*, all of these interpretations are equally important, and the forest embodies each of these identities simultaneously. Joyce's natural world exists physically and tangibly, but is always-already inscribed with linguistic, social, historical, ideological, and textual meaning. The fact that so much cultural material arises from human interactions with the nonhuman environment places the actual physical environment in the forefront of Joyce's "universal history." Joyce's interest in human adulterations of the physical world stems in part from the fact that we lose the initial context of so many of our metaphors, stories, cultures, and identities when such changes occur. In *Finnegans Wake*, geography is always a determinant. It is geography to which we must look to understand our differing languages and cultures and nature to which we must look to understand our similarities.

Finnegans Wake is not by any means the only work of modernist literature to engage with nature, but placing the *Wake* in a tradition of what I refer to as ecological modernism requires a reexamination of how modernism itself is defined and how its texts are read, studied, taught, and categorized. If modernism is a reaction to modernity, the fact that "nature" has so often been left out is baffling. Modernity is the condition wherein humans begin to separate from the earth that once defined their lives. Factors such as transportation, technology, energy, the sciences, philosophy, and government contributed to the reorganization of society in a way that helped to create the division between nature and culture and contributed to the genesis of the current global environmental crisis. An ecological modernism must address the genesis of modernity and locate the points of tension in the transitions; its aesthetic must be one where nature and culture, city and country, past and present, clash.

Begun largely by Raymond Williams, the project of reorienting modernism away from its definition as a solely urban, metropolitan, and cosmopolitan movement is slowly making progress. This is not to say that modernism will ever (or should ever) be conceived of as a provincial movement (though another current trend in modernist studies is the focus on individual countries and modernism), but that modernism, especially considering the time period covered by this term, begs to be examined in terms of the relationship between urban and nonurban, between technology and nature, between religion and science. *Finnegans Wake* explores these dualities under the larger umbrella of "culture versus nature," providing a much-needed acknowledgment of the natural world in a period when anxieties about the continuity of all life were high.

Finnegans Wake is unique in its exemplary representations of the nonhuman through linguistic and narratological technique. In the *Wake*, language is decoupled from the speaker, and the human morphs seamlessly into the nonhuman; nature is not treated as a setting but as a protagonist. The urban and the natural work together as communities, not as radically divided spheres. After one examines the notebooks, drafts, and proofs for the *Wake*, it becomes impossible to believe that Joyce's engagement with nature was merely ornamental; his extensive engagement with nature on several levels points to a "universal history" that is as equally dictated by natural history as by anything else. On many occasions, ecology, climate, and geography are conceived of as the dictating forces for other organizing principles such as nationhood, religion, or language.

Glen A. Love, in "Revaluing Nature: Toward an Ecological Criticism," argues, "The most important function of literature today is to redirect human consciousness to a full consideration of its place in a threatened natural world" (237). *Finnegans Wake* is admirable in its ability to place the "human consciousness" in this "threatened natural world"; Joyce revises the traditional stereotype of the Irish people and their landscape and focuses on the exploitations of nature in a global context. In his essay "A Wake in Chapelizod," Slote argues: "Inverting a formula popular in these ecologically sensitive times, in *Finnegans Wake* Joyce thinks locally yet acts globally" (48). Slote continues: "When Joyce refers to 'Howth Castle and Environs' (FW 3.3), the environs are as global as they are Hibernian, as if the whole world were a suburb of Dublin" (48). Joyce's discussions of weirs, hydroelectric schemes, dams, public health and housing, turf cutting, cloud seeding, bird sanctuaries, and forestry are all part of a global concern for the human and nonhuman world alike and are nearly always paired with the political ideologies from which these ideas of progress stem.

Articulating the presence of nature in modernist literature through the redefinition of the city as part of a larger global environmental network and refocusing the study of modernism and technology to include the environment specifically is also necessary for merging ecocriticism and modernism. Though not in the way that environmentalism is understood today, the environment is everywhere in literary modernism if one looks for it. The introduction of ecocriticism into modernist studies is essential not just to fill in the gaps of literary criticism, but also to locate the origins of, and to begin to mend, the drastic divide between city and nature in the twenty-first century.

Joyce's idea of a "universal history" is inextricably bound to the environment. This genetic analysis of nature in *Finnegans Wake* paves the way for further inquiry into ecocritical approaches to Joyce, Irish literature, and modernism. Additionally, an ecocritical examination of a text by a writer so often represented as the great champion of the city contributes also to the emerging field of urban ecocriticism. Examining not just the sidewalks and the buildings of cities, but the networks of natural resources and civil engineering supporting their existence, urban ecocriticism is indispensable for conceiving the role of nature in a world where the urban population is increasing by the second and humans are becoming ever more alienated from nature.

Serpil Opperman's 2006 article "Theorizing Ecocriticism: Toward a Postmodern Ecocritical Practice" dismisses Phillips's excoriation of postmodernist ideas of nature, calling it a "typical misjudgement," and argues for the ability "to conflate ecocriticism with an ecocentric postmodern theory" (104). Opperman continues to provide a brilliant account of the current debates in the field of ecocriticism and, most important to this study, to link ecocriticism with postmodernism and post-structuralism. Opperman's argument is quite simple, and it is curious that most practicing ecocritics have failed to recognize her main point. If we know, today, that nature is not the holistic unity it was once believed to be, why are ecocritics, who argue for the incorporation of environmental science into literary study, still largely operating as if it were? Instead of trying to find singularity in the practice of "reading a text like the world" or "reading the world like a text," why not try to find the multiplicity? Genetic criticism simultaneously allows for this multiplicity while also keeping the interpretation grounded enough to satisfy both ends of the ecocritical debate.

Ludwig Wittgenstein, in the fragmentary notes published and translated by Peter Winch in *Culture and Value*, discusses this false binary of culture versus nature that has been constructed in Western society: "It is very *remarkable* that we should be inclined to think of civilization—houses, trees, cars, etc.—as separating man from his origins, from what is lofty and eternal, etc. Our civilized environment, along with its trees and plants, strikes us then as though it were cheaply wrapped in cellophane and isolated from everything great, from God, as it were. This is a remarkable picture that intrudes on us" (50e, italics in original). Wittgenstein's general argument is that the modern sense of civilization as radically and irreversibly alienated from nature is false, that it is only a picture that we have created, a picture that intrudes on us. If we examine Joyce's composition methods in the *Wake* and apply this examination to close readings of Joyce's linguistic experiments, it becomes clear that *Finnegans Wake* seeks to unwrap the world from its cellophane.

This study reorients modernism away from the critical commonplace of being overwhelmingly urban and metropolitan and instead argues for an urban ecological criticism that focuses on the interdependence of the urban and the nonurban, city and country, culture and nature. An ecological modernism is key to understanding the origins of our current ecological crisis. With today's rising sea levels and global temperatures, decreasing biodiversity through species extinction and loss of habitat, and islands of plastic waste increasing in size by the minute, the impact of nature on human life is often front-page news. Studying the way in which nature has been culturally constructed during the period in which many of our current environmental concerns find their origin sheds light on how we continue to culturally construct nature as both the sustainer of life, deeply affected by human action and in need of "saving," and an uncontrollable force that brings catastrophe.

Finnegans Wake exquisitely embodies what Lawrence Buell has deemed "literature's capacity for articulating the nonhuman environment" (10). The genealogy of environmentalism, and the ways in which the environment is aesthetically and rhetorically constructed today, allows modernism to engage with nature, providing new explorations of realism on a stylistic level, and providing continuity between the late nineteenth and early twenty-first centuries on both the levels of literary history and environmentalist thought.

Notes

Introduction: An Ecocritical Joyce?

1. Merleau-Ponty's work has been quoted in several important recent works of ecocriticism, including David Abram's essay "Merleau-Ponty and the Voice of the Earth," in David Macauley's *Minding Nature: The Philosophers of Ecology*; Max Oelschlaeger's *Postmodern Environmental Ethics*; Sue Cataldi and William Hamrick's *Merleau-Ponty and Environmental Philosophy: Dwelling on the Landscapes of Thought*; and Louise Westling's essay "Literature, the Environment, and the Posthuman," in Catrin Gersdorf and Sylvia Mayer's *Nature in Literary and Cultural Studies: Transatlantic Conversations on Ecocriticism*.

2. Prior to the nineteenth century, forestry and wildlife management inadvertently contributed to the preservation of the environment and its flora and fauna, but not necessarily because of any intrinsic belief in the importance of nature for itself.

3. See "Our Past," *The Charity*, National Trust.org.uk, http://www.nationaltrust.org.uk/main/w-trust/w-thecharity/w-thecharity_our-past.htm (accessed 25 May 2011).

4. In contrast, many belief systems strongly opposed exploiting the earth and its resources, either because they believed the earth was a sentient being and experienced pain, or because they believed their gods would be angered and seek vengeance upon them. For more information on this topic, see Carolyn Merchant's *The Death of Nature* (29–41).

5. For an overview of these Christian beliefs, a famous essay by environmental historian Lynn White Jr., "The Historical Roots of Our Ecologic Crisis," seeks to trace the dislocation of culture from nature evident in discourse concerning science and technology back to Judeo-Christian tenets.

6. In addition to the behavior of insects, there were several popular studies of the behavior of birds and other animals. In 1934 a short film titled *The Private Life of Gannets* was the recipient of an Oscar (Alt 56), and "essays on nature subjects

by authors such as J. Arthur Thomson and E. M. Nicholson appeared regularly in generalist periodicals such as the *New Statesman* and *Time and Tide*" (Alt 57).

7. Additionally, Joyce's article on Henrik Ibsen's "When We Dead Awaken" was published in 1900 in the *Fortnightly Review*, so this journal would most likely have been on his radar throughout his life.

8. In 1869 Haeckel revised his definition slightly, bringing Darwin explicitly to the forefront: "By ecology we mean the body of knowledge concerning the economy of nature—the investigation of the total relations of the animal both to its inorganic and to its organic environment [. . .] in a word, ecology is the study of all those complex interrelations referred to by Darwin as the conditions of the struggle for existence" (qtd. in Merchant, *Columbia Guide* 160).

9. For a comprehensive overview of this relationship, please refer to the article "Tansley and Freud" by Laura Cameron and John Forrester in *History Workshop Journal*.

10. These studies include Henri Bergson's *Time and Free Will* (1889), Oswald Spengler's *Man and Technics* (1931), Lewis Mumford's *Technics and Civilization* (1934), Walter Benjamin's "The Work of Art in the Age of Mechanical Reproduction" (1936), and Martin Heidegger's "The Question Concerning Technology" (1954).

11. For example, John McCourt, in his introduction to *Roll Away the Reel World: James Joyce and Cinema*, describes Stanislaus Joyce's comments about films showing the devastation from the late 1908 earthquakes in Italy that killed "some 200,000 people" (6). In this same collection, Luke McKernan, in the essay "James Joyce and the Volta Programme," provides the detail that the Volta showed "newsfilms of the Paris floods" of 1910 (23–24).

12. "Nature may be speechless, without language, in the human sense; but nature is highly articulate" (qtd. in Grewe-Volpp 78).

Chapter 1. Reading the Landscape

1. In one of the earliest *Finnegans Wake* notebooks, VI.B.6, many of Joyce's notes from Stephen Gwynn's *History of Ireland* are related to Irish mythology and derive from Irish topography, displaying a relationship between the course of Irish history and the country's geography. These notes include: "Conn C & Mog Nuadat divide I. / by eskers (Dub to Gal)," "this Slighe Mor (Highroad)," "divides I into Conn's Half / & Mog's Half," "Leath Cuinn," "Usnach hill centre of I—," and "10 miles W of Mullingar" (VI.B.6: 180–81). These notes derive from two passages in Gwynn: "Conn's great opponent in Ireland was Mogh Nuadat, and tradition relates that after many battles they decided on a division of Ireland, following the Esker Riada or line of gravelly hillocks (still called eskirs) which runs across the central boggy plain from near Dublin to Maaree on the bight of Galway

Bay. From that time onward—marked off by this natural way, along which ran the Slighe Mor, chief road from east to west—the northern half of Ireland was called Leath Cuinn (Conn's Half), and the southern Leagh Mogha" (12-13) and "Tuathal extended [Connaught's] frontier across the Shannon to the Hill of Usnach, the central point of Ireland, about ten miles west of Mullingar" (13).

2. For more information on Joyce's use of Jespersen, please see Wim Van Mierlo's "Neutral Auxiliaries and Universal Idioms: Otto Jespersen in 'Work in Progress,'" and his essay, "*Finnegans Wake* and the Question of Histry!?" (43–64).

3. The words that Joyce takes note of in this section relate to bodies of water, and shortly thereafter, Joyce records the name of three Dublin rivers: "Dodder," "Tolka," and "Poddle" (VI.B.6: 87).

4. This page continues with this theme, and we find the notes: "main sea," "river Finn /—valley," "level with W in / inches," "bailing out water," "snowflakes on R," "make a detour of—," and "river blotted out," and a bit later, "cross the stream to look for water" (VI.B.6: 90). The last entry derives, again, from Jespersen, from a passage describing how the English language looks to other tongues for its words and expressions; it (borrowing a Danish idiom) must "cross the stream to look for water," the water, in this case, being language.

5. Cf. 11 March 1923 letter to Weaver: "Yesterday I wrote two pages—the first I have written since the final *Yes* of *Ulysses*" (LI 202).

6. Joyce announced the date to Harriet Shaw Weaver in a letter dated 11 March 1923: "Yesterday I wrote two pages—the first I have written since the final *Yes* of *Ulysses*. Having found a pen, with some difficulty I copied them out in a large handwriting on a double sheet of foolscap so that I could read them" (LI 202). The typescript was not returned to again until September 1938.

7. McGovern's essay "Joyce's 'A Painful Case' and Chapelizod" provides a brief overview of the history of the Dublin and Chapelizod Distillery Company as well as other evidence of Joyce's familiarity with Chapelizod and its presence in Joyce's earlier works (45–47).

8. This phrase is from the fair copy of 1923 (BL 47480-269, JJA 55: 446b). The first draft (BL 47480-267, JJA 55: 446a) has "grand pile" only.

9. This phrasing comes from the note, "She died the year the sugar was scarce" (VI.B.10: 30).

10. For information on the historical Roderick O'Connor, see the exhaustive study *Irish Kings and High Kings* by John Francis Byrne.

11. Slote explains that II.4§3 (using VI.B.2: 133, 136) was first drafted in September 1923 (JJA 56: 57, Buffalo VI.B.2: 136, 133, FDV 213–16, FW 388.01–398.30) and that a second draft followed almost immediately. Then, in October 1923, Joyce drafted II.4§2–3A (BL 47481-2r, 2v, 3r, 3v, 4r, JJA 56: 26–36. See LI

9 October 1923). The fair copy was completed shortly after (BL 47481-13r, 14r, 7r, 8r, 9r, 10r, 10v, JJA 56: 39–48. Cf. LI 17 October 1923 and 23 October 1923).

12. Simplified. BL 47481-2v, 3r, JJA 56: 29–30, FDV 214.18-28, FW 387.14–388.10.

13. In the passage from which this notebook entry originates, Chart explains how Dublin maintained its power after the defeat of the Vikings and how "the sea still, in the phrase of the annalists, 'vomited floods of foreigners into Erin'" (4).

14. The notes relating to Noah's ark from VI.B.3 also continue into the next notebook, VI.B.2, with the note "Lough Neagh = Dead Sea" (VI.B.2: 17) suggesting that Lough Neagh is meant to hold a prime spot in the development of Irish civilization, as the Dead Sea did in Abrahamic religions. Lough Neagh is formed by the convergence of six rivers, and, according to the legend, the lough is the water-filled hollow left after the hero Finn MacCool lifted a piece of land and hurled it into the sea, where it became the Isle of Man. Perhaps it is supposed to be HCE (VI.B.2: 11, 13, 16, etc.) who is cast as Finn MacCool here, a "king of nations" (VI.B.2: 17), or a Noah ("Tree = Ark = Temple = Cross," VI.B.2: 14), "HCE drunk" (VI.B.2: 16), "play old Ham" (VI.B.2: 17), or "primogeniture / 'Israel'—family" (VI.B.2: 18). Joyce's notes concerning the role of the patriarch are also infused with notes concerning the possible figure of the "son." Beginning with VI.B.2: 14, more Noah- and flood-related notes begin to appear: "Tree = Ark = Temple = Cross," "give him of the tree" (VI.B.2: 14), "flood" (VI.B.2: 15), "ark = museum" (VI.B.2: 15), "riverworthy" (VI.B.2: 15), "ship HM himself" (VI.B.2: 15), "ark of shittim wood" (VI.B.2: 16), and "Liffey" (VI.B.2: 16). Together, these notes suggest that Joyce is toying with the idea of placing a biblical flood in an Irish context, using the Liffey or Lough Neagh as the body of water.

15. O.J.R. Howarth, in his *Geography of Ireland*, also explains that, in general, building "artificial islands in lakes" for the purpose of erecting dwellings was a common method for ensuring safety in ancient Ireland (145).

16. VI.B.3: 42–45. This draft of the Saint Kevin sketch is unique in that it was entered entirely into the VI.B.3 notebook.

17. Cf. Joyce's correction of the mistranslation of Aristotle: "'Art is an imitation of Nature.' Aristotle does not here define art, he says only 'Art imitates nature,' and meant the artistic process is like the natural process" (CW 145). For example, Daedalus crafted "wings" to fly in imitation of a bird's flight, and, reductively speaking, airplanes fly because of the imitation of aerodynamic forces exhibited by birds in flight.

18. BL 47488-24r–v, JJA 63: 38a–38b. After this draft, there are two fair copies from July 1923, as well as a third (unrevised) fair copy of August 1923, which Joyce had asked Harriet Shaw Weaver to type.

19. BL 47488-24, JJA 63: 38a, FW 605.19. The "circumfluent" was added on

the second draft (July 1923; cf. letter from 9 October 1923 [LI 203]), but the "watercourse" was not added until the next draft, the July 1923 fair copy.

20. In John Wilson Foster's essay "Encountering Traditions," he discusses the interaction of "saints and beasts" in the Irish hagiographical tradition. He cites a story involving Saint Kevin as being one of the most famous examples of this tradition: "One of the best known concerns St Kevin whose hand outstretched to heaven was chosen by a blackbird for her nest. The bird laid eggs and hatched young before the saint would bring himself to move, for fear of disturbing it" (36). Foster also discusses the influence of the Franciscan tradition on Saint Ciaran and Saint Cainnic (36).

21. Many letters of 1924 document Joyce's preoccupation with the "watches" of Shaun, and one example is provided here. Joyce wrote to Miss Weaver on 7 October 1924, from Paris: "We returned here a couple of days ago. Another mountain came to Muhammed—my brother from Dublin whom I had not seen for twelve years. He went away last night. Strange to say like Shaun his work is postal night duty" (LIII 107).

22. Added Nov–Dec 1924. BL 47482b-66, JJA 58: 11, FW 476.06.

23. Added Nov–Dec 1924. BL 47482b-89, JJA 58: 53, FW 475.22.

24. For example, John Feehan notes how "almost all giant deer remains in Ireland have come from the clays underlying the raised bogs" ("Heritage" 15). Also see the various bog fact sheets available through the Irish Peatland Conservation Council Web site, http://www.ipcc.ie.

25. Simplified.

26. For a basic introduction to Joyce's use of this text, see Atherton, *The Books at the Wake* (62–67).

27. One detail that this line may refer to is Sullivan's description of the Celts as possessing an "extraordinary aptitude for picking up ideas from the different people with whom war or commerce brought them into contact" (x) and his subsequent examples, translated by Joyce to "spiral from Scandinavia" and "amber route" (VI.B.6: 62).

28. Sullivan paraphrases the work of Professor Hartley, who has provided the following conclusions concerning the materials used for the ink: "The black is lamp black, or possibly fish-bone black; the bright red is realgar (arsenic disulphide, As/sub/2S/sub/2); the yellow, orpiment (arsenic tersulphide, As/sub/2S/sub/3); the emerald green, malachite; the deep blue, possible lapis-lazuli but owing to its transparency when overlying green, more likely not so [. . .]." Then, Hartley concludes that almost all components derive from Irish sources: malachite, green in color and found in County Cork and County Limerick; chrysocolla, green to blue in color and found in County Cork; chrome, hematite, and ochres, found in County Wicklow; and the red hematite "of an earthy nature," "found in the

County Antrim." The only colors that may be artificial or imported are the "orpiment and realgar" and the "purples" (qtd. in Sullivan 47).

29. Also relating to this theme, Joyce adds to the Jaun section "leaf creeping down" (BL 47483-23v, JJA 57: 188b, FW 467.10) and "Jaun just then I saw to collect from the gentlest weeper among the wailers, who by this were inhalf droop leaf half long mourning for the passing of the last post" (BL 47483-159, JJA 57: 189, FW 470.25).

30. "Honeysuckle" also appears at FW 588.4.

31. In *The Textual Diaries of James Joyce* (TDJJ), Danis Rose devotes an entire chapter to Joyce's note-taking on trees and the incorporation of these notes into the drafts in the mid-1930s. This project derived from his work in *The Index Manuscript*: Finnegans Wake *Holograph Workbook VI.B.46*, wherein he identifies and explicates a page of notes related to trees on VI.B.46: 121. In TDJJ, Rose comments on the index from VI.B.46 as well as on content from Fitzpatrick recorded in VI.B.36. The first notes from Fitzpatrick date back to 1934: "horsechestnut," "elm," "yews," "wehmouth pine / Balsam Popalar" (VI.B.36: 206), "& the 5 cedars of Mt Anville soughing syrially to his obeisance," "by Juniper," "cupress," and "larix o'tourist whetawhistling in astuntedness & tamboys a beeches tittertattering his tendronym" (VI.B.46: 207), but they were not used until Joyce returned to the Fitzpatrick text for VI.B.46 and for the 1938 galley proofs. All of the notes Rose presents from Fitzpatrick find their way into just four passages of the *Wake*, all added to the 1938 galley proofs: FW 100 (I.4), FW 159 (I.6), FW 235 (II.1) and FW 246 (II.1).

32. The "other spring offensive" line is also seen as a renewal in Bill Cadbury's essay "'The March of a Maker': Chapters I.2–4" (77). The Christ imagery is also noted in Campbell and Robinson, who write of I.4, "One gets the impression that HCE's trial and incarceration are intended to symbolize the crucifixion and entombment of Christ" (79n1).

33. Cf. VI.B.14: 199, "hysteric historic."

34. During his viceroyalty, Chesterfield "ornamentally planted and laid it [the Phoenix Park] out, constructed the Main Road, and erected the Phoenix column" (W. Joyce 419–20).

35. On the first draft of III.4, Joyce has written the permutations of HCE (CEH, EHC, and HCE) with the word "sodomy" in the margins of an earlier passage (BL 47482a-30v, JJA 60: 58).

36. Cf. 7 August 1924 letter from Stanislaus: "How are you enjoying yourself in Saint Malo? The famous Carnac must be somewhere near there, I suppose? You could take a leaf out of Renan's book and meditate on old ancient Celtic civilization there and in Ireland before Logue's predecessors came over in their come-to-bed half a tall hats to swap the kingdom of Heaven for the Kingdom of Ireland" (LIII 105).

37. Frazer quotes an account of the French peasantry as believing that their

priest "possesses a secret and irresistible power over the elements . . . he can, on an occasion of pressing danger, arrest or reverse for a moment the action of the eternal laws of the physical world. The winds, the storms, the hail, and the rain are at his command and obey his will. The fire is also subject to him, and the flames of a conflagration are extinguished at his word" (53).

38. On the first page of the notebook, Joyce also recorded a title mentioned by Abbé Millon called *La Terre du Passé* (VI.B.14: 1), or *The Land of the Past*, that may also tie in with this interest.

39. Deane, Ferrer, and Lernout provide overviews of several other texts in VI.B.14 that fit into this category: L.-F. Sauvé's *Proverbes et dictons de la Basse-Bretagne*, Anatole Le Braz's *Le Légende de la mort en Basse-Bretagne*, and Zacharie Le Rouzic's *Carnac: Légendes, traditions, coutumes, et contes du pays*.

40. See "Lithography, n.," def. 2, *Oxford English Dictionary*, 2nd ed., 1989.

41. "Originairement la langue *divine* ne pouvant se parler que par actions. Presque toute action était consacrée; la vie n'était, pour ainsi dire, qu'une suite d'*actes muets* de religion. De là restèrent dans la jurisprudence romaine les *acta legitima*, cette pantomime qui accompagnait toutes les transactions civiles" (Michelet qtd. in Treip 67).

42. The *Online Etymology Dictionary* (http://www.etymonline.com) explains that the surname "Burke" is "[n]ot common in England itself, but it took root in Ireland, where William *de Burgo* went in 1171 with Henry II and later became Earl of Ulster."

43. See "Burg, n.," def. 1, *Oxford English Dictionary*, 2nd ed., 1989.

44. See "Epitaph, n.," def. 1, *Oxford English Dictionary*, 2nd ed., 1989.

Chapter 2. City versus Country

1. "As a creative force," Frank Budgen paraphrases, the Liffey "is older and greater than Christ or Caesar. If Christ left Dublin the city would still exist" (128).

2. An ecotone is the border between two systems, the intermediary space where two communities blend. In *Ecology, Cognition, and Landscape: Linking Natural and Social Systems*, Almo Farina explains that the term originated from the plant ecologist Frederic Clements in 1905, and that the term derived from a combination of *oikos* (home) and *tonos* (tension). In 1933, Aldo Leopold described "the greater richness of wildlife at the edges (across the ecotone)" (qtd. in Farina 84), popularizing the term.

3. See "Shoal, n.," def. 1, *Oxford English Dictionary*, 2nd ed., 1989. Dick Warner, in his natural and cultural history of the River Liffey, cites such shoals and sandbanks as being the primary impetus for the construction of the North Wall and the South Wall in the early eighteenth century (108).

4. Simplified. BL 47471b-75, JJA 48: 9, FDV 125.25–28, FW 204.5–12.

5. VI.B.6: 77: "[G]et some fresh sea air up my hole."

6. Dikes can be either man-made or natural and are trenches to regulate water

levels, and they restrict the flow of rivers. Peat lands are natural regulators of water levels; a fen is filled with standing water all year round, and a bog is waterlogged for about 90 percent of the year (Doyle and Ó Críodáin 79). Peat lands are not inhibitors of water in the same way a dike or a canal is; they control the flow of water naturally, at times releasing water into the rivers and streams, and at other times absorbing water as a natural flood regulator (Warner 12).

7. Added to the galleys for *transition* 4. One of the notebooks in use during this period, VI.B.18, contains notes in relation to Scandinavian and Viking aspects of Dublin.

8. This information, although it has already been written, does not appear in the text of *Finnegans Wake* until I.8.

9. Simplified.

10. Epstein argues that the "whisper" of ALP "possesses powerful stimulative power, just as the voice of the consort Lakshmi can rouse the sleeping Vishnu to create the universe" (EFW 63).

11. The fourth characteristic (the "phillohippuc theobibbus paupulation") describes the people of Dublin: hard-drinking, God-fearing, and impoverished gamblers.

12. "Atlantic Salmon Trust," http://www.atlanticsalmontrust.org, accessed 23 October 2011.

13. "In history, as in nature, evolution never follows a linear path" (translation mine).

14. "To open an abyss between nature and man" (translation mine).

15. From August 1929 to February 1930, Joyce was using notebook VI.B.24, which contained notes for III.4, for II.1, for an expansion of I.6, and for galleys of *transition* 18.

16. The various uses to which water can be put in industry also appeared in "Ithaca": "its docility in working hydraulic millwheels, turbines, dynamos, electric power stations, bleachworks, tanneries, scutchmills: its utility in canals, rivers, if navigable, floating and graving docks: its potentiality derivable from harnessed tides or watercourses falling from level to level" (U 17.220–24).

17. Other notes here include "Coribsen" (VI.B.29: 46), which derives from a passage describing how, when the grave was dug for the Celtic sea god, Manannan Mac Lir, Lough Corrib "burst over the land" (83).

18. See "Washington, D.C." *Encyclopaedia Britannica*, 11th ed., vol. 28, 352b.

19. This addition is from a retyped version of the previous typescript (3A.8+).

20. The 1931 marked pages of *Haveth Childers Everywhere* are missing (JJA 61: 2, 300), but this phrase appears on the 1937 galleys for book III (BL 47487-104, JJA 62: 193, FW 553.9).

21. See "Suburb, *n.*," def. 1, *Oxford English Dictionary*, 2nd ed., 1989.

22. Balbus also appears in the first chapter of *Portrait*, when Stephen sees the following: "And behind the door of one of the closets there was a drawing in red

pencil of a bearded man in a Roman dress with a brick in each hand and underneath was the name of the drawing: *Balbus was building a wall"* (P 43).

23. Notes on the Thames appear in VI.B.29: 119–20.

24. "Swan Water" is not added until drafts of II.1 in 1931 or 1932, appearing as "Sweet swanwater!" (BL 47477-137, JJA 51: 126, FW 248.23).

25. The Dutch influence on New York City also appears in I.5 with the reference to Peter Stuyvesant, "Pieter's in Nieuw Amsteldam" (FW 117.24), and to the "dutchy hovel" (FW 117.31).

26. BL 47484b-428, JJA 59: 167, FW 533.17.

27. To develop this point, Joyce has two entire pages of notes listing various suburbs of Dublin: Artane, Balbriggen, Baldoyle, Ballybrack, Booterstown, Cabinteely, Carrickmines, Castleknock, Chapelizod, Swords, Tallaght, Clonsilla, Clonskeagh, Coolock, Cullenswood, Donabate, Dundrum, Foxrock, Gleenagary, Goldenbal, Loughlinstown, Milltown, Raheny, Ranelagh, Rathcoole, Rush, Saggard, Seapoint, Sandford, Santry, Skerries, Stillorgan (VI.B.29: 134–35).

28. Atherton covers this text in detail in *The Books at the Wake* (75–79).

29. This phrase also appears in "Ithaca," when Bloom is thinking of his dream home: "Not to inherit by right of primogeniture, gavelkind or borough English, or possess in perpetuity an extensive demesne of a sufficient number of acres, roods and perches, statute land measure (valuation £42), of grazing turbary surrounding a baronial hall with gatelodge and carriage drive nor, on the other hand, a terracehouse or semidetached villa, described as *Rus in Urbe*" (U 17.1499–1503).

30. Added to the typescript in 1927, BL 47472-155, JJA 45: 197, FW 71.2.

31. See "sweating sickness," *Encyclopaedia Britannica* online academic edition, http://www.britannica.com/EBchecked/topic/576469/sweating-sickness (accessed 9 Sept. 2011).

32. In 1784, John Foster's "Corn Laws" prohibited grain from being imported to Ireland (Cf. FW 76.35).

33. In "The Localization of Legend," Fritz Senn explains that the "Chapelizod" entry for *Thom's Directory* remained largely unchanged during Joyce's career, so he could have used one for any year. Senn, however, suspects that the *Thom's* Joyce consulted for this section "is likely to have been one from the early thirties" (11).

34. Ball also explains in his chapter on Chapelizod how the "Isolde" of Chapelizod was said to be the daughter of the Irish King "Anguisshe," and on the integrated typescript of II.2§1–3A, Joyce changed "Aengus" to "Aengoisse," merging Ossian's Aengus with the aforementioned king (4: 163).

35. In *The Neighbourhood of Dublin*, Weston St. John Joyce provides this detail: "At the close of the 18th century this village [Palmerstown] possessed six calico printing mills, two oil mills, one dye mill, three wash mills, as well as lead, iron and copper works" (348).

36. See *Liffey Valley Park Alliance*, "Strawberry Beds," http://www.lvpa.ie/strawberrybeds.html (accessed 26 July 2011).

37. This relationship between mills and Christianity was strong in Dublin city; for example, St. Mary's Abbey, the wealthiest Cistercian Abbey in Ireland, was located on the north bank of the Liffey and had an extensive mill system of its own (D'Alton 520).

38. In addition to the distance calculations, the General Post Office, built while Ireland was under English control, did not formally belong to the Irish until the 1980s. According to the 1981 proceedings of the *Dáil* Éireann, ground rent was still being paid to England and the United States. See "GPO Ground Rent," §§3092–3093, *Dáil* Éireann *Debate*, vol. 328, no. 15, 19 May 1981, http://oireachtasdebates.oireachtas.ie (accessed 26 July 2011).

39. See "Latifundia, *n.*," etymology, *Oxford English Dictionary*, 2nd ed., 1989.

40. See "Green belt, *n.*," def. 3, *Oxford English Dictionary*, 2nd ed., 1989.

Chapter 3. The Politics of Nature

1. "Numidia," *Encyclopaedia Britannica* online academic edition, http://www.britannica.com/EBchecked/topic/422426/Numidia (accessed 29 Sept. 2011).

2. "Park, *n.*," def. 1, *Oxford English Dictionary*, 2nd ed., 1989. See also the *OED* entry for "Hunting, n.," def. 1.

3. See "History of the Forestry Commission," United Kingdom Forestry Commission, http://www.forestry.gov.uk/forestry/CMON-4UUM6R (accessed 6 June 2011).

4. The alignment between the Joyce/Shem figure and a fox does resurface in I.7, in reference to Wyndham Lewis's 1927 *The Lion and the Fox* ("though he was fixed fux to fux like a bunnyboy rodger with all the teashop lionses" [*FW* 177.36–178.1]).

5. According to the *Online Etymology Dictionary* (http://www.etymonline.com), the French *renard* derives from "Reginhard," the name of the fox in old Northern European fables, which originally meant "strong in council" or "wily."

6. These notes are: "a meuse in the thorn," "casts along shore (fox)," "saves his brush," "play possum," "the worry," "turning down," "trailing of vixens," "dogfox," "ran him," "lady pack," "the whip," "fox & weasel eat moles," "to wind hounds," "runs downwind," "pointing for his kennel," "dog was speaking," and "old deaf fox" (VI.B.10: 5–6).

7. Later in the notebook, on VI.B.10: 80, there are four more notes that relate to hunting: "farmers' shoot / rough—ing," "mixed bag," "to flush pheasants" and "ground game."

8. From VI.B.2: 14, "grand old gardener."

9. In this final version of the *Wake*, this section is FW 566.07–570.14.

10. This method of giving distances appears again much later in the composition of the *Wake*, on drafts of II.1 that, according to *Thom's Directory*, locate

Chapelizod by citing a distance equal to that from the GPO to Chapelizod. The GPO's clock once read Dunsink Time (approximately 25 minutes behind GMT), but it was set to Greenwich Mean Time in 1916, an event seen by many as a reaction to the Easter Rising.

11. "Salmon" has many roles throughout the *Wake*. First and foremost, Irish waterways were once heavy with salmon, and their unique pattern of migration provides an apt metaphor for the entire structure of *Finnegans Wake*. Finn McCool gains his power from the "Salmon of Knowledge," and it is the name for a house in Sheridan Le Fanu's *The House by the Churchyard*. Frazer's *The Golden Bough* also mentions that many Native American tribes associated twins with salmon (66), and the introduction of salmon here in conjunction with Shem may be linked to this association as well.

12. Added to second draft, January 1924.

13. Also, one of the sources for VI.B.14, *Les livres de Saint Patrice*, a translation by Georges Dottin of Saint Patrick's writings, includes a passage that tells of "the pagan crew of the ship that helped him escape from Ireland" and then "Patrick tells how he refused to suck their breasts" (VI.B.14 10).

14. See "Bog, n.," def. 1a, *Oxford English Dictionary*, 2nd ed., 1989.

15. Frank McDonald, "Bogs could be used as carbon sink, says report," *Irish Times* 19 July 2012. Web. 11 March 2013. http://www.irishtimes.com/newspaper/ireland/2012/0719/1224320380058.html.

16. Frank McDonald, "Bogs could be used as carbon sink, says report," *Irish Times*, 19 July 2012, Web, 11 March 2013, http://www.irishtimes.com/newspaper/ireland/2012/0719/1224320380058.html.

17. Frank McDonald, "Bogs could be used as carbon sink, says report," *Irish Times* 19 July 2012, Web, 11 March 2013, http://www.irishtimes.com/newspaper/ireland/2012/019/1224320380058.html.

18. Cf. "shiners" (FW 465.18).

19. The additions I have focused on relating to "turf" and "bog" are only a couple of many. To drafts of I.2, III.3, and II.3§6 during this period, Joyce also adds: "pisononse coves (the wetter is pest, the renns are overt and come the voax of the turfur is hurled on our lande)" (BL 47476a-159, JJA 49: 339, FW 39.14–15), "the blog and turfs and the brandywine bankrompers" (BL 47487-72v, JJA 62: 140, FW 510.19), "up from the bog of the depths" (BL 47487-76v, JJA 62: 149, FW 516.25), "bogusbagwindburster" (BL 47480-197v, JJA 55: 342, FW 359.13), "thud of surf" (BL 47480-201v, JJA 55: 350, FW 363.25), and "he changes colours as he is lefting the gat out of the bog" (BL 47480-11v, JJA 55: 22, FW 344.10–11). To the third typescript of "Mamalujo" (BL 47481-136–56), in September 1938, Joyce adds: "and we outkicking coal to peater the grate" (BL 47480-284v, JJA 55: 488, not in FW). On the fourth typescript of II.3§6, from late 1938, Joyce adds: "wholebeit in keener notcase would I turf aside for pastureuration [. . .] healped"

(BL 47480-243v, JJA 55: 436, FW 356.23–26) and "topsawys" (BL 47480-317v, JJA 55: 536, FW 374.34–35).

20. Also see "Easter," *Encyclopaedia Britannica* online academic edition, http://www.britannica.com/EBchecked/topic/176858/Easter (accessed 29 Sept. 2011).

21. In *Irish Trees: Myths, Legends, and Folklore,* Mac Coitir explains that the yew tree was also a tree associated with war as it was a favorite wood for making bows and spears, and that "the association of yew with the themes of churchyards, sanctuary and war links it with the goddess of the land who both protected her own, living and dead, and waged war on their enemies" (142–43).

22. Sent to Weaver 16 May 1938.

23. Royal Geographical Society, "About Us," http://www.rgs.org/AboutUs/About+us.htm (accessed 5 April 2012).

24. In addition to the close relationship between geography and imperialism, the establishment of geography as an independent discipline was characterized by tensions between human geography and more "scientific" statistical geography. Moreover, geography was defined differently by each nation, and the aims of the discipline were not (and still are not) easily agreed upon.

25. The letter reads: "I have ordered a Danish Berlitz book from Berlin. It will be published in January. In six months I ought to be able to read the Danish writers. I would like to read some of those at whom Ibsen hints in *The Master Builder.* One is named Nansen, I think" (LII 201). Ellmann notes that while there is a Danish writer Peter Nansen, Joyce probably meant Knut Hamsun (LII 201n3). Knut Hamsun is a subject of *The Master Builder* because of his critique of Ibsen (at a lecture Ibsen attended) in early 1892.

26. See "Ursus maritimus," *IUCN Red List of Threatened Species,* http://www.iucnredlist.org/apps/redlist/details/22823/0 (accessed 23 February 2012).

27. Bryndis Snæbjörnsdóttir and Mark Wilson's *Nanoq: Flat Out and Bluesome—A Cultural Life of Polar Bears* (2006), for example, chronicles the importation of polar bears into England during the Victorian period for the purposes of taxidermy and decoration. Martin A. Danahay's essay "Nature Red in Hoof and Paw: Domestic Animals and Violence in Victorian Art" (in Danahay and Morse 97–120) discusses the cultural significance of polar bears and the Arctic region during this period. He discusses one particular painting by Edwin Landseer, *Man Proposes, God Disposes* (1877), in which a polar bear, "an exotic animal for the British," is the subject committing violence (107). Danahay argues that in this context, "the polar bears and the Arctic [. . .] function as admonitions against overweening human ambition" (107). "This violent polar landscape," he continues, "is the antithesis of the comforts of home; [. . .] these polar landscapes are removed in space. Violence is seen as inhabiting the remote and the distant, not the local and the present" (107). Landseer's painting, of two polar bears hungrily ravaging and devouring the remains of some unfortunate polar explorers, embodies what Russell A. Potter refers to as the "Arctic Sublime" (129). If we compare these two

sources, the polar bear is a representation of the anti-domestic, the anti-rational; it is a being that needs to be tamed and domesticated, whether by installation as taxidermy in a museum or a private home, or through exhibition in a zoo. The arctic regions were a location of fear and disorder, spaces that exist outside of the Victorian sphere of control, and the polar bear, the great predator of these regions, stood as a threat to human ability to dominate these last remaining areas of the world.

28. Ellmann cites this comparison as originating in a 1953 interview with John Prudhoe, who had spoken with Nora in Zurich (JJ 812n74).

29. Catherine de Courcy, eminent historian of the Dublin Zoo, informed me that polar bears were listed as a "desirable" animal as early as 1833, and that the Zoological Society minutes of October 1860 record the Dublin Zoo's acceptance of a polar bear (e-mail message to author, 4–5 April 2012). Polar bears were thus kept in the Dublin Zoo intermittently until 2003.

30. In Philip Herring's editorial commentary for this note, he too suggests that the reference is likely to Ernest Shackleton (517).

31. See Office of Public Works Ireland, "Towards a Liffey Valley Park," 32, http://planning.southdublin.ie (accessed 26 July 2011).

32. To the galley proofs for the section of III.2 concerning Jaun's plan for improving the city of Dublin, Joyce also adds "way, O way for the autointoxication of our town of the Fords in a huddle" (BL 47487-30, JJA 62: 59, FW 447.22–24, FW 447.29–30).

33. Thank you to Fritz Senn for providing a scan of this article. Tysdahl begins with references to Ibsen and to P. A. Munch, but devotes this article to the discussion of writers more minor than these two. In addition to Nansen, Tysdahl discusses Joyce's use of Björnstjerne Björnson, Olaf Bull, Knut Hamsun, Gunnar Heiberg, Jonas Lie, and Sigrid Undset.

34. Transferred to VI.C.6: 243(a). This citation refers to the VI.C series of notebooks, which were a compilation of the uncrossed notes from the VI.B notebooks and were completed by Madame Raphael in the mid-1930s.

35. Transferred to VI.C.6: 243(b).

36. Transferred to VI.C.6: 243(c).

37. In the introduction to *Farthest North*, Nansen describes his hypothesized polar current: "The polar current is no doubt fed by a branch of the Gulf Stream which makes its way up the west side of Spitzbergen; but this small stream is far from being sufficient, and the main body of its water must be derived from further northwards" (24–25).

38. Also appears in FW 317.9.

39. As mentioned previously, Herring believes that the reference is likely to Ernest Shackleton (517).

40. In 1937, Joyce revisits the first six disasters again, inserting them into I.6: "against lightning, explosion, fire, earthquake, flood, whirlwind, burglary, third party, rot [. . .]" (BL 47476a-77v, JJA 49: 174, FW 133.11–12).

41. "Blue Lagoon," *Irish Times*, 1929, *Irishtimes.com*, 4 November 2010, http://www.irishtimes.com/newspaper/opinion/2010 (accessed 22 March 2011).

Chapter 4. Religion and Ecology

1. Tom Hayden's *The Lost Gospel of the Earth* unintentionally continues to evoke this demeaning attitude toward cultures and faiths other than his, but he does make an interesting point about how the "location" of our gods has changed. "We have abandoned the rivergod," he writes, "for a skygod that is separate from the earth" (2). Berry's reference to the Judeo-Christian god as a "skygod" actually unravels his own assertions, putting forth the idea that the Judeo-Christian god's origins are just as environmentally determined as the gods of the so-called native peoples.

2. Vico also deals fairly extensively with the issue of divination, painting it as a nation-constructing force. For example, he writes: "The true God founded Judaism on the prohibition of divination. By contrast, all the pagan nations sprang from the practice of divination" (85).

3. The note appears as "a fork of hazel" in VI.B.33: 59, also deriving from Waite's *Occult Sciences*; a required material for the "evocation" of fiends is "a forked branch of a wild hazel which has never borne fruit, and which must be cut on the day of the evocation, when the sun is just rising" (Waite 59). This addition here follows from the development of the "growth" themes in the previous drafts, which will be discussed in the next chapter of this study, and aligns Shem's role in the sexual awakening of the young girls with the invasive cutting of the plant. There is also a note from VI.C.1: 209 that is crossed and reads "w divine hazel."

4. Later, in VI.B.47, Joyce returns to Finn MacCool and makes the note "nuts-nolleges" (VI.B.47: 43).

5. Clouds will be discussed separately in this chapter, but it may be useful to note here that this "Cumhal" as "cumulus" is not in isolation, but that there are a few additions to this draft relating to clouds: "in the nebohood" (BL 47477-111, JJA 51: 161, FW 235.16), "Ayatherept they / fleurly to Nebuose / Will & Rofucale" (BL 47477-94, JJA 51: 178, FW 250.27), and "That cry's not Cucules" (BL 47477-100, JJA 51: 191, FW 248.16). On the final typescripts of book IV in 1938, in conjunction with the addition of the lengthy cloud passage of FW 599, Joyce adds, along this same line: "it was Captain Finsen's cumhulments" (BL 47488-220v, JJA 63: 324, FW 624.28–29).

6. This discussion of deforestation can also be seen in the "tree-wedding" section of "Cyclops": "As treeless as Portugal we'll be soon, says John Wyse, or Heligoland with its one tree if something is not done to reafforest the land. Larches, firs, all the trees of the conifer family are going fast [. . .] The fashionable international world attended *en masse* this afternoon at the wedding of the chevalier Jean Wyse de Neaulan, grand high chief of the Irish National Foresters, with Miss Fir Conifer of Pine Valley [. . .]" (U 12.1258–95). In this passage, a parody of a society

column about an aristocratic wedding, the only place that that the couple can find to honeymoon is the Black Forest.

7. This passage is partially derived, as Edmund Epstein points out, from Byron's *Childe Harold* and from *Punch* magazine (EFW 160).

8. A note from Joyce's reading of Jules Michelet's Vico in VI.B.12, "enemy = stranger" (15), may provide some insight into the meaning of "Hosty" in I.2, as well as provide a key to a recurring play on words in the *Wake*. The context of the note is as follows: "Cet petites sociétés étaient essentiellement guerrières (polis, polemos). *Etranger (hostis)*, dans leur langage, est synonyme d'*ennemi*" (Michelet 295 qtd. in Treip 70). ("These small communities were essentially military. Foreigner (*hostis*), in their language, is synonymous with *enemy*" [translation mine].) Accordingly, it seems one of the reasons for the name "Hosty" in I.2 is this element of foreignness. In Irish, "foreigner" is *gall*, and from here, Joyce begins to develop a relationship between "*gall*," "gale," and "Gael."

This relationship may also help to explain the connection between Hosty and wind. In the lead-up to Hosty's ballad, wind becomes an important medium for the transmittance of the ballad: "This on a slip of blue paper headed by a woodcut soon fluttered to the rose of the winds from lane to lattice." The wind is a force of both creation and destruction, and it causes the message on this blue paper to be separated from its origin and subsequent destination, but it also causes the message to be ultimately preserved, albeit in an altered state. The relationship between atmospheric phenomena and the transmitting of messages continues with the next section to be drafted, I.3§1, in November 1923 (FW 48–50.32, 57.16–61.27; drafted in red-backed notebook). As the reader tries to understand the accusations levelled against HCE, the testimonies are increasingly confusing because of their obfuscation by clouds (BL 47471b-10, JJA 45: 141, FDV 69.1–12, FW 48.05).

9. Cf. "hole in space" (VI.B.6: 63).

10. According to *Le Nouveau Petit Robert*, the word *temps* (def. 2) acquired its meteorological sense in the twelfth century. In French, the definition for "weather" is much different than it is in English, and it is presented here in full: "État de l'atmosphère a un moment donné considéré surtout dans son influence sur la vie et l'activité humaines" (State of the atmosphere at a given moment, considering, especially, its influence on human life and activity [translation mine]).

11. Sullivan also refers to a theory of Zimmer's in *The Irish Element in Mediaeval Culture* that is in line with the hydrologically determined history of Mamalujo: "Ireland, secure from invasion in the shelter of the Four Seas, had long been a refuge of timid scholars of Gaul, driven like thistledown before the barbarian blast, and that even in the fifth century the Irish schools were notable" (xii). Repurposing previous economic relationships, Sullivan continues, explaining, "The scholars came by the old trade routes, the three days' journey from the Loire to Cork—in 550 a ship-load of fifty landed there—or up the Irish Sea to Bangor" (xii).

12. Later in the first draft of III.4, we also find "promethean paradonnerwetter" and "life's lovelightning" (BL 47482a-27, JJA 60: 51, FDV 265.19–21, FW 585.11–12), continuing to evoke the sense that a thunderstorm is occurring.

13. Referring to the "congested districts board," which refers to Ireland's Congested Districts Board, established in 1891 to alleviate rural poverty. For more information about the history and effectiveness of this governmental body, see Ciara Breathnach's *The Congested Districts Board, 1891–1923*.

14. "Beaufort" is particularly relevant here as it provides another connection to the Gaels/gales pun, as it was an Irishman, Sir Francis Beaufort, who devised the scale of wind speed known as the Beaufort scale.

15. Another famous shepherd of importance to *Finnegans Wake* is Saint Patrick, who, of course, is aligned with Shaun/Abel. Kidnapped by King Niall of the Nine Hostages, Patrick (originally "Succoth") was brought to Slieve Mish in County Antrim and forced to tend cattle (Flood 10).

16. Ellen F. Davis's study *Scripture, Culture, and Agriculture: An Agrarian Reading of the Bible*, provides a thorough reading of this relationship, calling on biblical scholars to reread the Bible through the lens of land use and the politics of land.

17. Def. 1, *Oxford English Dictionary*, 2nd ed., 1989.

18. Cf. "Hep = river in heaven" (VI.B.32: 169), "celestial Liffey" (VI.B.32: 170).

19. Some of the elements in this passage derive from notes in VI.B.14, such as "Kjoekkenmoedding" (VI.B.14: 110), "plants stick in Earth" (VI.B.14: 111), and "Upfellbowm" (VI.B.14: 223).

20. Cf. also the discussion of Shaun and the blackthorn tree in I.5§4.

21. "The Writing of Growth and the Growths of Writing: A Genetic Exegesis of *Finnegans Wake* 503.30–505.29," part 1, *Hypermedia Joyce Studies*, 8.2, Web, 2 April 2010, http://hjs.ff.cuni.cz/archives/v8_2/essays/fordham.htm.

22. All three of the "mistletoe" entries are uncrossed, but the clear addition of "mistletoe" at this draft level supports the necessity of paying attention to the uncrossed notes as well as the crossed ones.

23. For a detailed description of the Irish May Day and maypole celebrations, see J. Edward Milner, *The Tree Book* (143–44).

24. Added to first typescript in 1925, BL 47484a-45, JJA 58: 185, FW 505.4.

25. Another Perry note in VI.B.14 concerning the Mother Goddess is "barley mother" (VI.B.14: 140), Joyce's own brewing-inspired note, which was added to a list consisting of "Corn Mothers, Maize Mothers and Rice Mothers" (Perry 119–20).

26. Ferrer cites Stefan Czarnowski's *Le culte des héros et ses conditions sociales: Saint Patrick, héros national de l'Irlande* as perhaps the most "interesting" of Joyce's French Saint Patrick sources, and provides the following gloss on the text:

> Czarnowski attempts to account for the fabulous stories surrounding the historical Patrick as the work of the ancient Irish poets, who, he maintained,

sought to make Patrick the Christian equivalent of Finn or Cuchulainn. He then goes on to explore the role of such heroes as organizing forces in the societies that give rise to them, through various rituals of death and resurrection. Patrick takes on the attributes of the gods of feasts, feasts being the chief means of social interaction in a primitive culture without cities. The significant dates in Patrick's history are seen to correspond with natural phenomena: for example, 17 March, the date of his death, is seen to correspond with the spring equinox. (VI.B.14 11)

Referring to a text by Abbé Eugène Martin, *Saint-Colomban (Vers 540–615)*, Deane, Ferrer, and Lernout provide the following: "Martin also describes the audacity and sternness of Columbanus in reprimanding the powerful (whether King or Pope) and his prolonged bitter fighting with the bishops of the Gauls on the question of the date of Easter. Joyce seems to be particularly interested in this question, which, after the Council of Nicea, divided Ireland and Irish inspired monasteries in Europe from the rest of the Christians" (VI.B.14 8).

27. A major element necessary for the success of any early civilization and their agriculture was undoubtedly the presence of water. In Egyptian mythology, the Nile holds a central position and is often tied up with the other dominant myths of Egypt of Osiris and of Re. Hooke synthesizes the seasonal myths, the fertility myths, kingship beliefs, burial rites, and the recurring floods by explaining how "the turning points in the annual rising and falling of the Nile were mythologized as the drowning or death of Osiris, his finding by Isis, and his resurrection through the magical arts of Isis and Nephthys, and each detail of the myth was enacted in rituals whose scene was the Nile. Nor must it be forgotten that all this Osiris-Nile mythology as ritual was inseparably connected with the functions of kingship in Egypt" (77).

28. "Historic Archive: Interactive Map of Ireland," *Ordnance Survey Ireland*, 2011, http://maps.osi.ie/publicviewer.

29. See "Husband, v.," defs. 1, 2, *Oxford English Dictionary*, 2nd ed., 1989.

30. The first set of galley proofs for *transition* 3 was dated 28 April 1927 (BL 47472-330–48, I.1§1–3), and the second set of galley proofs for *transition* 3 was dated 3 May 1927 (BL 47472-349–66). From April to May 1927, Joyce was also completing the first and second typescript of I.4§1–2 (BL 47472-253–92 and BL 47472-268, 270, 279, 280–81, 294–314, respectively) and the galley proofs for *transition* 4 (BL 47472-367–83, Buffalo VI.G.1).

31. In addition to the obvious relevance of the bog as a feature of the Irish landscape, this interpretation is also supported by the fact that later changes to the text have the preceding line as "and watch her waters of her sillying waters of and there now brown peater arripple" (FW 76.28–30).

32. When preparing book III for the printer of *Finnegans Wake*, Joyce returned to revisions begun earlier in the 1930s, and the final set was completed and dated 1 July 1936.

33. See "Rusty, *adj.*," def. 2.7., *Oxford English Dictionary*, 2nd ed., 1989.

34. Two more notes relate to the conversion from the lunar to the solar calendar: "Sothic calendar / Sirius" (VI.B.14: 138) and "Nilometer" (VI.B.14: 139). Frazer also discusses how "May Day" (Beltane) and the Feast of All Souls, the other major Celtic feast day, stemmed from the pastoral life of these tribes, and these holidays "were the days on which the cattle went forth from the homestead in early summer and returned to it again in early winter" (633). Frazer concludes here with an important point: "Hence we may conjecture that everywhere throughout Europe the celestial division of the year according to the solstices was preceded by what we may call a terrestrial division of the year according to the beginning of summer and the beginning of winter" (633). Continuing with the discussion of "Mother Goddesses" in conjunction with early fertility myths in Perry and in Hooke, Frazer here discusses how, in some Beltane festivals, figures representing the "tree-spirit" or "corn-spirit" were burned to ensure fertility of the land (609–41).

35. Joyce records other notes concerning funerary rites in VI.B.14, including "roadside burial / so that after 4 days / spirit reenters / passing W" (VI.B.14: 140), "X totem (ass)" (VI.B.14: 140), "⊏ pretends to die" (VI.B.14: 140), "die & be immortal" (VI.B.14: 140), and "Melanesia" (VI.B.14: 141), among others.

36. After the notes from Perry end, Joyce abruptly returns to earlier sources concerning Saint Patrick, perhaps evidence of Joyce's search for similar traditions in Irish Christianity. The notes from Riguet's *Saint Patrice*, R. P. Fages's *Histoire du Saint Vincent Verrier*, and the *Catholic Encyclopedia* are varied in their focus, but it seems Joyce is hunting specifically for information linking Christianity and Catholicism in particular to other world belief systems. There are other notes such as "embalmed in honey" (VI.B.14: 150), "Druid = priest of Daro" (VI.B.14: 158; "Daro" being Breton for "oak"), and "Mother Carey (Mater Cara)" (VI.B.14: 160). The editors of VI.B.14 explain that "Mother Carey's Chickens" was a "name given by sailors" to "stormy petrels" or "falling snow." Through the *Oxford English Dictionary*, the editors further explain that this term most likely derives from *madra cara*, or "Mother Dear," an "epithet for the Virgin Mary used by Levantine sailors" (VI.B.14 216), thus providing a clear link to the location of the "Mother Goddess" tradition in Christian thought.

37. A significant number of the notes taken from this source concern stars and constellations named after animals and other natural elements. Other notes relevant to my argument include "partially he became faint" (VI.B.14: 197), wherein the "he" being discussed is *Ea*, the god of earth and water, and "floodstorm" (VI.B.14: 198), from the sixth tablet, relating to cyclones.

38. In "Ithaca," the passage concerning whether or not Bloom fell when he climbed over the railings of 7 Eccles Street contains the year 1904 in a few different forms, some of which are used in the calculation of Easter (U 17.91–99).

39. Also referenced in the Yawn section (FW 478.34).

40. Possibly begun in 1933 or 1934, but not dated by the printer until 1 July 1936 (JJA 61: 1).

41. Neil McCaw, in *Writing Irishness in Nineteenth-Century British Culture*, also discusses how the *Tír-na-nóg* myth is used by Oscar Wilde in his *Portrait of Dorian Gray* (203). *Tír-na-nóg*, McCaw argues, was particularly popular with the Anglo-Irish, for whom it represented a mysterious exoticism akin to the "Orient" during the Victorian period. Thus, the incorporation of *Tír-na-nóg* may be referring to the Anglo-Irish co-opting of Irish myth.

42. Transferred to the proofs for I.6§3 (FW 156.14).

43. "The artist, like the God of the creation, remains within or behind or beyond or above his handiwork, invisible, refined out of existence, indifferent, paring his fingernails" (P 15).

44. Species in the category "reluctant fliers" often adopt this "reluctance" because of environmental factors; they are either forest-dwellers and need only hop from tree to tree, are earth-dwellers and need only to scurry between patches of underbrush, or are species that have been domesticated for millennia, such as the chicken (Roots 129–30).

45. Unused notes from this notebook were transferred by Madame Raphael into VI.C.17: 64–150.

46. Hart refers to the scarab of Ancient Egypt who was "Khepera, the creator of the gods," and explains that Shaun, by referring to Shem as a "leetle beetle," unwittingly elevates him to this divine status (57). Atherton comments that "Hart sees this identification as explaining the interspersion into the text of the host of other gods that have at some time appeared in animal or vegetable form" ("Shaun A" 160).

47. In *The Fictions of James Joyce and Wyndham Lewis: Monsters of Nature and Design*, Scott W. Klein argues that "fables are bound up with *Finnegans Wake*'s issues of language and history" (181) and uses Vico's gestural linguistic theories to argue that Vico ties "fable" to the concept of "logos." Klein's argument supports Joyce's use of fables and myths as, along with contemporary science, alternative ways of reaching "truth."

Chapter 5. Growing Things

1. Other relevant notes in VI.B.6: 128 include "Water," "vertical rivers," "dark clouds," "mud," "potomoac," "Sea in fence," "Rock," "Plutonian eruptive— / Neptunian sedimentary," "mica / granite / silica / lima / chalk / marble," "Mudmud!" "fossil / crystals," "△ source," "bed," "mouth," "rapids," and "underground & out." This list continues onto the next page with "Mouthless rivers," "delta," "alluvial," "ocean R estuary not △," and "△ bobbed hair" (VI.B.6: 129). Throughout the remainder of the notebook, Joyce scatters notes relating to "△," such as "Wade across △" (VI.B.6: 134) or "△ clogs" (VI.B.6: 136). However, on VI.B.6: 148, a series of notes develops the relationship between "△" and the Liffey, as well as

strengthens the relationship between rivers and history: "garden of Erin = Wicklow Mts," "Liffey's detour / devil's glen," "haven" (cf. haven/havet from VI.B.6: 73), "Blackstairs Mt," "grotto Kilkenny," "marble," "canal crosses Δ," and "curragh."

2. This passage is transcribed from Hayman's *First-Draft Version*. In his "Reader's Key" at the beginning of the volume, Hayman explains that Joyce's additions are in italics, additions to additions are in brackets, cancellations are crossed out, and substitutions are in bold face (44).

3. See River Vartry Protection Society, "River's Story," accessed 7 October 2010, http://www.rivervartry.com.

4. Though the relationship between ALP, the triangular delta of a river, and the triangular Greek letter "delta" is very clear, Sullivan's *Book of Kells* also explains that the symbol of a triangle is "symbolical of the Trinity, and so of Christianity in general, in mediaeval times. For this reason perhaps it is that its use in the *Book of Kells* is confined to the garments, symbols, or surroundings of only holy personages" (30).

5. See "Littoral, *adj.*," def. 1a, *Oxford English Dictionary*, 2nd ed., 1989.

6. See "Paraheliotropism, *n.*," def. 1, *Oxford English Dictionary*, 2nd ed., 1989.

7. See "Photoperiodism, *n.*," def. 1, *Oxford English Dictionary*, 2nd ed., 1989.

8. Joyce took notes from Jousse in VI.B.18, VI.B.21, VI.B.23, and VI.A (Milesi, "Vico" 75).

9. The first draft and the first fair copy of II.1§3 were both completed in December 1930 (BL 47477-33–36 and BL 47477-38–41, respectively).

10. Though Luke McKernan does not advocate that Joyce had any relationship to or paid any attention to the films screened at the Volta after his return to Trieste ("James Joyce" 26), McKernan's appendix ("Volta Filmography") of these films is useful, even if just as an example of the type of films being shown during this period in cinematic history. The films Alt describes in her introduction would not be included in McKernan's appendix, as they are the shorts before the feature film. Some relevant feature films include *The Waterfalls of Tanforsen* (27–29 December 1909), *The Fascination of the Snowy Mountain Peaks* (27–29 December 1909), *A Storm at Sea* (20–22 January 1910), *A Grand Procession of Elephants* (27–29 January 1910), *First and Second Parts of the Dreadful and Disastrous Sicilian-Calabrian Earthquake! In two very fine films taken at Messina* (7–9 February 1910), *The Floral City* (14–16 February 1910), *Agricultural Industry in Denmark* (21–23 February 1910), *The Paris Floods, Entirely Different from Those Films Already Shown* (3–5 March 1910), *Crocodile Hunting* (7–9 March 1910), *The Aviator Blériot Showing Flights over Vienna* (10–12 March 1910), *Modern Agriculture* (14–16 March 1910), *Niagara* (17–19 March 1910), and *The Icefields of Finland* (31 March–2 April 1910).

11. See "Mimosa, *n.*," etymology, *Oxford English Dictionary*, 2nd ed., 1989.

12. Additionally, the French for "potato" is *pomme de terre*, and this reference to the famous Irish crop connects to Adam's curse.

13. The story ends with the painter Kraft's work, titled *Boadicea*. It is a representation of Milly's feminine, Edenic essence distilled onto canvas and another example of nature-as-female being "tamed."

14. See "Woodward, *n.*" and "Regarder, *n.*," def. 1, *Oxford English Dictionary*, 2nd ed., 1989.

15. See "Vert, *n.*," def. 1a, *Oxford English Dictionary*, 2nd ed., 1989.

16. See "Vert, *n.*," def. 2, *Oxford English Dictionary*, 2nd ed., 1989.

17. The forest management terms, in addition to their political implications, also refer back to the Garden of Eden and to larger questions concerning the management of nature. The complication of the "tree murderer" murdering the phallic tree in O. Henry is translated to HCE's being both tree murderer and tree in the revisions of II.1 for *transition* 22. Joyce adds a line concerning the male HCE/Finn figure just before the "tree murderer": "Why will thou earwaken him from his earth, O summonorother: he is weatherbitten from the dust of ages." HCE is described as being awoke "from his earth," as if he has been sleeping, embedded, like a tree, in the soil (similar to the description of his reawakening following his burial in I.4). He is described also as "weatherbitte" or weatherbeaten (referring to the earlier "Prost bitten"), meaning that he is to be felled because he is dying. The weather (and perhaps the aforementioned "Mermer," the Sumerian storm-God) has taken a toll on him, and he can no longer recover.

18. "Australopithecus," *Encyclopaedia Britannica* online academic edition, http://www.britannica.com/EBchecked/topic/44115/Australopithecus (accessed 2 Aug. 2011).

19. More generally, "Armorica" was also the name given to the coastal area of Gaul, and the region "Aquitania" was merely the Latin word for "Armorica" (Anthon 2: 116). There are other possible referents for "Armorica," such as Amory Tristram, who (in addition to having a surname pleasingly close to "Tristan"), according to Chart, was "one of the Norman adventurers, who followed Strong-bow, defeated the Danish inhabitants, who still lingered here after the fall of Dublin, and took their lands for himself" (342).

20. Added to the pages of *transition* 3. In addition to the reference to Darwin, the "testament of the rocks" line also returns to a source that Joyce culled years before for the line, "a day of dappled seaborne clouds" (P 160) of the "bird-girl" epiphany on Dollymount Strand in *A Portrait of the Artist as a Young Man*. The phrase Joyce uses is actually a misquotation from Hugh Miller's *The Testimony of Rocks; or, Geology in Its Bearings on the Two Theologies, Natural and Revealed*, and the passage from which this quotation is extracted "describes Satan contemplating, but unable to comprehend, the divine Creation" (Gifford, *Joyce Annotated* 219). The line actually reads "a day of dappled, *breeze*-borne clouds," and Stephen's misquotation implies a misreading of the larger passage, which concludes: "man, a creature in whom, as in the inferior animals, vitality was to be united to matter,

but in whom also, as in no inferior matter, responsibility was to be united to vitality" (Miller qtd. in Gifford, *Joyce Annotated* 219).

21. "Wold" is also an old Germanic word for "forest, forest land, wooded upland" (OED, def. 1), and "sleep" also implies a death; the "Oxmanswold" is a return of Dublin and HCE to their Viking forebears, but it is also the return, in the Viconian sense, to the beginning of civilization in the forests, to before "the green woods went dry" (FW 74.9–10).

Conclusion: New Boundaries of Ecocriticism

1. Cf. "babes in wood" (VI.B.47: 51).

2. As a point of interest, see "Stag Hunting Ban Debated in Dáil," *RTÉ News*, 25 June 2010, http://www.rte.ie/news/2010/0624/hunting.html (accessed 24 September 2011).

3. See "whip, *n.*," def. 5, and "whipper-in, *n.*," def. 1, *Oxford English Dictionary*, 2nd ed., 1989.

4. To the fifth typescript of this section, Joyce clarifies this familial relationship within the river with the addition: "And she'll be sweet for you as I was sweet when I came down out of me mother" (BL 47488-192, JJA 63: 282, FW 627.7–9).

Works Cited

Aalen, F.H.A., Matthew Stout, and Kevin Whelan. *Atlas of the Irish Rural Landscape*. Cork: Cork University Press, 1997. Print.
Abadie, Ann J., and Joseph R. Urgo, eds. *Faulkner and the Ecology of the South*. Oxford, MS: University Press of Mississippi, 2005. Print.
Abram, David. "Merleau-Ponty and the Voice of the Earth." Macauley 82–101. Print.
Adorno, Theodor W., and Max Horkheimer. *Dialectic of Enlightenment: Philosophical Fragments*. Trans. Edmund Jephcott. Ed. Gunzelin Schmid. Stanford: Stanford University Press, 2002. Print.
Aesop. *Aesop's Fables*. Trans. V. S. Vernon Jones. 1912. London: Collector's Library, 2006. Print.
Albright, Daniel. *Quantum Poetics: Yeats, Pound, Eliot, and the Science of Modernism*. Cambridge: Cambridge University Press, 1997. Print.
Allaby, Michael. *Atmosphere: A Scientific History of Air, Weather, and Climate*. New York: Infobase Publishing, 2009. Print.
Allison, Alexander W., et al., eds. *The Norton Anthology of Poetry*. 3rd ed. New York: Norton, 1983. Print.
Alt, Christina. *Virginia Woolf and the Study of Nature*. Cambridge: Cambridge University Press, 2010. Print.
Alter, Robert. *Imagined Cities: Urban Experience and the Language of the Novel*. New Haven: Yale University Press, 2005. Print.
Andersen, Mikael Skou, and Duncan Liefferink, eds. *European Environmental Policy: The Pioneers*. Manchester: Manchester University Press, 1997. Print.
Andrews, J.H.A. *A Paper Landscape: The Ordnance Survey in Nineteenth Century Ireland*. 1975. Dublin: Four Courts Press, 2001. Print.
Anthon, Charles. *A System of Ancient and Mediaeval Geography: For the Use of Schools and Colleges*. New York, 1850. Archive.org. Web. 2 April 2011.
Armbruster, Karla. "'Buffalo Gals, Won't You Come Out Tonight': A Call for Boundary-Crossing in Ecofeminist Literary Criticism." Gaard and Murphy 97–122. Print.

Armbruster, Karla, and Kathleen R. Wallace, eds. *Beyond Nature Writing: Expanding the Boundaries of Ecocriticism*. Charlottesville: University of Virginia Press, 2001. Print.

Armstrong, Tim. "Technology: 'Multiplied Man.'" Bradshaw 158–78. Print.

Association for the Study of Literature and the Environment (ASLE). "Ecocritical Library." Resources section. Web. 17 April 2010. http://www.asle.org/site/resources/ecocritical-library.

Atherton, James S. *The Books at the Wake: A Study of Literary Allusions in James Joyce's* Finnegans Wake. Carbondale: Southern Illinois University Press, 1959. Print.

———. "Shaun A/Book III, Chapter i." Begnal and Senn 149–72. Print.

———. "Sport and Games in *Finnegans Wake*." Dalton and Hart 52–64. Print.

Attridge, Derek. *Joyce Effects: On Language, Theory, and History*. Cambridge: Cambridge University Press, 2000. Print.

Attridge, Derek, and Daniel Ferrer, eds. *Post-Structuralist Joyce: Essays from the French*. Cambridge: Cambridge University Press, 1984. Print.

Aubert, Jacques. "Breton Proverbs in Notebook VI.B.14." AWN 15 (1978): 86–89. Print.

Baker, Sir Samuel W. *The Albert N'Yanza, Great Basin of the Nile, and Explorations of the Nile Sources*. 2 vols. London: 1867. Print.

Bakhtin, M. M. *The Dialogic Imagination: Four Essays by M. M. Bakhtin*. Trans. Caryl Emerson and Michael Holquist. Ed. Michael Holquist. Austin: University of Texas Press, 1981. Print.

Ball, Francis Elrington. *A History of the County Dublin*. 6 vols. 1902–1920. Dublin: Gill and Macmillan, 1979. Print.

Barczewski, Stephanie L. *Antarctic Destinies: Scott, Shackleton, and the Changing Face of Heroism*. London: Hambledon Continuum, 2007. Print.

Barger, John. "A Preliminary Stratigraphy of *Scribbledehobble*." Treip 127–38. Print.

Barkan, Elazar, and Ronald Bush, eds. *Prehistories of the Future: The Primitivist Project and the Culture of Modernism*. Palo Alto: Stanford University Press, 1995. Print.

Barnhill, David Landis, and Roger S. Gottlieb, eds. *Deep Ecology and World Religions: New Essays on Sacred Ground*. Albany: State University of New York Press, 2001. Print.

Barr, Susan, and Cornelia Lüdecke, eds. *The History of the International Polar Years (IPYs)*. Berlin: Spring-Verlag, 2010. Print.

Barta, Peter. *Bely, Joyce, and Doblin: Peripatetics in the City Novel*. Gainesville: University Press of Florida, 1996. Print.

Bate, Jonathan. *Romantic Ecology: Wordsworth and the Environmental Tradition*. London: Routledge, 1991. Print.

Bazarnik, Katarzyna. *Joyce and Liberature*. Prague: Litteraria Pragensia, 2011. Print.
Beck, Harald, and Clive Hart. "Sunwise: The Sun in *Ulysses*." *Papers on Joyce* 10/11 (2004–2005): 15–28. Print.
Beer, Gillian. *Open Fields: Science in Cultural Encounter*. New York: Oxford University Press, 1999. Print.
Begnal, Michael H., ed. *Joyce and the City: The Significance of Place*. Syracuse: Syracuse University Press, 2005. Print.
Begnal, Michael H., and Fritz Senn, eds. *A Conceptual Guide to* Finnegans Wake. University Park: Pennsylvania State University Press, 1974. Print.
Benejam, Valerie, and John Bishop, eds. *Making Space in the Works of James Joyce*. London: Taylor & Francis, 2011. Print.
Benjamin, Walter. *Illuminations*. Trans. Harry Zorn. Ed. Hannah Arendt. London: Pimlico, 1999. Print.
———. "The Work of Art in the Age of Mechanical Reproduction." 1936. Benjamin 211–44. Print.
Bennett, Michael, and David W. Teague, eds. *The Nature of Cities: Ecocriticism and Urban Environments*. Tuscon: University of Arizona Press, 1999. Print.
Benstock, Bernard, and Shari Benstock. *Who's He When He's at Home: A James Joyce Directory*. Champaign: University of Illinois Press, 1990. Print.
Bergson, Henri. *Time and Free Will*. 1889. Trans. F. L. Pogson. London: Allen & Unwin, 1971. Print.
Berry, Thomas. Introduction. *The Lost Gospel of the Earth: A Call for Renewing Nature, Spirit, and Politics*. By Tom Hayden. Dublin: Wolfhound Press, 1997. ix–xv. Print.
Berry, Wendell. *The Unsettling of America: Culture and Agriculture*. San Francisco: Sierra Club, 1977. Print.
Bew, Paul. *Land and the National Question in Ireland: 1858–1882*. Dublin: Gill, 1978. Print.
Biagini, Eugenio. *British Democracy and Irish Nationalism, 1876–1906*. Cambridge: Cambridge University Press, 2007. Print.
Bielenberg, Andy. *The Shannon Scheme and the Electrification of the Irish Free State*. Dublin: Lilliput Press, 2002. Print.
Bilskey, Lester J., ed. *Historical Ecology: Essays on Environmental and Social Climate Change*. Port Washington, N.Y.: Kinnikat Press, 1980. Print.
Bishop, John. Introduction. *Finnegans Wake*. By James Joyce. New York: Penguin, 1999. vii–xxvii. Print.
———. Finnegans Wake: *Joyce's Book of the Dark*. Madison: University of Wisconsin Press, 1986. Print.
Bloom, Harold, ed. *George Orwell's* Animal Farm. Bloom's Guides: Comprehensive Research and Study Guides. New York: Infobase Publishing, 2006. Print.

Borach, George. "Conversations with James Joyce." Trans. Joseph Prescott. *College English* 15 (1954): 325–27. JSTOR. Web. 15 March 2011.
Boughey, A. S. "Environmental Crises—Past and Present." Bilskey 9–32. Print.
Bowen, Elizabeth. *The Last September*. London: Vintage, 1998. Print.
Bradbury, Malcolm. "The Name and Nature of Modernism." Bradbury and McFarlane 19–55. Print.
Bradbury, Malcolm, and James McFarlane, eds. *Modernism: A Guide to European Literature, 1890–1930*. 1976. London: Penguin, 1991. Print.
Bradshaw, David. *A Concise Companion to Modernism*. Oxford: Blackwell, 2003. Print.
Bramwell, Anna. *Ecology in the 20th Century: A History*. New Haven: Yale University Press, 1989. Print.
Breathnach, Ciara. *The Congested Districts Board, 1891–1923*. Dublin: Four Courts, 2005. Print.
Brewer, E. Cobham. *Brewer's Dictionary of Phrase and Fable*. New York: 1898. Archive.org. Web. 12 November 2010.
Brill's Encyclopedia of Islam. 2nd ed. Ed. P. Bearman, et al. *Brill Online*. 2006. Web. 10 July 2011.
Brooker, Peter, and Andrew Thacker, eds. *Geographies of Modernism: Literatures, Cultures, Spaces*. London: Routledge, 2005. Print.
Brown, Francis, S. R. Driver, and Charles Briggs. *The Brown-Driver-Briggs Hebrew and English Lexicon*. Peabody: Hendrickson, 1996. Print.
Brown, Laura. *Homeless Dogs and Melancholy Apes: Humans and Other Animals in the Modern Literary Imagination*. Ithaca: Cornell University Press, 2010. Print.
Brown, Terence. *The Life of W. B. Yeats*. Oxford: Blackwell, 2001. Print.
Browne, William James. *Botany for Schools and Science Classes*. Dublin: Sullivan Bros., 1881. *Archive.org*. Web. 15 September 2011.
Bryson, J. Scott, ed. *Ecopoetry: A Critical Introduction*. Salt Lake City: University of Utah Press, 2002. Print.
——. "Modernism and Ecological Criticism." Eysteinsson and Liska 591–604. Print.
Budge, Ernest Alfred. *The Book of the Dead: The Hieroglyphic Transcript and Translation into English of the Ancient Egyptian Papyrus of Ani*. 1895. New York: Gramercy, 1999. Print.
——. *The Rosetta Stone in the British Museum*. London: Religious Tract Society, 1929. Print.
Budgen, Frank. *James Joyce and the Making of* Ulysses. Bloomington: Indiana University Press, 1960. Print.
Buell, Lawrence. *The Environmental Imagination: Thoreau, Nature Writing, and the Formation of American Culture*. Cambridge: Belknap-Harvard University Press, 1995. Print.

Burgess, Ernest, Roderick McKenzie, and Robert Park, eds. *The City*. 1925. Chicago: University of Chicago Press, 1984. Print.
Burke, Edmund, and Kenneth Pomeranz, eds. *The Environment and World History*. Berkeley: University of California Press, 2009. Print.
Burke, Hilary. "Northern Ireland's Forest Service." *Forestry Journal* 9 (2009): 22–23. JSTOR. Web. 29 May 2011.
Burrells, Anna, Steve Ellis, Deborah Parsons, and Kathryn Simpson, eds. *Woolfian Boundaries: Selected Papers from the Sixteenth Annual International Conference on Virginia Woolf*. Clemson University Digital Press, 2007. Print.
Byock, Jesse L., ed. and trans. *The Prose Edda*. By Snorri Sturlson. New York: Penguin Classics, 2006. Print.
Byrne, John Francis. *Irish Kings and High Kings*. Dublin: Four Courts, 2004. Print.
Cadbury, Bill. "'The March of a Maker': Chapters I.2–4." Crispi and Slote 66–97. Print.
———. "Sequence and Authority in Some *transition* Typescripts and Proofs." Slote and Van Mierlo 159–88. Print.
Callanan, Frank. "James Joyce and *The United Irishman*, Paris 1902–3." *Dublin James Joyce Journal* 3 (2010): 51–103. Print.
———. *The Parnell Split, 1890–91*. Syracuse: Syracuse University Press, 1992. Print.
Cambrensis, Giraldus. *Topographia Hiberniae*. 1188. Trans. John J. O'Meara. Mountrath: Dolmen Press, 1982. Print.
Cameron, Laura. "Ecosystems." Harrison, Pile, and Thrift 55–56. Print.
Cameron, Laura, and John Forrester. "Tansley and Freud." *History Workshop Journal* 48 (1999): 65–100. JSTOR. Web. 10 August 2011.
Campbell, Joseph, and Henry Morton Robinson. *A Skeleton Key to* Finnegans Wake. 1944. Novato: New World Library, 2005. Print.
Campbell, SueEllen. *The Face of the Earth: Natural Landscapes, Science, and Culture*. Berkeley: University of California Press, 2011. Print.
———. "The Land and Language of Desire: Where Deep Ecology and Post-Structuralism Meet." *Western American Literature* 24 (1989): 199–211. Print.
Campbell, Thomas. "The Beech-Tree's Petition." *The Poems of Thomas Campbell*. Archive.org. Web. 4 February 2011.
Cantrell, Carol H. "The Flesh of the World: Virginia Woolf's *Between the Acts*." Coupe 275–81. Print.
Carter, R.W.G., and A. J. Parker, eds. *Ireland: A Contemporary Geographical Perspective*. London: Routledge, 1989. Print.
Cartmill, Matt. *A View to a Death in the Morning: Hunting and Nature through History*. Cambridge: Harvard University Press, 1996. Print.
Casey, Christine. *Dublin: The City within the Grand and Royal Canals and the*

Circular Road with the Phoenix Park. New Haven: Yale University Press, 2005. Print.
Castle, Gregory. *Modernism and the Celtic Revival*. Cambridge: Cambridge University Press, 2001. Print.
Cataldi, Sue, and William Hamrick, eds. *Merleau-Ponty and Environmental Philosophy: Dwelling on the Landscapes of Thought*. Albany: State University of New York Press, 2007. Print.
Chart, D. A. *The Story of Dublin*. London: J. M. Dent, 1907. Print.
Chesney, Helena C. G., and John Wilson Foster, eds. *Nature in Ireland: A Scientific and Cultural History*. Montreal: McGill-Queen's University Press, 1997. Print.
Christiani, Dounia Bounis. *Scandinavian Elements of* Finnegans Wake. Evanston: Northwestern University Press, 1965. Print.
Chryssavgis, John. *Beyond the Shattered Image: Insights into an Orthodox Christian Ecological Worldview*. Minneapolis: Light and Life Publishing, 1999. Print.
Clark, Hilary. "'Legibly depressed': Shame, Mourning, and Melancholia in *Finnegans Wake*." *James Joyce Quarterly* 34 (1997): 461–72. Print.
Clark, Samuel. *Social Origins of the Irish Land War*. Princeton: Princeton University Press, 1979. Print.
Clarke, Howard B., ed. *Irish Cities*. Cork: Mercier Press, 1995. Print.
Coats, Alice M. *Garden Shrubs and Their Histories*. New York: Dutton, 1965. Print.
Connolly, Thomas E., ed. *The Personal Library of James Joyce: A Descriptive Bibliography*. Buffalo: University of Buffalo Bookstore, 1957. Print.
———, ed. *James Joyce's* Scribbledehobble: *The Ur-Workbook for* Finnegans Wake. Evanston: Northwestern University Press, 1961. Print.
"The Conquest of the South Pole." *Manchester Guardian*. 9 March 1912. Web. 2 January 2012.
Cook, Judith. *Pirate Queen: The Life of Grace O'Malley, 1530–1603*. Edinburgh: Tuckwell, 2004. Print.
Cope, Jackson. *Joyce's Cities: Archaeologies of the Soul*. Baltimore: Johns Hopkins University Press, 1981. Print.
Cosgrave, Dillon. *North Dublin: City and Environs*. 1909. Dublin: Nonsuch-The History Press Ireland, 2005. Print.
Costello, Peter, and John Wyse Jackson. "Rifleman Buckley." *James Joyce Online Notes*. Web. 1 March 2013. http://www.jjon.org/.
Coughlan, Gerry, and Martin Hughes. *Irish Language and Culture*. Victoria: Lonely Planet Books, 2007. Print.
Coupe, Laurence, ed. *The Green Studies Reader: From Romanticism to Ecocriticism*. London: Routledge, 2000. Print.
Cox, Richard. *Hibernia Anglicana: or, History of Ireland, from the conquest thereof by the English, to this present time. With an introductory discourse touching the*

ancient state of that kingdom. 2 vols. London, 1689–1690. *Google Book Search*. Web. 10 January 2011.

Crispi, Luca. "A Commentary of James Joyce's National Library of Ireland 'Early Commonplace Book': 1903–1912." *Genetic Joyce Studies* 9 (2009): no page. Web. 3 Nov. 2010.

———. "Storiella as She Was Wryt: Chapter II.2." Crispi and Slote 214–49. Print.

Crispi, Luca, and Sam Slote, eds. *How Joyce Wrote* Finnegans Wake: *A Chapter-by-Chapter Genetic Guide*. Madison: University of Wisconsin Press, 2007. Print.

Croker, Thomas Crofton, ed. *Popular Songs of Ireland*. London, 1839. *Google Book Search*. Web. 15 March 2010.

Crosby, Alfred, Jr. *Ecological Imperialism: The Biological Expansion of Europe, 900–1900*. New York: Cambridge University Press, 1986. Print.

Curtin, Jeremiah. *Myths and Folk-Lore of Ireland*. Boston, 1890. Print.

Cusick, Christine, ed. *Out of the Earth: Ecocritical Readings of Irish Texts*. Cork: Cork University Press, 2010. Print.

Czerniak, Julia, and George Hargreaves, eds. *Large Parks*. New York: Princeton Architectural Press, 2007. Print.

D'Alton, Edward. "Daniel O'Connell." *The Catholic Encyclopedia*. Vol. 11. New York: Robert Appleton Company, 1911. Web. 29 Sept. 2011. http://www.newadvent.org/cathen/11200c.htm.

———. *A History of Ireland: From the Earliest Times to the Present Day*. London: Gresham, 1912. Print.

Dale, Thomas Francis. *The Eighth Duke of Beaufort and the Badminton Hunt*. Westminster: Archibald Constable, 1901. Print.

Dalton, Anthony. *Polar Bears: The Arctic's Fearless Great Wanderers*. Surrey, British Columbia: Heritage House Publishing, 2010. Print.

Dalton, Jack, and Clive Hart, eds. *Twelve and a Tilly: Essays on the Occasion of the 25th Anniversary of* Finnegans Wake. London: Faber and Faber, 1966. Print.

Daly, Mary E. *Industrial Development and Irish National Identity, 1922–1939*. Syracuse: Syracuse University Press, 1992. Print.

Danahay, Martin A. "Nature Red in Hoof and Paw: Domestic Animals and Violence in Victorian Art." Danahay and Morse 97–120. Print.

Danahay, Martin A., and Deborah Denenholz Morse, eds. *Victorian Animal Dreams: Representations of Animals in Victorian Literature and Culture*. Hampshire, England: Ashgate, 2007. Print.

Dante. *The Divine Comedy*. Trans. C. H. Cisson. New York: Oxford University Press, 1998. Print.

Darwin, Charles. *On the Origin of Species by Means of Natural Selection, or The Preservation of Favoured Races in the Struggle For Life*. 1859. London: Collector's Library, 2004. Print.

Darwin, Francis, ed. *The Life and Letters of Charles Darwin*. Vol. 2. London: John Murray, 1887. Archive.org. Web. 17 January 2015.
Davis, Alex, and Lee Jenkins, eds. *Locations of Literary Modernism: Region and Nation in British and American Modernist Poetry*. Cambridge: Cambridge University Press, 2002. Print.
Davis, Ellen F. *Scripture, Culture, and Agriculture: An Agrarian Reading of the Bible*. Cambridge: Cambridge University Press, 2008. Print.
Davis, John, ed. *Rural Change in Ireland*. Belfast: Queen's Institute of Irish Studies, 1999. Print.
Deane, Seamus. "Irish Poetry and Irish Nationalism: A Survey." Dunn 4–22.
Deane, Vincent, Daniel Ferrer, and Geert Lernout, eds. *The Finnegans Wake Notebooks at Buffalo*. Turnhout: Brepols, 2001– . Print.
De Courcy, Catherine. *Dublin Zoo: An Illustrated History*. Cork: Collins Press, 2009. Print.
———. Message to the author. 5 April 2012. E-mail.
De Courcy, J. W. "Bluffs, Bays, and Pools in the Medieval Liffey at Dublin." *Irish Geography* 33 (2000): 117–33. Print.
Deleuze, Gilles, and Félix Guattari. *Anti-Oedipus: Capitalism and Schizophrenia*. Trans. Robert Hurley, Mark Seem, and Helen R. Lane. London: Continuum, 2004. Print.
———. *A Thousand Plateaus*. Trans. Brian Massumi. Minneapolis: University of Minnesota Press, 1987. Print.
Deppman, Jed. "A Chapter in Composition: Chapter II.4." Crispi and Slote 304–46. Print.
Deppman, Jed, Daniel Ferrer, and Michael Groden, eds. *Genetic Criticism: Texts and Avant-Textes*. Philadelphia: University of Pennsylvania Press, 2004. Print.
Derrida, Jacques. *Dissemination*. Trans. Barbara Johnson. London: Continuum, 2008. Print.
———. *L'animal que donc je suis*. Paris: Galilée, 2006. *The Animal That Therefore I Am*. Ed. Marie-Louise Mallet. Trans. David Wills. New York: Fordham University Press, 2008. Print.
———. *Of Grammatology*. Trans. Gayatri Chakravorty Spivak. Baltimore: Johns Hopkins University Press, 1997. Print.
"Divination, n." Def. 1a. *The Oxford English Dictionary*. 2nd ed. 1989. OED Online. Oxford University Press. Web. 10 January 2010.
Dizard, Jan E. *Going Wild: Hunting, Animal Rights, and the Contested Meaning of Nature*. Amherst: University of Massachusetts Press, 1994. Print.
Dolan, Terence Patrick. *A Dictionary of Hiberno-English*. Dublin: Gill & Macmillan, 2000. Print.
Doyle, Gerard J., and Colmán Ó Críodáin. "Peatlands—Fens and Bogs." Marinus 79–108. Print.

"Dr. Nansen's Journey across Greenland," *Nature* 40 (1889): 103–4. Web. 10 January 2013.
Duffy, Enda. *The Subaltern Ulysses*. Minneapolis: University of Minnesota Press, 1994. Print.
Dunbar, Gary S., ed. *Geography: Discipline, Profession, and Subject Since 1870*. Dordrecht, The Netherlands: Kluwen Academic Publishers, 2001. Print.
Dunn, Douglas, ed. *Two Decades of Irish Writing: A Critical Survey*. Chester Springs, PA: Dufour, 1975. Print.
Eckley, Grace. "Looking Forward to a Brightening Day." Begnal and Senn 211–35. Print.
Edwards, Denis. *Ecology at the Heart of Faith*. Maryknoll, NY: Orbis Books, 2006. Print.
Eide, Marian. *Ethical Joyce*. Cambridge: Cambridge University Press, 2002. Print.
Elder, John. *Imagining the Earth: Poetry and the Vision of Nature*. 1985. Athens: University of Georgia Press, 1996. Print.
———. Introduction. Cusick 1–4. Print.
Eliot, T. S. "*Ulysses*, Order and Myth." Givens 480–83. Print.
———. "The Waste Land." *The Complete Poems and Plays*. London: Faber and Faber, 2004. 59–80. Print.
Encyclopaedia Britannica. 11th ed. 29 vols. General editor, Hugh Chisolm. Cambridge: Cambridge University Press, 1910–1911.
Epstein, Edmund. *A Guide through* Finnegans Wake. Gainesville: University Press of Florida, 2009. Print.
Erickson, Paul A., and Liam D. Murphy, eds. *A History of Anthropological Theory*. Toronto: University of Toronto Press, 2008. Print.
Evans, David. *A History of Nature Conservation in Britain*. London: Routledge, 1992. Print.
Evans, E. Estyn. *The Personality of Ireland: Habitat, Heritage, and History*. 1973. Dublin: Lilliput, 1992. Print.
Evernden, Neil. "Beyond Ecology: Self, Place, and the Pathetic Fallacy." Fromm and Glotfelty 92–104. Print.
———. *The Social Creation of Nature*. Baltimore: Johns Hopkins University Press, 1992. Print.
Eysteinsson, Astradur, and Vivian Liska, eds. *Modernism*. 2 vols. Amsterdam: John Benjamins, 2007. Print.
Farina, Almo. *Ecology, Cognition, and Landscape: Linking Natural and Social Systems*. Dordrecht: Springer, 2010. Print.
Feehan, John. "The Heritage of the Rocks." Foster and Chesney 3–22. Print.
———. "Threat and Conservation: Attitudes to Nature in Ireland." Foster and Chesney 573–96. Print.
Feehan, John, and Sadhbh McElveen. "The Changing Use of Raised Bogs." Aalen, Stout, and Whelan 114–17. Print.

Finnegans Wake *Extensible Elucidation Treasury*. Comp. Raphael Slipon. Web. 27 July 2011. http://www.fweet.org.

Fitzgerald, Walter. *The Historical Geography of Early Ireland*. London: G. Philip, 1925. Print.

Fitzpatrick, David. "Ireland since 1870." Foster 174–230. Print.

Fitzpatrick, H. M. *Trees and the Law*. Dublin: Incorporated Law Society of Ireland, 1985. Print.

———. "The Trees of Ireland: Native and Introduced." *Scientific Proceedings of the Royal Dublin Society* 20 (1933): 597–656. Print.

Fleming, Deborah. "Landscape and the Self in W. B. Yeats and Robinson Jeffers." Bryson 39–57. Print.

Flood, J. M. *Ireland: Its Saints and Scholars*. Dublin: Talbot Press, 1918. Print.

Fordham, Finn. *I Do I Undo I Redo: The Textual Genesis of Modernist Selves in Hopkins, Yeats, Conrad, Forster, Joyce, and Woolf*. Oxford: Oxford University Press, 2010. Print.

———. *Lots of Fun at Finnegans Wake: Unravelling Universals*. Oxford: Oxford University Press, 2007. Print.

———. "The Writing of Growth and the Growths of Writing: A Genetic Exegesis of Finnegans Wake 503.30–505.29." Part 2. *Hypermedia Joyce Studies* 9.1. Web. 2 April 2010. http://hjs.ff.cuni.cz/archives/v9_1/essays/fordham.htm.

Foss, Peter, and Catherine O'Connell. "Bogland: Study and Utilization." Chesney and Foster 184–98. Print.

Foster, John Wilson. "Encountering Traditions." Chesney and Foster 23–70. Print.

Foster, R. F., ed. *The Oxford Illustrated History of Ireland*. London: Oxford, 2001. Print.

Frawley, Oona. *Irish Pastoral: Nostalgia and Twentieth-Century Irish Literature*. Dublin: Irish Academic Press, 2005. Print.

Frazer, Sir James. *The Golden Bough: A Study in Magic and Religion*. 1922. Wordsworth Reference Series. Hertfordshire: Wordsworth, 1993. Print.

Frehner, Ruth, and Ursula Zeller, eds. *A Collideorscape of Joyce*. Dublin: Lilliput, 1998. Print.

French, Marilyn. *The Book as World: James Joyce's Ulysses*. Cambridge: Harvard University Press, 1976. Print.

Freud, Sigmund. *Totem und Tabu: Einige Übereinstimmungen im Seelenleben der Wilden und der Neurotiker*. 1913. *Totem and Taboo*. 1950. Trans. James Strachey. London: Routledge, 1999. Print.

Fromm, Harold, and Cheryll Glotfelty, eds. *The Ecocriticism Reader*. Athens: University of Georgia Press, 1996. Print.

———. "Introduction: Literary Studies in an Age of Environmental Crisis." Fromm and Glotfelty xv–xxxvii. Print.

Fujita, Motoko, ed. *The Shadow of James Joyce: Chapelizod and Environs.* Dublin: Lilliput Press, 2011. Print.
Fuse, Miko. "The Letter and the Groaning: Chapter I.5." Crispi and Slote 98–123. Print.
Fussell, Paul. *The Great War and Modern Memory.* 1975. Oxford: Oxford University Press, 2000. Print.
Fütterer, Dieter K., Detlef Damaske, Georg Kleinschmidt, Hubert Miller, and Franz Tessensohn, eds. *Antarctica: Contributions to Global Earth Sciences.* Berlin: Springer-Verlag, 2006. Print.
Gaard, Greta Claire, and Patrick D. Murphy, eds. *Ecofeminist Literary Criticism: Theory, Interpretation, Pedagogy.* Champaign: University of Illinois Press, 1998. Print.
Gallaher, Carol, and Mary Gilmartin, et al. *Key Concepts in Political Geography.* London: Sage Publications, 2009. Print.
Garrard, Greg. *Ecocriticism.* New York: Routledge, 2004. Print.
Garriott, Edward B. *Weather Folk-Lore and Local Weather Signs.* 1903. Ithaca: Cornell University Press, 2009. Print.
Gaskell, G. A. *Dictionary of the Sacred Languages of All Scriptures and Myths.* 1981. New York: Gramercy, 2003. Print.
Gay, Peter. *Modernism: The Lure of Heresy.* New York: Norton, 2007. Print.
Genet, Jacqueline, ed. *Rural Ireland, Real Ireland?* Irish Literary Studies 49. Gerrards Cross, Buckinghamshire: Colin Smythe, 1996. Print.
Gera, Deborah Levine. *Ancient Greek Ideas on Speech, Language, and Civilization.* Oxford: Oxford University Press, 2003. Print.
Gersdorf, Catrin, and Sylvia Mayer, eds. *Nature in Literary and Cultural Studies: Transatlantic Conversations on Ecocriticism.* Amsterdam: Rodopi, 2006. Print.
"Giant's Causeway." *Dublin Penny Journal* 5 (1832): 33–34. JSTOR. Web. 10 August 2011.
Gifford, Don. *Joyce Annotated: Notes for* Dubliners *and* A Portrait of the Artist as a Young Man. Los Angeles: University of California Press, 1982. Print.
———. *Ulysses Annotated: Notes for James Joyce's* Ulysses. 2nd ed. Berkeley: University of California Press, 1989. Print.
Gilbert, Stuart. *James Joyce's* Ulysses. New York: Vintage, 1952. Print.
Gilcrest, David W. *Greening the Lyre: Environmental Poetics and Ethics.* Reno: University of Nevada Press, 2002. Print.
Gillespie, Michael Patrick, ed. *James Joyce and the Fabrication of an Irish Identity.* European Joyce Studies 11. Amsterdam: Rodopi, 2001. Print.
Givens, Seon, ed. *James Joyce: Two Decades of Criticism.* New York: Vanguard Press, 1948. Print.
Glacken, Clarence J. *Traces on the Rhodian Shore: Nature and Culture in Western Thought from Ancient Times to the End of the Eighteenth Century.* Berkeley: University of California Press, 1976. Print.

Glasheen, Adaline. *Third Census of* Finnegans Wake: *An Index of the Characters and Their Roles*. Berkeley: University of California Press, 1977. Print.

Gluck, Mary. *Popular Bohemia: Modernism and Urban Culture in Nineteenth-Century Paris*. Cambridge: Harvard University Press, 2005. Print.

Gordon, Craig. *Literary Modernism, Bioscience, and Community in Early 20th Century Britain*. New York: Palgrave Macmillan, 2007. Print.

Gordon, John. Finnegans Wake: *A Plot Summary*. Dublin: Gill and Macmillan, 1986. Print.

Goudie, Andrew, ed. *Encyclopedia of Geomorphology*. 2 vols. New York: Routledge, 2004. Print.

Graham-Campbell, James. *The Viking World*. London: Frances Lincoln, 2001. Print.

Grant, Robert M. *Early Christians and Animals*. London: Routledge, 2002. Print.

Green, Miranda. *Animals in Celtic Life and Myth*. New York: Routledge, 1992. Print.

Gregory, Lady August. *Gods and Fighting Men: The Story of the Tuatha de Danaan and of the Fianna of Ireland*. London: J. Murray, 1904. Print.

Grewe-Volpp, Christa. "Nature 'Out There' and as 'A Social Player': Some Basic Consequences for a Literary Ecocritical Analysis." Gersdorf and Mayer 71–86. Print.

Grieve, James, trans. *In the Shadow of Young Girls in Flower*. By Marcel Proust. New York: Penguin Classics, 2005. Print.

Grim, John, and Mary Evelyn Tucker, eds. *Worldviews and Ecology: Religion, Philosophy, and the Environment*. Maryknoll, NY: Orbis Books, 1994. Print.

Groden, Michael. "The National Library of Ireland's New Joyce Manuscripts: A Statement and Document Descriptions." *James Joyce Quarterly* 39 (2001): 29–52. Print.

Guerber, H. A. *Myths of Northern Lands*. 1895. Detroit: Singing Tree Press, 1970. Print.

Gwynn, Stephen. *The History of Ireland*. New York: Macmillan, 1923. Archive.org. Web. 3 April 2010.

Haldane, John Burdon Sanderson. *Daedalus, or Science and the Future*. London: Kegan Paul, 1924. *The Online Books Page*. UPenn. Ed. Cosma Rohilla Shalizi. Web. 17 January 2015.

Haliday, Charles. *The Scandinavian Kingdom of Dublin*. Shannon: Irish University Press, 1969. Print.

Hamilton, Andrew. "6000-Year-Old Settlement Poses Tsunami Mystery." *Irish Examiner*. 9 May 2012. Web. 11 March 2013. http://www.irishexaminer.com/ireland/6000-year-old-settlement-poses-tsunami-mystery-193230.html.

Hanson, Gillian Mary. *Riverbank and Seashore in Nineteenth and Twentieth Century British Literature*. Jefferson, North Carolina: McFarland and Company, 2005. Print.

Haraway, Donna. *Primate Visions: Gender, Race, and Nature in the World of Modern Science*. New York: Routledge, 1989. Print.

———. *Simians, Cyborgs, and Women: The Reinvention of Nature*. New York: Routledge, 1991. Print.

Harding, Desmond. *Writing the City: Urban Visions and Literary Modernism*. New York: Routledge, 2003. Print.

Hardy, Thomas. "The Darkling Thrush." Allison 846. Print.

Hargreaves, George. "Large Parks: A Designer's Perspective." Czerniak and Hargreaves 121–74. Print.

Harmon, Maurice, ed. *The Irish Writer and the City*. Buckinghamshire: Colin Smythe, 1984. Print.

Harrison, Peter. "The 'Book of Nature' and Early Modern Science." Van Berkel and Vanderjagt 1–26. Print.

Harrison, Robert Pogue. *Forests: The Shadow of Civilization*. Chicago: University of Chicago Press, 1992. Print.

Harrison, Stephan, Steve Pile, and Nigel Thrift, eds. *Patterned Ground: Entanglements of Nature and Culture*. London: Reaktion Books, 2004. Print.

Hart, Clive. *A Concordance to* Finnegans Wake. Minneapolis: University of Minnesota Press, 1963. Print.

———. "His Good Smetterling of Entymology." *AWN* 4 (1967): 14–24. Print.

———. *Structure and Motif in* Finnegans Wake. London: Faber, 1962. Print.

Hart, Clive, and David Hayman, eds. *James Joyce's* Ulysses: *Critical Essays*. Berkeley: University of California Press, 1974. Print.

Haugen, Einar. "The Ecology of Language." *The Ecolinguistics Reader: Language, Ecology, and Environment*. Ed. Alwin Fill and Peter Mühlhäusler. London: Continuum, 2001. 57-66. Print.

Hayden, Tom. *The Lost Gospel of the Earth: A Call for Renewing Nature, Spirit, and Politics*. Dublin: Wolfhound Press, 1997. Print.

Hayman, David. *A First-Draft Version of* Finnegans Wake. Austin: University of Texas Press, 1963. Print.

———. "Reading Joyce's Notebooks?! *Finnegans Wake* from Within." Lernout 8–22. Print.

———. "To Make a List: Two Preparatory Puzzles on the Threshold of Book III." Hayman and Slote 255–79. Print.

———. "Tristan and Isolde in *Finnegans Wake*: A Study of the Sources and Evolution of a Theme." *Comparative Literature Studies* 1 (1964): 93–112. Print.

———. *The* Wake *in Transit*. Ithaca: Cornell University Press, 1990. Print.

Hayman, David, and Sam Slote, eds. *Probes: Genetic Studies in Joyce*. European Joyce Studies 5. Amsterdam: Rodopi, 1995. Print.

Heath, Stephen. "Ambivolences: Notes for Reading Joyce." Attridge and Ferrer 31–68. Print.

Heidegger, Martin. "The Question Concerning Technology." Kaplan 9–24. Print.

Heise, Ursula K. *Sense of Place and Sense of Planet: The Environmental Imagination of the Global.* New York: Oxford University Press, 2008. Print.
Hemingway, Ernest. *Hemingway on Hunting.* Ed. Séan Hemingway. Guilford, CT: Lyons Press, 2001. Print.
——. *Selected Letters of Ernest Hemingway, 1917–1961.* Ed. Carlos Baker. New York: Scribner, 1981. Print.
Henry, Holly. *Virginia Woolf and the Discourse of Science: The Aesthetics of Astronomy.* Cambridge: Cambridge University Press, 2003. Print.
Henry, O. "An Adjustment of Nature." *Cabbages and Kings, The Four Million, The Trimmed Lamp.* London: Collins, 1954. Print.
Herman, Daniel Justin. *Hunting and the American Imagination.* Washington, D.C.: Smithsonian, 2001. Print.
Herring, Phillip F., ed. *Joyce's* Ulysses *Notesheets in the British Museum.* Charlottesville: University of Virginia Press, 1972. Print.
Hesiod. *Theogony.* Trans. and ed. Richard Hamilton. Bryn Mawr, PA: Thomas Library Bryn Mawr College, 1990. Print.
——. *Works and Days.* Trans. and ed. Richard Hamilton. Bryn Mawr, PA: Thomas Library Bryn Mawr College, 1998. Print.
Hessel, Dietrich, and Rosemary Radford Ruether, eds. *Christianity and Ecology: Seeking the Well-Being of Earth and Humans.* Cambridge: Harvard University Press, 2000. Print.
Hickey, Kieran. *Wolves in Ireland: A Natural and Cultural History.* Dublin: Four Courts Press, 2011. Print.
Hickie, David. *Native Trees and Forests of Ireland.* Dublin: Gill and Macmillan, 2002. Print.
Higgins, Sir Godrefy. *The Celtic Druids.* New York: Cosimo Classics, 2007. Print.
Higginson, Fred. *Anna Livia Plurabelle: The Making of a Chapter.* Minneapolis: University of Minnesota Press, 1960. Print.
Holdridge, Jefferson. "Dark Outlines, Grey Stone: Nature, Home and the Foreign in Lady Morgan's *The Wild Irish Girl* and William Carleton's *The Black Prophet.*" Cusick 20–35. Print.
Hollingsworth, Christopher. *Poetics of the Hive: The Insect Metaphor in Literature.* Iowa City: University of Iowa Press, 2001. Print.
Hollis, Christopher. "Christopher Hollis on *Animal Farm*'s Literary Merit." Bloom 83–85. Print.
Holy Bible. New Revised Standard Edition (with the Apocryphal and Deuterocanonical Texts. Ed. Wayne A. Meeks. San Francisco: Harper, 1993. Print.
Hooke, S. H. *Middle Eastern Mythology.* New York: Penguin, 1963. Print.
Hopkins, David Moody, ed. *The Bering Land Bridge.* Stanford: Stanford University Press, 1967. Print.
Howard, Sir Ebenezer. *To-morrow: A Peaceful Path towards Real Reform.* 1898. London: Routledge, 2009. Print.

Howarth, O.J.R. *Geography of Ireland*. Oxford: Clarendon Press, 1911. Print.
Howarth, William. "Some Principles of Ecocriticism." Fromm and Glotfelty 69–91. Print.
Hume, David. *The History of England: From the Invasion of Julius Caesar to the Revolution in 1688*. Archive.org. Web. 14 March 2011.
———. *The Philosophical Works of David Hume*. 4 vols. Boston, 1854. Archive.org. Web. 14 March 2011.
Hurd, Barbara. *Stirring the Mud: On Swamps, Bogs, and Human Imagination*. Athens: University of Georgia Press, 2008. Print.
Irving, Washington. *A History of New York*. 1809. New York: Doubleday, 1928. Print.
Jacquet, Claude. "'In the buginning is the woid': James Joyce and Genetic Criticism." Lernout 23–36. Print.
———, ed. *Scribble 1: Genèse des Textes*. Paris: Minard, 1988. Print.
Jahn, Victoria, ed. *Simon and Schuster's Guide to Bonsai*. New York: Fireside, 1990. Print.
Jahnke bequest. Zürich James Joyce Foundation. Unpublished. August 2009.
Jespersen, Otto. *Growth and Structure of the English Language*. 9th ed. Garden City, NY: Doubleday Anchor Books, 1956. Print.
Jolas, Eugene. "Marginalia to James Joyce's *Work in Progress*." transition 22 (1933): 101–5. Print.
———. "My Friend James Joyce." Givens 11–12. Print.
Joyce, P. W. *A Short History of Ireland from the Earliest Times to 1608*. London: Longmans, Green, and Co., 1895. Print.
Joyce, Weston St. John. *The Neighbourhood of Dublin: Its Topography, Antiquities, and Historical Associations*. 1939. Yorkshire: S. R. Publishers, 1971. Print.
Kain, Richard. "James Joyce to John Eglinton: An Unpublished Letter." *James Joyce Quarterly* 12 (1975): 358–61. Print.
Kaplan, David M., ed. *Readings in the Philosophy of Technology*. Lanham, MD: Rouman and Littlefield, 2009. Print.
Kavanagh, Mary. *Galway-Gaillimh: A Bibliography of the City and County*. Galway: Galway County Council, 2000. Print.
Keating, Geoffrey. *The General History of Ireland*. 1723. Ed. David Comyn. London: Irish Texts Society, 1902. Print.
Kelly, Edward, and Edward Timms, eds. *Unreal City: Urban Experience in Modern European Literature and Art*. New York: St. Martin's Press, 1985. Print.
Kennedy-O'Neill, Joy. "'Sympathy between man and nature': Landscape and Loss in Synge's *Riders to the Sea*." Cusick 36–49. Print.
Kennedy, P. G. "Violation of Sanctuary." *Studies: An Irish Quarterly Review* 38 (1949): 37–45. JSTOR. Web. 3 March 2010.
Keown, Edwina. "New Horizons: Irish Aviation, Lemass, and Deferred Anglo-

Irish Modernism in Elizabeth Bowen's *A World of Love*." Keown and Taaffe 217–36. Print.

Keown, Edwina, and Carol Taaffe, eds. *Irish Modernism: Origins, Contexts, Publics*. Reimagining Ireland 14. Bern: Peter Lang, 2010. Print.Kerasote, Ted. *Bloodties: Nature, Culture, and the Hunt*. London: Kodansha International, 1993. Print.

Kerridge, Richard, and Neil Sammels, eds. *Writing the Environment: Ecocriticism and Literature*. London: Zed Books, 1998. Print.

Kiberd, Declan. *Irish Classics*. London: Granta, 2000. Print.

Kinane, Dean Thomas. *St. Patrick, His Life, His Heroic Virtues, His Labours, and the Fruits of His Labours*. Dublin, 1889. Print.

Kirsch, Johann Peter. "St. Dymphna." *The Catholic Encyclopedia*. Vol. 5. New York: Robert Appleton Company, 1909. Web. 19 Aug. 2011. http://www.newadvent.org/cathen/05221b.htm.

Kitcher, Philip. *Joyce's Kaleidoscope: An Invitation to Finnegans Wake*. Oxford: Oxford University Press, 2007. Print.

Klein, Scott W. *The Fictions of James Joyce and Wyndham Lewis: Monsters of Nature and Design*. Cambridge: Cambridge University Press, 1994. Print.

Kolodny, Annette. *The Lay of the Land: Metaphor as Experience and History in American Life and Letters*. Chapel Hill: University of North Carolina Press, 1975. Print.

Kroeber, Karl. *Ecological Literary Criticism: Romantic Imagining and the Biology of Mind*. New York: Columbia University Press, 1994. Print.

Lalor, Brian. *Dublin Bay: From Killiney to Howth*. Dublin: O'Brien Press, 1989. Print.

———, ed. *The Encyclopedia of Ireland*. Dublin: Gill and Macmillan, 2003. Print.

Lamhna, Éanna ní. *Wild Dublin*. Dublin: O'Brien Press, 2008. Print.

Landuyt, Ingeborg. "Cain-Ham-(Shem)-Esau-Jim the Penman: Chapter I.7." Crispi and Slote 142–62. Print.

———. "Tale Told of Shem: Some Elements at the Inception of FW I.7." Slote and Van Mierlo 115–34. Print.

Landuyt, Ingeborg, and Geert Lernout. "Joyce's Sources: *Les grandes fleuves historiques*." *Joyce Studies Annual* 6 (1995): 99–138. Print.

Langdon, Stephen. *Enuma Elish: The Babylonian Epic of Creation Restored from the Recently Recovered Tablets of Assur*. Oxford: Clarendon Press, 1923. Archive.org. Web. 15 November 2011.

Latour, Bruno. *We Have Never Been Modern*. Trans. Catherine Porter. New York: Harvester Wheatsheaf, 1993. Print.

Lauber, Volkmar. "Austria: A Latecomer Which Became a Pioneer." Andersen and Liefferink 81–109. Print.

Lawless, Emily. *The Story of Ireland*. London: T. F. Unwin, 1923. Print.

Lee, Joseph. *The Modernisation of Irish Society, 1848–1918*. Dublin: Gill and Macmillan, 1973. Print.

Le Fanu, Sheridan. *The House by the Churchyard*. 1863. London: Wordsworth, 2007. Print.

Lehan, Richard. *The City in Literature: An Intellectual and Cultural History*. Berkeley: University of California Press, 1998. Print.

Lernout, Geert, ed. Finnegans Wake: *Fifty Years*. European Joyce Studies 2. Amsterdam: Rodopi, 1990. Print.

———. "The *Finnegans Wake* Notebooks and Radical Philology." Hayman and Slote 19–48. Print.

———. *The French Joyce*. Ann Arbor: University of Michigan Press, 1992. Print.

———. Rev. of *Shane Leslie: Sublime Failure*, by Otto Rauchbauer. *James Joyce Quarterly* 47 (2009): 164–69. Print.

———. "Richard Wagner's 'Tristan und Isolde' in the Genesis of *Finnegans Wake*." *James Joyce Quarterly* 38 (2000–2001): 143–56. Print.

———. "Woman the Inspirer: Wagner in VI.B.3 and VI.B.35." *AFWC* 6 (1990–1991): 1–12. Print.

Lévi-Strauss, Claude. *The View from Afar*. Trans. Joachim Neugroschel and Phoebe Hoss. Chicago: University of Chicago Press, 1992. Print.

Lewis, Wyndham. *Time and Western Man*. 1927. Berkeley: Gingko Books, 1993. Print.

"The Liffey Valley Today." *Office of Public Works, Ireland*. Web. 26 July 2011. http://kildare.ie/CountyCouncil/LeisureServices/LiffeyPark.

Litz, A. Walton. *The Art of James Joyce: Method and Design in* Ulysses *and* Finnegans Wake. London: Oxford University Press, 1961. Print.

Long, Mark. "William Carlos Williams, Ecocriticism, and Contemporary American Poetry." Bryson 58–74. Print.

Lopez, Barry. "Landscape and Narrative." *Crossing Open Ground*. New York: Vintage, 1989. 61–72. Print.

Losey, Jay B. "Dream-Epiphanies in *Finnegans Wake*." *James Joyce Quarterly* 26 (1989): 611–17. Print.

Love, Glen A. "Revaluing Nature: Toward an Ecological Criticism." *Western American Literature* 25 (1990): 201–15. Print.

Lüdecke, Cornelia. "International Cooperation in Antarctica, 1901–1904." Barr and Lüdecke 127–34. Print.

Ludwig, Theodore M. *The Sacred Paths: Understanding the Religions of the World*. Upper Saddle River: Prentice Hall, 2001. Print.

Lynch, Kevin. *The Image of the City*. Cambridge: Massachusetts Institute of Technology Press, 1960. Print.

Lyotard, Jean-Francois. "Ecology as Discourse of the Secluded." Coupe 135–38. Print.

———. *Political Writings*. Trans. Bill Readings and Kevin Paul Geiman. Minneapolis: University of Minnesota Press, 1993. Print.
Macalister, Robert Alexander Stewart, ed. *Lebor Gabála Érenn: The Book of the Taking of Ireland*. Irish Texts Society by the Education Co. of Ireland, 1939. *CELT: Corpus of Electronic Texts*. University College Cork. Web. 15 May 2011. http://www.ucc.ie/celt/LGintro.pdf.
Macauley, David, ed. *Minding Nature: The Philosophers of Ecology*. New York: Guilford Press, 1996. Print.
Mac Coitir, Niall. *Irish Trees: Myths, Legends, and Folklore*. Cork: Collins Press, 2006. Print.
MacManus, M. J. *Eamon De Valera*. Chicago: Ziff Davis Publishing, 1946. Print.
Madrigal, Alexis. *Powering the Dream: The History and Promise of Green Technology*. Philadelphia: Da Capo, 2011. Print.
Magee, W. K. *Pebbles from a Brook*. Kilkenny: Standish O'Grady, 1901. *Hathi Trust*. Web. 17 January 2015.
Maier, Kevin. "Hemingway's Hunting: An Ecological Reconsideration." *Hemingway Review* 25 (2006): 119–22. Print.
Malory, Sir Thomas. *Le Morte D'Arthur*. Ed. Stephen H. A. Shepherd. Norton Critical Editions. New York: Norton, 2003. Print.
Mansfield, Katherine. *The Collected Stories of Katherine Mansfield*. London: Wordsworth, 2006. Print.
Manwood, John. *Treatise of the Forest Laws*. 1592. London: E. Nutt, 1717. *Archive.org*. Web. 15 April 2011.
Marinus, L. Otte, ed. *Wetlands of Ireland: Distribution, Ecology, Uses, and Economic Value*. Dublin: University College Dublin Press, 2003. Print.
Marsh, George Perkins. *Man and Nature, Or, Physical Geography as Modified by Human Action*. New York, 1864. Print.
Marx, Leo. *The Machine in the Garden: Technology and the Pastoral Ideal in America*. New York: Oxford University Press, 1964. Print.
Masueth, James D. *Botany: An Introduction to Plant Biology*. 3rd ed. Sudbury, MA: James and Bartlett, 2003. Print.
Mazel, David. "American Literary Environmentalism as Domestic Orientalism." Fromm and Glotfelty 137–46. Print.
McAsey, Carmel. "Chapelizod, Co. Dublin." *Dublin Historical Record* 17 (1962): 40–44. *JSTOR*. Web. 16 May 2011.
McCarthy, Patrick. "Making Herself Tidal: Chapter I.8." Crispi and Slote 163–80. Print.
McCaw, Neil. *Writing Irishness in Nineteenth-Century British Culture*. Burlington: Ashgate, 2004. Print.
McCourt, John. "Introduction: From the Real to the Reel and Back: Explorations into Joyce and Cinema." McCourt, *Roll* 1–14. Print.

———, ed. *Roll Away the Reel World: James Joyce and Cinema*. Cork: Cork University Press, 2010. Print.
McCracken, Eileen. *The Irish Woods since Tudor Times: Distribution and Exploration*. Newton Abbot: David and Charles, 1971. Print.
McCullen, John A. *An Illustrated History of the Phoenix Park: Landscape and Management to 1880*. Dublin: Celtic Press, 2009. Print.
———. "Chapelizod—The Shadow of James Joyce in Phoenix Park." Fujita 71–76. Print.
McFague, Sallie. *Life Abundant: Rethinking Theology and Economy for a Planet in Peril*. Minneapolis: Fortress Press, 2001. Print.
McGovern, Barry. "Joyce's 'A Painful Case' and Chapelizod." Fujita 45–47. Print.
McHugh, Roland. "Chronology of the Buffalo Notebooks." *AWN* 9 (1972): 19–31. Print.
———. "Jespersen's Language in Notebooks VI.B.2 and VI.C.2." *AFWC* 2 (1987): 61–71. Print.
———. *The Sigla of* Finnegans Wake. London: Edward Arnold, 1976. Print.
McKernan, Luke. "James Joyce and the Volta Programme." McCourt, *Roll* 15–27. Print.
———. "Volta Filmography." Appendix. McCourt, *Roll* 187–204. Print.
McLean, Stuart John. *The Event and Its Terrors: Ireland, Famine, Modernity*. Palo Alto: Stanford University Press, 2004. Print.
McLuhan, Eric. *The Role of Thunder in* Finnegans Wake. Toronto: University of Toronto Press, 1997. Print.
McManus, Ruth. *Dublin, 1910–1940: Shaping the City and Suburbs*. Dublin: Four Courts, 2002. Print.
Meeker, Joseph W. *The Comedy of Survival: Studies in Literary Ecology*. New York: Scribner's, 1972. Print.
Merchant, Carolyn. *The Columbia Guide to American Environmental History*. New York: Columbia University Press, 2002. Print.
———. *The Death of Nature: Women, Ecology, and the Scientific Revolution*. 1980. San Francisco: Harper Collins, 1989. Print.
Merleau-Ponty, Maurice. *Phénoménologie de la perception*. Trans. Colin Smith. London: Routledge Classics, 2002. Print.
———. *The Visible and the Invisible*. Evanston: Northwestern University Press, 1973. Print.
Metchnikoff, Léon. *La civilisation et les grands fleuves historiques*. Paris: Hachette et Cie, 1889. Print.
Mikhail, Alan. *Nature and Empire in Ottoman Egypt: An Environmental History*. Cambridge: Cambridge University Press, 2011. Print.
Milesi, Laurent. "Metaphors of the Quest in *Finnegans Wake*." Lernout 79–108. Print.

———. "Supplementing Babel: Paget in VI.B.32." *Genetic Joyce Studies* 1 (2001): no page. Web. 15 January 2015.
———. "Vico. Jousse. Joyce. Langue." Jacquet, *Scribble* 143–62. Print.
Mills, William J. *Exploring Polar Frontiers: A Historical Encyclopedia*. Santa Barbara: ABC-Clio, 2003. Print.
Milner, J. Edward. *The Tree Book: The Indispensable Guide to Tree Facts, Crafts, and Lore*. London: Collins and Brown, 1992. Print.
Milton, John. *Paradise Lost: A Norton Critical Edition*. 2nd ed. Ed. Scott Elledge. New York: Norton, 1993. Print.
Mink, Louis O. A *Finnegans Wake Gazetteer*. Bloomington: Indiana University Press, 1978. Print.
"The 'Missing Link' at Last? Discovery of Ape Man's Skull May Prove Theory That Africa Is the Birthplace of Man." *Popular Science Monthly* April 1925: 50–51. Web. 9 September 2011.
Mitchell, Don. *Cultural Geography: A Critical Introduction*. Oxford: Wiley-Blackwell, 2000. Print.
Monaghan, Patricia. *The Encyclopedia of Celtic Mythology and Folklore*. New York: Facts on File-Infobase, 2004. Print.
Montgomery, William Ernest. *The History of Land Tenure in Ireland*. Cambridge: Cambridge University Press, 1889. Print.
Moriarty, Christopher. *Dublin and North Wicklow*. Dublin: Gill and Macmillan, 1980. Print.
Mountfield, David. *A History of Polar Exploration*. London: Hamlyn Publishing, 1974. Print.
Mumford, Lewis. *The City in History: Its Origins, Its Transformations, and Its Prospects*. New York: Harcourt Brace, 1961. Print.
———. *Technics and Civilization*. 1934. London: Routledge & Kegan Paul, 1967. Print.
Murphy, Michael. "Index." Macalister 4. Web. 15 May 2011. http://www.ucc.ie/celt/LGintro.pdf.
Murphy, Patrick D. *Literature, Nature, and Other: Ecofeminist Critiques*. Albany: State University of New York Press, 1995. Print.
Nansen, Fridtjof. *Farthest North*. 1897. New York: Cambridge University Press, 2011. Print.
———. *The First Crossing of Greenland*. Vol. 2. 1890. Trans. Hubert Majendie. New York: Cambridge University Press, 2011. Print.
Nash, Roderick. *Wilderness and the American Mind*. New Haven: Yale University Press, 1982. Print.
National Library of Ireland (NLI). "Joyce Papers 2002." Unpublished.
———. "Joyce Papers 2006." Unpublished.
Neeson, Eoin. *A History of Irish Forestry*. Dublin: Lilliput, 1991. Print.

Nelson, E. Charles, and Wendy F. Walsh. *Trees of Ireland: Native and Naturalized*. Dublin: Lilliput, 1993. Print.
Nolan, Brendan. *Phoenix Park: A History and Guidebook*. Raheny: Liffey Press, 2006. Print.
Norris, David. "Re-verberations—Joyce, Chapelizod, Motoko Fujita." Fujita 43–44. Print.
Norris, Margot. *The Decentered Universe of* Finnegans Wake: *A Structuralist Analysis*. Baltimore: Johns Hopkins University Press, 1974. Print.
Nouveau petit Robert: Dictionnaire alphabétique et analogique de la langue française. Paris: Dictionnaires Le Robert, 2009. Print.
O'Brien, Joseph V. *"Dear, Dirty Dublin": A City in Distress, 1899–1916*. Berkeley: University of California Press, 1982. Print.
O'Dwyer, Riana. "Czarnowski and *Finnegans Wake*: A Study of the Cult of the Hero." *James Joyce Quarterly* 17 (1980): 281–91. Print.
Oelschlaeger, Max. *The Idea of Wilderness: From Prehistory to the Age of Ecology*. New Haven: Yale University Press, 1991. Print.
———. *Postmodern Environmental Ethics*. Albany: State University of New York Press, 1995. Print.
Office of Public Works Ireland. "The Phoenix Park Conservation Management Plan." March 2009. *OPW.ie*. Office of Public Works. Web. 22 Sept. 2011.
O'Flaherty, Liam. "Spring Sowing." *The Short Stories of Liam O'Flaherty*. London: Jonathan Cape, 1924. 11–18. Print.
O'Hanlon, Rev. John. *Lives of the Irish Saints: With Special Festivals, and the Commemorations of Holy Persons, Compiled from Calendars, Martyrologies, and Various Sources, Relating to the Ancient Church History of Ireland*. 4 vols. Dublin: 1873. Print.
O'Hanlon, John, and Danis Rose. *Understanding* Finnegans Wake: *A Guide to the Narrative of James Joyce's Masterpiece*. London: Farland, 1982. Print.
O Hehir, Brendan. *A Gaelic Lexicon for* Finnegans Wake, *and Glossary for Joyce's Other Works*. Berkeley: University of California Press, 1967. Print.
Ó hÓgáin, Dáithí. *The Sacred Isle: Belief and Religion in Pre-Christian Ireland*. Cork: Collins Press, 1999. Print.
Opperman, Serpil. "Theorizing Ecocriticism: Toward a Postmodern Ecocritical Practice." *ISLE* 13 (2006): 103–29. Print.
Ordnance Survey Ireland. Web. 2 April 2011. http://maps.osi.ie/publicviewer/.
Ortega Y Gasset, José. *Meditations on Hunting*. Belgrade, MT: Wilderness Adventures Press, 1995. Print.
Ossianic Society. "Transactions of the Ossianic Society." Vol. 2. Dublin, 1855. *Archive.org*. Web. 2 September 2011.
Oxford English Dictionary (OED). 2nd ed. Oxford: Oxford University Press, 1989. Web.

Paget, Richard. *Babel, or, The Past, Present, and Future of Human Speech*. London: Kegan Paul, 1930. *Hathi Trust*. Web. 17 January 2015.

———. *Human Speech: Some Observations, Experiments, and Conclusions as to the Nature, Origin, Purpose, and Possible Improvement of Human Speech*. London: Kegan Paul, 1930. *Hathi Trust*. Web. 17 January 2015.

Perry, W. J. *The Origin of Magic and Religion*. London: Methuen, 1923. Print.

Phillips, Dana. *The Truth of Ecology: Nature, Culture, and Literature in America*. New York: Oxford University Press, 2003. Print.

Platt, Len. "Madame Blavatsky and Theosophy in *Finnegans Wake*: An Annotated List." *James Joyce Quarterly* 45 (2008): 281–300. Print.

Pliny the Elder. *Natural History*. Ed. Harris Rackham. 37 vols. Cambridge: Harvard University Press, 1971. Print.

Ponting, Clive. *A New Green History of the World: The Environment and the Collapse of Great Civilizations*. London: Vintage, 2007. Print.

Potter, Russell A. *Arctic Spectacles: The Frozen North in Visual Culture, 1818–1875*. Seattle: University of Washington Press, 2007. Print.

Pound, Ezra. *Selected Poems and Translations*. Ed. Richard Sieburth. London: Faber, 2010. Print.

Power, Anne. *Hovels to High Rise: State Housing in Europe since 1850*. London: Routlegde, 1993. *Google Book Search*. Web. 6 March 2010.

Power, Arthur. *Conversations with James Joyce*. Dublin: Lilliput Press, 1999. Print.

Prendergast, John P. "Some Notice of the Life of Charles Haliday." Haliday iii–cxxiii. Print.

Proceedings of the Royal Irish Academy. Vol. 9. Dublin: M. H. Gill, 1867. *JSTOR*. Web. 24 February 2011.

Rabaté, Jean Michel. "The Fourfold Root of Yawn's Unreason: Chapter III.3." Crispi and Slote 384–409. Print.

Rasmussen, Larry L. *Earth Community, Earth Ethics*. Maryknoll, NY: Orbis Books, 1996. Print.

Rice, Stanley A. *Encyclopedia of Evolution*. New York: Facts on File-Infobase, 2003. Print.

Richardson, Angelique. "The Life Sciences: 'Everybody Nowadays Talks about Evolution.'" Bradshaw 6–33. Print.

Rickard, John. "'A Quaking Sod': Hybridity, Identity, and Wandering Irishness." Gillespie 83–100. Print.

Riordan, Colin. "German Literature, Nature, and Modernity Before 1914." Gersdorf and Mayer 313–30. Print.

Rivkin, Julie, and Michael Ryan, eds. *Literary Theory: An Anthology*. 2nd ed. Malden, MA: Blackwell, 2004. Print.

Ronsley, Joseph, ed. *Myth and Reality in Irish Literature*. Waterloo, ON: Wilfrid Laurier Press, 1977. Print.

Roots, Clive. *Flightless Birds*. Westport, CT: Greenwood Publishing, 2006. *Google Book Search*. Web. 1 September 2011.
Rose, Danis. *Chapters of Coming Forth by Day*. Colchester: A Wake Newslitter Press, 1982. Print.
———. *The Index Manuscript*: Finnegans Wake *Holograph Workbook VI.B.46*. Colchester: A Wake Newslitter Press, 1978. Print.
Rosendale, Steven. *The Greening of Literary Scholarship: Literature, Theory, and the Environment*. Iowa City: University of Iowa Press, 2002. Print.
Ross, Andrew. Interview by Michael Bennett. "The Social Claim on Urban Ecology." Bennett and Teague 15–30. Print.
Rubin, Gayle. "The Traffic in Women." Rivkin and Ryan 770–94. Print.
Rueckert, William. "Literature and Ecology: An Experiment in Ecocriticism." Fromm and Glotfelty 105–23. Print.
Ryden, Kent C. *Mapping the Invisible Landscape: Folklore, Writing, and the Sense of Place*. Iowa City: University of Iowa Press, 1993. Print.
Schama, Simon. *Landscape and Memory*. New York: Knopf, 1995. Print.
Schumm, Stanley Alfred. *River Variability and Complexity*. Cambridge: Cambridge University Press, 2005. Print.
Scott, Bonnie Kime. *In the Hollow of the Wave: Virginia Woolf and Modernist Uses of Nature*. Charlottesville: University of Virginia Press, 2012. Print.
———. "Virginia Woolf, Ecofeminism, and Breaking Boundaries in Nature." Burrells et al. 108–15. Print.
Senn, Fritz. "The Localization of Legend." *AFWN* 8 (1971): 10–13. Print.
Shakespeare, William. *Macbeth*. *The Oxford Shakespeare: The Complete Works*. 2nd ed. Ed. John Jowett, William Montgomery, Gary Taylor, and Stanley Wells. Oxford: Clarendon Press, 2006. 969–94. Print.
Shepard, Paul. *Man in the Landscape: A Historic View of the Esthetics of Nature*. New York: Ballantine, 1967. Print.
Shiva, Vandana. *Staying Alive: Women, Ecology, and Development*. London: Zed Books, 1989. Print.
Sienaert, Edgar Richard. "Marcel Jousse: The Oral Style and the Anthropology of Gesture." *Oral Tradition* 5.1 (1990): 91–106. *JSTOR*. Web. 5 May 2010.
"Sixth International Geographical Congress, London 1895." *American Geographical Society of New York* 27 (1895): 226–38. *JSTOR*. Web. 16 February 2012.
Sjoestedt, Marie-Louise. *Celtic Gods and Heroes*. Trans. Myles Dillon. 1949. Mineola, NY: Dover Publications, 2000. Print.
Slote, Sam. "Blanks for When Words Gone: Chapter II.1." Crispi and Slote 181–213. Print.
———. "Prolegomenon to the Development of Wakean Styles: New Acquisitions at the National Library of Ireland." *James Joyce Quarterly* 42/43 (2004–2006): 21–30. Print.
———. "A Wake in Chapelizod." Fujita 48–50. Print.

Slote, Sam, and Wim Van Mierlo, eds. *Genitricksling Joyce*. Amsterdam: Rodopi, 1999. Print.

"Small Boat First to Circle Franz Josef Land." *Popular Mechanics* 59 (1933): 359. Web. 13 September 2011.

Snæbjörnsdóttir, Bryndis, and Mark Wilson. *Nanoq: Flat Out and Bluesome—A Cultural Life of Polar Bears*. London: Black Dog Publishing, 2006. Print.

Snyder, Gary. *The Practice of the Wild*. San Francisco: North Point Press, 1990. Print.

Solomon, Margaret C. *Eternal Geomater: The Sexual Universe of Finnegans Wake*. Carbondale: Southern Illinois University Press, 1969. Print.

Soper, Kate. *What Is Nature? Culture, Politics, and the Non-Human*. Oxford: Blackwell, 1998. Print.

Southworth, Helen, and Elisa Kay Sparks, eds. *Woolf and the Art of Exploration: Selected Papers from the Fifteenth International Conference on Virginia Woolf*. Clemson, SC: Clemson University Digital Press, 2006. Print.

Spears, Monroe K. *Dionysus and the City: Modernism in Twentieth-Century Poetry*. New York: Oxford University Press, 1970. Print.

Spengler, Oswald. *Man and Technics: A Contribution to a Philosophy of Life*. Trans. Charles Francis Atkinson. London: Allen & Unwin, 1932. Print.

Spinks, Lee. *James Joyce: A Critical Guide*. Edinburgh: Edinburgh University Press, 2009. Print.

Squire, Charles. *Celtic Myths and Legends*. Broxburn, Scot.: Lomond Books, 2000. Print.

Staley, Thomas F., ed. *Joyce Studies Annual* 6. Austin: University of Texas Press, 1995. Print.

Steel, Duncan. *Marking Time: The Epic Quest to Invent the Perfect Calendar*. Hoboken: John Wiley, 2000. Print.

Stookey, Lorena Laura. *Thematic Guide to World Mythology*. Westport, CT: Greenwood Publishing, 2004. Print.

Strachan, Rob, and Nigel Woodcock, eds. *Geological History of Great Britain and Ireland*. Oxford: Blackwell, 2002. Print.

Sullivan, Edward. *The Book of Kells*. 1920. London: Studio Editions, 1986. Print.

Sultzbach, Kelly. "The Fertile Potential of Virginia Woolf's Environmental Ethic." Southworth and Sparks 71–77. Print.

Swan, James A. *The Sacred Art of Hunting: Myths, Legends, and the Modern Mythos*. Minocqua, WI: Willow Creek Press, 2000. Print.

Tambling, Jeremy. *Dante and Difference: Writing in the "Commedia."* Cambridge Studies in Medieval Literature. Cambridge: Cambridge University Press, 1988. Print.

Tansley, A. G. "The Use and Abuse of Vegetational Concepts and Terms." *Ecology* 16 (1935): 284–307. JSTOR. Web. 20 August 2011.

Theall, Donald. "Joyce, Eros, and 'Array! Surrection!'" *Myth and Reality in Irish*

Literature. Ed. Joseph Ronsley. Waterloo, ON: Wilfrid Laurier Press, 1977. 239–54. Print.

———. *Joyce's Techno-Poetics*. Toronto: University of Toronto Press, 1997. Print.

Thom's Irish Almanac and Official Directory for the Year 1903. Dublin, 1903. Print.

Tindall, William York. "James Joyce and the Hermetic Tradition." *Journal of the History of Ideas* 15 (1954): 23–39. Print.

———. *A Reader's Guide to* Finnegans Wake. Syracuse: Syracuse University Press, 1996. Print.

"Towards a Liffey Valley Park." *Office of Public Works Ireland*. Web. 26 July 2011. http://planning.southdublin.ie.

Travis, Charles. *Literary Landscapes of Ireland: Geographies of Irish Stories, 1929–1946*. Lewiston, NY: Edwin Mellen Press, 2009. Print.

Treip, Andrew, ed. Finnegans Wake: *Teems of Times*. European Joyce Studies 4. Amsterdam: Rodopi, 1994. Print.

———. "Recycled Historians: Michelet on Vico in VI.B.12." *AFWC* 4 (1989): 61–72. Print.

Tuan, Yi-Fu. *Space and Place: The Perspectives of Experience*. Minneapolis: University of Minnesota Press, 1977. Print.

Tysdahl, B. J. "Joyce's Use of Norwegian Writers." *English Studies* 50 (1969): 1–13. Print.

United Nations. International Labour Organization. Web. 10 March 2013. https://www.ilo.org.

Van Berkel, Klaas, and Johan Vanderjagt, eds. *The Book of Nature in Early Modern History*. Leuven: Peeters Publishers, 2008. Print.

———. Introduction. Van Berkel and Vanderjagt, *Book of Nature* ix–xi. Print.

Van Hulle, Dirk, ed. *James Joyce: The Study of Languages*. New Comparative Poetics 6. Brussels: PEI/Peter Lang, 2002. Print.

———. "The Lost Word: Book IV." Crispi and Slote 436–61. Print.

———. "Reveiling the Ouragan of Spaces in Less Than a Schoppinhour." Slote and Van Mierlo 145–58. Print.

———. *Textual Awareness: A Genetic Study of Late Manuscripts by Joyce, Proust, and Mann*. Ann Arbor: University of Michigan Press, 2004. Print.

Van Mierlo, Wim. "*Finnegans Wake* and the Question of Histry!?" Slote and Van Mierlo 43–64. Print.

———. "Neutral Auxiliaries and Universal Idioms: Otto Jespersen in 'Work in Progress.'" Van Hulle, *James Joyce* 55–70. Print.

———. "Shaun the Post: Chapters III.1–2." Crispi and Slote 347–83. Print.

———. "The Subject Notebook: A Nexus in the Composition History of *Ulysses*—A Preliminary Analysis." *Genetic Joyce Studies* 7 (2007): no page Web. 18 March 2009. http://www.geneticjoycestudies.org.

Verene, Donald Phillip. *Knowledge of Things Human and Divine*: Vico's New Science *and* Finnegans Wake. New Haven: Yale University Press, 2003. Print.

Vico, Giambattista. *New Science*. 3rd ed. 1744. Trans. David Marsh. New York: Penguin, 2001. Print.

Viney, Michael. "Native's Return: After Many Centuries of Deforestation Trees Are Now Making a Comeback." *Irish Times*, 7 April 2005. Web. 29 June 2011. http://archive.today/Ib2S4.

———. *A Smithsonian Natural History of Ireland*. Washington, D.C.: Smithsonian Institution Press, 2003. Print.

Voltaire. *Candide and Other Stories*. Trans. Roger Pearson. Oxford: Oxford University Press, 2006. Print.

Waite, Arthur Edward. *The Occult Sciences*. London: Kegan Paul, 1891. *Archive.org*. Web. 17 January 2015.

Wales, Katie. "Stagnant Pools in the Waning Moon: The Poetry of the 'Ithaca' Episode of *Ulysses*." Frehner and Zeller 156–70. Print.

Warburton, John, James Whitelaw, and Robert Walsh. *A History of the City of Dublin: From the Earliest Accounts to the Present Time*. 2 vols. London, 1818. Print.

Ward, Stephen Victor, ed. *The Garden City: Past, Present, and Future*. Oxford: Taylor and Francis, 1992. Print.

Warner, Dick. *The Liffey: Portrait of a River*. Donaghadee, N. Ireland: Cottage Publications, 2007. Print.

Watson, G. J. *Irish Identity and the Literary Revival: Synge, Yeats, Joyce, and O'Casey*. Washington, D.C.: Catholic University of America Press, 1979. Print.

Wells, H. G. *A Short History of the World*. 1922. New York: Cosimo Classics, 2005. Print.

Wenzell, Tim. *Emerald Green: An Ecocritical Study of Irish Literature*. Newcastle upon Tyne: Cambridge Scholars Publishing, 2009. Print.

Werness, Hope B. *The Continuum Encyclopedia of Animal Symbolism in Art*. New York: Continuum, 2003. Print.

Westling, Louise. *The Green Breast of the New World: Landscape, Gender, and American Fiction*. Athens: University of Georgia Press, 1998. Print.

———. "Literature, the Environment, and the Posthuman." Gersdorf and Mayer 25–47. Print.

Weston, Jessie L. *From Ritual to Romance*. 1920. New York: Cosimo Classics, 2005. Print.

Westropp, Thomas Johnson. "Will-o-the-Wisp and Corpse-lights: Underground Folk." *A Folklore Survey of County Clare*. Clare Public Library. Web. 5 December 2009.

Whelan, P. T. "The Hunting Metaphor in *The Fox* and Other Works." *D. H. Lawrence Review* 21 (1989): 275–90. Print.

White, Lynn, Jr. "The Historical Roots of Our Ecologic Crisis." *Science* 10 (1967): 1203–7. Print.

Whitworth, Michael H. *Einstein's Wake: Relativity, Metaphor, and Modernist Literature*. Oxford: Oxford University Press, 2001. Print.

——, ed. *Modernism*. Blackwell Guides to Criticism. Oxford: Blackwell, 2007. Print.

Wilde, Oscar. *The Importance of Being Earnest and Four Other Plays*. Ed. Kenneth Krauss. New York: Barnes & Noble Classics, 2003. Print.

Williams, Raymond. *The Country and the City*. New York: Oxford University Press, 1975. Print.

——. *Keywords: A Vocabulary of Culture and Society*. London: Flamingo, 1983.

Williams, William Carlos. *Imaginations*. 1938. New York: New Directions, 1970. Print.

Wilmer, Pat. *Pollination and Floral Ecology*. Princeton: Princeton University Press, 2011. Print.

Winston, Greg. "George Moore's Landscapes of Return." Cusick 66–84. Print.

——. *James Joyce and Militarism*. Gainesville: University Press of Florida, 2012. Print.

Wirth-Nesher, Hana. *City Codes: Reading the Modern Urban Novel*. Cambridge: Cambridge University Press, 2006. Print.

Wittgenstein, Ludwig. *Culture and Value*. Trans. Peter Winch. Ed. Heikke Nyman and G. H. Von Wright. Chicago: University of Chicago Press, 1980. Print.

Woodcock, Nigel. "Ordovician Volcanism and Sedimentation of Eastern Avalonia." Strachan and Woodcock 153–65. Print.

Worster, Donald. *Nature's Economy: A History of Ecological Ideas*. Cambridge: Cambridge University Press, 1977. Print.

——. *The Wealth of Nature: Environmental History and the Ecological Imagination*. New York: Oxford University Press, 1993. Print.

Yeats, William Butler. *Irish Fairy and Folk Tales*. New York: Modern Library, 2003. Print.

Young, Charles R. *The Royal Forests of Medieval England*. Philadelphia: University of Pennsylvania Press, 1979. Print.

Zapf, Hubert. "The State of Ecocriticism and the Function of Literature as Cultural Ecology." Gersdorf and Mayer 49–69. Print.

Index

Aalen, F.H.A., 9, 135
Abram, David, 4
"An Adjustment of Nature" (Henry), 214
Adventure-time, 165
Aeromancy, 162
Agency: of "ALP," 99; of nature, 16–17, 42, 165, 193, 204, 210–11, 216
Agri/culture, 113, 185; in Cain and Abel story, 96, 130, 133–34, 173–75; civilization and, 173, 175–76, 180, 182–83; ecology, religion and, 172–83, 199; fertility myths and, 172–76, 179–83, 199; "Norwegian Captain" sketch and, 181–82
A la recherche du temps perdu ("In the shadow of young girls in flower") (Proust), 208
"ALP" (fictional character), 64, 71, 116, 121, 179, 185; agency of, 99; coming of age and, 201–3; letter and, 60, 63, 166, 173; as Liffey, 15, 21, 85–90, 93, 95, 99, 118, 132–33, 176, 203, 223, 226–27, 254n4; as nature, 71, 85–90, 93, 95–96, 99, 149, 173, 198, 202–3, 212, 223–25; roles of, 91–93, 168
Alt, Christina, 11–12, 209, 252n10
Alternative energy resources, 17, 29–30
The American City Novel (Gelfant), 20
Amundsen, Roald, 146–47, 150, 155
Andersen, Mikael, 8
Anglo-Irish: conservation and, 8, 111–12; culture, 7–8, 44, 71–72, 110–12, 124–26, 164, 251n41; landlord, 71, 112, 126
"Anna Livia Plurabelle" chapter, 21, 28, 30–31; coming of age in, 200–212; Dublin's natural setting in, 85–90
Anthon, Charles, 220
Anti-Oedipus: Capitalism and Schizophrenia (Deleuze and Guattari), 14–15
Aristotle, 18, 24, 26, 236n17
Armbruster, Karla, 3, 129
Armorica, 219–20, 253n19
Armstrong, Tim, 14
Art, 18, 24, 131–32, 236n17
Arthur (king), 51, 176
Ash tree, 93
Atherton, J. S., 151, 210, 251n46
Atlas of the Irish Rural Landscape (Aalen, Stout, and Whelan), 9
Attridge, Derek, 22
Autumn, 184
Avant-texte, 25–26, 102, 126

Babel, or, The Past, Present, and Future of Human Speech (Paget), 206–7
Badminton Hunt, 170
Bakhtin, Mikhail, 165
"Balbus" (fictional character), 104, 240n22
Ball, Francis Elrington, 118, 241n34
Ballast Office, 99–101
Barger, John, 221
Barnacle, Nora, 148, 212
Barnhill, David, 160–61
Beaufort, 170, 248n14
Beckett, Samuel, 139
Bennett, Michael, 20
Bering Strait, 217

Berry, Thomas, 160, 246n1
"Beyond Ecology: Self, Place, and the Pathetic Fallacy" (Evernden), 41–42
Beyond Nature Writing: Expanding the Boundaries of Ecocriticism (Armbruster and Wallace), 3
Biagini, Eugenio, 155–56
Biocentric mythology, 161
Biological holism, 11
Birds, 190–94
Blackthorn tree, 66–67
Blue Lagoon Scheme, 157–58
"Bogland: Study and Utilization" (Foss and O'Connell), 135
Bogs, 183, 189, 243n19, 249n31; ecology of, 136, 221; politics of nature and, 134–40; preservation in, 59–60, 62–63
The Book of Kells (Sullivan): inspiration from, 23, 42, 60–61, 66–68, 83, 132, 252n4; wolf in, 192
Book of the Dead, 176
The Books at the Wake (Atherton), 151
Botany for Schools and Science Classes (Browne), 80–81
Boughey, A. S., 114
Bradbury, Malcolm, 10
Bramwell, Anna, 11
Breton culture, 76–78, 82
Brian Boru (king), 120, 140, 143
British Democracy and Irish Nationalism (Biagini), 155–56
Broom, Robert, 218
Browne, William James, 80–81
Bryson, J. Scott, 6
Budgen, Frank, 86, 239n1
Buell, Lawrence, 6–7, 24, 26–27, 197, 231
Burgess, Ernest, 108
Burke, Edmund, 17–18
"Butt and Taff" sketch, 139, 144
"By the Way" (Joyce), 67–68

Cain and Abel story, 96, 130, 133–34, 173–75
Cainapple, 67–68, 173–75
Calendar, 180, 185–86, 250n34
Cambrensis, Giraldus, 35

Campbell, Joseph, 73, 119
Campbell, SueEllen, 21–22, 27
Casement, Roger, 53
Castle, Gregory, 43
Cave paintings, 78–79, 82
Celtic paganism, 50, 55, 66–67, 165, 187–88
Celtic society, 49–51, 55, 77, 178, 186
Celtic Tiger, 9, 158
The Changing World of the Ice Age (Daly, R.), 217
Chapelizod, 215, 226, 235n7, 241nn33–34, 243n10; Dublin and, 48–50, 104, 106, 115–21; River Liffey in, 116–18, 121; as transitional space, 104, 182
Chart, D. A., 53, 105, 107, 111–12, 236n13
Chesterfield Avenue, 76
Children, 201–2, 207, 211
Christianity, 119, 132, 242n37, 252n4; Celtic paganism and, 50, 55, 66–67, 165, 187–88; Easter in, 142–43, 188; ecology, religion and, 161, 173–75, 188–94, 233n5; landscape influencing, 55–56, 135; resurrection in, 73–74; Saint Patrick in, 55–56, 75–77, 186, 188–92, 199, 248n15, 248n26, 250n36
Christ imagery, 73–74, 238n32
"Chuff" (fictional character), 208–9
Cinema, 209–10, 252n10
City: country's relationship with, 20, 84–85, 96–98, 103–6, 110–12, 115, 121; literature, 20
The City (Burgess, McKenzie, and Park), 108
La civilisation et les grandes fleuves historiques (Metchnikoff), 14, 29, 31–38
Civilization: agri/culture and, 173, 175–76, 180, 182–83; nature exploited by, 214–16
Clark, Hilary, 132
Class, politics of nature and, 122, 125–26, 128–29
Climate: adaptation and, 32; Irish, 18, 34–35, 54, 141–44; war and, 141–43
Clouds, 166–67, 169–72, 246n5
Coats, Alice, 175
Collins, James, 105–6

Coming of age: growing things and, 200–212; rivers and, 200–202
Conservation: Anglo-Irish associated with, 8, 111–12; development vs., 8–9, 155–59; environmentalism and, 11, 156, 229, 231; modernization and, 137; origins of, 8, 17, 156; paradigm shift to, 10–11
Controlling myths, 186
Conversations with James Joyce (Power), 160
Cosgrave, Dillon, 105, 110
Country: city's relationship with, 20, 84–85, 96–98, 103–6, 110–12, 115, 121; in modernism, 85
The Country and the City (Williams), 126
Coupe, Laurence, 3–4
Cox, Richard, 189–90
Crabapple, 174
Creation myth, 186
Crimean War, 144
Crispi, Luca, 202
Cultural ecological criticism, 9
Culture: Anglo-Irish, 7–8, 44, 71–72, 110–12, 124–26, 164, 251n41; Breton, 76–78, 82; nature's relationship with, 1–3, 5, 14, 19, 39–40, 71, 134–36, 140, 177–81, 187, 216, 226–28, 230–31, 233n5; "primitive," 160–63. *See also* Agri/culture
Curragh, 90, 128–29
"Cyclops" (Joyce), 138, 141, 215, 246n6

Daedalus, 191, 236n17
Daedalus (Haldane), 28–31
Daisy, 211
Daly, Mary E., 137
Daly, Reginald, 217
Danish language, 63–64, 170, 244n25
Dante Alighieri, 130, 190, 226
Dante and Difference (Tambling), 190
Dart, Raymond, 218
Darwin, Charles, 97, 207, 217–18, 234n8; *Descent of Man* by, 195; "Movement of Plants" by, 205; *On the Origin of Species* by, 12, 117–78, 194–95; *The Power of Movement in Plants* by, 210; *Variation of Plants and Animals under Domestication* by, 194

Dawson, G. M., 217
"The Dead" (Joyce), 18
Deane, Vincent, 99, 105, 150, 180, 207; on Breton culture, 77–78; on mythology, 185–86
Decomposition: in ecology of *Finnegans Wake*, 30, 60, 65–66, 73, 131–32, 176, 184, 223; politics of nature and, 131–32, 134
Deep Ecology and World Religions (Barnhill and Gottlieb), 160–61
Deforestation, 125–26, 135, 215, 246n6
Deleuze, Gilles, 14–15, 108
"The Delivery of the Letter" sketch, 60–63, 66–68, 83
Delta, 33, 93, 95, 203, 252n4
Democritus, 198
Deppman, Jed, 52
Derrida, Jacques, 3–4, 129–30, 160
Descent of Man (Darwin), 195
De Valera, Éamon, 137, 141
Development, conservation vs., 8–9, 155–59
Dickens, Charles, 110
Dictionary of Celtic Myth and Legend (Green), 143
Dike, 90, 239n6
Disease, 107–15
Divination: ecology, religion and, 161–72, 199; Vico on, 161, 246n2
"Dream-Epiphanies in *Finnegans Wake*" (Losey), 148
Dublin, 157, 172, 205; Chapelizod and, 48–50, 104, 106, 115–21; environs and, 85, 95–107; founding of, 64, 93, 95, 116, 227; "HCE" as, 15, 85–86, 89, 92, 95–96, 99, 104–6, 223–24, 254n21; Liffey's relationship with, 23, 32, 64, 85–86, 88–91, 93, 95, 99–102, 118, 151, 201–2, 222; physical setting of, 18–19, 23, 85–91, 93–95, 109–12, 189, 222, 225; in *Ulysses*, 42, 48; water supply of, 36, 107–9
Dublin: A Historical and Topographical Account of the City (Fitzpatrick, S.), 71, 105, 189
Dublin Bay, 89, 95, 99–102, 182, 202–3
Dublin Bay (Lalor), 95

Dubliners (Joyce), 48
Dubois, Eugene, 218
Ducks, 191
Dumuzi and Enkimdu myth, 173–74
Dutch language, 46

Easter, 142–43, 188
Ecocriticism: Buell on, 6–7, 24, 26–27, 197, 231; defined, 2; genetic criticism and, vii–viii, 1, 22, 25–28, 39, 211–12, 221, 229–30; Irish literature and, 7–10; Joyce and, 1–2, 4–5, 7–8, 18–24; modernism and, 5–7, 9–10, 17, 20–21, 39–40, 84–85, 98, 115, 227; new boundaries of, 221–31; overview of, 2–5, 22–24; post-structuralism/postmodernism interacting with, 3–5, 25, 177, 229; urban, 20, 23, 40, 84, 229–30. *See also* Ecology, of *Finnegans Wake*
The Ecocriticism Reader (Fromm and Glotfelty), 2
Ecolinguists, 45–47
Ecological modernism, 6, 227–28, 230
Ecology: bog, 136, 221; defined, 12; in Joyce's lifetime, 10–18; outdated models of, 27; urban, 23, 40, 84, 121
Ecology, of *Finnegans Wake*: children in, 201–2; decomposition in, 30, 60, 65–66, 73, 131–32, 176, 184, 223; disease and, 107–15; Dublin's environs in, 85, 95–107; environmental history and, 17–18; famine and, 15, 107–15, 156; housing and, 107–15; introduction to, 1–5, 7, 12, 14–15, 17–28, 31, 39; nature's agency in, 16–17, 42, 165, 193, 204, 210–11, 216; new boundaries of ecocriticism and, 221–31; notebooks and, 22, 25–26, 28–40, 54, 221; rivers in, viii, 5, 7, 15, 21–23. *See also* Growing things; Landscape; Nature, politics of; Religion, ecology and
Ecology in the 20th Century: A History (Bramwell), 11
The Ecology of Language (Haugen), 45
Ecosystem, 12–13
Ecotaph, 80–83, 221

Ecotone, 87, 203, 239n2
Eden, 55, 174, 192, 194–95, 211, 226
Egypt, 34, 176, 180–82, 185, 196, 251n46
Eide, Marian, 62
Elder, John, 21
Elder tree, 184
Electric streetlights, 205
Eliot, T. S., 16, 21, 51
Ellmann, Richard, 22, 122, 139, 149, 213, 244n25
Elm trees, 108, 215
Encroachment, 157–58
Encyclopaedia Britannica, 38, 101, 106, 108–10, 113, 189
England: Ireland and, 125–26, 130–31, 190; polar exploration by, 147
Entomology, 12, 196–97
Enuma Elish: The Babylonian Epic of Creation (Langdon), 185–87
Environment, 2, 84–85. *See also* Conservation; Landscape; Nature
"Environmental Crises—Past and Present" (Boughey), 114
Environmental determinism, 13–14, 31, 53–55, 79, 227
Environmental history, 17–18
The Environmental Imagination (Buell), 6–7, 26
Environmentalism, 11, 156, 229, 231
The Environment and World History (Burke and Pomeranz), 17–18
Environs, 84–85, 95–107, 121
"Epiphanies" (Joyce), 148
Epstein, Edmund, 200, 240n10, 247n7
Epstein, Jean, 210
Esker Ridge, 35–36, 57–58, 135
Estuaries, 109, 182, 202, 222, 225
Ethical Joyce (Eide), 62
Ethology, 11–12
Evans, David, 126
Evans, E. Estyn, 59
The Event and Its Terrors: Ireland, Famine, Modernity (McLean), 114
Evernden, Neil, 41–42
Evolution, 11, 97, 194; of growing things,

207, 209, 211, 216–21; language and, 207, 211, 216, 218
Exploration, 145. *See also* Polar exploration

Fabre, Jean-Henri, 12
The Face of the Earth: Natural Landscapes, Science, and Culture (Campbell, S.), 21
Famine, 15, 107–15, 156
Feehan, John, 8, 112, 137, 237n24
Ferrer, Daniel, 99, 105, 150, 180, 207; on Breton culture, 77–78; on mythology, 185–86
Fertility: floods and, 182–83, 213; myths, 172–76, 179–83, 199
Finnegans Wake (Joyce): "Anna Livia Plurabelle" chapter in, 21, 28, 30–31, 85–90, 200–212; *avant-texte* of, 25–26, 102, 126; city and country interacting in, 20, 84–85, 96–98, 103–6, 110–12, 115, 121; early sketches for, 1–2, 23–24, 42–43; environs in, 84–85, 95–107, 121; genetic criticism and, vii–viii, 1, 22, 25–28, 39, 211–12, 221, 229–30; heroes of, 1; "The Ondt and the Gracehoper" in, 12, 133, 196–97; as representative work, viii; suburbs integral to, 120–21; "Upfellbowm" passage of, 80–81, 187; as *Work in Progress*, 28, 32. *See also* Ecology, of *Finnegans Wake*; Notebooks, for *Finnegans Wake*; Sketches, for *Finnegans Wake*; *specific characters*
Finnegans Wake: A Plot Summary (Gordon), 54
Fir Bolg, 49–51
Fitzpatrick, H. M., 71–72
Fitzpatrick, Samuel A., 71, 105, 189
Flood, J. M., 56, 60–62, 114
Floods, 32, 168, 180, 185; fertility and, 182–83, 213; Noah and, 33–34, 162, 184, 236n14
Flower girls, 71, 184, 204, 208, 210, 213
Flowers, 103–4, 162, 175; as growing things, 200–202, 204–5, 207–11, 213–14, 216, 223; Joyce's distaste for, 18, 200, 204; Quinet and, 38, 72, 116, 204
Foehn wind, 141–42

"The Foggy Dew," 142
Folklore, 43, 78
Fordham, Finn, 20, 177–78, 194–95
Forest, 227, 253n17, 254n21; deforestation and, 125–26, 135, 215, 246n6; ecology, religion and, 164, 188–94; Laws, 124–27, 129; Saint Patrick and, 188–92; as *selva oscura*, 130, 190, 226
Fortnightly Review, 12, 234n7
Foss, Peter, 135
Fossils, 217–19
Foster, John, Wilson, 193, 237n20
Four historians, 52–53, 94
Four Waves of Erin, 52, 57, 165
Fox, 126–28, 242nn4–5
Franz José Land, 153
Frazer, James, 181, 195, 238n37, 250n34. See also *The Golden Bough*
Freud, Sigmund, 13
Fromm, Harold, 2
From Ritual to Romance (Weston), 51, 173, 175–76
Fussell, Paul, 142

Galway, 95, 106, 155–56
Galway-Gaillimh: A Bibliography of the City and County (Kavanagh, M.), 106
Gardening, 210–12
Gelfant, Blanche Housman, 20
The General History of Ireland (Keating), 58
General Post Office, 119, 130–31, 242n38
Generelle Morphologie der Organismen (Haeckel), 12
Genesis, 185
Genetic criticism: benefits of, 22; ecocriticism and, vii–viii, 1, 22, 25–28, 39, 211–12, 221, 229–30; growing things and, 211–12
Geographical Congress, 146
Geography of Ireland (Howarth), 59–60, 236n15
Geopolitics, Geographical Materialism, and Marxism (Wittfogel), 14
George IV (king), 127–29, 131, 170
Gifford, Don, 204
Gilbert, Stuart, 62

Gilgamesh, 104–5
Glacken, Clarence, 10
Gladstone, William, 181, 190
Glendalough, 55–56
Glotfelty, Cheryll, 2
"Glugg" (fictional character), 162, 207–8
The Golden Bough (Frazer), vii, 51, 163, 172, 177–79, 181; on Breton culture, 77; insects in, 197; salmon in, 243n11
Goose, 191
Gordon, John, 54
Gottlieb, Roger, 160–61
Graves, Robert, 186
The Great War and Modern Memory (Fussell), 142
Green, Miranda, 143
Green belt, 120, 224
The Green Breast of the New World (Westling), 5
The Greening of Literary Scholarship (Rosendale), 3
The Green Studies Reader (Coupe), 3–4
Green technology, 17
Grewe-Volpp, Christa, 16
Griffith, Arthur, 141, 157
Growing things: coming of age and, 200–212; evolution of, 207, 209, 211, 216–21; flowers, 200–202, 204–5, 207–11, 213–14, 216, 223; genetic criticism and, 211–12; Joyce's love for, viii, 18, 24, 200; language and, 204, 206–7; marriage, trees and, 212–16; sexuality and, 204, 206, 208–9, 211–16; in *Ulysses*, 204–6
Growth and Structure of the English Language (Jespersen), 45
Guattari, Félix, 14–15
Gwynn, Stephen, 35–36, 45, 58, 234n1

Haeckel, Ernst, 12–14, 234n8
Haldane, J.B.S., 28–31
Haliday, Charles, 99–101
Haraway, Donna, 16
Hardiman, James, 105–6
Hargreaves, George, 74, 76
Harrison, Robert, 104, 128, 164, 190, 226
Hart, Clive, 19, 22, 196–97, 251n46

Haugen, Einar, 45
"Haveth Childers Everywhere" sketch, 96–98, 115
Hawkins, John, 113
Hayman, David, 48
Hazel, 163, 246n3
"HCE" (fictional character), 21, 52, 55, 109, 119, 121, 220; as Arthur, 51, 176; bottom of, 74–76, 130; burial of, 73–74, 76, 183–84; Christ imagery of, 73–74, 238n32; as cultivator, 181, 183; as Curraghman, 90; as Dublin, 15, 85–86, 89, 92, 95–96, 99, 104–6, 223–24, 254n21; encroachment and, 157–58; as explorer, 154; as Gilgamesh figure, 105; Hunt and, 127–30, 224–25; as landlord, 71–72, 112; as landscape, 86, 212, 223–24; letter and, 60, 166; Phoenix Park and, 74, 76, 120, 130; politics of nature and, 127–30; as "Pop," 48; pub of, 62, 169–70; railroad and, 107; rise and fall of, 74, 127, 214; roles of, 91, 168; trees and, 70–71, 225, 253n17; universe fixed by, 198
Heidegger, Martin, 4
Heidelberg Man, 218–19
Heise, Ursula, 20–22, 141
Heliotrope, 162, 207–8
Henry, O., 214–15, 253n17
Henry II (king), 54
"Here Comes Everybody" sketch, 129
Heroic language, 79
Hibernia, 123, 144, 181, 226, 229
Higgins, Godfrey, 93
Hill of Usnach, 57–58
History: cyclical movements of, 96, 107; environmental, 17–18; landscape and, 41–42, 54–55, 62, 64–65, 76, 222–23; preservation of, 59–60, 73; universal, 12, 18, 42, 227, 229
History of Ireland (Cox), 189–90
The History of Ireland (Gwynn), 35–36, 45, 234n1
The History of Land Tenure in Ireland (Montgomery), 119
A History of Nature Conservation in Britain (Evans), 126

A History of New York (Irving), 105, 109–10
A History of Polar Exploration (Mountfield), 146
A History of the County Dublin (Ball), 118
The History of the Town and County of Galway (Hardiman), 105–6
Hitler, Adolf, 141, 145
Holy Spirit, 193, 196, 224
Hooke, Samuel H., 173–74, 186, 249n27
Hopkins, D. M., 217
Housing, 107–15
Howard, Ebenezer, 103, 120, 171
Howarth, O.J.R., 59–60, 236n15
"How Buckley Shot the Russian General" sketch, 24, 139–41
Humans: as animal, 219; language detached from, 4–5; nature inseparable from, 2–3, 6–7, 10–11, 14–16, 39, 159; prehistoric, 78, 218–20
Human Speech (Paget), 206–7
Hume, David, 124–26
Hunt, 242n7; Badminton, 170; fox in, 126–28; "HCE" and, 127–30, 224–25; Phoenix Park and, 23–24, 124–31; violence in, 124–25, 129
Huntington, Ellsworth, 14
Hurd, Barbara, 134
Hydroengineering, viii, 98, 156

The Idea of Wilderness (Oelschlaeger), 174
The Image of the City (Lynch, K.), 42
Imagining the Earth (Elder), 21
Imperialism: control over landscape as, 164, 189; polar exploration and, 150–51, 155, 164
Industrial Development and Irish National Identity, 1922–1939 (Daly, M.), 137
Inferno (Dante), 190
Inner landscape, 41–42, 44
Insects, 12, 196–97
"In the shadow of young girls in flower" (*A la recherche du temps perdu*) (Proust), 208
Invasion: by invasive species, 71–72, 212; of Ireland, 46–47, 51, 53, 54, 64, 71, 107, 170, 212, 222, 224
Invisible landscape, 42–44

Ireland: agricultural practices of, 113; art of, 131–32; biodiversity of, 136; Breton culture and, 77–78; climate of, 18, 34–35, 54, 141–44; England and, 125–26, 130–31, 190; exploration translated to, 154–55; as Hibernia, 123, 144, 181, 226, 229; invaders of, 46–47, 51, 53, 54, 64, 71, 107, 170, 212, 222, 224; mythology of, 42–44, 49–50, 78, 234n1; nationalism in, 133–34, 138, 141–42; railroad in, 107; self-sufficiency of, 131–34; "Shem" as threat to, 131–34; waterways of, 35–36
Ireland: Its Saints and Scholars (Flood), 56, 60–62, 114, 188
Irish Free State, 8–9, 24, 131–40, 156–59
Irish literature: ecocriticism and, 7–10; revival of, vii, 19, 43–44
Irish Trees: Myths, Legends, and Folklore (Mac Coitir), 163, 186, 244n21
Irrigation, 180
Irving, Washington, 105, 109–10
"Issy" (fictional character), 71, 201–2, 213, 226
"Ithaca" (Joyce): in *Ulysses*, vii, 57, 149, 156, 159, 204–5, 208, 240n16, 241n29, 250n38; water in, 240n16

Jacob and Esau story, 175
"Jaun" (fictional character), 82, 137, 238n29
Jespersen, Otto, 45–46, 142, 223, 235n4
Johanson, Donald, 218
Jolas, Eugene, 1
Jousse, Marcel, 79, 206–7, 218
Joyce, James: "By the Way" by, 67–68; "The Dead" by, 18; *Dubliners* by, 48; ecocriticism and, 1–2, 4–5, 7–8, 18–24; ecology in lifetime of, 10–18; "Epiphanies" by, 148; flowers disliked by, 18, 200, 204; growing things loved by, viii, 18, 24, 200; as hunted animal, 127; marriage of, 212; "The Mirage of the Fisherman of Aran" by, 156; "A Painful Case" by, 48; polar exploration paralleling life of, 147–48; *A Portrait of the Artist as a Young Man* by, 18, 193, 240n22, 253n20; *Stephen Hero* by, 18; umbrellas disliked by, 122;

Joyce, James—*continued*
  universal history of, 12, 18, 42, 227, 229; as urban writer, vii, 19. *See also Finnegans Wake; Ulysses*
"Joyce's Use of Norwegian Writers" (Tysdahl), 151–52
Jupiter (god), 33

Kane, Matthew, 53
Kant, Immanuel, 30–31
"Kate Strong" (fictional character), 60, 73–74
Kavanagh, Mary, 106
Kavanagh, Patrick, 8, 44
Keating, Geoffrey, 58
Kennedy-O'Neill, Joy, 44
Kerridge, Richard, 21
Kettle, Thomas, 157
Kingship, 163–64, 178, 180
Koh-I-Baba, 33

Lalor, Brian, 95
"The Land and Language of Desire" (Campbell, S.), 27
Landlords, 71–72, 112, 126
Land ownership, 119–20, 183
Landscape: Christianity influenced by, 55–56, 135; as decisive factor, 121; ecotaph, 80–83, 221; in first sketches, 47–58; "HCE" as, 86, 212, 223–24; history and, 41–42, 54–55, 62, 64–65, 76, 222–23; identity and, 158; imperialism and, 164, 189; inner, 41–42, 44; invisible, 42–44; language and, 43–47, 59–65, 71, 73, 76, 78–80, 82–83, 114, 222; legibility of, 42, 47, 60, 73, 82–83; letter and, 59–63, 65–67, 73, 83; mountainy mots, 79–80; mythology and, 42–44; outer, 41–42, 44; as palimpsest, 73–79; trees in, 67–73, 80–81; in "Upfellbowm" passage, 80–81; visible, 42–44; "Yawn" in, 23, 52, 57–58, 91. *See also* Bogs
Landuyt, Ingeborg, 31, 173
Langdon, Stephen, 185–87
Language: as consumable, 132; Danish, 63–64, 170, 244n25; as decisive factor, 121; divination as, 161; Dutch, 46; evolution and, 207, 211, 216, 218; growing things and, 204, 206–7; heroic, 79; human detached from, 4–5; landscape and, 43–47, 59–65, 71, 73, 76, 78–80, 82–83, 114, 222; marriage and, 212; nature and, 2–4, 43–47, 182, 204, 206, 222–24, 226, 228, 234n12; rivers and, 38; sedimentation of, 62, 134; Vico on, 23–24, 46–47, 64–65, 79–81, 161, 206, 218, 251n47
"Language and Environment" (Sapir), 46
"Large Parks: A Designer's Perspective" (Hargreaves), 74
Lawless, Emily, 54
Leakey, Mary, 218
Legibility, 42, 47, 60, 73, 82–83
"Leopold Bloom" (fictional character): growing things and, 204–6; in *Ulysses*, 22, 36, 89, 149–50, 159, 204–6, 241n29
Lernout, Geert, 31, 99, 105, 126, 150, 180, 207; on Breton culture, 77–78; on *Daedalus*, 28–29; on mythology, 185–86
Leslie, Shane, 126
"Lestrygonians" (Joyce), 22
Letter: "ALP" and, 60, 63, 166, 173; in "The Delivery of the Letter," 60–63, 66–68, 83; landscape and, 59–63, 65–67, 73, 83; in "The Revered Letter," 166; "Shaun" and, 60–61, 66–67; "Shem" and, 60–61, 173–74; weather and, 70, 165–67
Liefferink, Duncan, 8
Life in Old Dublin (Collins), 105–6
Life sciences, 11
Liffey. *See* River Liffey
Literature: city, 20; defined, 2; Irish, vii, 7–10, 19, 43–44
London, 108–9
Lopez, Barry, 41
Losey, Jay B., 148
Lots of Fun at Finnegans Wake (Fordham), 20
Love, Glen A., 228
Lynch, Kevin, 42
Lynch, Tom, 21

Macbeth (Shakespeare), 163–64
Mac Coitir, Niall, 163, 186, 244n21

MacCool, Finn, 76, 91, 127, 167, 236n14, 243n11
Madrigal, Alexis, 17
Magee, W. K., 87–88
"Mamalujo" sketch, 47, 57, 74–75, 155, 243n19; sea in, 52–54; "Yawn" and, 176–77
Man and Nature, Or, Physical Geography as Modified by Human Action (Marsh), 11
Marcus, Laura, 209–10
Marriage: of Joyce, 212; trees and, 212–16
Marsh, George Perkins, 11, 13–14
Mathematics, 194, 202–3
May Day, 177–79, 250n34
Mazel, David, 84–85
McAsey, Carmel, 50–51
McCann, Philip, 212–13
McCourt, John, 210, 234n11
McFarlane, James, 10
McGovern, Barry, 48, 235n7
McKenzie, Roderick, 108
McLean, Stuart John, 114
McLuhan, Eric, 46–47
Merchant, Carolyn, 12
Merleau-Ponty, Maurice, 4–5, 134, 233n1
Metchnikoff, Léon: *La civilisation et les grandes fleuves historiques* by, 14, 29, 31–38; inspiration from, 14, 29, 31–38, 53–54, 86–87, 97, 123; *Le progrés* by, 97
Meteorology: ecology, religion and, 161–72; thunder in, 161–62
Meteoromancy, 162–64, 169
Midden, 63–64, 221
Middle Eastern Mythology (Hooke), 186
Milesi, Laurent, 207
Millon, Abbé, 77–78, 239n38
Mimosa, 210
"The Mirage of the Fisherman of Aran" (Joyce), 156
Mistletoe, 178–79
Modernism: country in, 85; defined, 10; ecocriticism and, 5–7, 9–10, 17, 20–21, 39–40, 84–85, 98, 115, 227; ecological, 6, 227–28, 230; Irish revival and, 43–44; paradigm shift in, 10; romanticism and, 16; technology and, 14–15

"Modernism and Ecological Criticism" (Bryson), 6
Modernism and the Celtic Revival (Castle), 43
Modernization, 137, 159
"Molly Bloom" (fictional character), 89, 149–50
Monaghan, Patricia, 50
Montgomery, William Ernest, 119
Moon, 187
Moore, George, 44
Moriarty, Christopher, 181
Moses, 33–34
Mountainy mots, 79–80
Mountfield, David, 146
"Movement of Plants" (Darwin), 205
"Mr. Duffy" (fictional character), 48–49
Mythology, 185, 190–91, 251n47; biocentric, 161; controlling, 186; creation, 186; of Dumuzi and Enkimdu, 173–74; fertility, 172–76, 179–83, 199; of Ireland, 42–44, 49–50, 78, 234n1; syncretism of, 78

Nansen, Fridtjof, 145–48, 150–55, 245n37
Nationalism: Irish, 133–34, 138, 141–42; of polar exploration, 147
Nationality: politics of nature and, 122–23, 126, 131, 133–34, 138–39, 141–42, 145; weather and, 122–23
Natural disasters, 15
Natural History (Pliny), 178–79, 220
Natural History of Ireland (Viney), 8
Nature: agency of, 16–17, 42, 165, 193, 204, 210–11, 216; "ALP" as, 71, 85–90, 93, 95–96, 99, 149, 173, 198, 202–3, 212, 223–25; art imitating, 18, 24, 236n17; children and, 201–2; conflict with, 114; control of, 14, 50–51, 102–3, 124, 158, 164, 189, 198, 212–13; culture's relationship with, 1–3, 5, 14, 19, 39–40, 71, 134–36, 140, 177–81, 187, 216, 226–28, 230–31, 233n5; engineering by, 107; exploited, 98, 158, 214–16, 229, 233n4; films, 209–10, 252n10; humans inseparable from, 2–3, 6–7, 10–11, 14–16, 39, 159; language and, 2–4, 43–47, 182, 204,

Nature—*continued*
  206, 222–24, 226, 228, 234n12; naming of, 129–30; technology and, 14–15, 17, 196; in *Ulysses*, 18–19, 156, 159; Vico on, 23–24, 46–47, 79–81, 161, 164, 167–69, 182–83, 197, 216, 224, 254n21; war and, 140–45. *See also* Landscape
Nature, politics of: bogs and, 134–40; class and, 122, 125–26, 128–29; conservation vs. development in, 155–59; decomposition and, 131–32, 134; exploration and, 145–55; "HCE" and, 127–30; hunt and, 23–24, 124–31; Irish Free State and, 131–40, 156–59; nationality and, 122–23, 126, 131, 133–34, 138–39, 141–42, 145; Phoenix Park and, 23–24, 124–31; self-sufficiency in, 131–34; Sinn Féin in, 131, 138–39, 141–42; violence in, 124–25, 127, 129; weather in, 122–23
The Nature of Cities: Ecocriticism and Urban Environments (Bennett and Teague), 20
Navel, 35–36
A New Green History of the World (Ponting), 113–15
New Science (Vico), 46, 64, 79–80, 175, 218, 227
New York City, 109–10, 241n25
Night, 30–31
Nile River, 33–34, 180–82, 185, 203, 249n27
Noah, 33–34, 82, 162, 184, 219, 236n14
Norris, David, 48
North Dublin: City and Environs (Cosgrave), 105, 110
North Strand, 100
"Norwegian Captain" sketch, 216–17; agri/culture and, 181–82; marriage and, 212–13; polar exploration in, 24, 150–55, 152; weather and, 164, 168–70
Notebooks, for *Finnegans Wake*: ecology and, 22, 25–26, 28–40, 54, 221; methods of, 39, 96; scientific terminology in, 194–95; sketches and, 47

Oak trees, 179
O'Brien, Flann, 44

The Occult Sciences (Waite), 162, 246n3
O'Connell, Catherine, 135
Oelschlaeger, Max, 82, 174
O'Flaherty, Liam, 44
Ogham alphabet: calendar and, 186; trees in, 51, 54, 67–71, 93, 143–44, 186
O'Hanlon, John, 63
"The Ondt and the Gracehoper" (Joyce), 12, 133, 196–97
On the Origin of Species (Darwin), 12, 117–78, 194–95
Opperman, Serpil, 229–30
Original sin, 74, 130, 215
The Origin of Magic and Religion (Perry, W.), 78–79, 179–80, 185
Outer landscape, 41–42, 44

Paget, Richard, 206–7, 218
"A Painful Case" (Joyce), 48–49
Palimpsest: landscape as, 73–79; Phoenix Park as, 74–76
Paraheliotropism, 204–6, 210
Park, Robert, 108
Parks, 23–24, 48, 102, 124, 126. *See also* Phoenix Park
Parthalonians, 49–51
Partridge, 190–91
Peat, 131, 134–36. *See also* Bogs
Peat lands, 90, 240n6
Pebbles from a Brook (Magee), 87–88
Perdix, 191
Perry, John, 100
Perry, William James, 78–79, 179–80, 185–87
The Personality of Ireland: Habitat, Heritage, and History (Evans, E.), 59
Phillips, Dana, 12–13, 27
Phoenix Park, 48, 94, 117, 226; as artifact, 65; "HCE" and, 74, 76, 120, 130; hunt and, 23–24, 124–31; original sin and, 74, 215; as palimpsest, 74–76; as suburban, 104, 110–11; as transitional space, 104, 124; weather and, 54, 170
Photoperiodism, 205
Les Pierres Bretons et leurs legendes (Millon), 77–78
Pliny, 178–79, 220

Plumbing, 107–8
Polar bears, 149, 244n27, 245n29
Polar exploration, 244n27, 245n37; imperialism and, 150–51, 155, 164; Joyce's life paralleling, 147–48; nationalism of, 147; in "Norwegian Captain" sketch, 24, 150–55, 152; politics of nature and, 145–55; in *Ulysses*, 148–50
Politics. *See* Nature, politics of
Pollination, 174, 207, 209
Pomeranz, Kenneth, 17–18
Ponting, Clive, 113–15
"Pop" (fictional character), 47–48
A Portrait of the Artist as a Young Man (Joyce), 18, 193, 240n22, 253n20
Post-structuralism/postmodernism, 3–5, 25, 177, 229
Potatoes, 113–14, 211, 252n12
Poverty: A Study of Town Life (Rowntree), 105, 111–12
Power, Arthur, 160
Powering the Dream: The History and Promise of Green Technology (Madrigal), 17
The Power of Movement in Plants (Darwin), 210
Prehistoric humans, 78, 218–20
"A Preliminary Stratigraphy of *Scribbledehobble*" (Barger), 221
Prendergast, John, 99–100
"Primitive" cultures, 160–63
Le progrès (Metchnikoff), 97
Prophecy, 161, 163–64, 169–70
"Proteus" (Joyce), 61–62, 70, 89, 148
Proust, Marcel, 208
Providence: ecology, religion and, 160–72, 199; weather and, 16, 24, 161–67, 199, 224
Pub, of "HCE," 62, 169–70

"'A Quaking Sod': Hybridity, Identity and Wandering Irishness" (Rickard), 19
Quarterly Review, 126–28
Quinet, Edgar, 38, 65, 72, 115–16, 204

Rabaté, Jean Michel, 96
Race, fossils and, 218–19
Railroad, 107

Reforestation, 190
Religion: Celtic paganism, 50, 55, 66–67, 165, 187–88; environmental determinism and, 55, 79; fossils and, 218–19. *See also* Christianity
Religion, ecology and: agri/culture in, 172–83, 199; birds in, 190–94; Christianity and, 161, 173–75, 188–94, 233n5; divination in, 161–72, 199; forests in, 164, 188–94; meteorology in, 161–72; "primitive" cultures and, 160–63; providence, 160–72, 199; science and, 24, 194–99; seasons, 183–88
Resurrection, 73–74, 76, 186, 249n26
"Revaluing Nature: Toward an Ecological Criticism" (Love), 228
"The Revered Letter" sketch, 166
"Reynard the Fox," 126–28
Rickard, John, 19
Riders to the Sea (Synge), 44
River Liffey, 22, 34–35, 56, 82, 109, 211; "ALP" as, 15, 21, 85–90, 93, 95, 99, 118, 132–33, 176, 203, 223, 226–27, 254n4; in Chapelizod, 116–18, 121; coming of age and, 200–202; Dublin's relationship to, 23, 32, 64, 85–86, 88–91, 93, 95, 99–102, 118, 151, 201–2, 222; hydroengineering and, viii, 98, 156; politics of nature and, 132–33, 137, 151, 156–57; walling in of, 100, 102, 239n3
Rivers: coming of age and, 200–202; in ecology of *Finnegans Wake*, viii, 5, 7, 15, 21–23; notes on, 32–39; transitional spaces of, 87–88. *See also specific rivers*
River Shannon, 35–36, 135, 137–38, 155–57
River Vartry, 200–201
Robinson, Henry Morton, 73, 119
Rocks, 219–20, 253n20
"Roderick O'Conor" sketch, 47–52, 54, 60, 77, 163, 165
The Role of Thunder in Finnegans Wake (McLuhan), 46–47
Roll Away the Reel World: James Joyce and Cinema (McCourt), 210, 234n11
Romanticism, 5–6, 8, 16, 112
Rome, 104

Rose, Danis, 63, 238n31
Rosendale, Steven, 3
Rowntree, B. Seebohm, 105, 111–12
Ryden, Kent, 42

"Saint Kevin" sketch, 47, 55–57, 66, 71, 171, 188
Saint Patrick: in Christianity, 55–56, 75–77, 186, 188–92, 199, 248n15, 248n26, 250n36; forests and, 188–92
"Saint Patrick" sketch, 119, 188
Salmon, 132, 156, 163, 243n11
Sapir, Edward, 46
The Scandinavian Kingdom of Dublin (Haliday), 99–101
Science, 6, 29–30, 202; life, 11; religion and, 24, 194–99
Scott, Robert, 147, 150–51, 154
Sea, in "Mamalujo," 52–54
Seasons: cycles of, 213; ecology, religion and, 183–88; spring, 184, 186
Sedimentation, 62, 134, 222
Self-sufficiency, 131–34
Selva oscura, 130, 190, 226
Semple, Ellen Churchill, 14
Sensitive plants, 210
Sexuality, 204, 206, 208–9, 211–16
Shackleton, Ernest, 150–51
Shackleton, George, 151
Shakespeare, William, 163–64
Shannon, 35–36, 135, 137–38, 155–57
"Shaun" (fictional character), 73, 131, 190, 201, 208, 237n21; letter and, 60–61, 66–67; questions answered by, 91–94; "Shem" criticized by, 133–34, 137; in "The Triangle," 202–3
"Shem" (fictional character), 28, 75, 180, 201, 225–26; as Cain, 133–34, 173–75; in darkness, 208; letter and, 60–61, 173–74; questions asked by, 91–94; "Shaun" criticizing, 133–34, 137; as threat to Ireland, 131–34; in "The Triangle," 202–3; "Yawn" and, 190–91
Shiva, Vandana, 172
Shoal, 87–88
A Short History of the World (Wells), 218
"Sigurdsen" (fictional character), 62–63

Sinn Féin, 9, 72, 131, 138–39, 141–42
Sjoestedt, Marie-Louise, 49–50
A Skeleton Key to Finnegans Wake (Campbell, J., and Robinson), 73
Sketches, for *Finnegans Wake*: "Butt and Taff," 139, 144; "The Delivery of the Letter," 60–63, 66–68, 83; early, 1–2, 23, 42–43, 47–58, 82, 188; "Haveth Childers Everywhere," 96–98, 115; "Here Comes Everybody," 129; "How Buckley Shot the Russian General," 24, 139–41; landscape in, 47–58; "Mamalujo," 47, 52–54, 57, 74–75, 155, 176–77, 243n19; notebooks and, 47; "The Revered Letter," 166; "Roderick O'Conor," 47–52, 54, 60, 77, 163, 165; "Saint Kevin," 47, 55–57, 66, 71, 171, 188; "Saint Patrick," 119, 188; "The Triangle," 63–64, 202–3, 212; "Tristan and Isolde," 47–48, 128–29, 164–66, 168. *See also* "Norwegian Captain" sketch
Slavery, 219
Slote, Sam, 116, 207, 226, 229
Soldiers, trees as, 143–44
Source texts, 2, 25–26, 28, 57, 69, 96. *See also specific sources*
Souvenirs entomologiques (Fabre), 12
Spring, 184, 186
Staying Alive: Women, Ecology, and Development (Shiva), 172
"Stephen Dedalus" (fictional character), 240n22; growing things and, 204, 206; in *Ulysses*, 57, 61–62, 70, 148–49, 204, 206
Stephen Hero (Joyce), 18
Stirring the Mud: On Swamps, Bogs, and Human Imagination (Hurd), 134
Stones, 39, 57, 65, 78, 186–87, 215
Storm, 167–68
The Story of Dublin (Chart), 53, 105, 107, 111–12
The Story of Ireland (Lawless), 54
Stout, Matthew, 9
Streetlights, 205
Suburbs, 106, 229, 241n27; importance of, 120–21; Phoenix Park as, 104, 110–11; as transitional spaces, 104, 124, 182. *See also* Chapelizod

Sullivan, Edward, 23. See also *The Book of Kells*
Sweeney (king), 192–93
Synge, J. M., vii, 19, 43–44

Tambling, Jeremy, 190
Tammuz, 180, 186–87
Tansley, A. G., 13–14
Taylor, Thomas Griffith, 14
Teague, David, 20
Technology: cinema, 209–10; electric streetlights, 205; green, 17; nature and, 14–15, 17, 196
Textual Awareness (Van Hulle), 25, 28
Textual memory, 28, 32
Thames, 21, 108–10
"Theorizing Ecocriticism: Toward a Postmodern Ecocritical Practice" (Opperman), 229–30
Thom's Directory, 105, 112, 117, 119, 241n33, 242n10
Thoreau, Henry David, 26–27
"Threat and Conservation: Attitudes to Nature in Ireland" (Feehan), 8
Thunder, 46–47, 161–62, 182, 183, 224
Tides, 187, 222
Time-lapse photography, 209–10
Tindall, William York, 203
Topographia Hiberniae [Topography of Ireland] (Cambrensis), 35
Traces on the Rhodian Shore (Glacken), 10
Transitional spaces, 193; focus on, 7, 115; of rivers, 87–88; suburbs as, 104, 124, 182
Transition pages, 183, 218–19
Travel guides, 57
Trees, 195, 226, 238n31; appropriation of, 177–78; art from, 132; "HCE" and, 70–71, 225, 253n17; in landscape, 67–73, 80–81; marriage and, 212–16; in Ogham alphabet, 51, 54, 67–71, 93, 143–44, 186; plumbing and, 107–8; prophecy and, 163–64; as soldiers, 143–44. See also *specific trees*
"The Trees of Ireland: Native and Introduced" (Fitzpatrick, H.), 71–72
Treip, Andrew, 79
"The Triangle" sketch, 63–64, 202–3, 212

"Tristan and Isolde" sketch, 47–48, 128–29, 164–66, 168
The Truth of Ecology (Phillips), 12–13
Tuatha Dé Danaan, 49, 51, 192
Turf, 134, 136–40, 159, 243n19. See also Bogs
Tysdahl, B. J., 151–52, 245n33

Ulster, 192–93
Ulysses (Joyce), 35, 89, 107, 126; cinematic qualities of, 210; "Cyclops" in, 138, 141, 215, 246n6; Dublin in, 42, 48; growing things in, 204–6; "Ithaca" in, vii, 57, 149, 156, 159, 204–5, 208, 240n16, 241n29, 250n38; "Leopold Bloom" in, 22, 36, 89, 149–50, 159, 204–6, 241n29; "Lestrygonians" in, 22; "Molly Bloom" in, 89, 149–50; nature in, 18–19, 156, 159; polar exploration in, 148–50; "Proteus" in, 61–62, 70, 89, 148; "Stephen Dedalus" in, 57, 61–62, 70, 148–49, 204, 206; "Wandering Rocks" in, 19
Ulysses Annotated (Gifford), 204
Umbrellas, 122
Universal history, 12, 18, 42, 227, 229
Universe, fixed, 198
The Untilled Field (Moore), 44
"Upfellbowm" passage, 80–81, 187
Urban ecocriticism, 20, 23, 40, 84, 229–30
Urban ecology, 23, 40, 84, 121
Urban environment, 20
Urban writer, Joyce as, vii, 19

Van Hulle, Dirk, 25–26, 28, 32, 208, 223
Variation of Plants and Animals under Domestication (Darwin), 194
Verene, Donald Phillip, 161
Vico, Giambattista: cycle of, 22, 102, 197–98, 227; on divination, 161, 246n2; inspiration from, 23–24, 46–47, 79–81, 96–97, 102–4, 247n8; on language, 23–24, 46–47, 64–65, 79–81, 161, 206, 218, 251n47; on nature, 23–24, 46–47, 79–81, 161, 164, 167–69, 182–83, 197, 216, 224, 254n21; *New Science* by, 46, 64, 79–80, 175, 218, 227
Vinding, Ole, 18, 200, 204

Viney, Michael, 8, 158
Violence, in politics of nature, 124–25, 127, 129
Virginia Woolf and the Study of Nature (Alt), 11, 209
The Visible and the Invisible (Merleau-Ponty), 4
Visible landscape, 42–44

Waite, Arthur Edward, 162, 246n3
"A Wake in Chapelizod" (Slote), 116, 229
Wallace, Kathleen, 3
Walls, 100, 102, 104–5
"Wandering Rocks" (Joyce), 19
War, 244n21; climate and, 141–43; nature and, 140–45
Warner, Dick, 118
Washington, D.C., 101
The Waste Land (Eliot), 16, 21, 51
Water, 149, 168, 222, 240n16, 249n27; in "Ithaca," 240n16; in "Mamalujo," 52–54; romanticized, 55; supply, 35–39, 107–9, 118
The Wealth of Nature (Worster), 5
Weather, 54, 247n10; cyclical, 213; forecasts, 169–70, 199; letter and, 70, 165–67; nationality and, 122–23; "Norwegian Captain" and, 164, 168–70; Phoenix Park and, 54, 170; in politics of nature, 122–23; providence and, 16, 24, 161–67, 199, 224. *See also* Climate; Meteorology

Weaver, Harriet Shaw, 38, 69, 85, 128, 173
Wells, H. G., 218–19
Westling, Louise, 5
Weston, Jessie L., 51, 173, 175–76
Whelan, Kevin, 9
The White Goddess (Graves), 186
Wilde, Oscar, 129, 251n41
Wilderness, 189
William I (king), 124–27, 129
Williams, Raymond, 126, 228
Wind, 141–42, 166, 170–71, 192, 247n8
Winston, Greg, 141
Winter, 184
Wittfogel, Karl, 14
Wittgenstein, Ludwig, 230
Wohl, Ellen, 21
Wolf, 192
A Woman of No Importance (Wilde), 129
Wordsworth, William, 16, 88
Work in Progress (Joyce), 28, 32
World War I, 10, 17, 125, 142
World War II, 141, 145
Worster, Donald, 5, 14

"Yawn" (fictional character), 80, 176–77, 195; birds and, 190–93; in landscape, 23, 52, 57–58, 91
Yeats, W. B., vii, 19, 43, 70
Yew tree, 70, 143, 244n21
Yggdrasil, 80, 91, 179, 194

Alison Lacivita holds a PhD from Trinity College Dublin and held the position of assistant professor of Modern British Literature at the University of Southern Mississippi. She left academia to study wildlife management and emergency medicine, and now works as a mountain rescue tech, ski patroller, and paramedic in the Adirondack Mountains.

The Florida James Joyce Series
Edited by Sebastian D. G. Knowles

The Autobiographical Novel of Co-Consciousness: Goncharov, Woolf, and Joyce, by Galya Diment (1994)
Bloom's Old Sweet Song: Essays on Joyce and Music, by Zack Bowen (1995)
Joyce's Iritis and the Irritated Text: The Dis-lexic "Ulysses," by Roy Gottfried (1995)
Joyce, Milton, and the Theory of Influence, by Patrick Colm Hogan (1995)
Reauthorizing Joyce, by Vicki Mahaffey (paperback edition, 1995)
Shaw and Joyce: "The Last Word in Stolentelling," by Martha Fodaski Black (1995)
Bely, Joyce, and Döblin: Peripatetics in the City Novel, by Peter I. Barta (1996)
Jocoserious Joyce: The Fate of Folly in "Ulysses," by Robert H. Bell (paperback edition, 1996)
Joyce and Popular Culture, edited by R. B. Kershner (1996)
Joyce and the Jews: Culture and Texts, by Ira B. Nadel (paperback edition, 1996)
Narrative Design in "Finnegans Wake": The Wake Lock Picked, by Harry Burrell (1996)
Gender in Joyce, edited by Jolanta W. Wawrzycka and Marlena G. Corcoran (1997)
Latin and Roman Culture in Joyce, by R. J. Schork (1997)
Reading Joyce Politically, by Trevor L. Williams (1997)
Advertising and Commodity Culture in Joyce, by Garry Leonard (1998)
Greek and Hellenic Culture in Joyce, by R. J. Schork (1998)
Joyce, Joyceans, and the Rhetoric of Citation, by Eloise Knowlton (1998)
Joyce's Music and Noise: Theme and Variation in His Writings, by Jack W. Weaver (1998)
Reading Derrida Reading Joyce, by Alan Roughley (1999)
Joyce through the Ages: A Nonlinear View, edited by Michael Patrick Gillespie (1999)
Chaos Theory and James Joyce's Everyman, by Peter Francis Mackey (1999)
Joyce's Comic Portrait, by Roy Gottfried (2000)
Joyce and Hagiography: Saints Above!, by R. J. Schork (2000)
Voices and Values in Joyce's "Ulysses," by Weldon Thornton (2000)
The Dublin Helix: The Life of Language in Joyce's "Ulysses," by Sebastian D. G. Knowles (2001)
Joyce Beyond Marx: History and Desire in "Ulysses" and "Finnegans Wake," by Patrick McGee (2001)
Joyce's Metamorphosis, by Stanley Sultan (2001)
Joycean Temporalities: Debts, Promises, and Countersignatures, by Tony Thwaites (2001)
Joyce and the Victorians, by Tracey Teets Schwarze (2002)
Joyce's "Ulysses" as National Epic: Epic Mimesis and the Political History of the Nation State, by Andras Ungar (2002)
James Joyce's "Fraudstuff," by Kimberly J. Devlin (2002)
Rite of Passage in the Narratives of Dante and Joyce, by Jennifer Margaret Fraser (2002)

Joyce and the Scene of Modernity, by David Spurr (2002)
Joyce and the Early Freudians: A Synchronic Dialogue of Texts, by Jean Kimball (2003)
Twenty-First Joyce, edited by Ellen Carol Jones and Morris Beja (2004)
Joyce on the Threshold, edited by Anne Fogarty and Timothy Martin (2005)
Wake Rites: The Ancient Irish Rituals of "Finnegans Wake," by George Cinclair Gibson (2005)
"Ulysses" in Critical Perspective, edited by Michael Patrick Gillespie and A. Nicholas Fargnoli (2006)
Joyce and the Narrative Structure of Incest, by Jen Shelton (2006)
Joyce, Ireland, Britain, edited by Andrew Gibson and Len Platt (2006)
Joyce in Trieste: An Album of Risky Readings, edited by Sebastian D. G. Knowles, Geert Lernout, and John McCourt (2007)
Joyce's Rare View: The Nature of Things in "Finnegans Wake," by Richard Beckman (2007)
Joyce's Misbelief, by Roy Gottfried (2008)
James Joyce's Painful Case, by Cóilín Owens (2008; first paperback edition, 2017)
Cannibal Joyce, by Thomas Jackson Rice (2008)
Manuscript Genetics, Joyce's Know-How, Beckett's Nohow, by Dirk Van Hulle (2008)
Catholic Nostalgia in Joyce and Company, by Mary Lowe-Evans (2008)
A Guide through "Finnegans Wake," by Edmund Lloyd Epstein (2009)
Bloomsday 100: Essays on "Ulysses," edited by Morris Beja and Anne Fogarty (2009)
Joyce, Medicine, and Modernity, by Vike Martina Plock (2010; first paperback edition, 2012)
Who's Afraid of James Joyce?, by Karen R. Lawrence (2010; first paperback edition, 2012)
"Ulysses" in Focus: Genetic, Textual, and Personal Views, by Michael Groden (2010; first paperback edition, 2012)
Foundational Essays in James Joyce Studies, edited by Michael Patrick Gillespie (2011; first paperback edition, 2017)
Empire and Pilgrimage in Conrad and Joyce, by Agata Szczeszak-Brewer (2011; first paperback edition, 2017)
The Poetry of James Joyce Reconsidered, edited by Marc C. Conner (2012; first paperback edition, 2015)
The German Joyce, by Robert K. Weninger (2012; first paperback edition, 2016)
Joyce and Militarism, by Greg Winston (2012; first paperback edition, 2015)
Renascent Joyce, edited by Daniel Ferrer, Sam Slote, and André Topia (2013; first paperback edition, 2014)
Before Daybreak: "After the Race" and the Origins of Joyce's Art, by Cóilín Owens (2013; first paperback edition, 2015)
Modernists at Odds: Reconsidering Joyce and Lawrence, edited by Matthew J. Kochis and Heather L. Lusty (2015; first paperback edition, 2020)
James Joyce and the Exilic Imagination, by Michael Patrick Gillespie (2015)

The Ecology of "Finnegans Wake," by Alison Lacivita (2015; first paperback edition, 2021)

Joyce's Allmaziful Plurabilities: Polyvocal Explorations of "Finnegans Wake," edited by Kimberly J. Devlin and Christine Smedley (2015; first paperback edition, 2018)

Exiles: A Critical Edition, by James Joyce, edited by A. Nicholas Fargnoli and Michael Patrick Gillespie (2016; first paperback edition, 2019)

Up to Maughty London: Joyce's Cultural Capital in the Imperial Metropolis, by Eleni Loukopoulou (2017)

Joyce and the Law, edited by Jonathan Goldman (2017; first paperback edition, 2020)

At Fault: Joyce and the Crisis of the Modern University, by Sebastian D. G. Knowles (2018; first paperback edition, 2021)

"Ulysses" Unbound: A Reader's Companion to James Joyce's "Ulysses," Third Edition, by Terence Killeen (2018)

Joyce and Geometry, by Ciaran McMorran (2020)

Panepiphanal World: James Joyce's Epiphanies, by Sangam MacDuff (2020)

Language as Prayer in "Finnegans Wake," by Colleen Jaurretche (2020)

Rewriting Joyce's Europe: The Politics of Language and Visual Design, by Tekla Mecsnóber (2021)

Joyce Writing Disability, edited by Jeremy Colangelo (2022)

www.ingramcontent.com/pod-product-compliance
Lightning Source LLC
Chambersburg PA
CBHW031758220426
43662CB00007B/451